Nu

*Proceedings of the Oxford Symposium
on Food and Cookery 2003*

Edited by Richard Hosking

FootWork
2004

Published in the UK by Footwork
7 Stackpool Road
Bristol BS3 1NG

September 2004

© 2004 as a collection Footwork
(but © 2004 in individual articles rests with authors)

All rights reserved. No part of this publication may be reproduced without written permission from the author and publisher.

ISBN 0 9535057 2 3

Editor	Richard Hosking
Cover design	M-J Thornton
Typography	Footwork, after an original design by M-J Thornton

Cover images supplied by Ursula Heinzelmann.

Printed and bound in Great Britain by Antony Rowe Ltd.

Contents

Introduction

Baby-Food in the Middle Ages	1
Melitta Weiss Adamson	
'Please, Sir, I want some more'	12
Feeding of children in workhouses in the 19th century	
Joan P Alcock	
Flavour is Nurture – Not Nature	26
Anthony Blake	
Piki, Polenta, and Pellagra: Maize, Nutrition and Nurturing the Natural	36
Barrett P Brenton	
Slow Schooling	51
Franca Chiarle, Anya Fernald, Sophie Herron, Silvia Monasterolo	
Family meals, sharing and hierarchy in a West-African town	66
Liza Debevec	
In Sickness and in Health	78
Daphne L Derven	
A Nice Cup of Bovril in Utopia	84
Margaret Drabble	
Our first and sweetest nurture…'	90
Dreaming of food from Ancient Greek comedies to Russian folktales	
Alexandra Grigorieva	
"Quit Playing, You'll Spoil Your Dinner!"	98
The Impact of Youth Sports on Childhood Eating Behaviors	
Natalie Anne Halbach	
Children's Cookery Books: Nurturing Adults' Ideas About Society	112
Ursula Heinzelmann	

Slow Food, Slow School: Nurture and Education	124
Maurice Holt	
Food Guidance from my Grandparents	129
Philip Iddison	
Nurturing a Holiday: Christmas Foods in 18th and 19th Century America	146
Cathy K Kaufman	
The Flavour Continuum	157
Samantha Kilgour	
Picnics and Fairy Tales: or, Let them Eat Cake: Satisfy the Psyche and Starve the Child	167
Walter Levy	
The Business of Food: Preserving Culinary Traditions Keeps the Family Fed in the Philippines	180
Pia Lim-Castillo	
Mentoring: a model for the future nurturing of Culinary Talent	190
Máirtín Mac Con Iomaire	
The Earth's golden oil: the shelf-life of Nurture A vertical tasting of Manni extra virgin olive oil 2001 and 2002	204
Armando Manni	
Byron, Bread and Butter	211
Antony Peattie	
What Ibn Jazla Says You Should Eat	224
Charles Perry	
Images of Infant Nutrition: Sightings of food in group & child portraits	228
Gillian Riley	
My brother always made Blue Peter's potato curry. He still does. Cooks, Home-cooking and Becoming a Cook	241
Frances Short	
Commercial Nurturing: The Culinary Education of America's Youth	253
Andrew F Smith	
Mumbling	260
Colin Spencer	

Nuts for the children: the evidence of the Talmudic literature	264
Susan Weingarten	
But I saw it on TV!' - How do you get children to eat real food?	273
Mary Whiting	
Count Rumford's Soup	285
Bee Wilson	
Feeding the Artist	298
Carolin Young	
Symposium Events	306
About the Authors	313

Introduction

In many ways Oxford Symposium 2003 marked the end of an era, though participants were unaware of this at the time. It was to be the last time the Symposium was held at St Antony's College, our home of over 20 years. Soon after the conclusion of the Symposium, the Trustees decided that for many reasons, particularly those of size and facilities, we had outgrown St Antony's. The Symposium had to move; and we are moving to Oxford Brookes University.

It was also to be the last time that Alan Davidson, one of the joint founders of the Symposium, was to attend. Very sadly Alan died quite unexpectedly at the beginning of December 2003. How fortunate, then, that we had celebrated him and his award of the *Premium Erasminanum* in such grand fashion at the special lunch on the Sunday of the Symposium, and that we had presented him with a sheaf of warm tributes written by symposiasts and other friends and collected by Geraldene Holt, Chairman of Trustees.

This year the Symposium was held under the joint chairmanship of Paul Levy, Claudia Roden and Theodore Zeldin. The topic Nurture attracted fewer papers than usual and we have decided to publish them all, departing from the usual practice of only publishing a selection. It is hoped that this will not lower the high standard to which we have become accustomed, though it is regretted that in some cases the documentation did not reach the standard expected. We intend to remedy this in the future,

This year's keynote speech was presented by Andrew Prentice, and was entitled, "The surprisingly rapid subversion of Nurture: selected for fasting; seduced by feasting". The distinguished chefs Heston Blumenthal and Raymond Blanc led the discussion in a lively manner. Then in the afternoon Margaret Drabble spoke on "Nurture, Utopias and Dystopia", with the discussion led by Jonathan Meades and Ray Sokolov.

On Sunday morning there was a plenary discussion of the topic "The Politics, Psychology and Pathology of Nurture" conducted by Claudia Roden, Barbara Kafka and Michele Wood.

This year a notable feature of the Symposium Dinner on Saturday night and the Sunday Lunch in honour of Alan Davidson, were the high standard of food and the exceptionally attractive table settings. Caroline Conran and Elisabeth Luard for the Symposium Dinner, and Silvija Davidson and her team for The Alan Davidson Lunch, are to be congratulated on the success of their efforts. The menus are reproduced for your pleasure.

Another notable feature this year was the success of the Bring-and-Buy Sale. Patsy and Phil Iddison's efforts broke the record in profits of the sale and are to be warmly thanked and congratulated. As indeed is Silvija Davidson, our new Organiser, who worked extraordinarily hard to achieve a most successful outcome. The difficulties and frustrations of organising the Symposium are endless, and Silvija coped with them admirably, for which she has the sincerest thanks of all of us.

We must also heartily thank all those at St Antony's who have put up with us and done their best to help us over our long association with the College. In particular, Charles White, the Domestic Bursar; Tony Squirrell, the Steward; and Mark Walker, the Head Chef, did everything they could to help us, for which they have our hearty thanks.

Finally, as the new editor of the Symposium Proceedings I must confess what a daunting task it has been to try to maintain the high standard of editing that my predecessor, Harlan Walker, had achieved in the years of his editorship since 1989, when he took the work on. We are deeply grateful to Harlan for his hard work and outstanding achievement

Richard Hosking
June, 2004

Alan Eaton Davidson

1924–2003

Baby-Food in the Middle Ages

Melitta Weiss Adamson

In medieval Europe nutrition was regarded by the medical community as key to the maintenance of health.[1] Countless treatises were written and compiled that focused primarily on the dietary needs of healthy adults, but some also dealt with pregnant women and babies. To understand how they fit into the overall scheme of medicine it is necessary to first look at its theoretical underpinnings. Throughout the period, European physicians subscribed to the humoral theory of classical antiquity according to which foodstuffs were made up of a combination of two of the prime qualities hot, cold, wet, and dry. It was thought that in a healthy body an equilibrium existed between the four qualities, and that illness ensued when the equilibrium was upset in some way. In addition to these basic states of health and sickness, the theory included a third, neutral state, and people belonging to this state were pregnant women, children, the elderly, and convalescents whose condition was not that of a healthy adult which was the norm, nor was it that of a person suffering from an illness.

The genre of medical literature that dealt with the maintenance of health was known in medieval Europe as *Regimen sanitatis*. When in the early Middle Ages Arab physicians, among them Johannitius, Haly Abbas, Rhazes, and Avicenna put the preventive medicine of antiquity into a theoretical framework they used the six non-natural causes for health and sickness, namely 1. Air, 2. Food and Drink, 3. Exercise and Rest, 4. Sleep and Waking, 5. Repletion and Excretion, and 6. Passions and Emotions as ordering principles, and propagated a lifestyle of moderation in these areas. Initially applied to healthy adults, the six non-naturals, of which Food and Drink always occupied the biggest space, were in time applied to the neutral state, and regimens for these particular groups soon followed to which a regimen for the wet-nurse was added.

The two most influential works that were adopted as textbooks by many newly established medical schools in Europe were Rhazes' *Liber de medicina ad Almansorem*,[2] and Avicenna's *Canon medicinae*.[3] In the *Almansor*, as it was often referred to incorrectly by medical students and physicians alike who mistook the addressee for the author, the pregnancy regimen is followed by regimens for the parturient woman, the infant, and the wet-nurse.[4] In the *Canon* Avicenna organizes the material differently. Preventive medicine is treated in Book I, Fen III, Treatise1 to 5, and it is the birth of the child that opens the regimen-cycle. A set of regimens similar to those contained in Rhazes is found in the *Canon* in Book III, Fen XXI, Treatise 2, as part of Avicenna's treatment of sexuality, male and female reproductive organs and their diseases.[5] Much of what physicians in late-medieval Europe wrote concerning the food for pregnant women and young children ultimately goes back to these few chapters in Rhazes and Avicenna, who in turn derived a lot of their knowledge from the works of Hippocrates and Galen.

One of the most extensive treatments of the subject in German was by the physician Bartholomäus Scherrenmüller who according to his own words completed the text on 20 November 1493.[6] What he wrote, however, was by no means an original treatise but the German translation of part of a much larger and older Latin work entitled *Summa conservationis et curationis*, by the famous Italian physician and surgeon William of Saliceto.[7] Born around 1210 near Piacenza, Saliceto studied medicine and surgery at the famous medical school of Bologna where he also taught before he became physician to the city and the hospital of Verona. The *Summa* was probably written after 1275 at the request of Ruffinus, the prior of a monastery in Piacenza. The medical compendium consists of four "books", 1. Special diseases and their therapy, 2. Fevers, 3. Cosmetics, dermatology, and toxicology, and 4. Pharmacopoeia and an antidotary. The regimen-cycle, entitled "De conservatione sanitatis a die conceptionis usque ad ultimum vite senij" forms Chapter 1 of Book 1. This prominent position is an indication of the value Saliceto and his contemporaries put on prevention.[8] Saliceto used the general regimen for healthy adults as the core around which he grouped the special regimens for pregnant women, wet-nurses, children, travelers, and he concluded the cycle with a regimen against the Plague.

To find out what caused a German physician more than two hundred years later to translate Saliceto's regimen into German, we must take a closer look at the career of Bartholomäus Scherrenmüller.[9] Born around 1450 in Aalen in Swabia, Scherrenmüller appears as a medical student at the University of Erfurt in 1469. He received his Baccalaureus artium in 1471 or 1472, and his Magister artium on 2 February 1476. When in 1477 the Arts Faculty opened at the University of Tübingen, he was one of its teachers. Where exactly he studied medicine is not known but by 1492 he appears as a professor of medicine at Tübingen, together with Johann Widmann who was personal physician to Count Eberhard im Bart of Württemberg (1445-1496). Count Eberhard loved books, he loved Italy and the Italian Renaissance, and he needed to produce an heir. It is a combination of all these factors, it seems, that brought about the Saliceto translation. As a book lover he had one major problem, he did not speak Latin, and most of the books at the time were still in Latin. His solution was to hire translators. His love for Italy expressed itself in contacts with the likes of Marsilio Ficino, and culminated in a union with Barbara, the daughter of Margrave Ludovico Gonzaga of Mantua, whom he married on 4 July 1474. To help him produce an heir, Eberhard commissioned Bartholomäus Scherrenmüller to translate a medical text into German that just happened to be by a famous Italian physician.

How much procreation was on the mind of Eberhard, whose son and daughter had died early, can be seen from the fact that he had another important text translated by Scherrenmüller, the obstetrical portion of Abulcasis' *Chirurgia*. Furthermore it was during his reign that in 1491 the midwives of Ulm were regulated for the first time. In his introduction to the Saliceto translation Scherrenmüller mentions another little treatise on obstetrics which he claims to have sent to the count and countess previously. The prologue on folio 1v also identifies the author of the translated text: Gwilhelmus Placentinensis de Saliceto. Scherrenmüller dedicates the German version to both the count and his wife. Presumably to make the text more user-friendly, he divided Saliceto's compilation into small sections that are consecutively numbered and given headings. What follows is my summary of the dietary advice contained in the first forty-three sections.[10]

For the pregnant woman the text recommends light and subtle or delicate food that is well mixed or "tempered," food that creates moisture, is appetizing, and strengthens the mouth of the stomach, as is kid, chicken, and partridge. The pregnant woman should drink a little (white) wine that is of a good quality and color, and diluted with water, or clear, red wine. She should avoid filling the stomach completely with food and drink, and refrain from any bitter, or pungent foods, as are capers, *vygbonen*,[11] lupines, unripe fruits of the olive tree, sesame seed, and the like. She should also avoid those foods that provoke urine and the menstrual flow, such as chickpeas, celery, green beans, and rue. If she craves coals or clay, she should eat bitter foodstuffs as a remedy, among them onions, mustard, watercress or other cress together with a little vinegar. Or on an empty stomach she should eat quinces, pears, and the like, and drink the juice of acidic and styptic fruits mixed with a variety of drugs. Invoking Hippocrates as the authority, the text claims that if milk is flowing from the breasts of the pregnant woman, the birth will be a "weak" one, if the breasts are hard, it will be a healthy birth. [As an aside, intercourse and bathing during pregnancy are discouraged, but recommended shortly before birth to open the birth canal] If while giving birth the woman is beside herself with pain, she should be given good wine or a broth made from lamb and egg yolk. To speed up the birth, a concoction of warm wine and rue helps, to which myrrh can be added.

A good wet-nurse should fulfill the following criteria: she should be young, of medium height, and of a rosy complexion.[12] Her breasts should be big and wide, and she should not have given birth more than two or three months prior because before that time the milk is not well purified and digestible, and bad for the baby. Under no circumstances should the wet-nurse have sexual intercourse because it clouds the blood and generates bad, rotten milk. The wet-nurse should also not be pregnant herself, or suffer from a genital disease[13] because these things destroy the milk and cause it to spoil. She should beware of sharp foods such as onions and garlic, of vinegar and constipating things, of pepper and the like, and of pungent, strong, undiluted wine. She should carefully avoid celery, rue, and wild mustard because they turn milk into menstrual flow, make it runny, and cloud and dilute the blood.

The wet-nurse should eat good food in moderate quantity, such as lamb from a year-old wether, capon, hen, chicken, partridge, pheasant, and veal of three to four month old calves, mixed with egg yolk, warm goat milk, and sugar. Her wine should be white, neither pungent nor strong, and diluted with water. If the wet-nurse falls ill, she should stop breast-feeding and take medication appropriate for her disease. If she is in need of more milk, she should twice a day eat a dish made from bean meal, rice, wheat, and oat, milk, or meat broth of hen or capon. And with it she should drink clear white wine diluted with water. If the child is in pain and cries because the breast-milk coagulates or causes wind in the stomach, it should be given sugar or honey together with the breast-milk. And if in the fourth month the baby develops pustules or feverish swellings, the wet-nurse should consume pomegranate wine, barley flour, lettuce, and squash until the heat goes away. Then she should go back to her normal diet. If the child suffers from diarrhea, the wet-nurse is advised to eat styptic food.

When the child starts teething, the gums should be anointed daily with butter to take the pain away, and from time to time the gums should be rubbed with barley corns so that the teeth break through more easily. When the child begins to speak, the gums and tongue should be rubbed gently with salt and honey. If the child half a year or a year old, it should eat and chew mild food, and should be given rice cooked in milk, or breadcrumbs soaked in chicken broth, or the soft breast meat of birds and chickens. And the wet-nurse should wean it off wine as much as possible, and should give it water or honey to drink. And if she cannot get the child off wine, she should give it wine that is white, light, and well-diluted. The child should not be breast-fed longer than two years, and it is preferable to wean the child at the beginning of winter, on St Andrew's Day at the end of November.[14] The weaning should be done slowly and not abruptly so that the child does not fall ill because of the abrupt change. At the point when the child starts walking it should eat of all things so that in time it gets used to all foods.

Compared to his source, Scherrenmüller has streamlined the material and has removed or shortened some of the references to the three authorities used for the Latin text: Avicenna, Rhazes, and Hippocrates.[15] The dietetic advice given by Rhazes and Avicenna reflects Middle Eastern culinary customs, and foodstuffs such as limes, pomegranates, and sesame are frequently mentioned. As their medical works were translated into medieval Latin and subsequently into the vernacular languages, more and more of these foodstuffs that were exotic or completely unavailable to Europeans, especially those living north of the Alps, were either eliminated, or substituted with local foodstuffs that were similar in taste and humoral quality. Perhaps because Scherrenmüller's target audience was aristocratic and could afford expensive imports, he kept the references to pomegranate wine and sesame seed; alternatively he may as a translator have tried not to stray too much from his source.

For modern readers it may sound odd that blood and breast-milk are mentioned in the same breath, as happens repeatedly in the regimen. But this can be explained by the fact that classical and medieval medical theory considered breast-milk as a form of blood.[16] Most of the food recommended for pregnant women, wet-nurses, and infants in the text is the type of food that convalescents eat, and that regularly appears in the section on sick-dishes in medieval cookbooks such as the *Viandier* of Taillevent from fourteenth-century France.[17] Considering that all the groups of people addressed belong to the neutral state between health and sickness, this is not surprising. The ingredients listed in sick-dishes usually fall under the rubric "pure foods" in Haly Abbas' categorization, which means that they were hot, cold, wet, or dry in the first or second degree, rather than the extreme third or fourth which were the qualities of "medicinal foods", pepper and lettuce for instance. Pure foods were thought to increase the substance of the body without altering its humoral composition.[18] The idea that the wet-nurse with the help of a special diet can cure minor afflictions in the child, such as pustules, feverish swellings, and diarrhea, is worth noting in this context, since it implies that the medicinal foods consumed by the wet-nurse generate breast-milk with medicinal qualities which, when ingested by the baby, is capable of healing.

The following statement found in Saliceto and Scherrenmüller is puzzling when these texts are read in isolation," Is the child half a year or a year old [...] the wet-nurse should wean it off wine as much as possible, and should give it water or honey to drink. And if she cannot get the child off wine, she should give it wine that is white, light, and well-diluted." (See above) Nowhere in the preceding sections has the reader been told to give babies wine (unless, of course the diet of the mother and wet-nurse that contains wine is what the physicians refer to here, which is doubtful), so why at six or twelve months are some so addicted to alcohol that they cannot be weaned off it? Here my other German text, the *Regimen* of Heinrich Laufenberg, is able to provide an explanation.

Unlike Saliceto, and Scherrenmüller, who were physicians, Heinrich Laufenberg was a churchman. He was born in Freiburg around 1390, and died in a monastery in Strasbourg in 1460. His literary works include hymns, some didactic literature, and the *Regimen* which he claims to have completed in 1429.[19] Rather than prose, Laufenberg chose rhymed couplets for his German regimen which consists of seven parts: a "regimen duodecim mensium" or Labors of the Month; three treatises on the planets, the signs of the zodiac, and the four seasons and four temperaments; a general *Regimen sanitatis*; a regimen for pregnancy and child rearing; and a regimen against the Plague.[20] There are indications that the last two parts are later additions, and that the regimen for pregnancy and child rearing was written last but inserted before the Plague regimen, perhaps because the latter contained an accrostichon which gave away the identity of the author/compiler "HEINRICH LOVFFENBERG VON FRYBURG EIN PRIESTER."[21]

In the Prologue to Part 6, Laufenberg claims that he got the inspiration from God to write on pregnancy and child rearing, and that his advice is intended for pregnant women, parturient women, and mothers. Note that the wet-nurse is already missing from the list! For Laufenberg, the priest, pregnancy is a state blessed by God, and the growing up of a child "no small miracle."[22] Much of the dietary advice given in his pregnancy regimen is also contained in Scherrenmüller, Saliceto, Rhazes, and Avicenna, as the following brief summary will show. For the pregnant woman he recommends food in moderation, nutritious foods such as veal, kid, chicken, partridge, small birds, game, and soft-boiled eggs, and no coarse or harmful food. For the parturient woman he recommends hot milk and mush. [Naturally, the reference to intercourse and bathing at the end of a woman's term has been omitted by Laufenberg!] Once she has given birth, the woman should consume delicate food that is well prepared from hens and chickens, and fine white wine, but no honey.[23] When it comes to feeding the baby, he recommends breast-milk until teething sets in, since any other food could potentially kill the child or cause illness.

Unlike the physicians Saliceto and Scherenmüller, Laufenberg is not a fan of wet-nurses, however. He clearly considers a mother's milk as far superior. His only caveat is that the milk produced by the mother immediately following the birth is not healthy which is why another woman should nurse the child until the mother's breast has settled. In his defense of a mother's breast-milk, he argues that the child enjoys sucking it (presumably because it creates a bond between mother and child), and that it is the food the child is already used to from the womb. It is for this latter reason that he advises the mother to continue the diet she had while she was pregnant. The mother should nurse the baby two to three times a day until it gets stronger and then give it a lot of milk. For easier digestion of the breast-milk the infant should be given honey before breast-feeding starts. Laufenberg states that every morning the mother should drain the coarse milk from her breasts before she begins nursing. Referring vaguely to a "great master" he gives the advice that wine along with breast-milk is also healthy. Apparently feeling uncomfortable with this recommendation, he quickly returns to the topic of mother's milk, and repeats his conviction that no milk is better than it. At the end of the section on baby-food Laufenberg raises the issue of wine again and emphasizes that if a baby would like to drink wine, the wish should be granted, but that it should only be a very small amount diluted in clear water. Also discussed in connection with feeding is the question of overeating and the indigestion and wind that can ensue. Like Saliceto and Scherrenmüller, Laufenberg recommends a moderate quantity of food.[24]

With regard to teething, the cleric is more detailed than the physicians. His advice is to rub the gums with butter, chicken fat, olive oil, the brain of a hare, or herbs. Violet oil is also recommended for anointing the gums and the throat, and so is washing the head with a camomile infusion. At this stage in the development the child should be given light food that is neither hot nor cold, delicate meat that is well-cooked, boiled and fried pears, nuts and bread that are pre-chewed, breadcrumbs soaked in honey water or diluted wine, all of it in moderate quantity so as not to fill the stomach too much. When the child wants to start speaking, the tongue should be rubbed with salt, honey, incense, and a little liquorice, which supposedly will speed up the process.[25]

Despite the fact that Laufenberg clearly favors the milk of the mother over that of the wet-nurse, he recognizes that there are certain circumstances that require the services of a wet-nurse: if the mother suffers from a delicate (*zart*) constitution and cannot nurse the baby herself, or if for "God knows what" reason she does not want to, or if there are problems with her breast-milk. In these cases the child should be breast-fed by a wet-nurse that should meet the following criteria. She should be well-built, not too old or too young, between twenty-five and thirty-five to be precise, since that is the age at which she produces the best milk, have a rosy complexion, and breasts that are strong and big and of medium firmness. She should not be too far from having given birth herself, and not be sick. She should have kind eyes, and be neither too skinny nor too big because that is bad for the baby's health. She should be chaste, and have good manners, because the baby will take after her, rather than the father. Laufenberg describes the best breast-milk as white, sweet, not sour like wine, and not too thick or too thin. He warns of green and red milk which he claims is harmful. Not surprisingly, the wet-nurse, like the mother, has to be careful with her diet, and eat white bread with good meat, almonds, hazelnuts, rice, and lettuce, and drink good white wine. In order to produce more milk she should eat chickpeas and beans, and a lot of mush made with milk. He warns of onions, garlic, and all sour food, and food prepared with pepper, and food that contains too much salt or vinegar. If she has sexual intercourse too often the wet-nurse is in danger of becoming pregnant which makes her milk worthless and harmful to the baby.[26]

According to Laufenberg, the ideal age to wean a child off milk is two years. This should be done with delicate or dainty food dipped lightly in sugar. If the food is too coarse, it will lead to stones and cramps. He repeats the concern about weaning on hot summer days found in Saliceto and Scherrenmüller, and the choice of cool, breezy days. If the child does not want to let go of the breast but wants to nurse more, then a bitter-tasting plaster on the breast containing a mixture of ground myrrh and mint will serve as a disincentive. The child should then be fed fairly well and sometimes a little less, but food should not be used as a substitute for sleep, or a bath because that causes health problems. Still extremely troubled by the advice of giving young children wine Laufenberg found in his sources, he returns to the topic one more time at the end of the section on weaning. Instead of invoking some unnamed medical authority or authorities, as he does throughout the text, he now makes it clear that it is *his* opinion that he expresses ("Ouch so sprich ich ...", verse 4870). Children under four especially should be guarded against wine because it causes them pain, he says. Only rarely should they be given wine mixed with water, or better still, just water after their meal.[27] Finally, between the ages of six and ten the child is mature enough to eat coarser food.[28]

It is conceivable that Saliceto's *Summa* was also the source for Heinrich Laufenberg, judging from the degree of overlap in the material, which is greater than with any other regimen of this type I have come across so far. Where Scherrenmüller and Laufenberg differ enormously is in the treatment of the source text. The physician at the end of the fifteenth century aims at producing a faithful translation while the churchman molds the material to serve his agenda. Instead of naming the medical authorities, Rhazes, Avicenna, and Hippocrates, as Saliceto and Scherrenmüller do, Laufenberg speaks vaguely of "masters," or "great masters," and the knowledge he found in books. Given that God made him compose the work, as he says, he may have found it hard to credit all those medical authorities none of whom were Christian! But his recasting of received medical wisdom does not end with obscuring the sources, and turning Latin prose into German rhyme. His first-person narrator takes a firm stand on issues that he considers important, and at times plays coy when it comes to medical explanations for dietetic guidelines. More than once he tells the reader that he is not going to divulge that information. When it comes to the foodstuffs mentioned in the texts of Arab and Latin school medicine, Laufenberg replaces anything too exotic and completely out of reach to the average bourgeois consumer with familiar items. Gone are the references to capers, pomegranates, and sesame, and some of the expensive foodstuffs only the aristocracy could afford to indulge in. There are two issues that Laufenberg feels strongly about and to which he returns again and again. They have to do with the pros and cons of including wine in the diet of the infant, and of having a wet-nurse rather than the biological mother nurse the baby. I would argue that where the author stands on these issues has as much to do with class and religion as with medicine. Wine was the drink of choice of the aristocracy in the Middle Ages, and it is doubtful whether townspeople or peasants could have afforded to use it for such a purpose. On top of that, Laufenberg was a priest for whom wine represented the blood of Christ in the Eucharist. The thought of having it downgraded to baby-food, and drooling down a baby's face mixed with breast-milk quite possibly horrified him. Class and religion may also account for his opposition to the services of wet-nurses. Laufenberg's criticism of mothers who blame their dainty constitution for their inability to nurse or come up with God knows what lame excuses for not breast-feeding their babies speaks for such a reading. Laufenberg's intended audience is not the European aristocracy for whom money was not an issue and who subscribed to the ideals of the Italian Renaissance as Count Eberhard im Bart of Württemberg did, but bourgeois congregations in Freiburg and other small towns in southwestern Germany. His regimen expresses a deep distrust of wet-nurses and their potential for corrupting the body *and* soul of an infant. And how much greater the paranoia if the wet-nurse belonged to a different faith than the baby she was nursing! It was a practice that Church Council after Church Council in the Middle Ages tried to eradicate. At the Council of Rouen in 1074 Christians were forbidden to employ Jewish wet-nurses, and at the Third Lateran Council in 1179 Jews were no longer allowed to employ Christian wet-nurses. That these doctrines were controversial, can be seen from the fact that in 1090 the Bishop of Speyer allowed Jewish wet-nurses to feed Christian babies in Christian families despite the prohibition, and the ban on Christian wet-nurses in Jewish families had to be repeated at the Synod of Paris in 1213.[29] Pope Innocent III turned the rhetoric up a notch in a letter to the Bishops of Sens and Paris in which he made the following claim that clearly established a link between breast-feeding and the Eucharist:

> For we have heard that the Jews have become so insolent that they have resorted to offences against Christian belief, which we can only speak and think of with a shudder. For they instruct the Christian wet nurses of their children, if they have partaken of the Body and the blood of Christ on Easter Sunday, to drain their milk in the latrine for three days before they are allowed to breastfeed their children.[30]

Based on the literature on baby-food examined above that reflects the views of both the medical community and the medieval church, it seems fair to say that in the nature versus nurture debate the Middle Ages came down firmly on the side of nurture.

Notes

1. For a detailed study of food in the context of medieval medicine see Melitta Weiss Adamson, *Medieval Dietetics: Food and Drink in* Regimen Sanitatis *Literature from 800 to 1400* (Frankfurt am Main/Berlin/Bern/New York/Paris/Vienna: Peter Lang, 1995).
2. The edition used is entitled *Liber Rasis ad Almansorem* (Venice: Bonetus Locatellus per Octavianum Scotum, 1497).
3. Avicenna, *Liber Canonis* (Edition Venice 1507. Reprint Hildesheim: Olms, 1964).
4. In the edition of Rhazes' *Liber de medicina ad Almansorem* consulted for this study, they are Chapter 27 "De regimine infantis et pregnantis," Chapter 28 "De alleviatione partus et regimine parturientis," Chapter 29 "De regimine infantis," and Chapter 30 "De electione nutricis et eius regimine."
5. Avicenna's *Canon medicine*, Book III, Fen XXI, Treatise 2 begins with Chapter 1 "De impregnatione et partu," Chapter 2 "De regimine vniversali pregnantis," "De regimine enixe," and "De appetitu pregnantis."
6. The only known manuscript of the text is Berlin, Staatsbibliothek Preußischer Kulturbesitz, Ms. Germ. 4° 1020, fol. 1v-60v. Scherrenmüller's regimen is edited in Wolfram Schmitt, " Bartholomäus Scherrenmüllers Gesundheitsregimen (1493) für Graf Eberhard im Bart" (Med. Diss. Heidelberg 1970), pp.44-99.
7. The part of Saliceto's *Summa* that Scherrenmüller translated is edited in Schmitt, pp.105-146.
8. On Saliceto's life and work see Schmitt, pp.23-32.
9. On Scherrenmüller's life and work see ibid., pp.8-23.

10. Ibid., pp.45-60.
11. I have so far been unable to identify this foodstuff which is not listed in Saliceto. It may be a type of bean.
12. Literally "a light complexion with a little redness."
13. The reference to "genital disease" is not in Saliceto.
14. The Saint's Day was added by Scherrenmüller.
15. Saliceto began his compilation with extracts from Rhazes' chapter on the pregnant woman. He then turned to Avicenna's *Canon*, and extracted material from Book III on abortion, the general pregnancy-regimen, and the preservation of the embryo, which he interspersed with various notes from Hippocrates' *Aphorisms*. From Book III of the *Canon* he switched to Book I, and copied material on lactation, and the care of infants from birth until they start to walk. Returning to Rhazes, he used passages from the regimen for the wet-nurse and the infant, and then switched back to Book I of the *Canon*, and the chapters on children's diseases and lactation. Four more quotes from Hippocrates, and one each from Rhazes' chapter on the extraction of blood, and Avicenna's Book I of the *Canon* on children's diseases conclude the list of sources cited up to Section 43 that ends with the regimen of the child up to age seven. See Schmitt p.100f.
16. The German nun Hildegard of Bingen in alluding to the Hippocratic idea of a vein connecting the uterus and the breasts describes the production of breast-milk as follows: "*The milk*. When the woman receives seed from the man so that it begins to grow in her, then by that natural energy, too, the woman's blood is drawn up towards her breasts, and what was to become blood from food and drink now is turned into milk to nourish the child growing in the mother's womb. As the child keeps growing in its mother's womb the milk increases in her breasts to nourish the child with it." See Margaret Berger, trans. *Hildegard of Bingen: On Natural Philosophy and Medicine. Selections from* Cause et cure (Cambridge: D.S. Brewer, 1999), p.50. See also Joan Cadden, *Meanings of Sex Difference in the Middle Ages: Medicine, Science, and Culture* (Cambridge: Cambridge University Press, 1993).
17. Terence Scully, ed. and trans. *The* Viandier *of Taillevent: An Edition of All Extant Manuscripts* (Ottawa: Ottawa University Press, 1988), recipes pp.90-96.
18. Adamson, p.17.
19. Heinz H. Menge, Das 'Regimen' Heinrich Laufenbergs: Textologische Untersuchung und Edition (Göppingen: Kümmerle, 1976), pp.547-556.
20. For a detailed description of the contents of the *Regimen*, see Menge, pp.11-37.
21. Ibid.,p.437f.
22. Ibid., pp.362-364.
23. "Wie sich die swangern fruvwen halten söllent", ibid., pp.364-370.
24. "Wie man die kindlin Spisen sol oder söigen In Ir Iugent," ibid., pp.377-380.
25. "Wie man das kindly sol halten so yme die zenly uff gond," ibid., pp.380-382.
26. "Wie die amme sin sol," ibid., pp.383-386.
27. "Wie man dz kindli entwänen sol vnd halten," ibid., pp.387-390.
28. "Wie man das kinde leren soll," ibid., p.390f.
29. Winfried Frey, "Jews and Christians at the Lord's Table?," in *Food in the Middle Ages: A Book of Essays*, ed. by Melitta Weiss Adamson (New York and London: Garland, 1995), p.118f.
30. Quoted in Frey, p.119.

'Please, Sir, I want some more'
Feeding of children in workhouses in the 19th century

Joan P Alcock

The problem of the poor

One of the great problems which exercised social reformers in the 19th century was how to care for and provide useful employment for the poor and, in particular, for their children. Persons in poverty regarded children as an investment because their wages would contribute to household expenditure. Children could be apprenticed to employers to learn a trade, in which case the employer would be responsible for feeding and clothing them. They might also be sent to sea, placed in the army, put on the land, placed in domestic service or sent *en masse* into factories, often far removed from places of birth. Nathaniel Pattison took apprentices from the workhouse at Plumstead in Kent, to work in his silk mill in Congleton, Cheshire and Samuel Greg's mill at Style in Cheshire was serviced by children from the Woolwich workhouse, near London (Alcock, 2003, 44).

During the medieval period, monastic houses had provided alms and shelter for the poor. After the final dissolution of the monasteries in 1536, the poor gradually became the responsibility of the parish in which they lived. Eventually, in Elizabeth I's reign, Parliament passed the 1598 Poor Law Act and the 1601 Act of 43rd Elizabeth (Williams 1965, 26-35). Although these set up workhouses to house the poor (Leonard 1960, 55), they firmly established the principle that Justices of the Peace should administer a system of poor relief with money collected from the parish. In other words, the poor were to be given money, that is, outdoor relief, to relieve their lot, without being forced into any kind of confinement.

In 1782, Thomas Gilbert, M P for Lichfield, successfully introduced a Parliamentary bill for parishes to establish workhouses to shelter the non-able-bodied poor until steady work could be found for them (Bagley and Bagley 1966, 30). These housed the poor; they did not establish a prescriptive regime. Maintaining the poor with outdoor relief for an unlimited period was still the responsibility of the parish in which they lived, money being supplied by the Poor Rate or local funds (Bruce 1968, 55).

The cost of Poor Law funds rose enormously after the end of the Napoleonic Wars in 1815, when men were discharged from the army and navy without any hope of future employment. Agricultural labourers, who were tied to the land, also claimed that they were treated 'like potatoes in a pit', only taken out when the farmer could no longer do without them (Nicholls and Mackay, 1898-1889, 196). Towns were becoming crowded with people seeking work, but with no hope of a steady job. There might be serious unrest throughout England, if not revolution, and equally great alarm that unemployment could cause a massive rise in the Poor Rate (Digby 1982, 9). To prevent this the Government established a Royal Commission to examine the problem.

The Poor Law of 1834
Twenty-six Assistant Commissioners diligently visited 3000 towns and villages to enquire how they treated the poor. The Commissioners could be regarded as philanthropic amateurs warned to keep costs down, but their reports show their conscientious detail. 'What the Assistant Commissioners brought back from their tours was, in the main, an extraordinary full collection of particular instances of maladministration' (Webb and Webb 1927, 84), and details of how a new workhouse system could work. A major problem was that the Commissioners probably genuinely believed that Gilbert's workhouses were almshouses which kept both young and old in ignorance and idleness and that this should be remedied in any new accommodation.

Their findings led to the Poor Law Report (1834), one of the most detailed ever produced, which filled 26 folio volumes, covering 13,000 pages (Webb and Webb 1927, 51-55). This resulted in Parliament passing the Poor Law Amendment Act (1834), thereby changing the system and establishing two principles. The Principle of the Workhouse Test was that all able-bodied persons were not to be given outside relief. Relief was only to be provided in the workhouse. The Principle of Less Eligibility ensured that the position of able-bodied persons receiving relief in the workhouse was to be less desirable than that of the humblest worker outside. This led to an unstated third principle that those who were offered and accepted shelter in the workhouse were genuinely in need and want. As the Poor Law Report stated, 'if the claimant does not comply with the terms on which relief is given, i.e. if the person refuses the offer of shelter, nothing is given, and if the person does comply, this compliance proves the truth of the claim that he or she is destitute' (Bruce 1968, 97). The workhouse was 'thus a self-operating test, for only the truly indigent would wish to enter such an institution' (Digby 1982, 14).

Local workhouses, established under Gilbert's Act, were to be replaced by Union workhouses, some established in large towns, some formed from a union of several smaller towns and parishes. Families were to be separated, so that children were provided with separate accommodation, workhouse clothing worn, silence preserved at meals and smoking and beer drinking not allowed. 'Adequate food and shelter were to be provided, but that was all, and adequacy was not to be interpreted liberally' (Bruce 1968, 98). Elected Boards of Guardians appointed paid officials – a master, who was expected to be married so that his wife acted as an unpaid helper, a cook, a baker, a porter, a school master and a part-time medical officer.

Dietary in the workhouse

Three Poor Law Commissioners in London prescribed the preparation and serving of food. They issued dietary tables, which contained about 160-170 oz of solid food per week for adults and less for children. This was allotted on days of the week. Usually, the same meals were served on Sunday and Thursday, Wednesday and Friday, Tuesday and Saturday. Monday might have a separate menu. Inmates were divided into men and women, children aged 9-15, children aged 2-9, and infants. The menus and the quantities varied, however, according to how the different unions chose to administer them. In Norfolk Unions breakfast was bread, butter and cheese on four days a week, milk or water gruel on the other three. Supper was always bread, and cheese or butter. Dinner was dumplings, meat and bread on three days, broth and bread on two days, milk and water gruel on Wednesday and bread and cheese on Saturday, thus replicating the evening meal (Digby 1982, 2).

The Congleton Union Workhouse at Arclid in Cheshire, opened in 1844, served a union of 31 parishes and townships. Breakfast was the same every day. Children aged 9-16 got 5 oz bread and 1½ pints porridge; children aged 2-9 were given 4 oz bread and 1 pint of porridge. Tea, provided at 4 pm, was 4 oz bread and treacle for children aged 9-16 and 3 oz for children aged 5-16. This was an extra meal, not approved by the Poor Law Commissioners. It was discontinued by 1860 as the Board of Guardians complained that after this meal the children could not eat their supper. The insistence on exact quantities was because the 1834 Act allowed inmates the right to have their rations weighed in front of them.

Supper was the same food as provided at breakfast. Dinner was served at noon. On Sunday and Thursday there was rice pudding, 1½ lb for children aged 9-16, 1½ lb for the others. Monday was pea soup day, but it is not clear if this had a basis of a meaty pig's trotter or if it was just made with split peas and water. The quantities were 1½ pints for children aged 9-16, 1 pint for boys aged 2-9 and ½ pint for girls aged 2-9. Tuesday and Saturdays were red-letter days as meat and potatoes were served. Children aged 9-16 got 1 lb potatoes and 1½ oz meat; the other children got ½ lb potatoes and 1 oz meat. On Wednesday and Friday, dinner was potatoes and buttermilk in proportioned quantities.

Instructions from the London Poor Law Commissioners stated that neither beer nor spirits was to be issued to the children. Some workhouses ignored this and gave a small quantity of beer to children. The usual drink given was tea, which, as it was made with boiled water, was superior to water drunk from an impure source. Presumably Arclid did this.

By 1867 1½ oz cheese had been added to the ration for children aged 9-16 on two days a week. Meat was additionally provided for dinner on Monday and Friday, but the quantity of potatoes was reduced if bread was added. Bread was a vital necessity because it acted as a 'filler'. In 1867, the Arclid Board of Guardians employed a cook at a salary of £18 a year and a baker at a cost of two shillings and six pence a day. Five years later, in order to cut costs, they dismissed the baker and gave the post to the porter who also acted as the tailor. This proved too much for Frederick Pickering, who resigned, but his replacement was employed as a baker and a porter. The boys helped him in some of his baking duties.

Bread was vitally necessary in the diet, especially for children who were constantly hungry. The quantities eaten varied from 98-60 oz per week according to age. Quality was of a different matter; workhouse bread was often made of the cheaper forms of flour and with little fat (Crowther1981, 215). Most bread was adulterated with the addition of ground beans, peas or potatoes (Accum 1820). Alum was used to whiten inferior grades of flour, known as seconds (Burnett 1966, 74), usually in the ratio of 4 oz alum to a 240 lb sack. In 1870, the Arclid Workhouse Visiting Committee investigated a complaint that the bread was of inferior quality. A sample sent for analysis revealed that the flour contained almost 9 oz of alum to the 240 lb sack (Langley 1993, 54). Efforts were then made to improve the bread on the grounds that it could harm the children.

This diet could be compared with a pre-1834 diet issued in the Fulham workhouse in London. Quantities are not given but it provided children with a meat dinner on four days a week, and bread and cheese 'of good Gloucestershire quality' on the other three days. Milk porridge was provided five mornings and bread and butter on the other three days (Faulkner 1813, 162). In 1820 the Fulham Select Vestry Committee of the Poor decided that bread was to be of second quality, except for infants, who were to have best quality. This was continued in the new workhouse built in 1849.

The pre-1834 Fulham workhouse provided soup in the evening made with liquid from the boiled meat – a definite advance on the Arclid habit of throwing away the liquid. To the broth was added rice, scotch barley and peas in rotation. The meat dinner was 6 oz for children, which seems a large quantity compared to that provided at Arclid, but this should be considered in ratio to the other food. The meat was to be distributed at the discretion of the Master and Mistress of the workhouse, but unfortunately there is no reference to how this was done.

The children's diet at the Flegg Incorporation in Norfolk was a more nutritious one. This provided a pint of milk and 4 oz of bread for breakfast for the infants. For older children dinner on two days was 8 oz of meat pudding and 10 oz of vegetables and on another 8 oz of suet pudding and 10 oz of vegetables. On the other four days they had bread and cheese. Supper was always 4 oz bread, 1 oz of treacle and half a pint of milk and water. The 5-9 year olds got the same but in smaller quantities. This meal, which provided much needed vegetables and a decent amount of protein, was said to be superior to that given to children of rural labourers in Norfolk (Digby 1978, 157).

The rice pudding provided at Arclid on Sundays and Thursdays might have been made in accordance with a recipe akin to those provided by Mrs Beeton. Her one entitled *Plain and Economical; a nice pudding for children* (Beeton 1861 no 1343) included butter and sugar, which might be thought to have been too extravagant for workhouse children. Far more appropriate was *Plain Boiled Rice* Pudding (Beeton 1861 no 1344). Half a pound of rice was tied into a pudding cloth, put into cold water and boiled for at least two hours. As the rice swelled so was the cloth loosened and re-tightened. This quantity was stated to serve at least five to six children and might feed more. It would be eaten with warm or cold butter, jam or fruit, but as these were not included on the dietary, there was no need to provide them. Mrs Beeton noted approvingly that this pudding formed a 'valuable and nutritious addition to our farinaceous foods'. It would certainly be a filling meal for hungry children.

Gruel is often found on workhouse menus. The term is often substituted for porridge, as was the case in the Arclid workhouse diet in 1867. It was gruel, which was the downfall of Oliver Twist (Dickens 1837, Chapter 2). His gruel was prepared in a copper at one end of a large, stone hall, from which the workhouse master ladled it into each boy's porringer, which, as Dickens' wrote, 'never needed washing. The boys polished it with their spoons till they shone again and when they had performed this operation, they would sit staring at the copper, with such eager eyes as if they would have devoured the very bricks of which it was composed'. Oliver was chosen by lot to do the fatal deed. 'Child as he was, he was desperate with hunger and reckless with misery. He rose from the table; and advancing to the master, basin and spoon in hand said: somewhat alarmed at his own temerity: Please Sir, I want some more'. The result was a blow from the master's ladle, instant confinement and a bill posted outside the gate 'offering a reward of five pounds to anyone who would take Oliver Twist 'off the hands of the parish', that is to anyone who would apprentice him to any trade'.

Gruel was a standby in Victorian households. Mrs Beeton has two recipes. Her barley gruel (Beeton 1861, no 1856) was not one provided for workhouse children for it contained pearl barley, a pint of port wine, sugar water and lemon. Children would probably have been fed on recipe no 1868, which consisted merely of groats brought to the boil in cold water. A recipe book, published by the London School Board for teaching children in elementary schools, provided 3 oz porridge oats to a pint of water and for gruel one flat tablespoon of oatmeal to a pint of water (Briggs 1890, 88, 90). There is also a recipe for pea soup giving one pint of split peas to a quart of water (Briggs 1890, 20)

Mrs Beeton was not insensible to food provided for the poor. Her *Useful Soup for Benevolent Purposes* (no 165) contained meat and a variety of vegetables and herbs. She made this in the winter of 1858, in quantities of eight or nine gallons to distribute to the families in her village so that they 'would have a dish of warm comforting food in place of the cold meat and a piece of bread which form, with too many cottagers, their usual meal'. A modern critic condemned the 'sour smell of condescension which hangs about Mrs Beeton's appalling soup'. But this is to ignore the circumstances of the time and the excellent nourishment of the soup. Workhouse children would have benefited from eating bowls of this soup.

Later changes to the dietary

Alterations to the dietary tables at Arclid were made after the 1880s. Seed bread was given to children at 10 am, 4 oz for boys, 3 oz for girls. Potato Pie, served on Thursdays, provided variety; every pound of pie included 8 oz of potatoes and 3 oz of meat (Langley 1993, 55). In 1897 the pea soup dinner was replaced by one with extra meat. Children were provided with extra buttermilk; children under five got extra fresh milk. After 1890 puddings were added to dinner on Saturday – apple pie and plum pudding. Later more puddings were added, only to be removed during the First World War. A Local Government Board

Inspector in 1918 complained that the children's diet was 'monotonous and inadequate'. He was sharply reminded that the workhouse was simply following the Government's food instructions to save food and money in the interests of the war effort. Before the war the children had had puddings five times a week and seedcake on two days.

As early as 1844 Christmas at Arclid had been recognised as a special occasion with roast beef and plum pudding being served. Older children were allowed some ale, the quantity to be determined by the Master. In 1902 oranges and sweets were given to children on the coronation of Edward VII. The *Times* reported on 26 December 1849 that throughout London 90,000 people ate Christmas dinner served in workhouses in 28 parishes, many of these people not normally resident in the workhouse. As well as the adults the report gives a total of 170 boys and 200 girls having dinner in St Pancras' workhouse, 35 boys and 50 girls in the St Martin's in the Fields' workhouse, 180 children at Drouet's Establishment, Brixton, and 46 children and 52 infants in the St Luke's, Chelsea', workhouse. All had a meal of beef, potatoes and plum pudding. Porter was allowed to the children 'at discretion' but tea was the preferred drink. St Pancras provided fruit and sweetmeats for the children. This was in contrast to the Andover, Hampshire, workhouse, where the inmates had been refused any variation of their bread and cheese diet, in spite of the fact that the poor outside were provided with a Christmas dinner in the market square (Anstruther 1973, 89).

Feeding outside the workhouse

The comment that many people who would not normally be in the workhouse were attending the free Christmas dinners, is significant. If the diet in the workhouse was monotonous and sometimes badly cooked, at least meals were provided on a regular basis. Through the Victorian period, working-class diet in town and country was monotonous and sometimes extremely sparse. This raises the question as to whether children would have fared better outside the workhouse. In 1850 the Poor Law Commissioners refused to agree to a diet prepared by the Bradford Board of Guardians on the grounds that it was 'decidedly less nutritious than those of other unions'. The Bradford Guardians retorted that 'their diet gave paupers more to eat than independent labourers of the district could buy for themselves and their families out of their wages' (Woodward 1938, 435).

It is impossible to generalise about the standard of living of agricultural labourers in England in the 19th century. This would vary with the area of the country, the size of the family and the skill of the man who was usually the breadwinner. In textile towns both men and women worked in the mills and expected their children to do the same. As the various

Factory Acts were passed, so the age of the children working in factories rose. Their wages, however, were a significant factor in contributing to the family income.

Light was shed upon this in 1904 when a collection of letters and reports dealing with the 1840s, 'the Hungry Forties' as it came to be called, was published. Many of the people whose evidence was taken had been children during that period (quoted in Burnett 1966, 23). Throughout the country at that time there was a shortage of food. The reports contained references to doughy and 'ropey' bread, porridge of bruised beans, a meal of potatoes followed by one of potato peelings. Tea was eked out with burnt crusts; supper was vegetables stolen from neighbouring fields. The *Reports of the Special Assistant Poor Law Commissioners on the Employment of Women and Children in Agriculture* (1843) comment that in Wiltshire the food of the poor consists of bread, potatoes, a little butter and tea, with occasionally cheese and bacon. Bacon could be sliced thinly to make it go further. Children suffered from 'scrofulous' diseases and scurvy, caused by lack of fresh fruit and vegetables. A widow in Calne, Wiltshire said that she ate well while her husband was alive, but since his death, she and her eight-year son lived on potatoes, tea, butter and sugar, and bread made from flour she ground herself (Burnett 1966, 25).

After the 1850s, provision of food improved, but even so the death rate of children dying before the age of five reached 50 per cent in some areas and many of the survivors suffered from malnutrition and rickets. Even when the family lived relatively well, children ate less food than their parents and of a more doubtful quality. Dr Edward Smith's *Report on the Food of the Poorer Labouring Classes in England* presented to Parliament in 1863 gave examples of this. A Derbyshire man gave his children bread and milk, while he and his wife lived on bread, meat and butter. A Coventry worker gave his family bread and treacle for breakfast and bacon and potatoes for dinner with the water thrown away rather than being used as a stock for soup. As late as 1901 the list of budgets produced by Seebohm Rowntree's survey in York (Rowntree 1901) showed the monotony of the diet: bread, butter, occasionally bacon and tea for breakfast, meat and potatoes for dinner, bread and butter for tea; bread, butter, jam or potted meat for supper and sometimes cake for supper. Earlier, the diet of silk-workers in Congleton in Cheshire consisted of oatmeal porridge, bread, potatoes, a little meat and cheese. Breakfast time in the mills had been marked by a procession of children carrying cans containing bread and milk, often sweetened by treacle or syrup (*Macclesfield Courier*, 7 September 1844).

A comparison can be made with food provided in the late 19th century for boys, aged 14 and over, who were sent to join the training ship *Exmouth*, established by the Forest Gate School District (Hulbert 1968). It is quite clear that the District Committee wished to remove pauper boys from the area, but in so doing, they did provide them with a trade, if not a career, and with decent meals. The *Exmouth* was an old two-decker ship of the line, which had served in the Baltic. 600 boys could be accommodated in the vessel, which served as a training ship from 1870 to 1903. A three-decker iron ship then replaced her. The training was replicated in other ships – the *Arethusa* and the *Chichester* based at Greenwich, the *Warspite* at Woolwich, the *Indefatigable* at Birkenhead and the *Formidable* at Bristol. All these ships provided training for a life at sea for boys committed by magistrates under the Industrial Schools Act of 1870 (Chance, 1897, 253).

These boys received three adequate meals a day, which could include bread, fats, fish, meat, cheese, rice, potatoes and other farinaceous food. Vegetables seem to be lacking, but this was certainly the case in the workhouse and in much of the diet of the poor. Stewed fruits were, however, provided when in season (Hulbert 1968, 120).

The workhouse system

The workhouse system in England lasted until 1929 when the Local Government Act swept away the Boards of Guardians and the principles established by the 1834 Act. The cost of administering poor relief was transferred to County Councils and County Boroughs. Poor Relief was to be called Public Assistance to underline the fact that the poor were to be assisted not degraded. This particularly applied to children, who were no longer to be separated from their parents and were to be adequately fed.

The food provided for children in workhouses had included little meat, very few, if any, vegetables and hardly any fats. Much of the diet consisted of cheap carbohydrates. Cheese and the meat provided some protein, but the diet lacked fresh vegetables and was deficient in protein and vitamins. The basic staple foods were gruel (or porridge) and bread and these in portions, which were strictly rationed and often less than were provided in some prisons. Although the calorific content of the diet compares favourably with present day figures provided by the Department of Health, it is obvious that the workhouse diet was not a suitably nutritious one for growing children. Food was bought in bulk at the lowest possible tender and in the hands of untrained cooks would not only be badly cooked, but could also be dangerous. In summer, there were numerous complaints of children suffering from stomach pains. It is not, therefore surprising that Medical Officers of Health constantly reported cases of rickets, scurvy and malnutrition, especially in adolescent boys. These boys would have been better nourished in naval training ships or in army establishments. Even so children in workhouses would receive a more filling and regular diet than some children outside them.

There could be enormous problems. The most horrendous case was that of the scandalous conditions at the Andover workhouse (Anstruther 1973). Adults and children, forced to crush cattle and horse bones for manure, gnawed ravenously for the marrow and meat from the putrid bones. Yet the scandal was that, even after the investigation of the Select Committee of Inquiry in 1846, the regime was just as bad. The *Times* targeted its campaign on abolition of the Poor Law Commissioners, who were disbanded in July 1847; after that, the *Times* lost interest. Andover inmates were still refused a Christmas dinner of roast beef and plum pudding. Children still starved on meagre rations and the Reverend Mr Dodson, who had been forced to resign as Chairman of the Board, was unanimously elected as no one else would take on the position. He retired in 1876 lauded by the townspeople.

Not all children in the workhouse had the opportunity, as did Oliver Twist, of securing a happy future. Not all were apprenticed to caring employers. Few records were kept of their views on the regime they suffered. Allowance has to be made for the fact that little thought was given to nutrition and meal planning in the 19th century. The regime did not necessarily materially deprive but it did psychologically repress. Attention was concentrated on meals, which filled the stomach, and bread, potatoes and rice pudding certainly did this. The workhouse regime was degrading and humiliating. Yet, whatever may be the modern view of the workhouse, it did attempt to provide, in its contemporary context, a reasonable amount of food and shelter for the many families who were forced into poverty, often through no fault of their own and for children who might not otherwise have survived the rigours of life in Victorian England.

Bibliography
ACCUM, F., 1820 A treatise on the adulteration of food and culinary poisons : exhibiting the fraudulent sophistications, Philadelphia: A Small.
ALCOCK, J. P., 2003 *Congleton. history and guide,* Stroud: Tempus Publishing.
ANSTRUTHER, I., 1973 *The scandal of the Andover Workhouse*, London: Bles.
BAGLEY, J. J. AND BAGLEY, A. J., 1966 *The English poor law*, London: Macmillan
BEETON, I., 1861 *The Book of Household Management*; Facsimile Edition 1982, London: Chancellor Press.
BRIGGS, MISS, 1890 School book for London. Instruction in cookery. Book of receipts and axioms., London: Alexander and Shepheard.
BRUCE, M., 1968 *The coming of the Welfare State,* London: Batsford.

BURNETT, J., 1966 Plenty and want: A social history of diet in England from 1815 to the present day, London: Thomas Nelson.
CHANCE, W., 1897 Children under the Poor Law: their education, training and aftercare, London: Sonnenschein and Co.
CROWTHER, M. A., 1981 The workhouse system 1834-1929: the history of an English social institution, London: Batsford.
DICKENS, C., *Oliver Twist* 1837, Oxford World Classics 1966, Oxford: Oxford University Press.
DIGBY, A., 1978 *Pauper palaces,* London: Routledge and Kegan Paul.
DIGBY, A., 1982 The Poor Law in nineteenth-century England and Wales, London: Historical Association.
FAULKNER, T., 1813 An historical and topographical account of Fulham: including the hamlet of Hammersmith, London: J. Tilling for T. Egerton.
HULBERT, J., 1968 *A history of the training ship Exmouth, 1870-1919,* Unpublished dissertation submitted for the Degree of B Ed., University of London.
LANGLEY, M. AND LANGLEY, G., 1993 At the crossroads. A history of the Arclid Workhouse and Hospital, Nantwich: Johnsons.
LEONARD, E. M. 1900 The early history of the English poor law, London: Frank Cass
NICHOLLS, G. AND MACKAY, T. A. 1898-1899 A history of the English poor law, vol. III from 1834 to the present time, London: P. S. King and Son.
ROWNTREE, B. SEEBOHM, 1901 *Poverty. A study of town life* London: Macmillan.
WEBB, S. AND WEBB, B. 1927 English local government, vol. 07: English Poor Law history: Part I. The old Poor Law, London: Longmans Green
WILLIAMS, E., 1965 *A documentary history of England,* London: Penguin Books.
WOODWARD, E. L., 1938 *The age of reform, 1815-1870* Oxford: Clarendon Press.

Appendix 1
The Farnham Workhouse

In 1837 three boys were sent from Bishops Wareham Workhouse to Farnham Workhouse in the expectation that they would be taught a trade. One of the boys started wetting his bed and as a punishment all three boys were put on minimum rations. As the bedwetting continued they were confined in a small shed for ten days and given the rations specified below. No attempt was made to allow the boys to clean themselves or their place of confinement. When the boys were finally released, it was obvious that they were on the point of death. No action seems to have been taken against the workhouse.

Minimum rations, Farnham Workhouse

Weekly diet	Quantity	Calorific Content	Daily calorific content
Bread	2 lb 10 oz	2,772	
Mutton	5 oz	250	
Potatoes	1 lb	448	
Cheese	3.5 oz	420	
Pudding	12 oz	425	
Milk	3.5 pt	1,050	
Total		5,365	766

Appendix 2

Congleton Union Workhouse at Arclid: Children's Dietary
Estimated calorific content: daily allowance

Day	Children	Bread	Treacle	Porridge	Rice Pudding	Pea Soup	Potatoes	Meat	Buttermilk	Daily Total
Sunday & Thursday	Children 9-16	942	25	1035	287.5					**2.289.5**
	Boys 2-9	726	25	690	258					**1.699**
	Girls 2-9	660	25	690	258					**1.633**
Monday	Children 9-16	942	25	1035		1,065				**3.067**
	Boys 2-9	726	25	690		704				**2.145**
	Girls 2-9	660	25	690		528				**2.103**
Tuesday & Saturday	Children 9-16	942	25	1,035			368	75		**2.445**
	Boys 2-9	726	25	690			276	50		**1.767**
	Girls 2-9	660	25	690			276	50		**1.701**
Wednesday & Friday	Children 9-16	942	25	1,035			368		232	**2.602**
	Boys 2-9	726	25	690			276		116	**1.833**
	Girls 2-9	660	25	690			276		58	**1.709**

Appendix 3

Children's dietary, Congleton Union Workhouse at Arclid

Day	Children	Breakfast Bread (oz)	Breakfast Porridge (Pts)	Dinner Cooked Meat (oz)	Dinner Potatoes (lb)	Dinner Pea soup (pts)	Dinner Buttermilk (pts)	Tea Rice Pudding (lb)	Tea Bread & Treacle (oz)	Supper Bread (oz)	Supper Porridge (Pts)
Sunday & Thursday	Children 9-16	5	1.5					1.5	4	5	1.5
	Boys 2-9	4	1					1.25	3	4	1
	Girls 2-9	4	1					1.25	3	3	1
Monday	Children 9-16	5	1.5			1.5			4	5	1.5
	Boys 2-9	4	1			1			3	4	1
	Girls 2-9	4	1			0.75			3	3	1
Tuesday & Saturday	Children 9-16	5	1.5	1.5	1				4	5	1.5
	Boys 2-9	4	1	1	0.75				3	4	1
	Girls 2-9	4	1	1	0.75				3	3	1
Wednesday & Friday	Children 9-16	5	1.5			1	1		4	5	1.5
	Boys 2-9	4	1			0.75	0.75		3	4	1
	Girls 2-9	4	1			0.75	0.5		3	3	1

Flavour is Nurture – Not Nature

Anthony Blake

Introduction

It is exactly three years since I presented a paper to this symposium which was entitled "The language of Flavour: Learning and memory" (Blake 2000), and in it I discussed the way our senses of sight, smell, taste, sight and hearing give us information about our food. I speculated on how we learn to like the foods we do and the part that our brain must play in creating our memories of foods and flavours. My final phrase in that paper was "…the food you give to your toddler might already decide how much pleasure that child will get from food in later life". In the intervening three years there have been developments in several areas which have changed the entire understanding of what flavour is, how we come to have preferences for certain foods while excluding others, and we can now state not only that this fictional toddler's future food preferences will quite definitely be influenced by what he is given to eat but also that his learning process started much earlier in his life than I appreciated when I wrote that sentence. This paper fills in the last three years and reviews those issues which relate to this new understanding. It will necessarily stray into several scientific disciplines but I will try to keep the details of the science to a minimum and beg your patience while I first introduce several topics which may seem to be a long way from the enjoyment of food. One relates to the development of the human brain, another to some strange consequences of how the brain processes information received from our different senses and, finally, how the brain compiles the information which collectively decides whether our food is delicious or disgusting.

The Human Brain

An understanding of how the human brain performs its functions and a proper explanation of the phenomenon we know as consciousness has been described as one of the greatest unsolved problems of science. Many authors have written on this topic at a popular level and good reviews are (McCrone 1999), (Scientific 1999). Much of our knowledge of brain function has come from correlations made between damage to specific areas of the brain caused by trauma or stroke and the subsequent impairment of function. Experimental work has also been carried out on the living brain during surgery in order to establish the function of brain regions by direct stimulation and its consequence. However in recent years non-invasive scanning techniques have become available which allow direct observation of the brains of conscious, healthy individuals. It is now routine to 'look' inside an individuals head and watch the brain working as it performs some mental exercise and where the information which arrives from the different senses is processed. The notion that the brain has discrete areas that process a single sensory channel has been dramatically revised. The modern consensus of opinion is that all regions of the brain have the potential to be connected to all others and that this interconnectivity is essentially determined by experience. It is known that the brain has remarkable plasticity in the way it develops and restructures itself according to the sensory inputs it receives and this is particularly true for the developing brains of infants and children. It is also obvious that the parts of the brain which process the different sensory inputs have a much greater degree of interconnection than had been previously thought. It is estimated that at birth the brain of a baby has about 10^{11} (one hundred trillion) neurons, which is about the same as in an adult brain, but what changes dramatically as the child grows and its brain develops is the extent and nature of the interconnections between them. It has been estimated that any one neuron can be linked in this way with several thousand other neurons meaning more than 10^{14} connections within an adult brain (roughly equivalent in computer terms to a 10 terabyte hard disk!). Eating or drinking and the experience of the associated flavours will be as important to the structuring of a child's brain as are all the other sensations it receives while it matures, and it can even be argued that feeding will play a disproportionately greater degree of influence in the first few months simply because at that time it is such a major part of daily life. The sensations associated with feeding, together with internalised feelings of well-being and comfort, will be integrated within the baby's growing brain and it is during this process that its brain structure will change to form its memories and expectations for food enjoyment in the future.

Multi-sensory perception
Six years ago it was shown (Calvert 1997) that the hearing areas of the brain are activated as well as the visual areas when people are engaged in silent lip-reading even though there is no sound being heard. In other words there are sufficient connections between the vision and auditory regions of the brain such that the two function together. This is a clear case of what is now known as multi-sensory perception, a phenomenon already well known to

experimental psychologists and one which is very much involved in our new understanding of what flavours actually are and how we learn to like them. Almost thirty years ago it was found that the lip movements of a person speaking can change the audible perception of sounds (McGurk and MacDonald 1976). There are many examples where we are conscious of one sensory mode but what we perceive is changed by information which the brain obtains through the other senses even though we are not aware of this. (Driver and Spence 2000) and this is particularly true for flavour.

What flavour is and how we learn to like it

Flavour is a simple word which we all use in everyday language although often incorrectly or at best vaguely. We taste our food to see if we like the flavour, we talk of wines with the taste of oak, raspberries or spice and of course we all know where we experience the flavour of our food – in our mouths. The reality is that much of our information about food derives from our sense of smell detected high up in our nose; it is estimated that as much as 80% of the information about our food depends on olfaction (Murphy 1977). The olfactive epithelium is in fact a direct extension of the brain and is the only part of it which protrudes from the skull into the outside world. Even though we are not conscious of its location (behind the eyes and roughly midway between the ears) it is from the receptor cells in this organ that signals are sent to the brain giving information about the changing pattern of volatile molecules being released from food during eating. We may sniff our food before putting it in our mouth as a preliminary and cautious step to checking its quality but it is during eating, drinking and swallowing that the volatile components of the food are transported in the breath to the olfactive receptors and it is this which provides most of the information about our food which we consciously perceive as flavour. The fact that we cannot 'taste' our food when we have a cold (another example of the inaccurate way we use these words) means that the volatile molecules cannot get up into the nose and we lose the olfactive signals. Of course even with a blocked nose we can in fact still taste our food because this sense is truly located in our mouth but limited to just five informational components – sweet, sour, bitter, salty and umami. Our perception of taste is very important to the overall flavour but it is the olfactive signal which gives the brain the information which allows it to discriminate and recognise what it is that we are eating. Flavour does not rely solely on taste and olfaction; the mouth also sends information via the trigeminal nerve, one of the main nerves leading from the face to the brain. It is through this that we know whether our food is hot or cold, whether it is spicy (as with chilli or pepper) or cooling (as with peppermint), and what texture it has. Our mouths are incredibly good at assessing the textural characteristics of food via our sense of touch but it is only in recent years that we have come to understand that this also plays a key role in the perception of flavour. Scientists at the University of Nottingham (Hollowood, Linforth et al. 2002) have shown that the thickness of a flavoured sauce has a direct influence on the strength of its flavour but that this has nothing to do with olfaction. Flavour also depends on vision and the colours of food or drinks are an important factor in flavour learning. A recent report discusses how a group of experienced wine tasters were asked to describe the quality and characteristics of a selection of white wines which they did expertly; when the same wines were again presented but now coloured red by the addition of a flavourless food dye, the experts were quite unable to correctly identify the same wines and could only describe them in terms of quite inappropriate red wine descriptors (Morot 2001).

'Flavour' is therefore a synthesis of all the associated sensory signals received during eating and drinking including the internally generated emotions associated with the occasion. Very simply when we eat a particular food on a regular basis then our brain combines all the signals received from the different senses, restructures itself and creates the memory we recognize as the 'flavour' of that food. The acceptability of food is therefore a fundamentally personal thing and will depend very much on how familiar it is to us and our previous histories of eating it. If we eat a food and its flavour is even slightly different from what we expect then our brain will tell us to pause and consider what it is that we have in our mouth; if the flavour is associated with a previously bad eating experience, such as nausea or vomiting, or is totally different from anything eaten before, then almost certainly our reaction will be to spit it out. Flavour is Nature's way of letting food communicate with us in order that we know what it is that we have in our mouth and can decide whether or not we continue to eat it. Since the multi-sensory perception of flavour is learned then how this happens will play a determining role in deciding what foods we enjoy eating in later life.

Learning to Like Flavour
Americans in general like the flavour of wintergreen which is used in many foods and drinks in the United States, particularly in sweet confectionery and most notably in root beer. Europeans normally do not like these products and associate the smell of wintergreen with liniment, skin creams and other medications, but certainly not food. Clearly this is not a phenomenon which depends on genetic differences since both populations derive essentially from the same gene pool. This is a clear example where nurture rules over nature and the

flavours liked by a group of people are consequent on their collective experiences as children. It is apparent from recent work that we start to experience flavour much earlier than has generally been considered to be the case; already at eleven weeks after conception (six months before birth) the human foetus has a functioning olfactory epithelium (Doty 1992). During pregnancy the foetus continually swallows amniotic fluid which contains flavour molecules transferred from the mother's blood and by the time that it is born the baby has already experienced many of the flavours which derive from the mother's diet. Pregnant mothers who consume carrot juice in their last three months of pregnancy give birth to babies which will respond more positively to carrot flavoured cereal after birth (Menella, Jagnow et al. 2001).

After the baby has been born a whole new world of sensory input opens for it and of particular relevance to this discussion is the fact that it starts to drink and to experience the sensations of feeding, the flavours that come with the milk and all the other sensory and emotional aspects of the feeding occasion: nourishment, security, contact, warmth and attention. Breast feeding gives the benefit that the baby's diet is not monotonous since the foods eaten by the mother will affect the flavour of the milk and provide variety, and it has been shown that mothers who consume specific flavours during breast feeding will enhance acceptance of those flavours in their child's diet at the time of weaning (Menella, Jagnow et al. 2001). Breast fed infants are also reported to be more willing to accept a novel vegetable on first presentation than are formula fed infants (Sullivan 1994). Bottle fed infants are also affected by the flavour of the feed and the acidity or bitterness of it creates preferences at weaning for foods with the same tastes (Menella 2002).

In early infancy the bonding between mother and child will play a uniquely important role and influence future food preferences of the child far more than is generally assumed to be the case. It has been reported that the sight of a mother eating a particular food can positively influence a child to try that food as well (Harper and Sanders 1975). If we consider the wide range of foods eaten by all human groups on earth one must ask the question whether any edible material which provides nourishment and no ill-effects can be regarded as inherently disgusting, since if presented at a sufficiently early age with positive reinforcement from the child carer it would become an accepted part of the diet. The eating of insects is a good example because while in most European and North American cultures this is regarded as disgusting it is nevertheless perfectly acceptable in parts of South America, Australia and Asia. The influence of parent-child relationships and observational learning by the child from siblings and other adults appears to have been only rarely investigated in the case of eating habits but may prove to be one of the most important factors for food acceptance and flavour learning by young children. A mother's expression of disgust at something her young infant is attempting to eat may well provide a powerful and negative association for the future acceptability of that item as a food. A fascinating study at the Monell Chemical Senses Center has looked at the liking which youngsters have for the smell of alcoholic beverages (Menella and Garcia 2000); the children fell into two quite separate groups, those which reacted positively to the smell of drinks such as beer and those quite negatively. The most interesting finding was that in the families of the children which liked the smell, alcohol had a neutral role in family life; in the families of those which reacted negatively to the smell of beer there was evidence of alcohol abuse or dependency on it in the family group. It is assumed that the children had never themselves experienced the alcohol but were remembering its smell in the context of unpleasant family situations.

Much work has been done on what is needed to get a small child to try and then come to like a new food. Familiarity and repeated exposure appear to be the key requirements for overcoming neophobia (Sullivan 1994), (Birch, Gunder et al. 1998) and peer pressure appears to play a role even in preschool life (Birch 1980). However it is not sufficient simply to see the food being consumed by others, it has actually to be tried by the child on several occasions (Birch 1987), (Birch 1990) and will then be gradually accepted. Many parents fail to get their children to like new foods because their strategies usually involve either coercion, punishment or even bribery. It has been shown that all these strategies fail because the stress of the situation or the parent's displeasure simply become associated with the food and equally importantly its flavour. A better strategy for encouraging the consumption of vegetables might be "If you don't finish all your ice cream you won't be able to have some of this lovely broccoli".

Many omnivorous animals show a dislike for trying new foods and in humans this starts at about the age of two. This behaviour is explained in terms of the evolutionary benefits to be had from only eating foods proven to be safe and to avoid anything new which might be harmful. Many animals which have a choice of potential foodstuffs in fact restrict their diet to only a handful of these; the Californian sea otter has a selection of more than twenty foods available to it but each pup is taught by its mother to select only three or four of these which it then sticks to for the rest of its life (Monterey 2003). It is not difficult to understand why neophobia in humans should exist, what is much more difficult to understand is the fact that human beings both individually and collectively do not stick to eating the same foods throughout their lives. Even with young children we see patterns of food experimentation which are hard to understand, for example they eat and apparently enjoy confectionery products with levels of sourness which are totally unacceptable to their parents. Charles Darwin (Darwin 1877) commented on his own children's preferences for rhubarb, unripe gooseberries and Holz apples which he found disgusting. It is reported that over one third of five to nine year old children show preference for highly acidic confections and that this correlates with lower levels of neophobia (Liem 2003). What is puzzling is that the children should show this behaviour at all since it is hard to explain it in terms of any real benefit other than the gratification of behaving differently from older people and of seeking novelty.

Flavour Learning in Adults

Clearly when children reach their teens they are encouraged to try new foods and grow to like flavours which they never did as children. It is an intriguing and puzzling aspect of human behaviour that many of our most preferred flavours have features which are intrinsically unpleasant.

Indeed the most popular beverages in the world, tea, coffee, beer, are all found to be distasteful on first exposure and there has been much written on the curiously popular appeal of chilli (Rozin 1990). Our liking for coffee is interesting since it has been shown that our initial acceptance of it has nothing to do with its caffeine content, which is a popular misconception. One possible explanation, which does not appear to have been investigated, is that as children we learn to associate coffee, and in particular its powerful and characteristic smell with positive emotional situations which are essentially adult. Thus the smell of freshly brewed coffee at the start of a new day when breakfast is being prepared, the experience of adults enjoying coffee together at the end of a meal might be markers for contentment and maturity. Has the smell of coffee and its association as an essentially adult flavour made the eventual acceptance of it in a drink a ritual of passage from childhood to maturity? It is a peculiar fact that many of the flavour molecules to which we are most sensitive, i.e. the ones to which we have the lowest threshold levels, are only generated by cooking and are not found as such in nature. It is hard to explain how we have evolved exquisite sensitivity to molecules found in the odours of coffee, bread and roast beef which did not exist before man first used fire and started to cook. In spite of these gaps in our understanding there has nevertheless been a lot of work done on how we can modify and train our liking for foods and their associated flavours. Just as with children the key requirement for acquiring a liking for new flavours is that they are experienced over several eating or drinking occasions; even if they are disliked and rejected on a first tasting, regular exposure can ultimately lead to liking. In our own laboratory we have selected people with specific dislikes for certain fruits (rhubarb, durian) and with less than ten exposures shifted this to acceptance and even appreciation of their flavours.

It is hard to see why a society with an adequate and nutritious diet would spontaneously change its food and flavour preferences from generation to generation. In 1920 there were more than 200 shops preparing and selling tripe in Manchester and now there are essentially none (Mason 2002). Who would have thought 20 years ago that Americans would now be eating raw fish and that sushi bars would be found in most towns in the USA? Such shifts in food preferences are not new, the flavours of tomatoes, chillis, vanilla, potatoes and maize were unknown outside the Americas until the 15th century but became totally assimilated into the other cuisines of the world. One well-researched study (Cwiertka 1999) looks at changes in eating habits in Japan over the last 100 years, which had more to do with fashion and status than nutrition. Although it has been said that our food preferences are defined by socio-cultural rules rather than being influenced by physiological need (Rozin 1982) this does not explain why we shift away from the tried and proven foods we know, which would be the expected behaviour for a truly neophobic animal.

Many flavours uniquely belong to specific societies where children's early exposure to them is the key to their acceptance. A classic example is the liking for autolysed yeast. In some countries waste yeast from breweries is processed into a characteristically sticky, savoury, brown paste which is particularly rich in B-vitamins and sold as a nutritious spread (Marmite® in the UK, Vegemite® in Australia and New Zealand, Cenovis® in Switzerland). Many children in these countries are introduced to these products as a thin filling in sandwiches or spread on toast and they then remain popular at all age levels. However to people brought up outside these countries their flavour is generally regarded as quite disgusting.

At this symposium in 1997 Peter Barham deeply offended two Norwegian symposiasts when he described the flavour of Lutefisk as "his worst nightmare" (Barham 2001). There should have been no offence; Peter's brain was not programmed to like Lutefisk in the way that the brains of Norwegians are.

Young people fed a monotonous but nutritionally adequate diet show a dramatic increase in food cravings which disappear when they return to a varied diet, whereas older people in their seventies do not show an increase in craving different foods under these conditions (Pelchat 1997), (Pelchat 2000). Other studies also report an age related decline in food cravings (Hill 1991), (Basdevant 1993). One is left with the conclusion that in spite of our inherent neophobia, we show a unique behaviour as human beings in that we need to try new foods and flavours and that this characteristic declines as we get older. Ironically olfactive discrimination also decreases with age (Schiffman 2000) so that elderly people in spite of a reduced incidence of food cravings are nevertheless more willing to try novel foods (Pelchat 2000). Some very recent work has used modern imaging techniques to study the brains of people who experience food craving and there are some very preliminary but fascinating suggestions that the brain regions which are active during this are those which are also involved with drug addiction (Pelchat 2002), (Pelchat and Ragland 2003).

I will end this article with the thought that perhaps the evolutionary changes which allowed human beings to adapt so effectively to their environment also created an animal with a brain which demands continually changing sensory stimuli. There are many things we do which have no intrinsic evolutionary advantage but we get great pleasure out of them; our earliest ancestors drew and we still hang pictures on our walls, we listen to music and maybe our brains need to have the sensory stimulation of different, interesting and novel flavours just as much as it does that of art and song. The description of Eve's craving for the fruit on the tree of knowledge was a very shrewd perception of the human character.

The author would like to acknowledge the very helpful discussions with the scientists at the Monell Chemical Senses Centre in Philadelphia during the preparation of this article.

References

BARHAM, P., My worst nightmare - Lutefisk. *The Science of Cooking*, (Berlin: Springer Verlag, 2001), pp.103-105.

BASDEVANT, A. e. a., Snacking patterns in obese French women, *Appetite* 21(1993), pp. 17-23.

BIRCH, L. L., (1980) Effects of peer model's food choices and eating behaviors on preschoolers' food preferences, *Child Development* 51, pp. 489-496.

BIRCH, L. L., Ed., (1987) Children's Food Preferences: developmental patterns and environmental influences, *Annals of Development*, (Greenwich: JAI Press,).

BIRCH, L. L., (1990) The control of food intake by young children: the role of learning, *Taste, Experience and Feeding*, D. Capaldi and T. L. Powley, (Washington D.C.: American Psychological Association), pp.116-135.

BIRCH, L. L., L. GUNDER, et al., (1998) Infants' consumption of a new food enhances acceptance of similar foods, *Appetite* 30(3), pp. 283-295.

BLAKE, A., The Language of Flavour: Learning and Memory, *Food and the Memory*, Proceedings of The Oxford Symposium on Food and Cookery, (Totnes: Prospect Books, 2000).

CALVERT, G. A., BULLMORE et al., Activation of auditory cortex during silent lipreading, *Science* 276:(1997) pp. 593-596.
CWIERTKA, J. K., *The making of modern culinary tradition in Japan*, (Leiden: University of Leiden (1999).
DARWIN, C., Biographische Skizze eines kleinen Kindes. *Kosmos*, (1877) pp. 367-376.
DOTY, R. L., Olfactory function in neonates, *The Human Sense of Smell*, D. G. Laing, R. L. Doty and W. Breipohl, (Berlin: Springer-Verlag Berlin/Heidelberg,1992), pp. 155-165.
DRIVER, J. AND C., SPENCE, Multisensory perception: Beyond modularity and convergence, *Current Biology*, vol.10(20) (2000), R731-R735.
HARPER, L. AND K. M. SANDERS, The effect of adults' eating on young children's acceptance of unfamiliar foods, *Journal of Experimental Child Psychology*, vol. 20 (1975), pp. 206-214.
HILL, A. J. e. a., Food craving, dietary restraint and mood, *Appetite*, vol. 17(1991), pp. 187-197.
HOLLOWOOD, T. A., R. S. T. LINFORTH, et al., The effect of viscosity on the perception of flavour, *Chemical Senses*, vol.27 (2002) pp. 583-591.
LIEM, D. G. M., J.A., Heightened sour preferences during childhood, *Chemical Senses, vol.* 28 (2003) pp.173-180.
MASON, L., Mancunian Foods, *The International Herald of Taste*, no. 24 (2002).
MCCRONE, J., Going Inside: a tour round a single moment of consciousness, (London: Faber & Faber, 1999).
MCGURK, H. AND J. MACDONALD, Hearing lips and seeing voices, *Nature* 264, (1976), pp. 746-748.
MENELLA, J. A. AND P. L. GARCIA, (2000) Children's Hedonic Response to the Smell of Alcohol: Effects of Parental Drinking Habits, *Alcoholism – Clinical and Experimental Research* 24(8), pp. 1167-1171.
MENELLA, J. A., C. P. JAGNOW, et al., (2001) Prenatal and postnatal flavor learning by human infants, *Pediatrics,* 107(E88).
MENELLA, J. A., BEAUCHAMP, G.K., Flavor experiences during formula feeding are related to preferences during childhood, *Early Human Development* vol.68 (2002) pp.71-72.
Monterey, Personal Discussions with the Staff of the California Sea Otter Protection Programme, Monterey Bay Aquarium, (2003).
MOROT, G., BROCHET et al., The Color of Odors, *Brain and Language*, (Academic Press, 2001).
MURPHY, C. e. a., Mutual Action of Taste and Olfaction, *Sensory Processes* 1 (1977), pp. 204-211.
PELCHAT, M. L., (1997) Food cravings in young and elderly adults, *Appetite* 28, pp. 103-113.
PELCHAT, M. L., (2000) You can teach an old dog new tricks: olfaction and responses to novel foods by the elderly, *Appetite* 35(2)), pp. 153-160.
PELCHAT, M. L., (2002) Of human bondage: Food craving, obsession, compulsion, and addiction, *Physiology and Behaviour* 76, pp. 347-352.
PELCHAT, M. L. AND J. D. RAGLAND, (2003) *Images of Desire: fMRI and Food Craving.* Paper presented at the American Chemical Society meeting in Sarasota.
PELCHAT, M. L. AND S. SCHAEFER, (2000) Dietary monotony and food cravings in young and elderly adults, *Physiology and Behaviour,* no. 68, pp. 353-359.
ROZIN, E., The structure of Cuisine. *The Psychobiology of Human Food Selection*, L. M. Barker, (Westport: AVI Publishing Co., Inc.,1982).
ROZIN, P., Getting to like the burn of chili pepper: Biological, psychological and cultural perspectives, *Chemical Senses* 2: Irritation, (1990), pp. 231-269.
SCHIFFMAN, S. S., Taste quality and neural coding: Implications from psychophysics and neurophysiology, *Physiology & Behavior* 69(1-2), (2000), pp.147-159.
SCIENTIFIC AMERICAN, *The Scientific American Book of the Brain*, Scientific American, (1999).
SULLIVAN, S. A. B., L.L.BIRCH, Infant dietary experience and acceptance of solid foods, *Pediatrics* 93, (1994), pp. 271-277.

Piki, Polenta, and Pellagra: Maize, Nutrition and Nurturing the Natural

Barrett P Brenton

A focus on maize as a central food in human diets can provide a number of case studies within a loosely defined field of ethnonutrition. I define ethnonutrition as the information specific to a given culture that allows its members to recognize, categorize, and explain the impact of their diet and foodways on maintaining or restoring order in natural, social or spiritual realms. I would also add to this a biocultural perspective, a view that integrates scientific understandings of human nutrition with the cultural dimensions of its use in a society.

Let me state at the beginning that I'm not a big fan of reductionist nature vs. nature debates, or vulgar neo-Darwinian models of evolutionary nutrition. Humans have far too much of an evolutionary history with associated cultural baggage to condense it all down to either genes or gastronomy. In this paper the term nature and natural refers to the biological principles of digestion and nutrition that we cannot avoid or ignore. Nurture serves as a term implying both what is culturally learned, as opposed to innate, along with its meaning as a source of nourishment (both literally and figuratively) provided in cultural contexts that reflect patterns of consumption.

What follows traverses the world in an attempt to reveal how the culinary traditions associated with one crop, maize, have had a profound impact on the diet, health and destiny of countless humans since it left the shores of the New World over 500 years ago. Additional insights can be found in the extensive works of Coe (1994), Fussell (1992), Warman (2003), and Weathermax (1954). I argue here that the biocultural evolution of food processing traditions can only be understood with a holistic approach that integrates the nurturing of food as a symbol of cultural identity with the natural constraints and realities of human biology, diet and nutrition.

This journey into ethnonutrition is done by contrasting the traditions of Native Americans (Brenton 2003), whose alkali and other cooking traditions allowed them to consume maize as a primary dietary staple, with those peoples who did not adopt such a nurturing conquest of the natural limitations of maize nutrition. And by no fault of their own they suffered from the dietary malady of *pellagra*. To grasp the full complexity of this history an additional emphasis is placed on the problem of conflating natural and nurtured categories of sex and gender. The paper ends with a discussion on the use of genetically modified maize as an ongoing contested nexus of nature and nurture in human societies.

A Pellagra Primer

Put plainly, pellagra is a disease of poverty and social inequality (Brenton 1998). It has affected primarily the world's poor for centuries, and far more women than men. The disease results primarily from deficiencies in the B-vitamin niacin, and the amino acid tryptophan. Both of these nutrients are limiting factors in maize intensive diets. Pellagra has been generally correlated to high-maize and low-protein diets over the past three centuries. Indigenous New World peoples are believed to have been protected from this disease by the use of alkali processing techniques in the making of such foods as hominy and tortillas. In short, the addition of culinary ash (potassium or sodium hydroxide) or lime (calcium hydroxide) during the process of cooking increases the bioavailability of both niacin and tryptophan (Bressani 1990; Katz et al. 1974). The paper-thin blue maize flat bread *piki*, made by the Hopi Indians of Arizona, is another example of an alkali processed maize product with an enhanced nutritional value, discussed in greater detail below.

Not surprisingly, the first descriptions of pellagra were in the Old World during the 18th century as maize was becoming more common as a staple food. This "plague of corn," as Daphne Roe so wonderfully put it in her 1973 book title, was rampant in many southern European marginalized peasant populations for centuries and prevalent among poor U.S. southerners in the early decades of the twentieth century (Etheridge 1972; Roe 1973).

It is without the benefit of an alkali cooking tradition that scores of impoverished peoples consumed primarily maize-based diets and suffered its consequences. This ranged from the "polenta eaters" of Italy to the consumption of grits in southern U.S. cuisine. Pellagra continues to be a problem in refugee populations and is still endemic in some southern Africa communities (Brenton 1998). It is hard to imagine that over the centuries tens of thousands of people lost their lives to pellagra, while hundreds of thousand suffered from the malady.

Pellagra is one of the great detective stories in the history of nutrition (see Carpenter 1981; Etheridge 1972; Roe 1973; Terris 1964). Early on, an association was made between a high-maize diet and poverty among those with the greatest affliction, but for over two centuries many other theories were put forth to explain this malady. This included: 1) a high maize diet with little or no milk, meat or fresh vegetable supplements; 2) spoiled or rotten grain; 3) a disease spread by insects; 4) bad heredity, a question of eugenics, and 5) an overall consequence of poverty. Studies begun in 1914 by Dr. Joseph Goldberger, a US Public Health Service officer, came to the conclusion that pellagra was related to a poor diet lacking good sources of protein, which was in part a consequence of poverty (Goldberger 1918; Terris 1964). Yet his ideas did not receive widespread acceptance for almost 20 years given the competing theories stated above.

One thing that was fairly consistent was the description of this disease. Pellagra literally translated as "rough or angry skin" became popularly known as the affliction of the four "D's." Each "D" characterized one of the classic symptoms of the debilitating sequence of the disease: Dermatitis, Diarrhea, Dementia, with the fourth and final "D," Death. In short, the worse case scenario would progress as follows: the severe burning and itching of the dermatitis is later accompanied by bloody stools. This is followed by periods of dementia and if left untreated results in inevitable death. It should be emphasized that more often than not pellagrins suffered, but did not die. If their diet was altered to include sources of niacin or tryptophan, often unknowingly, the signs of pellagra disappeared. This often occurred on a seasonal basis with fluctuations in the availability of fresh fruits and vegetables.

The following two sections will highlight examples of Native American traditions that transcended the nutritional limitations of maize in a way that inextricably linked the symbolic importance of this food with cooking technologies that prevented pellagra.

Piki: The Lifeline of Hopi Traditional Foodways

Piki is a wafer-thin, perhaps more appropriately stated, paper-thin maize bread. It is prepared initially as a batter by taking finely ground (powder-like) blue maize meal and placing it in a bowl to which hot water and culinary ash are added until a blue hue is achieved. As a source of alkali the ash (*chamissa*, made from burning the four-wing saltbush) fixes the blue hue. The batter is then taken by hand out of the bowl—quickly spreading a thin layer onto a polished sandstone griddle. The blackened piki stone, cured traditionally by burning melon seeds and rubbing it down with fats from the brain and spine of a sheep, has an intense wood fire stoked underneath of it during the cooking process. One avoids the severe burning of the fingers by years of practice and the build up of heat resistant calluses. After it quickly cooks it is either rolled up or folded into a packet. This activity traditionally took place in a piki house or special room designed for a woman to kneel or sit down at the piki stone. Some have made piki using baking soda as the source of alkali and a Teflon griddle in place of the piki stone, but the altered taste and absence of smoky flavor gives its lack of authenticity away. The ability to make piki is clearly a culinary art. Women who have mastered it take great pride in the status it confers.

Today piki is still being made by the Hopi, a group of traditionally Native American farmers numbering over 10,000 strong, most of whom live on a one and a half million acre reservation in the desert and mesa region of northeastern Arizona, USA Over the centuries the matrilineal clan system of the Hopi has maintained a traditional system of dryland farming based primarily on the cultivation of maize, beans and squash.

The greatest change in Hopi diet has been a movement almost completely away from traditionally grown and prepared foods towards store-bought processed foods (Brenton 1992, 1993, 1994). The overall drawbacks of this transition are a diet that now contains high levels of salt, fat, and sugar, and is lacking many micronutrients that were plentiful in traditional foods (Brown and Brenton 1994; Kuhnlein and Calloway 1977, 1979; Kuhnlein *et al.* 1979). This overall dietary change has had a real impact on the Hopi in terms of the high rate of diabetes they now endure.

Still, the Hopi retain a sort of optimistic fatalism in a prophecy that has predicted that these changes will occur and they are expected to resist them. Hopi farmers now plant fewer types of crops and varieties and the decision of what type of maize to plant is based more on the color/variety needed for social and religious occasions than for a staple food. However, these actions are still central for nurturing Hopi identity. For example, maize is the one product that cannot be substituted with something store-bought. Grinding up a bag of commercially-made blue-corn tortilla chips does not confer the same meaning as the wafer-thin piki. The use of maize in its various colors is crucial to the maintenance of all traditional religious and social activities among the Hopi. The most important of all varieties is maize that is blue.

The Hopi have a very clear sense of the social and spiritual duties there are to fulfill until the end of this their fourth world, having survived the destruction of three previous worlds. When the creator set down the tribes of the region he presented them with maize of various colors and size. One by one the various tribes took them away. With great humility the Hopi waited until the very end when all that was left was a short ear of blue maize. Looking favorably on this action the creator told the Hopi that this would sustain them in the harsh life ahead of them in the desert. Without any pretense or arrogance Hopi prophecy also holds that it will be that blue maize that will allow them and the entire human race to survive into the fifth world, after this one is destroyed.

Blue maize also represents the westerly direction from which the prevailing winds bring clouds and rain. In the desert southwest this means life. It is no surprise then that when one speaks of piki one is primarily referring to its being made from blue maize. Other colors of piki do exist (white, yellow, and red), and are brought to Hopi children as gifts by masked men who are physical embodiments of *Katsina* spirits. It should also be noted that evidence for the *Katsina* cult is seen in the archaeological record around the same time as piki stones.

An unmarried woman's ability to learn the culinary art of making piki was an important criterion for her marriage. Engagements and weddings are surrounded by blue maize flour and the making of piki. The linkage of this foodstuff to a Hopi woman's gender identity cannot be understated. Young boys (and the occasional male anthropologist) showing an interest in wanting to take part in their mother's piki making are often looked upon as having some cross-gendered issues, much like boys who play with dolls.

A quick glance at Hopi society today would give one the impression that the making of piki is becoming a lost art. This is true in many other pueblos of the southwest, and one would think that its limited production by Hopi teenagers would support this claim. However, many young Hopi women after becoming married, having children, and perhaps even now divorced, in time learn the art of piki making as they come to realize their central role as a women in a matrilineal society. The symbolic centrality of piki to Hopi traditions is grounded in a food that was their daily bread and has now become a symbolic lifeline. This link is even more impressive when one considers the nature of this unique form of alkali processing.

The traditional methods of Hopi food processing seem to have been well adapted to a desert environment and a high maize diet. They used little water and included a number of methods to enhance nutrient processing (Katz 1989). Piki is only one of many alkali processed maize products made by the Hopi, but as discussed above, none hold the same symbolic importance as it does.

As stated earlier, pellagra is prevented by the presence of alkali cooking techniques that increase the bioavailability of niacin and tryptophan. On the other hand, if the alkalinity or pH is too high this can lead to both the degradation of niacin and essential amino acids. My own research on this issue with Solomon Katz (see Katz 1989) has shown that the alkali processing of piki involves a form of pH titration, wherein the blue color is linked to the optimal pH at which niacin is released. Essentially, the anthocyanin pigments that make blue maize blue are the same that are used in the classic pH litmus test strips, blue is basic - red is acidic. Too little alkali and the fine blue corn meal color stays a pinkish-red (pH 6) or slightly acidic with no effect, too much alkali (pH 9+) and the product turns green along with the degradation of niacin. If the source of alkali that Hopi women use is too strong they will often get the green color at which point they will usually throw out the batch and start over. When pressed for time or lack of milled maize, they may titrate back in more maize meal but it never seems to come out the same.

In short, the piki litmus test can be hypothesized as the biocultural evolution of a cuisine that incorporated the centrality of the color blue and its pellagra-preventative value with the nurtured value of this food, embedded in the symbolic context of Hopi tradition. The ethnonutritional dimensions of piki must also consider the role that gender and biological sex may have had in its development. But, before elaborating any more on this issue, I will present next another example of a Native American maize cuisine that reveals the symbolic and nutritional dimensions of pellagra-preventative cooking traditions.

Green Corn Ceremonialism: A Universal First Fruits Celebration

Most Native American horticultural societies throughout North America have traditionally taken part in ceremonies focused on the harvest and consumption of green corn (unripened maize). These rituals range from small family gatherings to community-wide celebrations. Culinary traditions for processing extend from the pit-baked sweet corn of the Hopi to the roasted unripened "field" corn of the Mandan. Perhaps more aptly put, these events are in recognition of the ripening of corn, a developmental process through which an assured harvest is both expected and celebrated.

The ethnonutritional and biocultural significance of green corn displays a pellagra-preventative alternative to alkali processing, that like piki holds deep symbolic and ceremonial significance (Brenton 1995). As the name implies, "Green Corn" ceremonies take place while corn is about to begin its final stages of maturation from an unripened or green state, where the corn is in its milky stage, with the cob and kernels nearly fully developed in size, to a ripened or matured state. It is also the time at which the sugar content of corn is quickly being enzymatically converted to starch.

In the temperate climates of North America the ceremonies generally take place in late summer from August through September, depending mostly on the latitudinal-dependent growing season of corn. The most extensive ceremonies and best recorded are those found within the Southeast ceremonial complex. So important were these ceremonies to Native American groups of the Southeast, that their New Year was brought in during the "Green Corn" ceremonies or 'Busk,' incorporating the "Green Corn" dance. Even the Mashantucket Pequots of Connecticut, once thought to be extinct as a tribe and now owners of the largest casino in the world, hold an annual event in September called the "Feast of Green Corn and Dance" or *Schemitzun*.

Hall (1997) has suggested that the importance of corn mother or *selu* among the Cherokee is related to the introduction of the "Green Corn" Goddess from Mexico during Toltec times (AD 900-1200). For many groups of the Eastern Woodlands "Green Corn" rituals were more significant than either planting or harvest rituals. In all cases, the harvest and preparation of green corn is followed by extensive feasting and gorging. Rituals involved with "Green Corn" ceremonialism are generally related to giving thanks for the expected harvest, providing assurance that the corn crop will continue on to maturity. This of course could be correlated to those "first fruits" rituals associated with major cultigens around the world.

The importance of ritual surrounding "Green Corn" ceremonialism is clear to see in the context of recognizing and nurturing an important stage in the developmental lifecycle of maize. The most intriguing nutritional dimension of green corn was suggested by Kodicek *et al.* (1974) who reported that roasting sweet corn leads to the conversion of bound niacin to a free form. This transformation has been subsequently supported by others (Brenton 1984; Carter and Carpenter 1982).

The key to understanding the differential availability of niacin is found in the developmental stages of maize. As maize goes from the stages of 1) milky, 2) dough, 3) denting, and 4) maturity, over a period of roughly 30 days, the bioavailability of niacin becomes less as it becomes biochemically bound (Wall *et al.* 1987). Again, an alkaline solution can lead to the release of some of this niacin in ripened corn, but it will destroy the niacin in green corn.

It can be argued that the cooking of green corn provided an anti-pellagragenic factor to Native Americans by increasing the amount of available niacin. This was accomplished by choosing to harvest and consume maize at different points in its developmental cycle. Its ceremonial significance nurtured a process that overcame the nutritional limitations of maize.

I've witnessed street vendors selling roasting ears of maize from Nairobi to Cuzco, and have come to expect the use of "baby corn" (primarily grown in Thailand) in Asian-American cuisine. These examples speak to ingenious and innovative culinary traditions that bypass the nutritional problems associated with matured maize without an alkali tradition, and should be explored further.

The biocultural importance of maize processing techniques and their associated symbolic meaning offers a strong case for how Native Americans nurtured the natural. They are case studies that highlight the interface of the sacred and the scientific. Further explorations on this topic can be found in the insightful writings of Sophie Coe concerning the tortilla, an alkali processed maize food (Coe 1994). But what about societies who did not have the same sacred ties to maize and whose misfortune was a product of history and social inequality? Such is the case of pellagra amongst the "polenta eaters" of Northern Italy and poor southerners in the American south.

Polenta, Grits, and Beyond: When Cornmeal and Pellagra Converge

Peasants of Northern Italy suffered from the malady of pellagra for centuries, only to find relief with food reform in the 20th century (Whitaker 1992). It truly was a "plague of corn" (Roe 1973). But unlike the plagues that had swept through their villages in centuries past, this one was more selective. It primarily afflicted only the poorest of the poor. Unable to afford wheat, meat or almost any other source of quality food, they were forced to subsist on a crop that their own countryman Christopher Columbus had introduced during his "discoveries" of the New World. Unfortunately for them, what Columbus had failed to do was to bring back the alkali processing key that was held by the indigenous peoples of the New World.

For centuries Italian physicians were among many throughout southern Europe that tried to understand why pellagra prevailed. Almost everyone came to the conclusion that maize was to blame but could not decipher why. What did become synonymous with pellagra was the basic peasant food, polenta. Polenta, simply a boiled corn mush, had sustained peasant populations for centuries. Add a little meat protein, cheese, or fresh fruit and vegetables on the side and it's still a diet of no great consequence, but you might avoid pellagra. If you were forced as a matter of landless poverty to have meals consisting primarily of polenta, then pellagra was inevitable. To be referred to as a "polenta eater" by your countrymen from the south is not a compliment.

In many ways polenta then becomes the antithesis of piki. Lost in its transfer to the Old World was a way of processing wherein nature became nurtured by its symbolic linkages to the sacred. Nevertheless, not all symbols have to be steeped in the divine. The migration of polenta foodways and traditions out of Italy has led to gentrified culinary traditions that left behind its pellagra roots to be with nutritionally secure generations that nurture it with great secular nostalgia while embracing the traditions of the old country.

In another context, the nurtured embrace of hominy grits (coarsely ground corn) provides a similar case of "after the fact" secularized nostalgia. It was the impoverished populations, as in Italy, of the American south during the first few decades of the 20th century that suffered most from Pellagra. To folks from the northern US states, grits continue to give a stigma of southern poverty along with being a "redneck" (a condition that was made more severe by the sun sensitive skin on the back of a pellagra victim's neck, which literally gave them a red neck). Yet, grits today are central to southern food identity, a national cuisine of the old Confederacy.

The stark distinction from the Italian experience however is that in the case of hominy grits American colonists had unknowingly adopted the Native American traditions of alkali processing and thus avoided pellagra for centuries. This all changed when the modern world of industrialized food processing took over at the turn of the 20th century. The industrial milling and dehulling/degerming processes of maize, which completely removed most of the niacin, became common around 1905 when US pellagra rates also began to rise.

In southern states where pellagra rates were the highest, grits were no longer being made as "hominy grits," which involved the alkali processing of maize into hominy. Hominy is a term derived from the Algonquian word *rockahominie*, which was used to refer to corn that was soaked in lye to remove the hull. Now they were only grits as a product of this new milling process. Unfortunately, these grits were still being sold as hominy grits, having lost the benefit of alkali processing. In short, the hominy was taken out of the grits but the name stayed, and pellagra became endemic in the American south for over a quarter century, killing thousands each year, and afflicting tens of thousands.

Pellagra mortality and morbidity rates quickly subsided during the late 1930s to early 1940s. By that time niacin had been isolated as a B complex vitamin which could be provided to patients in the form of yeast cakes, and by 1943 maize and wheat flours in the US were being fortified with niacin by law.

In both the case of polenta and grits, secular nostalgia was only later nurtured in an eating and nutritional environment that did not have to face the harsh natural realities of pellagra. In other contexts around the world pellagra and the use of maize meal has had a variety of consequences. Historically it most likely contributed to the deaths of Civil War prisoners at Andersonville, GA (Brenton 2000) and to victims of the Irish famine when maize was used as a relief food (Crawford 1981; Brenton 1998). Throughout southern Africa pellagra became common by the middle of the 20th century as traditional grains such as sorghum and millet were being replaced by maize or "mealy meal." The Apartheid era of South Africa was no doubt responsible for a disease that was only seen as a malady of black south Africans (Brenton 1998).

In places like Kenya and Ghana, traditions emerged that fermented maize meal into products like *uji* and *kenkey*, respectively. A slight lactic acid fermentation process is usually enough to aid in the release of bound niacin as well as providing additional niacin as a byproduct of microbial activity.

Beer of course is another way of overcoming the niacin problem without the aid of alkali processing. Various forms of maize beer are ubiquitous throughout Latin America. Before the Spanish conquest it essentially supported the great works of the Incan empire in the form of *chicha*. Maize beers can also be found in various forms throughout Africa, but often have various governmental restrictions put upon their manufacture. Native Americans developed some fermentations of maize, too (Brenton 1988). However, the mystery of why essentially no alcoholic fermentations were found historically north of Mexico goes unsolved.

What follows is not as much of a disjuncture with the rest of the paper as one might think.

My main objective is to highlight how clear the evidence is for differential pellagra mortality rates between males and females based on digestion and diet, nature and nurture. This is yet another dimension of pellagra that we need to consider when looking not only at the origin of a cuisine but the transformation of a staple food from one social context to another.

Pellagra, Sex and Gender

I have argued elsewhere (Brenton 2000) for a biocultural approach and hypothesis that investigates the clear difference and synergism of pellagra rates related to sex *and* gender. Putting a theoretical debate on the conflation of sex and gender aside, this proposal operates on the condition of distinguishing between: gender (defined as one's sexual identity as woman, man, etc.), *and* sex (defined as one's being biologically male or female).

One of the most striking characteristics of pellagra mortality in the U.S. from 1900-1950 (a time during which pellagra was most prevalent) is that rates for women were consistently nearly double to triple that of men (Miller 1978). Even more alarming is the fact that pellagra morbidity rates (those diagnosed with the disease) could be up to 20 times greater for women, with a common two- to threefold difference being prevalent. We have to ask why.

Overall, pellagra morbidity and mortality rates for females eating high maize and low protein diets are greater than males, owing to a complex biocultural interaction. It is a clear case where both nature (biological sex) and nurture (culturally defined gender roles and food consumption patterns) work as a synergism that is far more destructive than either of the factors taken alone. The two components are as follows:

    a. Unequal access to nutrient quality foods, and therefore inadequate intakes of niacin and tryptophan by women, owing to poverty, gender inequality, and household consumption patterns, and

    b. Estrogen's demonstrated inhibitory effect on converting the amino acid tryptophan to niacin, a major pathway for meeting our daily niacin requirements.

Pellagra's Nurtured Environment

Gendered explanations for why women suffered from pellagra much more than men in the US south during the first half of the 20th century are focused on differential and unequal access to quality foods within the household. For example:

    a. Often, as primary wage earners, men were given consideration and preference at the dinner table; they also had pocket money to spend on foods outside of the home.

    b. Women as wage earners made less than men, thus decreasing their spending power for food items.

    c. Women would give protein quality foods, especially milk, to their children first.

    d. Women would generally eat last after everyone else in the family had a chance to eat.

    e. Women, especially in southern states, strongly upheld the culinary triad of the 3 "Ms": maize (in the form of grits), molasses, and meat (really fat-back pork); a combination that clearly contributed to pellagra.

Pellagra and the Nature of Sex

Although the conversion rate of tryptophan to niacin is only 60:1 (Henderson 1983), our dietary requirements of niacin are usually met in this way. This pathway is especially important in diets which are low in niacin, as is the case with intensive maize eaters. It has been shown that estrogen can block or inhibit the biochemical conversion of the essential amino acid tryptophan to the B-vitamin niacin when diets are minimally adequate for tryptophan (Bender and Totoe 1984; Shibata and Satoko 1997).

A strong argument for the impact of estrogen on differential pellagra rates can also be found when one notes that in the US during some of the worst outbreaks of pellagra, the maximum number of pellagra deaths were for females between the ages of 20 and 40. This can clearly be seen in the age-dependent role of estrogen during the female lifecycle (from menarche to menopause). The onset of pellagra shows a dramatic increase around the age of menarche (first menses) and drops off sharply by age 50 and the onset of menopause. For males, pellagra rates are fairly steady during their adult years.

These observations are consistently noted in both mortality and morbidity rates for the US and in other countries as well. A 1990 survey of a pellagra outbreak among Mozambican refugees in Malawi showed that the morbidity rate was almost 8 times higher among women than men (Malfait et al. 1993). In sum, morbidity and mortality rates for females closely follow an age-related curve from menarche to menopause linked to life history levels of estrogen (Brenton 2000).

With the synergism of sex and gender in action, it is tempting to question the role of Native American females/women in the biocultural evolution of maize culinary traditions that stressed the use of alkali processing techniques to prevent the onset of pellagra and allow higher maize consumption. The importance of piki to the gender identity of Hopi women cannot be lost in an understanding of the selective forces at stake in nurturing a food processing technology that ushered in an even greater sanctity for the role of maize products in the secular and sacred life of the Hopi. Women simply had a lot more at stake.

Cyborg Diets and the Future of Maize

The current controversy surrounding the risks of using and consuming genetically modified organisms (GMOs), in this case maize, ushers in a new era for a wonder crop that has been both worshipped and associated with death and disease. Many are concerned with the speed at which our technological culture can tinker with natural biological processes. In all of the examples presented above *time* was the very ingredient needed to be able to develop a nurturing control over the natural. Biotechnology and bioengineering confront us with many new challenges as a nurturing species. The long-term affect of GMOs on human nutrition and health are at present unknown, but we are well aware of the negative political-economic and social costs GMOs have incurred.

When it comes to the use of various forms of genetically modified maize, conflicts have emerged ranging from establishing EU regulations over U.S. food imports, to the refusal of genetically modified maize as a much needed source of food aid in Zambia, to concerns by indigenous peoples over the defiling of their sacred maize by profane air-born genetically modified pollen, not to mention the patents now held on those ancient strains of maize by multinational corporations.

In a globalized world of GMOs there is no doubt that we need to explore in greater detail both the historical and contemporary nurturing of maize. We must also show how societies can be aided in facing the natural biological barriers to eating that they encounter, along with those imposed upon them by Cyborg driven social orders. I'm using the term Cyborg diet to refer to the new era of technologically enhanced diets and foods. But how is this any different, for example, from introducing the benefits of alkali processing? The main distinction is that those traditional diets and methods of food processing developed in a special relationship that nurtured the natural. In this new form there is no need for nurturing; in many cases people do not have any choice or are unaware of the choices they have. In addition, most of the enhancements are a matter of economic efficiency and corporate profits, and are anything but sustainable. The natural transformations are those of the crop and often do not have any direct nutritional benefit to the consumer. European resistance to GMOs obviously involves concern with a disjuncture at the nexus of nature and nurture that flies in the face of cooking traditions and cultural meanings ascribed to foods.

I'm not a futurist but I do think that as we continue to reveal past culinary traditions we can apply those lessons in order to resist a future of Cyborg diets rife with technologies that are out of sync with nurtured cultural environments, however futile that might be.

Perhaps it is most fitting to end this paper with a summary of comments that Hopi women expressed to me when I provided them with scientific explanations for piki's blue color and enhanced nutritional value. "Of course we know it's the best thing for you. That's why we have always eaten it and that's why it was given to us by the creator to sustain us in this world. We also know that by eating less of it today we have health problems like diabetes. Yes, your nutrition stuff is interesting, but just remember, Don't Worry, Be Hopi.

References Cited

BENDER, D. A. AND L. TOTOE, (1984), Inhibition of Tryptophan Metabolism by Oestrogens in the Rat: a Factor in the Aetiology of Pellagra. *British Journal of Nutrition* 51:219-224.

BRENTON, B.P., (1984), *Preliminary Investigations in the Nutritional Significance of Indian Maize Processing*. B.A. Thesis, Department of Anthropology, University of Nebraska-Lincoln.

BRENTON, B.P., (1988), Fermented Foods in New World Prehistory: North America. In *Diet and Subsistence: Current Archaeological Perspectives*. Brenda V. Kennedy and Genevieve M. Le Moine, eds. Pp. 329-337. Calgary, Alberta: University of Calgary.

BRENTON, B.P., (1992), An Analysis of Hopi 5th and 6th Grade Student Diets: Implications for Diet-Related Disease and the Role of Traditional Foods [Abstract]. *American Journal of Physical Anthropology*, Supplement 14:53.

BRENTON, B.P., (1993), An Analysis of Hopi Women's Diets: Implications for Diet-Related Disease and the Role of Traditional Foods [Abstract]. *American Journal of Physical Anthropology*, Supplement 16:62.

BRENTON, B.P., (1994), *Hopi Foodways: Biocultural Perspectives on Change and Contradiction*. Ph.D. Dissertation, Department of Anthropology, University of Massachusetts: Amherst, MA. Ann Arbor, MI: University Microfilms.

BRENTON, B.P., (1995), Green Corn Ceremonialism and Ethnonutrition: the Biocultural Evolution of Maize Use [Abstract]. *Journal of Ethnobiology* 15: 288-289.

BRENTON, B.P., (1998), Pellagra and Nutrition Policy: Lessons from the Great Irish Famine to the New South Africa. *Nutritional Anthropology* 22(1):1-11.

BRENTON, B.P., (2000), Pellagra, Sex and Gender: Biocultural Perspectives on Differential Diets and Health. *Nutritional Anthropology* 23(1):20-24.

BRENTON, B.P., (2000), *Death by "Dixie" Diet: Did Pellagra Kill Many Civil War POWs and Who's to Blame?* Paper presented at the Annual Meeting of the Medical History Society of New Jersey, Princeton, NJ. October.

BRENTON, B.P., (2003), American Indians: Contemporary Issues. In *Encyclopedia of Food and Culture*, Vol.1. S.H. Katz, ed. Pp. 75-79. New York: Charles Scribner's Sons.

BROWN, A.C. AND B. P. BRENTON, (1994), Hopi Native American Elementary Students: Current Diet and Recommended Changes to Decrease Dietary Risk Factors. *Journal of the American Dietetic Association* 94(5):517-522.

BRESSANI, R., (1990), Chemistry, Technology, and Nutritive Value of Maize Tortillas. *Food Reviews International* 6(2):225-264.

CARPENTER, K. J. (ed.), (1981), *Pellagra*. Stroudsburg, PA: Hutchinson Ross.

CARTER, E.G. AND K.J. CARPENTER, (1982), The Available Niacin Values of Foods for Rats and Their Relation to Analytical Values. *Journal of Nutrition* 112:2091-2103.

COE, S.D., (1994), *America's First Cuisines*. Austin: University of Texas Press.

CRAWFORD, E.M., (1981), Indian Meal and Pellagra in Nineteenth-Century Ireland. In *Irish Population, Economy, and Society*. J.M. Goldstrom and L.A. Clarkson, eds. Pp.113-133. Oxford: Clarendon Press.

ETHERIDGE, E.W., (1972), *The Butterfly Caste: A Social History of Pellagra in The South*. Westport, CT: Greenwood.

FUSSELL, B., (1992), *The Story of Corn*. New York: Alfred A. Knopf.

GOLDBERGER, J., (1918), Pellagra: Its Nature and Prevention. *Public Health Reports* 33:481-488.

HALL, R.L., (1997), *The Archaeology of the Soul: North American Indian Belief and Ritual*. Urbana and Chicago: University of Illinois Press.

HENDERSON, L.M., (1983), *Niacin*. Annual Review of Nutrition 3:289-307.
KATZ, S.H., (1989), Biocultural Evolution of Cuisine: The Hopi Indian Blue Corn Tradition. In *Handbook of the Psychophysiology of Human Eating*. R. Shepherd, ed. Pp 115-140. New York: John Wiley & Sons.
KATZ, S. H., M.L. HEDIGER, AND L.A. VALLEROY, (1974), Traditional Maize Processing Techniques in the New World. *Science* 184:765-773.
KODICEK, E., D.R. ASHBY, M. MULLER, AND K.J. CARPENTER, (1974), The Conversion of Bound Nicotinic Acid to Free Nicotinamide on Roasting Sweet Corn. *Proceedings of the Nutrition Society* 33:105A.
KUHNLEIN, H.V. AND D.H. CALLOWAY, (1977), Contemporary Hopi food intake patterns. *Ecology of Food and Nutrition* 6:159-173.
KUHNLEIN, H.V. AND D.H. CALLOWAY, (1979), Adventitious Mineral Elements in Hopi Indian Diets. *Journal of Food Science* 44:282-285.
KUHNLEIN, H.V., D.H. CALLOWAY, AND B. HARLAND, (1979), Composition of Traditional Hopi Foods. *Journal of the American Dietetic Association* 75:37-41.
MALFAIT, P. et al., (1993), An Outbreak of Pellagra Related to Changes in Dietary Niacin among Mozambican Refugees in Malawi. *International Journal of Epidemiology* 22: 504-511.
MILLER, D. F., (1978), Pellagra Deaths in the United States. *American Journal of Clinical Nutrition* 31:558-559.
ROE, D.A., (1973), *A Plague of Corn: The Social History of Pellagra*. Ithaca, NY: Cornell University Press.
SHIBATA, K. AND TODA, S., (1997), Effects on sex hormones on the metabolism of tryptophan and niacin and to serotonin in male rats. *Bioscience, Biotechnology, and Biochemistry* 61:1200-1202.
TERRIS, M. (ed.), (1964), Goldberger on Pellagra. Baton Rouge, LA: Louisiana State University Press.
WALL, J.S., M.R. YOUNG, AND K.CARPENTER, (1987), Transformation of Niacin-Containing Compounds in Corn During Grain Development: Relationships to Niacin Nutritional Availability. *Journal of Agricultural Food Chemistry* 35:752-758.
WARMAN, A., (2003), *Corn & Capitalism: How a Botanical Bastard Grew to Global Dominance*. Chapel Hill, NC: University of North Carolina.
WEATHERMAX, P., (1954), *Indian Corn in Old America*. New York: Macmillan.
WHITAKER, E.D., (1992), Bread and Work: Pellagra and Economic Transformation in Turn-of-the Century Italy. *Anthropological Quarterly* 63(2): 80-90.
WOLF, H., (1971), Hormonal Alteration of Efficiency of Conversion of Tryptophan to Urinary Metabolites of Niacin in Man. *The American Journal of Clinical Nutrition* 24:792-799.

Slow Schooling

Franca Chiarle, Anya Fernald, Sophie Herron
Silvia Monasterolo

"A mother recently said to me: 'I've given up fighting with my kids over food. I just let them eat what they like – chips, pizza, and hot-dogs – and feed them a vitamin each day"

Janet Chrzan, quoting an American mother in *Slow* magazine[1]

"Since the family meal has become more and more rare, we must start thinking about what the schools can do to teach these lessons"

Alice Waters[1]

Slow Food was founded in the Italian region of Piedmont in 1986. The fundamental importance of conviviality and the right to pleasure are the basic principles upon which all Slow Food events and activities are built. The movement believes that any traditional product encapsulates the flavors of its region of origin, not to mention local customs and ancient production techniques. Slow Food's main offices, situated in Bra (Cuneo), a small town in southern Piedmont, employ 130 people. The office is the hub of a close-knit network of local grassroots chapters in Italy and abroad, called 'convivia'. Over 700 convivia exist in 83 countries; 330 of them are in Italy, where Slow Food has more than 35,000 members. Today Slow Food boasts 75,000 members in all five continents and national offices have been opened in Germany, France, Switzerland, Spain, and the United States. In its 17 years of activity, Slow Food has blossomed into an international movement of food and wine culture and a champion of biodiversity, sustainable agriculture, education and rural development.

Introduction

One of the paramount objectives of the international Slow Food movement is the promotion of sensory education activities to foster an understanding and appreciation of food culture. To this end, Slow Food has proposed projects in schools that teach the value of taste and enjoying food and enrich the sensory aspect of education in schools. Slow Food's philosophy of education is based on the concept that the best way to instill a 'thoughtful' approach to food – where eating is associated with mental, sensory and physical satisfaction, not just with satiety – is by stimulating curiosity about food. The movement has developed a number of models for taste education in the past decade, for age groups ranging from under-10-year-olds to adolescents and adults. Here we present the history of these various initiatives, as well as giving constructive comments on the effectiveness of the approaches developed by Slow Food. Slow Schooling had its start in the schools themselves, with the organization of teacher education programs, farmer visits to cafeterias, and the publication of a textbook on how to teach food appreciation: Rossano Nistri's *To Say, To Do, To Taste – Taste Education Routes at School* [2]. This book was a tool for teachers, as well as parents, to encourage a proper relationship between young people and food, using the pleasure of eating as its main teaching instrument to build a grammar and syntax of taste, and thus communicate the cultural values connected to diet and food, and today this textbook is used by 5,100 teachers in Italy. Aside from these school initiatives, Slow Food has also developed numerous other projects to help young people stimulate their curiosity and appreciation of food. These include the Weeks of Taste[3]: dinners for under-26-year-olds at special prices in Italy's finest restaurants; Taste Workshops: lectures on food education; and teaching manuals. The newest Slow Food ventures for adult and young adult education are the Master of Food Program and the University of the Science of Gastronomy.

Why Educate?

Can education in schools instill a love of, attachment to, and a caring approach to eating in children? Slow Food believes so.

Slow Food educational activities are constructed on the premise that sensory education about food is an essential to guaranteeing a nurturing approach to food preparation. Its educational programs build shared activities that teach young people about their own gastronomic culture and their role in producing food. The deplorable state of knowledge and understanding of food among young Europeans and Americans is only getting worse. The results of a study carried out in 1999 of 2,400 nine- and ten-year-olds throughout the

European Union by the Conseil Européen des Jeunes Agriculteurs (CEJA) on their knowledge about food issues and comprehension of agriculture show an alarming ignorance.

One out of four children in the United Kingdom believes that oranges and olives grow in their country, one half of European children do not know where sugar comes from, and a quarter believe that cotton comes from sheep. A quarter of children in the European Union cannot think of any way to conserve food apart from freezing it and two thirds of young Europeans do not know what pesticides do.[4] The coordinator of the study remarked, "One lesson from the survey is that children are keen to know more about life in the countryside and how food is produced, the other is that children now learn about agriculture mainly through school".[5] Increasingly, the classroom is the primary source of knowledge about agriculture and food. The casual attitude that many young people have today about understanding the source of their food is reflected in their attitudes towards mealtimes and food consumption. Even in Italy, once a mainstay of the 'family meal', children are increasingly eating alone.

In a study carried out by the Italian agricultural association Coldiretti of 30,000 seven- to thirteen-year olds, about 60% said they ate breakfast in five minutes, and lunch and dinner in less than half an hour. They often ate alone, and rarely with their whole family (12 percent of the time at breakfast, and 30 percent of the time at lunch).[6]

Slow Food's educational mission has become urgent. The home is no longer a place to learn about food, and schools must adapt quickly to the new needs of their students. Continuing lack of interest on the part of educators in the important subjects of 'eating', 'farming', 'tasting' will only add to these trends – and to the secondary effects of obesity, eating disorders, and nutritional deficiencies. The risk is great: future generations that simply do not understand the pleasure that good food can bring.

Slow Food's Education Initiatives for under 18-year olds: an Overview

One of the most important main goals of Slow Food is the promotion and development of teaching activities on the subjects of sensory education and food culture.[7] In 1993, the movement began an educational project in Italian schools using taste as a learning tool and studying food products as one of the components of a society's culture.

For educators at every level, Slow Food has organized courses for training and further study all across Italy, authorized by the Ministry of Public Education and the various educational authorities, with the goal of furnishing teachers with teaching models to help convey a vision of food as culture while maintaining a scientific and experimental approach.

Beginning with the 1998-1999 school year and as part of the Communication and Food Education[8] program promoted by the Ministry of Agricultural and Forest Policies, the Piedmont Regional Authority asked Slow Food to organize a project to introduce diet and food into the curriculum of the region's schools, beginning with real situations of agricultural food production in Piedmont and Italy. In the first phase, aimed specifically at teachers, five theoretical and practical meetings were organized to focus on typical products from Piedmont. The second phase has now begun, supplying practical support for school staff to create food education courses with students, including classroom Taste Workshops meetings with artisan producers, the creation of school events and the educational CD-ROM *A Journey through the Magic of Taste*,[9] which has been distributed at the training meetings planned for every province in Piedmont.

During the 1998-1999 academic year, Slow Food organized 12 training courses for teachers, with the approval of the Ministry of Education, in various provinces of Italy, with a high rate of participation. The courses were repeated in 12 other cities during the academic year 1999-2000.

Since 1999, several Italian Regional Agriculture Departments have been collaborating with Slow Food to plan and implement projects within Italian schools. These projects are part of the program Nutrition Communication and Education,[10] designed to promote local foods and traditional farm production.

Experiences in the Italian schools

After four years, the results of the in-school teaching courses are positive and encouraging. Now, in the 12 'project schools', food and taste education are part of the official prospectus and many schools develop projects and events that reinforce and even go beyond the activities of cooking workshops.

Teachers learn during training classes that to teach students how to use their senses, they themselves must go through a learning process of their own. For example, we cannot learn how to 'smell' without thinking about our own olfactory perception and the factors that influence our senses. To help students in the search for a more balanced relationship with food, we must reflect on the meanings they attribute to food and sensory stimuli. Educating the senses means freeing oneself from prejudices and learning to tackle new experiences. The Slow Food teaching approach is multidisciplinary, beginning with practical examples supplied during the courses and continuing with support for teachers to help plan their programs. During the course, when teachers were presented with foods modified in appearance (for example, color), attitudes of suspicion or bewilderment often emerged. One's own senses play tricks on perception; and when colors changed, participants in the teacher's course often stated that foods tasted saltier, or spicier and others lost their taste altogether. So, recognizing that our eyes can confuse us becomes important in guiding students through their own prejudices.

The courses have stimulated many initiatives in Italian schools. For example, all the classes at the A Bruni Elementary School in Casale, Prato, dedicated a school year to the topic of the relationship between man and food in various historic periods. Beginning with sensory games, each class developed a course connected to different disciplines: languages, science, geography, statistics and computer studies. Periods for music and the teaching of image and movement were dedicated to creating a theatrical performance, A Tasty Walk through History,[11] which showed the children working on foods and recipes from each historical period represented. Students went from prehistory, with grubs and honey, to our era, with our grandparents' snacks of bread and jam, and the frozen foods and fried potatoes preferred by teenagers.

Another significant project was carried out at the Istituto Comprensivo at Vernio, a mountain village again near Prato. Teachers and students conducted research on diet and food during the period between the two world wars. Sensory literacy and the attention paid to the pleasure of taste, were aspects particularly appreciated by the students. Parents collaborated on this project and organized festive social occasions. Meetings on sensory education and the relationship between food and emotion were concluded by tasting dishes prepared by parents. At the end of the classroom course in July, students participated in a Gourmet Vacation,[12] an ecological-gastronomic week – which substituted for the usual week-long school holiday – spent discovering the environmental and cultural heritage and traditional cuisine of the Prato Mountains.

Similar programs were held in the provinces of Reggio Emilia, Bergamo, Venice, Treviso, Catanzaro, Syracuse, Oristano, Benevento and Terni. Others are under way in Comacchio, Isola d'Elba, Parco del Cilento and various towns in the regions of Liguria, Piedmont, Tuscany and Lazio, where special attention is paid to studying the agricultural-food heritage of the territory, its products and their production techniques.

At a pre-school in the hills of Pino Torinese, about 10 kilometers from Turin, the local community has undergone a gradual transformation over the last 30 years, shifting from an agricultural economy to become a predominantly residential area, hence with an agricultural history and past unknown by its children. For some years now, a group of teachers has developed teaching projects with the objective of bringing children, and subsequently their parents, back to knowledge of the territory and its remaining agricultural activities, the cultivation of corn, strawberries and grapes.

Over the past three years, the program has involved all children attending the school, from three- to five- years old. It is divided into two subject groups: corn and strawberries. In the first, the educational course began with a visit to local farms where children witnessed activities such as tilling the land, and planting and milling the grain. Two varieties of corn were planted in the school garden: marano, suitable for polenta, and a hybrid used for producing popcorn. The ripe ears were shucked, the corn was ground, the meal was cooked and the children finally – and very enthusiastically – ate a plate of their own polenta. The group involved with strawberries followed the same cycle. In this case, it concluded with the tasting of products from different varieties and production areas.

Students in the following year took a course on grapes that lasted from September to June. A winemaker illustrated the phases of producing wine in the cellar and the children repeated them in school until they obtained a wine that was tasted at the various phases of fermentation and then bottled. In the spring, the children worked at pruning and tying in the vineyards.

Involving Children in 'Adult' Food Events

Slow Food first achieved renown with its international food fairs: Salone del Gusto and Cheese. Given the high attendance numbers in these events, it was only natural to try to involve children as well.

A section of the second biannual Salone del Gusto in Turin in 1998 was a classroom for children to taste different food and food combinations, the Taste Play Room.[13] 800 children participated over the course of five days (schools were alerted ahead of time and allowed to reserve full-class spaces) in a sit-down tasting followed by discussion.

The Salone del Gusto also hosted a seminar called Taste Education and the Next Generation[14] and the presentation of the book *To Say, to Do, to Taste – Education Routes at Schools*[15].

At the next edition of the Salone, the approach was more refined and interactive, with the Tasting Itineraries[16] organized in the main hall of the Salone. This space for children featured five 'stations': Milk, Salami, Grains, Fruits and Vegetables, and Sweets. Over 2,000 children participated in this event, and were very enthusiastic about the 'stations ' – each staffed by a farmer – where they could taste different flavors and talk to the food producer. Marcello Marengo, Slow Food's coordinator for children's events says that, "The fact that the kids taste traditional products and at the same time they meet the producers is fundamental. This guarantees an experience that is memorable, and also encourages children to be more adventurous in what they are willing to try."

Owing to budget constrictions, the children's section at the Salone del Gusto 2002 was more limited, with a 'Sensory Education Station' at the fair that drew 1,200 children from Turin. In this stand, children were challenged to identify foods blindfolded using only smell, taste, and touch.

At the biennial Cheese event, children's participation is also a priority. Cheese for Kids[17] was launched in 1999 with a kitchen lesson on how to make pasta. In 2001, children participated in taste 'classrooms' where they ate cheese in all of its phases: milk, curd, whey, ricotta, young cheese, and aged cheese. Slow Food also organized buses for 500 schoolchildren to visit local dairy farms. At this year's edition of Cheese, the lessons will be based on the historic combination of honey and cheese (presented by cheesemakers and apiculturists) followed by a debate about favorite combinations.

From the pedagogical standpoint, these activities were used to develop further knowledge of science, logic and history along with artistic and sensory creativity. This method utilizes the knowledge progressively acquired by the children to initiate discussions, comparisons, changes and activities, with the teacher as a mediating element. The positive results are confirmed by the students' pleasure in retelling their experiences with drawings and conversations in the classroom and at home. Parents have confirmed that the children received these sensory and taste experiences positively. The children, in turn, involved and stimulated the interest of their families.

The Edible Schoolyard: A Hands-On Model for Slow Food

The Edible Schoolyard model was developed in Berkeley California by chef and Slow Food International Governor Alice Waters. The Edible Schoolyard is a practical approach to the problem of educating future generations about how to care for, select, prepare and enjoy food on a daily basis. An Edible Schoolyard is simply a garden in a schoolyard, which the students themselves care for and tend, and which is used as the base for a series of classes, lessons, and hands-on learning experiences. The gardens construct a practical pathway from seed to garden to kitchen and table – specifically to allow children to learn patience, compassion, inspiration and an appreciation of the importance of food, food cultures and a shared table.

The idea for an Edible Schoolyard in Berkeley, California came about through the collaboration of Alice Waters and School Principal of Martin Luther King Middle Jr. Middle School. Created in 1995 by Waters, the garden includes an acre of beds planted with seasonal produce, herbs, vines, berries and flowers and fruit trees. Students and adults work together to prepare the beds, sow the seeds, transplant, compost, water, weed, and harvest. Through their participation in every aspect of the seed-to-table experience, students learn to understand the full cycle of food production, seasonality and ecology. The experience is completed with shared periods in the kitchen, learning how to prepare and cook their harvest, and then enjoying it at set tables. Edible Schoolyards, says Waters, "turn pop culture upside down. They teach redemption through a deep appreciation for the real, the authentic and the lasting".[18] The idea of the Edible Schoolyard is in total synthesis with the Slow Food approach to education, and now the promotion and diffusion of the Edible Schoolyard model is developing through the Slow Food movement.

Another successful implementation of the Edible Schoolyard model can be found in the inner city Melbourne suburb of Collingwood. Here Stephanie Alexander had been inspired by Waters' work at Kings school and had long been concerned with the importance of food education. The project has been active since July 2001, so far involving 120 students in gardening, cooking, preparing and cooking fresh food. Both Edible Schoolyards show significant beneficial effects on the schoolyard environment they share. One of Waters' driving motivations was to create a school environment that would inspire and nurture the students; 'children deserve to be educated in places they feel proud of', she says.[19]

Developing Edible Schoolyards through Slow Food

Slow Food is now taking steps to develop the Edible Schoolyard model created by Waters at an international level. The movement has become very involved in the diffusion of this concept, and has facilitated the development of the gardens by procuring sponsorship, distributing educational models, and finding partners for potential projects. The first Edible Schoolyard in Italy will be launched this September in Piedmont, with many more to follow in European countries such as England, Germany, and Switzerland with a strong Slow Food membership base.

Slow Food's Education Initiatives for Young Adults: an Overview

Brief events like the Weeks of Taste[20] program has met with great success. These weeks are dedicated to the 26-and-under age group, which is given a chance to meet chefs and food experts, discover the world of quality artisan foods, learn about the production and processing of raw materials, and experience large-scale catering, eating in the finest restaurants in Italy at promotional prices. Other Slow Food initiatives are longer-term projects such as the University of Gastronomical Sciences and the Master of Food program, a series of evening classes on every conceivable subject related to food.

Involving Young Adults in Food Events: The Taste Workshop

The Taste Workshop is Slow Food's 'classroom' for taste education. This model was developed to answer the need for a format for educating people of all ages about gastronomy. The model is simple: experts from the association offer guided tastings of various enogastronomical products such as cheese and cured meats, rice and pasta, cakes and wine, beer and spirits, and so on. Several varieties of the same product are tasted by participants using comparison to arouse their curiosity for and appreciation of a higher quality standard, and to improve their tasting skills. The tasting seminar begins with theories of tasting techniques and a brief description of the product in question – often with a personal presentation by the producers themselves whenever possible – and remarks about the most suitable food-drink combinations. Then the real tasting begins; the speaker questions the participants about their preferences and guides them in recognizing aromas, visual sensations and taste, as well as the overall quality of the product. In the Taste Workshop, it is important to maintain an aspect of seriousness, which is important in encouraging the participants to think critically and honestly about their food. However, the pleasure aspect of what is being tasted should be emphasized as well, through a thoughtful, appreciative presentation and discussion.

How is a taste workshop organized?

The workshop can only work effectively if certain conditions are respected, such as:

- the products to be examined must be of high quality;

- the products must be served with wine or other suitable accompanying beverages;

- they must be tasted in a comfortable, quiet, environment without intrusive odors;

- the participants must be seated facing the panel or speaker;

- the place settings – including plates, glasses, cutlery, and napkins – must be of restaurant standard. The wine glasses, in particular, must be the standard degustation kind;

- the service must be efficient and professional;

- the pace of service and tasting must be quick and rhythmical. A laboratory must never exceed one and a half hours;

- the event must be announced in plenty of time and in such a way that it arouses curiosity and attracts participants.

Night School for Aficionados: the Master of Food Program[21]

In 2002, Slow Food initiated the Master of Food program, a teaching project for food, wine and sensory understanding. The aim is to recover taste-related knowledge and to spread awareness of production and tasting techniques, along with the history and culture of food, wine and gastronomy. All across Italy, courses are held on: beer; coffee, teas and infusions; meats; cereals, pasta, bread; sweets, chocolate, honey and fruit preserves; cheeses; distilled and alcohol based products; oil; fruit and vegetables; fish; salami and cured meats; food science and technology; spices, aromas and vinegar; the history and culture of gastronomy; cooking techniques; wine; and world food. The courses comprise three to six evening classes within the context of the Slow Food philosophy and style. In other words, rather than being exclusively academic in design, they strike a balance between scientific content and an appealing teaching style. The Master of Food program offers specialization for those who, for their own personal pleasure, have acquired some knowledge of taste and desire to place that knowledge in a broader framework through further study in a non-institutional context. Participants tend to be young, with a large number in the under-35 age group. The courses are reasonably priced (45 – 65 euros each. In 2001, 192 courses were offered, in 2002, 502, and in the first six months of 2003, 345. A total of 18,400 students have participated in Master of Food courses since the program's inception. About 25% of students decide to take additional courses in other subjects after one course. The Master of Food has also helped bring together a group of almost 300 teachers unified by a single program to present new courses of study. The Master of Food program will hopefully shift the dynamic of the 'food expert' community, creating a growing number of young adults informed and aware about fine artisan food production.

The University of Gastronomic Sciences[22]

The University of Gastronomic Sciences was founded by Slow Food to address a specific need: the reshaping of gastronomy as a serious subject of academic inquiry. The University intends to educate the next generation of leaders in the food world by using an interdisciplinary approach that encompasses everything from food science to semiotics; from nutrition to enology; from the history and geography of agriculture to the principles of sensorial evaluation. Yet a profound knowledge of food is incomplete without the experience of tasting products and understanding ingredients in their places of origin, so the students of the University will also be constantly engaged in the process of tasting, as well as studying and visiting the places where our food comes from, whether they be vineyards or cornfields, factories or mountain tops. These travels to different regions throughout Italy, Europe and around the world, collectively known as stages, will offer students an innovative and rigorous education in local realities in agriculture and food, both through a regional format (studying the gastronomic characteristics of a particular area) and a theme format (studying a particular category of food or food production, from cured meats to organic agriculture).

An extensive faculty has been assembled to teach and conduct research in two areas of study: Gastronomy and Agroecology. The Regional Authorities of Piedmont and Emilia-Romagna have provided considerable support in establishing two campuses, one in Pollenzo (near Bra, hometown of Slow Food, in Piedmont) and the other in Colorno (near Parma, in Emilia-Romagna). The Pollenzo campus will welcome the first class of 60 students in the Gastronomy program in October of 2004, while the Agroecology program will begin at a later date. Each program will offer a basic three-year training degree and a two-year specialization degree (roughly equivalent to a BA and a MA), as well as a one-year Master course and intensive seminars for working food professionals.

Master of Food: Sample Course Descriptions

Wine - First level course

Finding out more about something we like is, in itself a way of enjoying and appreciating it more. This course is tailor-made for people who say, 'I know nothing about wine. I know there are wines I like and others I don't like, but that's all', and would like to be more discerning in their choices and opinions.

This series of lessons teaches correct wine tasting techniques. It will place the onus on visual, olfactory and gustatory analysis, but without overlooking other aspects, such as service, wine-food combinations, conservation and legislation.

In the six lessons, the finest Italian wines will be tasted and discussed. Alongside practical tips about tasting and recognizing wines, with the help of technicians and producers the course will also seek to convey the characteristics of 'wine culture', from quality to consumption.

Meats

Meat is a ticklish question at the moment, what with the ongoing alarm and controversy over quality and wholesomeness. The survival of the finest breeds, such as the Piedmontese cow, is being jeopardized by the invasion of animals of foreign origin, bred on vitamin integrators and sold as quality meat. Furthermore, the lack of adequate structures to stave off the competition of large-scale industrial production and the fact that very few youngsters are prepared to carry on the trade of their fathers risks compromising the future of this fundamental foodstuff.

The course sets out from these basic considerations to consider different breeds, their feed, livestock farms, cuts of meat and preparation techniques. In short, it will provide all the basic knowledge needed to appreciate good meat. It will also feature guided tastings in the presence of technicians and breeders.

Chocolate, cakes and biscuits, honey and jams

If Dante had attended a course like this, there is no way he would have put the gluttons in Hell; they would be up there in the empyrean rapt in blissful contemplation! The course on chocolate and cakes is designed to make consumers more aware (recent European legislation means that we have to study labels carefully!) and capable of recognizing quality, different product typologies and regional traditions.

The course breaks down into four lessons. The first is dedicated to honey and jams, the second and third to traditional Italian cakes and biscuits from Piedmont to Sicily in a journey through the Italian regions the fourth to artisan and factory-made chocolate. At each, you can sweeten your palate with a number of tastings under the expert guidance of the lecturer, producers and technicians.

Conclusions: Brazil, the British Isles, and Beyond[23]

The Slow Food Manifesto states that "real culture is all about developing taste rather than demeaning it. And what better way to set about this than an international exchange of experiences, knowledge, projects?"[24] The essence of taste education is expressed in these words. Since the Manifesto was drawn up in 1989, Slow Food has been committed to spreading the movement's philosophy through its network of Convivia. The influence of the Edible Schoolyard is a fine example of what this network can do, in finding a good idea and assembling the right actors to make it materialize. No philosophy can be applied around the world, however, and no model is universal. Slow Food hopes, though, that sharing information and experiences, as we have done in this paper, will contribute to the realization of education projects around the world.

Let us take Brazil as an example. Rio de Janeiro's Convivium leader Margarida Nogueira is working with anthropologist and Slow Food member Daisy Justus on proposing an interesting project on behalf of the Gol de Letra Foundation. The Foundation currently organizes educational and sporting activities for about 600 underprivileged youngsters, 300 in São Paolo and 300 in Niteroi, in the state of Rio. What Slow Food does for them is to organize a series of cooking courses into into a full-fledged Escola de Gastronomia aiming to provide youngsters with knowledge that can give them a better chance of gaining entry into the job market.

As well as lessons in cooking theory and practice, and notions of courtesy, respect and care for customers, the youngsters will also be offered workshops in educação do paladar (taste education) and apuração dos sentidos (sensory appreciation). According to Nogueira, the project should be up to speed by the end of 2003.

Another important Rio project, this time more closely linked to food traditions, is the Projeto Mandioca created by chef and Slow Food member Teresa Corção. Manioc is a native South American plant from which flour is obtained to make tapioca, Brazil's traditional daily bread. During Corção's lessons, held in a Rio primary school, she tells pupils native Brazilian legends about manioc and teaches them how to cook tapioca and other dishes.

It's a long way from Brazil to the Republic of Ireland, but a general philosophy connects Slow Food activities in those two countries. During the fourth year of secondary school in Ireland, pupils have to design mini-enterprises as an exercise in acquiring business skills. Last year, during a lesson on the Slow Food approach at a local community college organized by Giana Ferguson (Cork Convivium leader and cheesemaker), a proposal was made for a Slow-style mini-enterprise and the pupils themselves subsequently took up the challenge. How could local ingredients be transformed into tasty, authentic dishes, according to seasonal availability? The students began to plan a project around high quality products, with the ultimate objective of 'promoting local potatoes in a unique, revolutionary way'.[25] To show that this project could be implemented nationwide, they planned and developed the relevant business activities, organizing the sale of products both locally and at fairs and markets. To make a long story short, in May last year the students entered BUPA, a national competition held in Dublin, with their 'Slow' project. They were successful – their 'super-potato' won first prize!

In Scotland, two Convivium leaders (John Tiller and Wendy Fisher) have designed an innovative approach to instilling the Slow philosophy in schools. Their project, Cooking for Kids, aims to help children experience the pleasure of preparing, eating and enjoying good food together. The project works in a simple way: Slow Food members in the restaurant business invite a small group of children from a local school to their business to organize an event aimed at giving the children an insight into the benefits of choosing simple and healthy food, and the experience of cooking and eating a homemade meal. Nick Nairn, chef and owner of a cookery school, ran the pilot in 2002. The children taking part in the pilot session were aged nine to ten, and were involved in activities such as preparing pizza with fresh vegetables and mozzarella, a healthy drink composed of carrots, oranges and apples, and, finally, a carrot, ginger and honey soup. So far, there have been three similar events, and more are planned for 2003.

The disparate experiences recounted in this paper are all individual approaches to a common philosophy. Hopefully this diversity of approaches will continue to function and inspire others, Slow Food Convivia, other associations, and other schools, to attempt similar work.

With thanks to: Vittorio Manganelli, Erika Lesser, John Irving

Notes
1. Janet Chrzan, Nutrition Education in the US, Slow 7(2002), p. 22.
2. Alice Waters, A World of Possibilities' in The Edible Schoolyard, ed. Margo Crabtree (Berkeley: Center for Ecoliteracy, 1998), p. 13.
3. Nistri Rossano, Dire Fare Gustare, Percorsi di Educazione del Gusto nella Scuola, (Bra: Slow Food Editore, 1998).
4. Original Title: Settimane del Gusto

5 Holst, Christian, Report of a Representative Survey on 'Children's Knowledge on Agriculture' (INRA Deutschland Mölln, Stiching vor CEJA Education) August 1999, updated June 2003, pp. 4 – 9.
6 Quote from Arnold Puech d'Alissac, President of CEJA, at presentation of update Report of a Representative Survey on 'Children's Knowledge on Agriculture', June 24, 2003.
7 Dimmi come mangi, ti dirò come cresci, (Campagna: Amica, 2002)
8 Article 4, International Statute of the Slow Food Movement, 2003
8 Original Title: Comunicazione ed Educazione Alimentare
10 Original Title: Viaggio nella Magia del Gusto
11 Original Title: Comunicazione ed Educazione Alimentare
12 Original Title: Passeggiata Gustosa nella Storia
13 Original Title: Vacanza Golosa
14 Original Title: Sala Giocagusto
15 Original Title: L'educazione del gusto e le giovani generazioni
16 Rossano, Dire Fare Gustare, Percorsi di Educazione del Gusto nella Scuola.
17 Original Title: Gusti in Pista
18 Original Title: Cheese Bimbi
19 Waters, 'A World of Possibilities' in The Edible Schoolyard,, p. 15.
20 Waters, 'A World of Possibilities' in The Edible Schoolyard,, p. 17.
21 Original Title: Settimana del Gusto
22 Contributions in this section by Alberto Capatti, director of Slow magazine.
23 Contributions in this section of Vittorio Maganelli and Erika Lesser, respectively Director and Stage Coordinator at the University of Gastronomic Sciences
24 Contributions in this section by John Irving, English-language editor of Slow magazine
25 From The Official Manifesto of the International Movement for the Defense of and the Right to Pleasure signed on November 9, 1989 at the Opera Comique in Paris by delegates from Argentina, Austria, Brazil, Denmark, France, Germany, Holland, Hungary, Italy, Japan, Spain, Sweden, Switzerland, United States and Venezuela.
26 Informal quote from Giana Ferguson's meeting with students.

Family meals, sharing and hierarchy in a West-African town

Liza Debevec

One of the first things that a foreigner who comes in contact with the local population in Burkina Faso will be told is that here 'one cannot eat on one's own.' Food is meant to be shared.[26] When in a street restaurant, if your neighbour was served before you, he will offer you food, saying 'Dumuni bey', which means 'There's food'; it is an invitation to eat with him.

Whenever a stranger arrives in a house, it is through food and drink that people express their welcome. Food brings people together and if your host does not offer you water to drink and food to eat, they are considered to have bad manners. Even in poor families one should never refuse food to a visitor and everyone who lives under the same roof should be provided for. Hospitality for the visitor is something that the Burkinabé, like other West Africans[27], take great pride in.

However this paper is not about the hospitality offered to a stranger, but the welcome given to one's own kind. It is about how large families in urban Burkina Faso cope with the number of relatives they need to feed and why there may be unequal distribution of food among the people living in the same family compound. I wish to explore the role that hierarchy plays in the family feeding process and what values related to food sharing and hierarchy are passed on to the children through food related situations. I am interested in the disparity between what people say to be proper behaviour when it comes to food sharing and what their actions tell us.

In an urban setting food is inextricably linked with material resources and poor people are left at the mercy of those around them who have enough food for themselves and others.

In Muslim societies *zakat*[28] is one of the five pillars of Islam and as such a requirement for every good Muslim, but Burkina Faso, a largely Muslim country, is full of mal-nourished and undernourished people, while there are people who have plenty of food to eat and share. One problem that arises when one wants to speak about the normal everyday interaction is that as a foreign visitor, one is not automatically privy to it. In the first months of my fieldwork, whenever I visited people's homes, they would welcome me with a big smile on their face and bring me food and drink. People were being friendly with me and among themselves. It always seemed that I was visiting one happy family after another. It was only through time, when I moved into a compound with local people and my presence became less conspicuous, that I had a chance to observe the great disparity in the treatment that people receive.

Life in a Family Compound in Bobo-Dioulasso

The paper is based on longterm fieldwork in Burkina Faso during which I was living with a large family in Bobo-Dioulasso. The head of the family is a widowed woman in her 60s. People in the compound refer to her as Mama or Grandemama[29].

Like most Bobolese, she comes from an ethnically mixed background. Mama's husband, who was a head-teacher in a primary school before taking his retirement, passed away seven years ago and was originally from a different part of Burkina. She has eight children, who are between 28 and 43 years old, 19 grandchildren[30] and one great-grandchild. She is a devout Muslim, who prays regularly and also attends classes of Koranic reading and discussion with other older women from the surrounding area.

She has a pension from her husband and also gets money from renting a compound in another part of Bobo. She runs a small business, which sells *shea* butter for personal use[31] and also sells prayer beads.

Mama is often away attending funerals at villages around Bobo. According to her she needs to do this in order to please Allah before her time comes[32]. Her two unmarried daughters who live in the compound often criticise her for being away[33] and leaving them with the responsibility of feeding the family[34]. Because Mama's oldest male child is unemployed, Mama is the one who provides most of the food for the family, which she buys with the money from her pension and the rent she gets for her plot. Because the plot belonged to the father of the family, the children see it as their birthright[35] to benefit from the rent money.

Mama buys most of the sacks of rice and corn flour and she allocates the daily food allowance referred to as *naan songo* or the price of sauce. In an average family it is the man who gives the *naan songo* to the wife on a daily basis. Mama's age and social status prevent her from cooking for the family and the preparation of the daily meal is entrusted to one of the younger unmarried women in the family. The only thing that Mama does cooking-wise is cutting up large pieces of meat, if they have slaughtered an animal. Otherwise she will only oversee the preparation and give advice. She never stirs the pot herself, unless there is no younger woman around to do so.

There are usually three young women living in the compound, two of whom do three cooking shifts per week each and one who does the Sunday shift, because she attends classes at high school during the rest of the week. The three young women are treated equally, despite their rather different origin and position in the family.

Celestine, the youngest of three, is the daughter of Mama's deceased son. Her mother lives in a village further south and Celestine lives in Bobo-Dioulasso in order to attend the local high school.

Madina, who is a few years older, is a daughter of one of mama's brothers in law, whose family lives in Côte d'Ivoire. She was brought to the compound about 12 years ago when she was just 12 years old and she has not been back to Côte d'Ivoire since. Out of the three girls, she is probably the worst off [36], because she has nowhere to go if things get difficult in the compound. She is not educated and speaks only very basic French and doesn't have the means to go back to her family in Abidjan.

The third one is Assetou, who is the mother of Mama's youngest grandson. Assetou is the partner of Yacouba, Mama's deaf and dumb son, but she is not his wife, neither in the traditional nor in the official way, because Mama has not offered the kola nuts[37] to Assetou's family. Assetou is the only rebellious one, the only one who tries to stand up against the authority of Mama's eldest daughters who seem more or less successfully to terrorise most of the people in the compound. She often packs her bags and leaves if she feels she is not being treated correctly, but she soon comes back to her 'husband', who always takes her side, whatever the cause of the argument.

Acquisition, Preparation and Distribution of the Main Daily Meal

While, for a married couple, it is the woman who decides what meal shall be cooked that day, in this case, the girls have only a partial say in the final decision. The choice of the dish depends on several things. The first thing that needs to be considered is what ingredients are already available in the compound. The hot climate limits this to less perishable items, such as onions, garlic, beans and dried or smoked fish. Meat is sometimes deep-fried and kept in a basket or a pot overnight, but that can attract ants or flies, of which the first are considered to be more of a nuisance. Rice and maize or other flour are kept in big sacks and are usually stored for months[38].

Heat and insects cause problems, but the main reason behind the everyday visit to the market is financial. Especially in the households where the man hands out the money, the women cannot afford to buy more than what is needed on the day. Some of the men I interviewed had mentioned that they would prefer to give a monthly lump sum to their wives, yet they agreed that the woman may be tempted or in need of spending the money on something else, which would result in the *naan songo* running out before the end of the month. Because of this most ingredients are bought on a daily basis.

In my host family it is either Mama, or the girl who is cooking that day, who goes to the market. While Mama might take a taxi and go to the central market, referred to as *logobaa* in Jula[39], the girls will walk to one of the two small markets, referred to by the French term *cinq heures*[40].

There isn't a great variety in the dishes being prepared every day. The staple food is rice or a maize porridge, both of which are accompanied by a sauce. The sauce may vary from one season to another according to the vegetables that are being harvested, but every family will have a repertoire of about six or fewer different dishes that will appear on the menu over the year, sometimes the same type of dish is eaten for a week. In my host family the most common dishes were rice with onion sauce called *jabajii*, rice with peanut sauce – *tigedigenaan*, maize porridge with sauce made of various greens – *tô ani furaburunaan*, or maize porridge with an okra[41] or baobab leaf sauce accompanied by a gravy-like meat sauce, known locally as *la soupe* or *naanjii*.

As the meal has to be ready by noon, a traditional lunch hour, the girl will start cooking between 9 and 10 a.m. She will light the fire and put the water to boil in a large pot, in which she will later cook either rice or porridge. Despite the fact that the number of people eating the meal may vary, the quantity of rice and sauce does not. In her study of the Bemba of Northern Rhodesia, Audrey Richards notes that the woman will not increase or reduce the amount of food she prepares according to the number of people she is cooking for, as she is used to having the numbers vary on daily basis, she prepares a set amount and then divides the food into the common dishes (Richards 1961[1939]:152). The same holds true for most households in Bobo-Dioulasso. The woman who is cooking does not measure the ingredients, but has an idea of how much food should be more or less enough for the number of people in the compound give or take a few. Quite often the quantity of ingredients depends on the price at the time of purchase, an onion sauce is much thicker when onions are in season, and much thinner when they become scarce just before the start of the rainy season.

Once the meal had been cooked it is time to divide it between the different eating groups. This seems to be the most delicate part of the feeding process as there are many rules and elements that need to be considered if one wishes to do it correctly so as not to offend any of the people who are above one in the family hierarchy.

My host family is one of the more 'Western' oriented families when it comes to food and eating as they no longer eat in the 'traditional' way[42] which consists of women and children eating together from one dish and men eating from a different one. According to the eldest son of the family, it was their father, a primary school headmaster, who encouraged them to eat from separate dishes and sitting at a table.

Because of that, food is divided in several dishes, according to eating groups. The best choice of meat and largest quantity of sauce and staple food will be given into a dish, which serves Mama and her two unmarried daughters. The second eating group is the one that includes the oldest son, who is in his early forties, his wife and their two children. They also get a good choice of meat and sauce and a lot of rice or porridge. These two groups get their food served in nicer pots than the rest of the family, because the women have purchased special pots and will eat their food only from their dishes, while the younger people get the meal served in simpler dishes that Mama bought for the family.

The third eating group consists of Mama's oldest daughter, a widow with 5 children, 3 of whom live and eat with her. She moved back into the compound recently, after life in the compound of her deceased husband became too difficult due to rivalry with co-wives. The fourth group consists of one of the younger brothers, his fiancé Assetou and their child. The fifth eating group is composed of Madina and Celestine. The rest of the people get individual food bowls, and while they might sit and keep each other company while eating, they do not eat from the same bowl.

The distribution of sauce and meat into serving bowls is considered to be the most difficult and most important part of the cooking process and the wife of the oldest son will supervise it, unless she is away at work. She takes great pride in making sure that everyone gets the share they deserve.

While it is clear that every person living in the compound will get a meal at lunch time and that they were probably given enough to have a small amount left over for their evening meal, it is also obvious that the amount and the quality varies from person to person, mostly according to age. Older people get a better choice of food than the younger ones, which is a common practice in many African societies[43]. Age stratification is evident in everyday interaction[44] and it doesn't seem to be ever really questioned by anyone. Adults sometimes explain the great amount of housework that children have to do as something quite acceptable, something they've all been through and now they can enjoy adulthood, which means that they can ask anyone who is younger to do their housework for them. While there is a clear sexual division of labour and adult men will never do any the household duties, the age hierarchy allows women to assign household chores such as fetching the firewood, or cooking water, to adolescent boys.

Audrey Richards noted that there was no such thing as equality in food distribution with the family or larger community. While she observed that 'nobody eats alone' she also noted that not every eating group is catered for in the same way (Richards 1961[1939]: 122-23). And the group that was probably least catered for were adolescent boys. She writes that '[b]oys of 9 or 10 are considered too old to eat with the women and are expected to forage for themselves. They trap birds and moles, sit hungrily around the young men's *nsaka*[45] waiting for remains, and only occasionally are lucky enough to get a special dish cooked for themselves' (ibid: 123).

In the case of my host family the children who are the worst off are the orphans who have been entrusted into the care of the family after their parents had passed away. There are quite a few children like this in the compound as Mama's first child, who was not her biological child, but a child who was entrusted to her, died of AIDS a few years ago and left several children. Three of his children lived in the compound during my fieldwork and their two unmarried aunts particularly mistreated two of them. Another daughter arrived from her village during my stay and was sent off to look after an elderly great-aunt, who lived in a compound nearby.

People insulted these children on daily basis, calling them stupid, dirty, lazy and greedy. Myriam Roger-Petitjean who studied childcare and nutrition in Bobo-Dioulasso noted that children who were entrusted in the care of relatives were usually less well nourished and often neglected. According to some of her informants it depends on who is entrusted with the child. If it is a grandmother, the child should, in their view, be better off than if it is a more distant relative, but most importantly children suffer most if they are in the hands of their stepmother (Roger-Petitjean 1999: passim). This of course is an obvious concern in view of the fact that there are many polygamous marriages in Burkina Faso and that rivalry between co-wives is a source of many domestic problems. Children often become the ammunition in the fights between co-wives and in case of a death or divorce of one of the co-wives, the children who stay in the family may become the innocent victims of the resentment of their stepmothers. In these cases feeding or more precisely non-feeding may be the way the person exercises their control.

Greed and the Morality of Sharing

Greed is frowned upon[46] in Bobo-Dioulasso and children are told off for having voracious appetites. From a very early age children are told that they must share food and if a child is eating on his/her own s/he will be told off by being asked a simple question '*I tina mogo son?*' Aren't you going to invite anyone? This is a way for a child to learn to share food, as a person is not supposed to eat on one's own, but has to invite others around him/her[47].

While it is polite to invite people to eat with you, if you are caught with a full plate, it is considered impolite to come round to someone's house at mealtime, because you put people in a difficult position. And moreover, while children are being taught to share their food, on most occasions adults do no practice what they preach. This is the case especially at breakfast and dinner.

While lunch is provided for everyone in the compound, at breakfast and dinner people are left to their own devices and financial means. The only people who regularly eat breakfast are Mama, her two unmarried daughters, their sister in law and her husband. The sister-in-law will usually also feed her children, although they might sometimes leave for school without eating. The girls who cook lunch may be given some left over bread and coffee by the sister-in-law, but never from the two unmarried women. While these two have a breakfast that consists at least of bread, butter/margarine and coffee, on occasion accompanied by fried eggs, sardines or avocado and they serve the same to their mother, they never share it with any of the orphaned children, who cannot afford to buy their own breakfast, nor do they offer it to the children of their widowed sister, who is too poor herself to buy breakfast for them.

The two women have recently started providing breakfast for Assetou's baby son, who is the youngest child in the family and is two and a half years old. Despite their on and off arguments with Assetou, they treat her baby with lots of tenderness. They call the baby Papa, because he is named after their father. They also sometimes give some bread and milk to their favourite niece and nephew, the youngest son of their oldest brother and the daughter of their youngest brother. These two will also be given daytime snacks, while the children of their widowed sister, who are of the same age group and play with their two cousins, will be ignored.

The reason behind this is the fact that there has been an ongoing dispute between the two unmarried sisters and the widow, and because they are not on speaking terms, the spinsters use the children as a tool in their dispute. As I have mentioned before, such behavior is often the case among co-wives in polygamous marriages where the man fails to treat the wives equally[48], but such behaviour, while it does exist, is more rare among the siblings.

It is quite possible that the two spinsters resent the fact that since their widowed sister moved back into the compound, the family budget has been stretched further and this may mean fewer extras for the two of them, but in conversation they will never admit that. They would also never admit to having preferences among their nieces and nephews and will argue that they treat everyone equally.

The adolescent children and the young women who prepare the main meal, all of whom are used to such behaviour, sometimes comment on the meanness of the two aunts and say that there is no point in worrying about it, because they will never change. They try and avoid dealing with them as much as possible and try and find ways of getting a few pennies from Mama or an older sibling in order to buy some breakfast or dinner foods that keep them going in the hours before or after lunch.

In the evenings, when the two women prepare their dinner, which consists of warming up the leftovers from lunch and most of the time also an additional dish, the young people, who sit around the TV, eat their leftovers from lunch. When the women's food is ready, they will offer it to their sister-in-law, send a plate over to the mother, who sits in the other side of the compound and depending on the quantity of the food that was prepared, they may give some to their oldest and youngest brothers. I also received a share, the size of which depended on the quantity of the food prepared.

Mama's Side of the Yard

The one person whose role I have not explored so far, but who is essential for understanding the dynamics of the compound, is Mama. She is the one that provides the money for the daily meal and she is the one who decides how many people should be living in the compound. She was the one who invited her widowed daughter back into the compound, she was the one who brought home the orphaned children and she is the one who has the final say in everything. While she does not expose herself or argue with her opinionated daughters, it is clear that she will put them straight if they exaggerate their mean and bossy behaviour[49]. Yet when it comes to sharing morning or evening meals[50], Mama is almost as strict and mean as her two daughters.

Because she is a respected elderly woman in the local community, she often receives food offerings from the people in Bobo-Dioulasso and surrounding villages. As these are most often cooked meals or fresh fruit and cannot be conserved, she divides them among the people of the compound. She usually reserves the largest part of the offering for herself and gives a nice share to her two single daughters and also to her first son and his wife. The rest is divided among her children and grandchildren[51]. The way in which she divides the food is influenced by many things. The oldest ones get a larger share than the adolescent ones, while the youngest ones get a share that is bigger than that of the teenagers. Grandchildren will stand around her and teasingly plead with her to give them a larger share, to which she usually replies with a comment that they should be happy they got anything at all and that they are being greedy. But this is not a harsh criticism of their behaviour and the grandchildren are grateful for what they receive. They would also never dare to ask for more if they were given food by their aunts, which is a proof of a more relaxed relationship with the grandmother. The origin of this rather special relationship can be found in the practice of the joking relationship.[52]

Conclusion: A Morality of 'Fairness'

As should be seen from the ethnographic data above, sharing food with a Burkinabé family is never a straightforward matter. It involves a lot of negotiation and the actors must follow many unwritten rules, especially concerning age stratification. It is also clear that while children are taught to become generous and sharing people, adults may choose to bend these requirements according to their own needs and desires. While no one is left to starve, there is clearly great inequality present in terms of food distribution. The inequality touches especially those children whose parents are not present, or cannot provide for their family. The children whose parents are present are especially well provided for (if the parents have financial means) until around the age of 12 when they start secondary school. After that age, they are no longer the first in line when it comes to snacks and food treats. The issue of morality comes into play a lot when it comes to teaching children about sharing food. Sharing food is seen as the most basic social value in Burkina Faso and people who do not offer food to others are frowned upon. Children are expected to learn that they must offer food to people around them and since they are the youngest they must offer food to all the adults around them. The adults on the other hand only need to offer food to their superiors and equals. All the others are at the mercy of the state of their mood at the time. Small children will usually receive a share of a special out-of-mealtime snack, but only a really small portion, which will not deprive the adults of their 'fair' share.

Bibliography

CAPLAN, ANN P., Choice and constraint in a Swahili community: property, hierarchy and cognatic descent on the East-African coast. (London: Oxford University Press for the International African Institute, 1975).

CARLONI, ALICE S., Sex disparities in the distribution of food within rural households, FAO Food and Nutrition, Vol.7 (1):3-12, (1981).

DEBEVEC, LIZA, African Family Meals First Hand: How West African Novelists See Family Food. Asian and African Studies Journal: Asia and Africa: Tradition and modernity. Vol.1, pp.2-5. (Ljubljana: Filozofska fakulteta, 2001).

GOODY, JACK, Cooking, cuisine and class: A study in comparative sociology. (Cambridge: Cambridge University Press, 1982).

GRUENAIS, MARC-ERIC, Aînés, aînées; cadets, cadettes: Les relations aînés/cadets chez les Mossi du centre (Burkina Faso). In Abeles, M. and Chantal Collard (ed.) Age, pouvoir et société en Afrique Noire (Paris: Karthala, 1985).

HARTOG, AIDAN, Unequal distribution of food within the household. FAO Nutrition Newsletter, Vol.10 (4) pp. 8-17 (1972).

JACQUEMIN, M.Y.,'Petites nièces' et petites bonnes: le travail des fillettes en milieu urbain de Côte d'Ivoire. Journal des Africanistes. Vol 70 (1-2) pp.105-122, (2000).

MCINTOSH, WILLIAM AND MARY ZEY. Women as gatekeepers of food consumption: a sociological critique. Food and Foodways Vol. 3 pp. 140-153. (1989).

RICHARDS, AUDREY I., Land, labour and diet in Northern Rhodesia. (Oxford: Oxford University Press, 1961[1939]).

ROBERTSON, ALEXANDER F. Greed: gut feelings, growth and history. (Cambridge: Polity Press, 2001).

ROGET-PETITJEAN, MYRIAM, Soins et nutrition des enfants en milieu urbain africain. (Paris: L'harmattan, 1999).

STOLLER, PAUL The taste of ethnographic things. The senses in Anthropology. (Philadelphia: University of Pennsylvania Press, 1989).

Notes

1. The importance of commensality has been recognised since the very early days of anthropological research, with W. Roberston Smith's 1889 book The Religion of the Semites. Goody notes that it was seen as 'the great promoter of solidarity, of community; the communion of brethren establishes and reinforces common ties' (1982:12).
2. See Stoller (1989:15)
3. Zakat comes from Arabic for giving alms. A practising Muslim should give one fortieth of his income to the people in need and if one doesn't have an income, they should be a giving and sharing person encouraging other people to do good deeds.
4. They use French terms.
5. Some of her grandchildren are not her biological grandchildren, as they are the children of a man who was taken in as a little boy by Mama and her husband before they had their first biological child. This fact was only brought up by Mama's third daughter when she argued that the children should be lucky that

they have a family in the first place, as their father, who was fostered by Mama, never showed what she considered to be the appropriate gratitude.

6   Shea butter can be used as grease for cooking, but in a slightly processed form (by mixing it in a bowl to smooth its texture) it is used as a body lotion, because it prevents skin from drying (which is a serious problem especially in the dry season, when the desert wind Harmattan brings a lot of sand and dust, which dries out the skin).
7   Young people can be excused from attending lengthy funerals, because they need to work and provide for their families. Older people generally have more spare time and are expected to attend.
8   Funerals can take days or even weeks (40 days after the burial there is a special sacrifice and if the funeral takes place in a remote village, Mama would stay there until this was over).
9   They have to provide the money for the sauce while Mama is away.
10 The widow is entitled to a pension and a place in the family, but it is the children who inherit their father's property.
11 Madina's situation is similar to that of the child servants that are found all over West Africa. She is better off only because the family has a maid who does all the most demeaning jobs, like sweeping and cleaning the compound and scrubbing the bathroom and toilet. For more on child maids see Jacquemin (2000).
12 If a man wants to mary a woman, his family must send a representative to the bride's family and if they accept, then the man's family sends over the kola nuts to share as a sign of the engagement of the couple. This is called worotlan in Jula (woro-kola nut, tlan- to share).
13 It is only the very poor families that are obliged to buy the flour on daily basis.
14 Jula, a language from the Mande language group, is the lingua franca of the south western part of Burkina Faso.
15 These are small markets found all around Bobo-Dioulasso and their name refers to the fact that they were originally opened in the afternoon, when the market sellers from the central market came around with what was left over.
16 Fresh okra is called gwan and dried okra powder gwanmugu, while baobab leaves are referred to as sirafuraburu.
17 On how West African novelists perceive traditional family meals, see Debevec 2001.
18 See Carloni (1971), Hartog (1972), McIntosh and Zey (1989).
19 See Gruénais (1985).
20 Men's club houses (original italics).
21 For more on greed see Robertson (2001).
22 Richards notes the same for the Bemba who train children to share food very early on in their life (1961[1939]:197).
23 According to the Koran a man is allowed up to four wives, but he has to be able to provide for them equally.
24 The children and also the oldest son's wife will refer to the two sisters as trouble makers, who complain all the time and are acting in a jealous way towards everybody in the compound, except towards Mama and the oldest and the youngest brother.
25 Morning and evening meals are 'individual meals', people who can afford them will buy them.
26 It is important to note that mama's youngest son is only a few years older than her oldest grandchild.
27 This practice is spread widely around Sub-Saharan Africa and in the case of Burkina it includes among others the relationship between cross cousins, grandparents and grandchildren, sisters and brothers in-law. People involved in such a relationship may tease and even insult each other, without any repercussions. The grandmother may refer to her grandson as her husband and the grandson may refer to his grandfather

as his rival. Caplan, writing about this practice in Tanzania, notes that 'this indeed may be one reason why grandparents welcome their grandchildren to bring up – they do not need to maintain as formal a relationship with them as they did with their own children.'(1975:49)

In Sickness and In Health

Daphne L Derven

"He has discovered the art of making fire, by which hard and stingy roots can be rendered digestible and poisonous roots or herbs innocuous. This discovery of fire probably the greatest ever made by man excepting language, dates from before the dawn of history."

    Charles Darwin

"the jaguar gave him a lesson in cooking 'if you are in a hurry, light a fire, put the meat on a spit, and grill it; if you have time cook it in an oven that has been hollowed out in the ground and previously heated; put foliage around the meat to protect it, and earth and hot ashes on top."

    Part of the origins of fire myth from the Opaye people of South America.
    Levi Strauss

Archaeologists study the past by working all over the world and throughout time. Some explore the earliest evidence of our species while others examine recently discarded garbage. Advances in scientific techniques, particularly dating technologies, have resulted in more comprehensive and interdisciplinary analyses of new and already existing data. The always fragmentary archaeological record becomes even more limited as we look backward toward the very distant past, early hominids and the origins of culture. Data can be and is interpreted to support innumerable and radically different explanations.

This year's symposium topic of "Nurture" caused me to revisit my on-going archaeological research into the origins and evolution of the use of fire and cooking. This brief review of evidence explores the use of fire, cooking, the effects of cooking on food and the relationship of cooked food to the concept of nurturing. Indications for fire reoccur throughout our record of the past. Many scientists believe that the opportunistic use of naturally occurring fires by hominids came first, followed by manipulation and finally deliberate control. There is much disagreement as to the application(s) for early fire. Some archaeologists believe its initial use was for heat and light. The theory advanced here is that its primary purpose was to cook food.

There is general agreement that early humans were cooking food 300,000 years ago. A smaller, but substantial group of scientists feel data supports cooking food as early as 500,000 years ago. However, a few archaeologists believe food was being cooked in Africa as long ago as 1.5-1.7 million years ago. (Wrangham et al) Many researchers believe that it was at about this time, if not earlier, that Homo erectus moved out of Africa and proceeded to colonize the world. This outward migration is variously attributed to an adaptation to a largely animal based diet, the quest for sufficient food supplies to support expanding populations and/or advancements in technology resulting in more efficient tools. All of these explanations have their supporters and detractors. The explanation advanced here is that we had already started cooking our food, thereby extending the available food supply, which in turn supported growth, both in territory and numbers. Certainly, a variety of other factors also come into play; climatic shifts, the evolving diversity of hominids, and changes in dentition, among others. Owing to space constraints, a full discussion is not possible here.

Why cook? Early hominids could and did survive and multiply without cooking their food, and without heat or light. There is agreement that the early hominid was both omnivorous and gratuitous, consuming anything to stay alive. This broad and flexible diet, then as now, would eventually allow our species to thrive in all parts of the world. A continual quest for food included foraging, gathering, fishing, trapping, hunting and collecting all in a world and under conditions that the viewers and participants of today's popular "Survivor" show can not even begin to imagine. Virtually anything that might provide nourishment was ingested. Evidence from existing hunter gatherers indicates that, in order to acquire sufficient food for survival, each individual must cover 6-8 miles every day, all while carrying food, tools and supplies (Leonard). There is no agreement, in fact there is extensive disagreement, about whether meat or plant foods were dominant in the early diet. Tools figure prominently in procurement strategies for plants and animals. An improved tool kit enhances food acquisition (Brothwell, Leonard, Richards et al, Shea, Wrangham et al). It is interesting that several current fads advocate a return to variations of supposed early diets.

Many plant foods, particularly certain tubers and roots (which archaeologists call underground storage organs), are not readily digestible, are toxic, or have limited food value in their natural state. Cooking food can increase its digestibility. According to Wrangham et al, "In our survey of underground storage organs eaten by African foragers, 21 (43.8%) of the 48 edible species identified required cooking to become palatable." (1999:570). In addition, they assert that cooked cassava has 76.1% more available gross energy than raw cassava in support of increased food values resulting from the process of cooking. Along with enhanced food values, cooking increases the available food supply by expanding pantry options. Of particular pertinence to this discussion, cooking renders foods easier to chew, swallow and assimilate. Cooking can also enhance the "shelf life" of perishable food. In a world where survival was an on-going and daily struggle, cooking food would have made a significant difference. But the act of cooking, however minimal, does require a location. A site, whether transitory or in relatively continuous use, allows the control of fire, and some form of hearth and kitchen.

The early evidence for fire in the archaeological record is ephemeral. Our ability to separate deliberate fire from the naturally occurring one is quite limited. Evidence for cooking is found in burnt bones, soils, rocks and sometimes hearths. A variety of archaeological sites, all dating from about 300-500,000 years before present (BP) have hearths which indicate the roasting of food. While most of these early kitchens have been found in the protected deposits of caves, there is also evidence for cooking inside portable tent like structures. (Schick and Toth pp.280-281)

Data that indicates cultural practices, such as nurturing is even more transient. Archaeologists can deduce a great deal from bones, but early hominid finds are rare. The existing sample is quite incomplete and disconnected. Relatively complete early specimens or evidence of daily life and culture are rarely found, and unfortunately in the archaeological record frequently represents compromised data. We know that early hominids survived, but our evidence for their lives is minimal at best. How then to argue for the deliberate care of those in need? Most would agree that early hominids generally lived in small groups aligned by blood or affiliation. Complex cultural concepts, which extend beyond direct family relationships are difficult to demonstrate with the existing archaeological evidence, but are inferred from carvings, art, ornamentation, specialized items, objects that have no specific use, grave goods, and burial of the dead (Shea).

Our limited evidence for care giving and nurturing demonstrates a cultural construct with social beliefs and concepts. Living a nomadic life requires equal participation by all. Everyone contributes. If we believe that even healthy *Homo sapiens* had to struggle to survive, then the chances for survival without nurturing intervention for the young, injured, old or sick would be slim to nonexistent. Lactating or pregnant women, small children, anyone at risk would have had a minimal chance without support from others. Nutrition and diet would be even more critical in these cases. The decision to expend the limited resources available through specialized diet and care giving indicates a conscious commitment to the overall vitality of the group.

The following evidence has been selected to demonstrate nurturing behavior by early hominids. Each of these individuals would have required a diet easily ingested, with little or no chewing, which was nourishing and sustaining. They were unable to feed themselves, or could have done so only with difficulty. Their food had to be specially prepared and differs from the evidence for the diet of healthy hominids. Cooking food would allow this to happen by providing a location for multiple food preparations as well as care giving.

In France, in 2000, a jawbone was found which dated to between 169,000 and 191,000 BP. The extent of tooth loss and damage during his lifetime meant that this individual would have been unable to chew his food. His survival would have required that others intervene. A diet of very soft foods, resulting from cooking would have provided the nutrients necessary in a form he could consume. Evidence for fire, charcoal, burnt bone and stone are all present, although specific evidence for a hearth is not. As mentioned earlier, evidence for cooking is generally poorly represented in the archaeological record. (Lebel et al:11101; Bower)

Shanidar Cave in the Zagros Mountains of Iraq also provides supporting evidence for consideration. Sixty thousand years ago an individual who was about 40 years old at the time of his death was deliberately buried. At that time, anyone 40 years of age would be extremely elderly. His skeleton indicated he had had an atrophied leg and arm (possibly from birth), a foot fracture that had healed and an injury to his left eye that meant he only had sight in his right eye. Another burial in the same cave was a male whose penetrating injury to his side had both damaged his rib and pierced his lung. Healing was present; he lived on for a time despite an injury that even today would be considered potentially fatal. At La Chapelle aux Saintes in France, a site over 50,000 years old, an individual was interred who was also in his forties when he died. In his lifetime, he had severe arthritis in his neck, a deformed hip, crushed toe, broken rib and damaged patella. Only extreme intervention by others would explain his reaching such advanced (for the time) old age. At the site of La Roche à Pierrot near St Césaire, France, a fragmentary skeleton was recovered in a context dated to about 36,000 BP. Recent computer analyses have reconstructed the skull and provided evidence which indicates a severe blow to the head by a sharp instrument. The resulting damage and indication of healing point toward an injury "probably serious, implying heavy bleeding, cerebral commotion and temporary impairment" followed by healing and recovery. (Zollikofer et al, 6447) Extreme intervention, feeding, soft and digestible foods and treatment of the injury would have been necessary for any healing to take place.

These individuals would have had limited mobility, have been unable to eat without assistance, and in fact could not have existed without nurturing behavior. That they lived at all and in some cases for long years indicates an extreme level of intervention. Feeding, special diets, more digestible and easily ingested food were all a necessity. Individuals who are elderly, injured or ill, frequently have to be fed. In spite of disputed and fragmentary evidence, it is certainly possible to hypothesize that members of the group would tend the fire, cook the food and care for the infirm as their contribution to overall survival. A hearth would provide the setting for care giving as well as cooking. Possibly these duties fell to women who were pregnant or nursing, or perhaps each member took their turn. Perhaps those who, although frail, too old, or too young for a normal day of hunting, gathering, walking and carrying, were still able to be of assistance, aided the cook/caregiver. The physical evidence, such as specialized wear marks on teeth, indicates that some of the debilitated continued to contribute to daily activities.

Of course, cooking is only one explanation for a special diet and survival. There are other possible ways of providing specialized nourishment: soft foods, others pre-chewing the food, or pulverizing the food. Further, a combination of some or all of the above may have been practiced. However, this hypothesis suggests that while these other possible dietary interventions assume nurturing behavior, they do not address all of the changes that occur around the time of the earliest evidence for cooking. Survival in spite of an incapacitating injury, or illness, would indicate nurturing by others and survival had to be the result of intervention by others who provided the necessary care and nourishment.

References
BOWER, BRUCE, *Neanderthals Show Ancient Signs of Caring*, Science News, 160:11:167, (9/15/2001).
BROTHWELL, DON AND PATRICIA BROTHWELL, *Food in Antiquity: A Survey of the Diet of Early Peoples*, (Baltimore: The Johns Hopkins University Press, 1998).
DARWIN, CHARLES, *The Descent of Man*, (New York: Appleton,1871).
LEONARD, WILLIAM, Food for Thought; Dietary Change Was a Driving Force in Human Evolution, Scientific American, November 12, 2002.

LEBEL, SERGE, ERIK TRINKAUS, MARTINE FAURE, PHILIPPE FERNANDEZ, CLAUDE GUÉRIN, DANIEL RICHTER, NORBERT MERCIER, HELÈNE VALLADAS AND GÜNTHER WAGNER, *Comparative Morphology and Paleobiology of Middle Pleistocene Human Remains from the Bau de l'Aubesier, Vaucluse, France*, Proceedings of the National Academy of Sciences (PNAS) 98: 20:11097-11102 (9/25/2001).

LEVI STRAUSS, CLAUDE, *The Raw and the Cooked: Introduction to A Science of Mythology*, (London: Pimlico, Random House, 1994).

RICHARDS, MICHAEL, PAUL PETTITT, MARY STINER AND ERIK TRINKAUS, *Stable Isotope Evidence for Increasing Dietary Breadth in the European Mid-Upper Paleolithic*, PNAS:98:11:6528-6532, (5/22/2001).

RIGOUD, JEAN-PIERRE, JAN F. SIMEK, THIERRY GE, *Mousterian Fires from Grotte XVI, Dordogne, France*,1995, Antiquity, 69(266):902-912.

ROSSOTTI, HAZEL, 1993, *Fire*, Oxford University Press. Oxford.

SCHICK, KATHY AND NICHOLAS TOTH, 1993, *Making Silent Stones Speak: Human Evolution and the Dawn of Technology*, Touchstone, Simon and Schuster, New York.

SHEA, JOHN, 2002, Modern Human Origins and Neanderthal Extinctions in the Levant, Athena Review, 2:4:21-32.

WRANGHAM, RICHARD W., HAMES HOLLAND JONES, GREG LADEN, DAVID PILBEAM AND NANCY LOU CONKLIN-BRITTAIN, 1999, *The Raw and the Stolen: Cooking and the Ecology of Human Origins*, Current Anthropology, 40 (5):567-594.

ZOLLIKOFER, CHRISTOPH, MARCIA PONCE DE LEÓN, BERNARD VANDERMEERSCH, FRANÇOIS LÉVÊQUE, 4/30/2002, *Evidence for Interpersonal Violence in the St Césaire Neanderthal*, PNAS:99:9:6444-6448.

A Nice Cup of Bovril in Utopia

Margaret Drabble

If you ask people to think of Utopian food or meals in literature, they come up with a rich spread of suggestions. The much-quoted Sydney Smith (1771-1845), self-styled "diner-out, wit and popular preacher", thought that heaven might consist of "eating patés (sic) de foie gras to the sound of trumpets", a wonderfully worldly counterblast to more disembodied concepts of Christian afterlife. The perfect boeuf en daube in Woolf's *To the Lighthouse* (1927) summons up an epiphany of family harmony, good company, and French farmhouse fare: the great brown dish, prepared by the cook over three days, exudes "an exquisite scent of oil and olives" as Mrs Ramsay peers into the dish "with its shiny walls and its confusion of savoury brown and yellow meats, and its bay leaves and its wine". The "lucent syrops, tinct with cinnamon" of the banquet in Keats's *The Eve of St Agnes*; the simple but elegant *omelette aux tomates* on which Strether lunches with Madame de Vionnet in Henry James's *The Ambassadors;* the manly slice of bread and raw onion so praised in Hemingway's battlefront idylls all offer different visions of delight, from the extravagant to the austere.

Writers love writing about food, and criticising one another for the manner in which they do it: the only comment a friend of mine made on one of my recent works was "I think your *salade tiède* was an anachronism". Some years ago, I asked the foodie-philosopher Paul Levy for his expert help in planning a repast that was to serve both as a celebration and a last supper for one of my characters [in *The Witch of Exmoor*]. The menu we devised consisted of *ravioli aux trompettes des morts, pieds de porc Saint-Menehould,* and a little of the soft cheese known as the *Caprice des Dieux*, which sports pretty cherubs on its packaging.

We didn't get round to naming any wines, surely an oversight on my part, as there must be many heavenly vintages with appropriately suggestive designations. Perhaps Nathan should have gone home to a mug of Bovril, instead of jumping into the Thames, for Bovril is one of the very few true Utopian foods - it was named after a mysterious life essence called Vril in Bulwer-Lytton's science fiction work *The Coming Race* (1871) ("Love is swifter than Vril!" cries the heroine, at one point).

A Nice Cup of Bovril in Utopia

Utopia, to some, is an endless feast of self-renewing plenty. In the classical version of Lucian of Samosata, whose satires influenced Sir Thomas More and Jonathan Swift, you can pluck self-filling wineglasses from the trees. More coined the word Utopia in 1516 to describe an imaginary island with an ideal social and political organisation. The middle ages created the idle land of Cockaigne, which features in innumerable anonymous poems, stories and illustrations. There, the houses were made of barley sugar and cakes and sausages, the streets were paved with pastry, and the ever-present threat of starvation and hunger was unknown.

This medieval vision of indulgence, so attractive in the post-war years of austerity, is no longer so appealing to us, because it has become too close to a reality. We now (perhaps wrongly) blame fatty and oversweetened fast foods, sugary soft drinks, and gigantic restaurant portions for growing obesity in the United States and elsewhere, while eating disorders are seen by many as the embodiment of abundance-anxiety. We are overwhelmed by choice, and have begun to perceive it as a threat. Anita Desai's novel *Fasting, Feasting* (1999) subtly contrasts attitudes to food and nurture in small-town India, in a culture which is accustomed both to deprivation and to fasting, with those of suburban America, with its overloaded shopping trolleys and its bulimia. Plenty creates its own hell.

Some Utopian schemes, including More's, concede the need to feast and celebrate, but for many of us Christmas has become an indigestible dystopian nightmare. My sugar-starved, Spam-fed generation used to look forward to December 25 as an interval of luxury and extravagance, but now we can all eat whatever we want all the year round, Christmas makes us hot, cross, fat and ill.

Of course children still dream, as John Keats once did, of unlimited pocket money to buy unrestricted sweets, but our culture of excess has produced, at the other extreme of nutritional fantasy, such extreme practices as the cult diet of breatharianism and the pranic light, which encourages its devotees to live on breath alone. Byron was anorexic, and his dislike of watching women eat was notorious, but many of us find some aspects of eating and drinking abhorrent.

Decades ago, somebody who had been watching the Booker prize dinner live on TV said to me "Never agree to eat on television". I wasn't pleased at the time, but I have never forgotten the rebuke. You do not have to be a breatharian to envisage Utopia as a freedom from the body. In most religions and mythologies, *pace* Sydney Smith, there is not very much eating and drinking in the afterlife, just as there is no marrying and giving in marriage there. Heavenly foods tend to be cool and ethereal and self-supplying manna, ambrosia, the milk of paradise. Spit-roasting is an activity that belongs strictly to hell.

But the earthly Utopian does not live disembodied on blue satin in the clouds, or sit at home planning the ideal menu. He chooses wholesome foods and worries about the ethics and responsibilities of eating. More's Utopia had more to do with renewable resources, a planned economy and communal labour than with enjoyment. His Utopia, the best known of all English Utopias (though it was written in Latin) has its legacy in the patriarchal, town-planning school of Letchworth Garden City, and has nothing to do with Cockaigne.

In his imagined land, cooking is done by women, and the slaughtering of livestock and the cleaning of carcasses is undertaken by prisoners and slaves. Hunting is beneath the dignity of free men, because it encourages blood lust. (Sir Thomas More was fond of animals, and his own large London household accommodated a monkey, a fox, a beaver and a weasel.) The Utopians drink wine, cider and perry, but not, curiously, beer, and they prefer to eat in communal dining halls, though they are allowed to take food home if they want to.

"No one likes eating at home," More's narrator Raphael Hythloday confidently states, "although there's no rule against it." Eating is allowed to be enjoyable, because life would be dull if hunger and thirst could be cured only by foul-tasting medicines - "They believe in enjoying food, drink and so forth, but purely in the interests of health."

We can see in More's moderately collective regime the seeds of attitudes that have flourished in many avant-garde planned communities, from the kibbutzim of Israel to the modernist Isokon flats in Hampstead, home to Agatha Christie's Hercule Poirot. In many of these attempts at social organisation, communal eating was considered the norm, and private kitchens banned, to the relief of many a working wife and mother. Experimental communities like Bournville, Welwyn Garden City and Letchworth all espoused the thrifty, communal ideal, where conviviality and a certain frugality went side by side.

Some Utopian dreamers managed to combine economy with a sense of luxury and occasion. In his famous romance, *Looking Backward* (1887), the American novelist and political theorist Edward Bellamy portrays an attractive futurist post-capitalist society in which the civic-minded citizens enjoy good wine and dining in company, in a setting of some architectural grandeur. The Rip Van Winkle narrator finds himself invited out to dinner by his charming hosts "in an elegant dining room containing a table for four. Windows opened onto a courtyard where a fountain played to a great height and music made the air electric.

> 'You seem at home here,' I said, as we seated ourselves at table, and Dr Leete touched an annunciator.

'This is, in fact, a part of our house, slightly detached from the rest,' he replied. 'Every family in the ward has a room set apart in this great building for its permanent and exclusive use... the meal is as expensive or as simple as we please, though of course everything is vastly cheaper as well as better than it would be if it were done at home. There is actually nothing which our people take more interest in than the perfection of the catering and cooking done for them... ah, my dear Mr West, though other aspects of your civilisation were more tragical, I can imagine that none could have been more depressing than the poor dinners you had to eat.'

Dr Leete goes on to explain that his society has no menials, and that in his world of equal wealth and opportunities all live reciprocally. The highly-educated waiters in the restaurant belong to an "unclassified grade of the industrial army" and every young recruit is given a taste of waiting at table. "I myself," says Dr Leete, "served as a waiter in this very dining house some 40 years ago." Unfortunately, the menu is not described in as much detail as the other arrangements of the meal.

Similarly, in William Morris's *News from Nowhere* (1890), set in a backward-looking world of craftsmanship, health, outdoor life and art, our time-traveller is offered a pleasant dinner "with a bottle of very good Bordeaux wine", but Morris spends more time describing the crockery ("lead-glazed though beautifully ornamented") and the glassware ("somewhat bubbled and hornier in texture than the commercial articles of the 19th century") than the food.

We are assured, merely, "that there was no excess either of quantity or of gourmandise; everything was simple, though so excellent of its kind; and it was made clear to us that this was no feast, only an ordinary meal". Elsewhere, Morris describes a young girl carrying a big basket of early peas, but she clearly appears for decorative rather than gastronomic reasons. However, Morris's narrator enthuses at one point, "If ever I drank a glass of fine Steinberg I drank it that morning", and lets us know that the children of Nowhere prefer, like children everywhere, to drink lemonade and ginger beer.

One wonders what Bellamy and Morris would have made of the GM crop debate, and the search for the perfect vegetable. Are the fruits of Utopia necessarily organic? The jury is out on this one, just as opinions are divided as to whether the fabled fruits of the Scottish community of Findhorn are delicious or tasteless. The new GM Frankenfoods certainly bear little resemblance to the science fiction diets of pills and plasma that were considered inevitable 20 or 30 years ago. Nothing dates faster than the future, as Shaw may have said, and we are now much more concerned with the rights and wrongs of spectacularly red, perfectly formed and imperishable tomatoes than we are with those space-saving time-saving dehydrated space travel astronaut meals of yesteryear.

And yet, and yet... the appeal of a butchery-free, kitchen-free, grub-free, and food-free future persists. Samuel Butler in his 1872 Darwinian fantasy *Erewhon* (the word derives from "nowhere" spelled backwards) follows his chapter on "Rights of Animals, by an Erewhonian prophet" with a chapter on "Rights of Vegetables", and although the Erewhonians finally revolt against the prophet's puritanism, Butler is not being wholly playful. The vegetarian George Bernard Shaw was one of the greatest advocates of the food-free Utopia, and despite what Dr Johnson said, most of us would rather go without beef than kill a cow.

The ethical problems of the food chain are not always easy to solve. In *The Shrimp and the Anemone,* LP Hartley demonstrates the ugliness of the moral law of "Eat and be eaten, be killed or kill" through the image of the boy Eustace and his sister Hilda failing to save a half-devoured shrimp. Eustace loses a little of his innocence as he stares at the shrimp with its mangled tail, "a sad, disappointing sight", and at the disembowelled anemone, which has lost its grip on life and on the rock to which it had been attached. Hilda "did not shrink from the distasteful task of replacing the anemone's insides where they belonged, but her amateur surgery failed to restore its appetite". The children proceed to quarrel about whether or not eating is synonymous with hurting, and eventually Eustace hysterically accuses his sister of being a murderer.

Is it not better simply to accept our carnivorous and carnal nature? No, said Shaw, who, in *Back to Methuselah*, takes us back to the primal murder in the Garden of Eden. In one scene he shows Eve, long bored by her seemingly interminable life in paradise and on earth, expressing her disenchantment with both Adam and Cain: "I hardly know which of you satisfies me least," she complains to Adam; "you with your dirty digging, or he with his dirty killing... you dig roots and coax grains out of the earth: why do you not draw down a divine sustenance from the skies?"

Shaw imagines a distant future where we hatch fully-grown from eggs, in a much pleasanter birth mode than the present "unspeakable" arrangement on which Eve looks back with such horror. There, we evolve into a disembodied race where "all the machinery of flesh and blood," which "imprisons us on this petty planet and forbids us to range through the stars," dies away, and we are liberated.

Contrast this with the drawbacks of the heaven of material wish fulfilment proposed by Julian Barnes in the last section of *The History of the World in Ten and a Half Chapters*. Here, an average sort of chap wakes up in an afterlife where he can do more or less exactly what he wants, forever. He can drive fast cars, have varied sex with innumerable partners, improve his golf handicap, and chat with celebrities for century after century. He can also eat what he likes.

Barnes describes in lyrical prose the perfect breakfast provided by room service on the first morning in heaven: the pink grapefruit, the three slices of grilled streaky bacon, the two fried eggs with "the yolk looking milky because the fat had been properly spooned over it in the cooking, and the outer edges of the white trailing off into filigree gold braid". Naturally, he orders breakfast for lunch, and breakfast for dinner, until eventually he is tempted out to shop in the heavenly supermarket. But alas, inevitably, as the millennia pass, he grows bored with reducing his golf handicap, and indeed sees the logical absurdity of attempting to do so forever. Satiety overwhelms him. You cannot eat forever, even in Utopia.

But you can enjoy heaven on earth, if you have the right attitude. One of Barnes's characters declares "When I die, I don't want to go to Heaven, I want to go shopping in America." My aunt, who died two years ago in her 90s, never went to America, but her idea of happiness was taking her shopping trolley round Safeway at Grantham. She could never get over the choice. She had lived through two world wars, and she remembered - with some relish, it must be said - the shortages and substitutes. In Safeway you could get what you wanted. You could get more than you wanted. She was no great gastronome, but she enjoyed her dinner. For her, Utopia was here and now, in Safeway, and she was lucky enough to know it.

© Margaret Drabble
The Guardian: Saturday December 20, 2003
Guardian Unlimited © Guardian Newspapers Limited 2003

This essay originated in a paper given to the Oxford Symposium on Food and Cookery 2003.

'Our first and sweetest nurture…'
Dreaming of food from Ancient Greek comedies to Russian folktales

Alexandra Grigorieva

The notion of nurture that is always to be found in abundance, a kind of nurture-around-the-clock nirvana for humankind overlaid with phantasmagoric and utopian characteristics, has existed in various cultures and at various periods of world history. Ancient, medieval, renaissance and other literatures profited from this concept born and maintained by the popular tradition. But notwithstanding the authorship, textual presentation of the nurture paradise has many startling similarities even if, as is shown here, this idea seems to revert to two different origins.

Dreams of nurture without effort, nurture without a care, easy and ever-present must have accompanied the human race from the very beginning. Presumably, when only a few days after strenuous mammoth killing the wretched prehistoric man had to leave his relatively comfy cave for the bitter cold and the dangers of the outside in search of new food he already tried to formulate in his mind ideas like, 'If only this dratted mammoth could come up to my cave every day skinned and roasted on its own what a life it would have been!'

But that's just wild speculation - unfortunately prehistoric times haven't provided us with textual evidence that could support it. What we have however is a fine legacy of Ancient Times, namely Greek and Latin literature. The concept of effortless nurture is already present in the 'Works and Days' of the Greek poet Hesiod (about 700 BC) as he describes[53] the rapid decline of human race from the Golden Age (when the corn-lands bore fruit on their own) to the modern bitter Iron Age (when the men have to toil hard before they obtain any food). The Roman poet Ovid (43 BC-AD 17) in his 'Metamorphoses' developed the same myth of the Golden Age,

> the ground untouched by any hoe and wounded by no plough gave everything itself,
> men were content with the foods created by nobody forcing them,

then he described men happily gathering some wild fruit and acorns and enjoying constant spring and fields ever-full of corn and concluded

> for there flowed rivers of milk alternated with rivers of nectar and yellow honey dripped from the green oak[54].

This is without doubt as close an idea of ideal nurture in the primordial paradise, as we will ever find in ancient literature.

Of course this concept was also present in other cultures, but somewhat differently. For instance in Hebrew texts God promised Moses to deliver his people from the Egyptians and bring him '*unto a land flowing with milk and honey*'[55]: this image of the *Promised Land* is present throughout the Old Testament sometimes with slight variations like '*the brooks of honey and butter*'[56] or '*many fountains flowing with milk and honey*'[57]. Actually, it's the same concept of nurture-abundant paradise, the only difference is that in the Hebrew tradition *Promised Land* (alias paradise) can and must be created on Earth and the paradise of the Past unlike that of the Future has no great attraction, in other words they don't wish Eve back to Adam's rib.

In the meanwhile the idea of paradise with simple wild foods in abundance could begin losing its allure for the Greeks with the development of their eating habits. As one of the characters of Dorothy L. Sayers' detective fiction once remarked: '*I have never regretted Paradise Lost since I discovered it contained no eggs-and-bacon*'[58]. So the Greek comedy with its admirable use of bathos refurbished the concept with modern culinary detail making it closer to the hearts and bellies of its contemporaries.

Actually, this was the achievement of the so-called Old Comedy (5th century BC) intent on satire and buffoonery, which is known to us mostly by the works of Aristophanes. We have no other comedies of his fellow-writers left, at best - scattered fragments of theirs in later Greek literature of grammatical persuasion. Some of these fragments[59] however turn out to be highly relevant to our subject of discussion.

Thus a fragment of Cratinus ('*Plutoi*') tells about the happy reign of Cronos[60], when people used to play dice with bread, and fine barley mash found its way to wrestling-schools. A longer and more detailed fragment contains a description of the paradise of old by Telecleides ('*Amphiktyones*'): every stream flowed with wine, fine barley mash fought bread for man's attention, fish came up to the houses, roasted itself and served itself on the table, rivers of sauce ran amid the banquet-couches trailing with them pieces of hot meat, roast thrushes flew into the mouth together with the cakes and so on.

But among such references to the blissful past of the human race there are some other comic fragments in which the topic of abundant effortless nurture (all foods and drinks vying with each other to tempt man's appetite) is treated much in the same manner but with different implications. For instance, in a fragment of Pherecrates' ('*Metalleis*') one can also see the roast thrushes fluttering around diners' mouths, flowing channels of black broth complete with the spoons, sliced sausages covering the river-banks like shells, beautiful fruit hanging out of nowhere and so on (and as soon as anything is eaten or drunk it reappears doubling its previous volume) — but this turns out to be the description of the Land of the Dead and it's the dead that dine[61]... The primordial historical food paradise of this world here is transformed into the geographical food paradise of the other world, the image of ever-present nurture remaining much the same but acquiring new semantics.

On first sight the same applies to the fragment of Metagenes ('*Thuriopersai*') where food paradise is situated in the South of Italy between the rivers Crathis and Sybaris (indeed the other world for the Athenians), the one flowing with fine barley mash (that has kneaded itself), the other with dainties to accompany it: boiled rays, meat, roast squid, sea-bream, langoustine, sausages, anchovies and many other dishes including self-stewed pieces of salted fish. But by the time of this play (end of the 5th - beginning of the 4th century BC) Sybaris of old (which is implied in the quotation), the proverbial luxurious city of gluttony and dissipation, had been wiped from the face of Earth for about a century. So this is both historical and geographical and is another twist of the nurture paradise idea: it's the mocking of the paradise of the others that will shortly turn hell on them[62].

Other fragments of the Old Comedy describing the abundance of nurture (Pherecrates' '*Persai*' and Nikophon's '*Seirenes*') unfortunately are short of context. In the first among other things Zeus will rain smoked wine and the trees in the mountains will put forward leaves of roast kids' guts, tender squids and boiled thrushes, in the second somebody invokes a food-tempest: '*Let it snow barley-meal, drizzle bread, rain pease-porridge, let sauce trail meat along the streets, and cake order its eating*'. As far as one may judge by the future tense of the first and the imperative mode of the second fragment they don't concern either the topic of the nurture paradise of old or that of the nurture paradise of the dead, but use the image of food abundance yet for some other motive. It is perhaps connected with comic futuristic projects of new life for men as in another Old Comedy fragment, this time by Crates ('*Theria*'), where the character who wants nobody to have slaves professes his intention to make all objects capable of walking and obeying oral instructions: the table arrives when called, the cup washes itself on order and so on, and the fish when asked to walk up answers that it's not yet done on the other side and receives the command to turn over, salt and anoint itself…

After the 5th century BC the theme of nurture paradise fades from Greek Comedy. From blatant public satire using elements of phantasmagoria and parody it turns to depiction of 'realistically' typical characters of contemporary life (miser, unhappy lover, devious slave etc.) and aspects of their private existence without burning invectives and bawdy jokes. However one of the Roman comedies of Plautus[63] (254-184 BC) based on the later Greek originals mentions among other exotic lands *Perbibesia* (Drink-through-land) and *Peredia* (Eat-through-land), but no more is said about them, so we are only left to wonder whether they were like the food and drink paradise of the Old Attic Comedy or not.

The rest of Ancient literature both Greek and Roman, as far as I know (and I'll be very glad to be enlightened if I've omitted anything), doesn't provide important insights into our topic. The concept of nurture paradise is much more common in Medieval European literature in Irish legends, French fabliaux, English satirical poems and German ballads appearing there under such names as *Cockaigne*, *Schlaraffenland* and so on.

In the Renaissance one of the most colourful representations of this theme belongs to the first half of the 16th century: it was the poem '*Schlaraffenland*' by the German *meistersinger* Hans Sachs, who wrote many songs (some of them religious, including his homage to Martin Luther 'Die Wittembergisch Nachtigall') and buffoon comedies for the carnival period, widely using the popular tradition.

In his poem *Schlaraffenland* is the name of a country for the lazy that is placed three miles behind Christmas and to get there one must eat through a mountain of millet porridge (three miles thick). Houses there are thatched with flatbread, the doors and windows made with gingerbread, the fence with grilled sausages (*Bratwurst*). There are streams of best wines which flow of themselves into one's mouth, on the fir-trees there hang many sweet doughnuts (*Krapfen*) and the meadow-trees let fall their wheat rolls (*Semmel*) into the ponds of milk to feed everybody. There are also lakes where boiled, fried, salted and baked fish swim up close to man's hands. Above fly roast chickens, geese and doves and if one is too lazy to raise a hand they fly straight into the mouth. Well-fattened roast pigs roam about with knife in the backside, anyone who wants can carve himself a slice of pork and then stick the knife back into the pig. As for the cheeses – they grow on trees and when they are ripe they fall and lie about like boulders…A similar image of *Schlaraffenland* (embellished with open eggs walking around on short legs and offering their content) is displayed in the 16th century Flemish painting of the same name by '*the most perfect artist of the century*'[64] Pieter Bruegel the Elder, Hans Sachs' younger contemporary.

The roots of the food paradise concept lie in popular tradition, whether it appears in Ancient Greece, Medieval Ireland, Renaissance Germany or some other place and time. So I was interested to see whether it manifests itself in Russian folktales, seeming to remember some promising instances from my childhood. Where does one find abundant ever-present nurture in Russian tradition and what does it mean?

For example[65] in '*Divo divnoye, chudo chudnoye*' there is a magical goose that comes up to its master when called, suffers itself to be killed and roasted and then comes back to life, and as soon as his master is hungry again the story repeats itself. In '*Petukh i zhernovtsy*' a poor old couple living off acorns gets from the sky (after climbing an oak tree grown from a lost acorn) a cock and some magical 'golden and blue' millstones, one turn of which produces a pie (*pirog*), and another — a pancake (*blin*) and so it continues ad infinitum. And of course many tales have *skatert'-samobranka*, a magical 'self-serving' tablecloth that on being spread out is ever loaded with food and drink.

But all these appearances in the pattern of the folktale have only the meaning of a magical object the same as a flying carpet or invisibility cap could have, and according to Russian 20th century folklorist V. Propp[66] they represent one of the basic elements of the folktale narrative, the magical object is always found, used, then lost (usually to the bad hero) and afterwards recuperated by the good hero or his helper. Thus, the millstones when stolen by an envious rich man are won back by the cock, and the magical goose when put to use by the master's wife and her lover, glues her and then him to the frying-pan, exposing them to its master's rightful anger (the goose here is both a magical object and the good hero's helper).

Some other nurture contexts turn out to be more interesting. In a collection of short nonsense tales called '*Ne liubo — ne slushay*', one is reminiscent both of Schlaraffenland and Hansel and Gretel's gingerbread house. The hero after walking along the milk river with *kisel* (starch-based jelly) banks sees a church built of pies and pancakes: inside the icons are of gingerbread, church vessels of turnips, candles — of carrots, and when he meets the "priest oat flour front" (*pop tolokonny lob*, a frequent character in Russian folktales) he swallows him in one bite. On the bank of the river grazes a roast bull with a sharp knife in his side, and anyone who wants to have some *zakuska* ('snack', presumably for vodka-drinking purposes) is welcome to carve away.

The other accumulation of apparent gastronomic nonsense is also a part of '*Ne liubo — ne slushay*'. The vigorous pea grows up to the sky much in the manner of the famous beanstalk, and the hero having climbed up discovers an oven-stove full of food guarded by a seven-eyed she-goat. He lulls asleep the six eyes of the goat naturally forgetting about the seventh and consumes all pies, roast geese and suckling pigs that are in the oven and then falls asleep. The owner of the oven directed by the goat finds the culprit and gives him a good beating, he tries to escape from the sky but as the pea-stalk has disappeared, he gets down with gossamer webs and more improbable comic adventures follow.

It is currently acknowledged by the folklorists that in Russian folktales the oven is a metaphor of death, so it's again the abundance of food that signals nurture paradise — but the nurture paradise of the dead. The nurture metaphor becomes even more pronounced in the tale '*Gusi-Lebedi*'. A girl seeks her abducted young brother passing an oven full of just baked rye pasties (*pirozhki*), a wild apple-tree laden with sour apples and a river of milk with *kisel* banks. She asks them where he's been carried by the *Gusi-Lebedi* (geese-swans, that were thought in Russia to be child-snatchers), they tell her to taste of them or she won't get an answer, but being a spoiled child she declines the offer; at her father's she has no appetite even for wheat pasties, sweet garden apples and cream. She finds her brother at *Baba-Yaga*'s, a specific Russian witch that lives alone in the forest in a crooked *izba* hut (that can turn around on its hen feet) and when she goes outside, flies about in a mortar, helping herself and obliterating the traces of her passage with a broom. In many folktales where she appears she is also called *Baba-Yaga Kostianaya Noga* ('bone leg'), because originally in Slavic mythology (from where she came into the folktales) she was thought to be the mistress of the underworld and half of her body was really a rotting corpse, with the bones showing through. The girl manages to snatch her brother before he is eaten and they run home, but *Baba-Yaga* sends her servants *Gusi-Lebedi* after them. Now the girl has to curb her pride; she eats some *kisel* from the milk river; it conceals the siblings under its high *kisel* bank and the *Gusi-Lebedi* pass overhead unaware of them. The same happens with the apple-tree that covers them with its branches and the oven, that hides them inside from pursuit, so they return home safely. The journey to the Land of the Dead (*Baba-Yaga*'s land) is marked by the borderline appearance of abundant nurture (of a sort) that claims human attention and appetite; it is also a variation of food paradise, but seen through by the hero for what it is.

'Our first and sweetest nurture…'

Another characteristic example of effortless nurture of much the same significance although doubtless having its origin in some Ukrainian folktale, belongs to one of the greatest Russian 19th century writers N. V. Gogol. In his 'Night before Christmas'[67] a smith named Vakula, desperate to win his love comes for advice to the village wise man and reputed sorcerer on Christmas Eve (a period of strict fasting for the Orthodox Church). As he enters the hut he is struck dumb with horrified surprise: the sorcerer is sitting at the table with a bowl of *smetana* (sour cream) and a bowl of *vareniki* (dumplings) before him: one by one they fly out of the bowl, bathe themselves in rich sour cream and then pop straight into the mouth of the complacent sorcerer. Seeing Vakula's mouth open with wonder, one of the dumplings looses no opportunity to force itself in, but the smith quickly recovers and spits it out, not breaking his good Christian's fast, incidentally making his later victory over a captured demon assured...

Apparently most instances describing food and drink paradise in European literature can be divided into two categories. One, the more frequent is that of effortless abundant nurture representing the Land of the Dead. The surfeit of copious food and drink and their almost forcing themselves on everybody present — that's actually a developed and much embellished image born of pagan fertility festivities and Christian Carnival practices: according to human perception the borderline times between life and death fighting each other for possession over man. This nurture paradise though most often full of gusto and revelry, always has the slight undertone of death, whether in Christian or in pagan culture.

The other category is the primordial nurture paradise with its rivers of milk, honey, wine etc. as its main characteristic. This is modelled on the world of infant innocence, full of love and peace, lacking teeth and impure foods, a world that everybody on Earth has known. And though of very short duration it remains in the recesses of the human mind, for the rest of our lives it is something to be dreamed of and at times longed for. It is indeed a personal paradise lost irrevocably by each of us for good or for bad, as Lord Byron[68] eloquently expressed:

> Full swells the deep pure fountain of young life,
> Where on the heart and from the heart we took
> Our first and sweetest nurture, when the wife,
> Blest into mother, in the innocent look,
> Or even the piping cry of lips that brook
> No pain and small suspense, a joy perceives

Man knows not, when from out its cradled nook

She sees her little bud put forth its leaves —

What may the fruit be yet? I know not — Cain was Eve's.

Notes

1. Hesiod, Works and Days, 106-201.
2. Ovid, Metamorphoses, I, 101-112.
3. Exodus 3,8.
4. Job 20,17.
5. II Esdras 2,19.
6. Dorothy L. Sayers, Busman's Honeymoon, ch. IV.
7. The following instances are fragments of the six Old Comedy writers reproduced in Athenaeus, Deipnosophistai, 267e–270a ('The sophists at dinner', beginning of the 3rd century AD) as a part of talk about slavery: all of these in some way depict nurture ever-present and in abundance thus abolishing toil and leaving no grounds for the existence of slavery.
8. Saturn according to the Roman tradition: it was generally thought that the Golden Age was the period of his rule (he had no baleful influence on humankind just then), after him came Zeus (Jupiter) and the Silver Age.
9. The same theme was possibly developed in 'Tagenistai' (mentioned in this passage of Athenaeus after Pherecrates' comedies), one of Aristophanes' lost plays, unfortunately due to Aristophanes' popularity it wasn't quoted in this context. However several other fragments of it have been preserved elsewhere: there are mentions of various dishes and invocations of the underworld Pluto and Hecate, but no definitive proof of their connection.
10. Not unlike Jean-Paul Sartre's line of reasoning that 'hell is the others' but for different causes.
11. Plautus, Curculio, 444.
12. Words of his patron, the famous cartographer and antiquarian, Abraham Ortelius.
13. All folktales mentioned in this paper are from the classical 'Russian Folktales' collection published by A. N. Afanasyev (collected from 1855 to 1864 and including more than 600 tales).
14. V. Propp, Morphologia skazki ('Morpology of the folktale').
15. N. V. Gogol, Vechera na khutore bliz Dikan'ki (collection of phantasmagoric tales 'Evenings at a hamlet near Dikan'ka village').
16. G. Byron, Childe Harold's Pilgrimage, IV, CXLIX.

"Quit Playing, You'll Spoil Your Dinner!" The Impact of Youth Sports on Childhood Eating Behaviors

Natalie Anne Halbach

"Whatever the cause, the kids in the neighborhood knew that missing dinner meant trouble. In those days, there were no Little League games nor soccer practice nor any of that organized by adults stuff to get in the way. When it was dinnertime, you dropped the bat, called time-out and hiked home. There would be time to finish the game after dinner."[69]

Whether real or imagined, the family dinner has long stood as a pillar of American family life. Black and white images of 1950s sitcom mothers, serving steaming casseroles to the delight of their polite children and grateful husbands seem almost laughably idyllic in comparison with our hectic lifestyles. Yet, we yearn for the structure and happiness that such meals seemed to provide to those scripted families. Indeed, recent studies by sociologists and psychologists show that the family meal does in fact provide tangible and important benefits. These scholars continue to defend the family dinner as an institution vital to the health and socialization of children into the nuclear unit and broader society.

Despite our continued desire for the security of the family meal, "Social changes of the last few decades have altered and continue to alter our habits."[70] Competitive youth sports, highly organized and more intense than ever before, play a central role in complicating the over-committed schedules of the modern family. The changes in youth sports as they have evolved from child-organized, back yard recreation to the adult-structured and time intensive "career" form that they follow today, impact not only the character and frequency of the family meal, but also the nutrition and activity level of American children.

Taught at the table

To comprehend the uproar surrounding the apparent loss of the family meal, we must examine its benefits. First, consistent family meals function as a ritual activity. According to research by Wolin and Bennett, rituals enhance family life by enacting values and providing predictability, emotional bonding and identity with a unique family.[71] By creating this framework for structuring family life, social scientist William Doherty argues that faithful rituals act as, " . . . the glue of family life."[72]

Dinnertime conversations shape a child's emotional well-being. Conversations that invite children's participation promote family cohesiveness by creating an egalitarian framework between parents and children. When "everyone is accorded the right to talk as well as listen . . . to be encouraged and treated with respect,"[73] conversation lessens the power disparity within the family. The sharing of family histories, recipes and food memories also enhances a sense of intergenerational identity.[74] Also, when cultural history and pride are handed down during the preparation of family favorites, " . . . food serves as the primary conduit for learning ethnic traditions."[75]

Dinnertime conversation and the act of sharing food also teach manners. Dinners necessitate what Blum-Kulka terms *social control acts*, directives that shape individual behavior for communal interest. From *situational discourse*, or conversation surrounding the preparation and eating of a meal, children learn to eat slowly, or to say "please" and "thank you". Parents also teach portion control and healthy eating habits. Though children don't learn conversational skills through this situational discourse, " . . . it serves at least one important goal of pragmatic socialization . . . for both verbal and non-verbal politeness."[76] Furthermore, observing manners and participating in clean up provide children with an opportunity to mimic roles played by adults and begin to bridge the gap between childhood and adulthood.[77]

Through conversation, the family meal also enhances academic achievement of children. A 1995 Reader's Digest poll of 2,130 high school seniors showed that students with a strong family life leapt ahead of their peers when examined. The poll found that 60% of the students who said their entire family shared meals at least four times a week scored high scores on a special academic test, while only 42% of students whose families ate together three times a week or fewer scored high. Furthermore, though girls consistently scored lower than boys, those who shared family meals scored high 51% of the time as compared to 32% in the fewer meal category.[78]

Families who consistently share meals together also decrease the incidence of delinquency in their children. University of North Carolina sociologist Kathleen Harris studied parental monitoring, involvement, and democratic decision-making as attributes found to decrease teen violence, substance abuse, sexual intercourse and delinquency. She concluded that, " . . . when families share all or most dinners together, substance abuse is lowest," and though, "increased parental monitoring lessens the probability of sexual activity, shared dinner meals have a larger impact."[79]

> In the small college town of Northfield, Minnesota, a mother counted fourteen community activities for three- year-olds.[80]

Despite the studied benefits and widely heralded emotive value of family dinners, the growing number of families with two working parents and increasingly harried schedules of the American youth lack the time needed for the ritual. An estimated 40 million American children now participate in organized sports. To understand why families embrace activities that threaten rituals, we examine the transformation of sandlot games to, " . . . the mania of kids' athletics as they are conceived in the late 1990s: hyperorganized, hypercompetitive, all consuming and often expensive."[81]

In the early 20th century, urbanization pushed families together geographically. Parents took advantage of new organizations such as the Young Men's Christian Association (YMCA) and the Playground Association of America to teach their *boys* discipline and teamwork.[82] Organized activity expanded rapidly during the 1950s and 1960s as the baby-boom generation spent an increasing amount of time playing sports that became, " . . . extraordinarily popular, and a staple of the American way of life, an accepted way for families to have fun with their children."[83]

Broader societal changes accelerated this growth. First, as two-earner households increased, parents needed after school programs and perceived organized sport as one that taught values and fun while protecting children from an ever more dangerous world.[84] Second, the expansion of youth sports followed the dramatic, media-driven growth of professional sports. Dr. Shane Murphy argues that both professional and youth sports are important because of their psychological hold over us. Sports attract us because, " . . . it's about real life. It has drama and significance."[85] Furthermore, sports foster a sense of group identity in cheering for and "belonging to" a certain team. The growth in youth activities has mirrored this popularity of professional sports.[86]

As organized youth sports have grown, the nature of play has also changed. Though participation grows each year, "there has been a decline in the number of publicly funded programs with free and open participation policies."[87] Privitization reflects a cycle of rising expectations characteristic of American life in the late 20th century. "More and more parents and kids want better coaching, more of a challenge and the prestige that comes from playing with the best."[88] The willingness of parents now to pay exorbitant club dues and traveling expenses, reflect the importance of the "performance ethic" in youth sports. Fun in youth sports is increasingly defined in terms of skill advancement and competitive success rather than participation. The number of children enrolled in traveling teams to reach this athletic prowess has doubled to 2.5 million since 1995.[89] The long hours and traveling squads that affect the frequency of the family meal result from this focus on performance.

With the growth of the performance ethic, sports have increasingly become a means to an end. Though less than 1% of children playing organized sports earn a college scholarship, parents worried about the economy or financial aid cuts might encourage participation at increasingly younger ages. For, " . . . if a kid waits till she's 10 to decide she wants to compete at an advanced level, the travel team will have already left the station."[90] In our achievement oriented society, parents consider themselves "brokers of community services for children," and worry that, " . . . [they] are not keeping up with the output of other parents."[91] Yet parents, though they feel frazzled at times, hardly realize how dramatically the changing structure of youth sports and family schedules can alter both the contents of the foods eaten by athletes and their families and the contexts in which they are consumed.

Parents can't say no to a new enrichment activity such as karate or traveling soccer on the grounds that it interferes with family dinners.[92]

Aside from the personal frustration of parents such as a mother of three basketball-playing girls who counted only three days a month without practice and complained of "meals on the fly," why should we be concerned that these opportunities are taking so much of our children's lives, their free time decreasing 16% between 1981 and 1997?[93] Meals on the go decrease bonding time around the table, cited above as central to developing a sense of security and family cohesiveness. One mom said wistfully, "It seems like Anna is running off almost every night . . . I miss seeing her. I miss talking to her."[94]

In fact, a survey published in the 1999 edition of the Statistical Handbook on the American Family reveals that only 22% of parents of 5-17 year old children questioned ate dinner with their child every day over a three-month period. A full 44% of respondents ate with their child once a month or never! The handbook further cites a mere 22% of parents that talk with children several times per week about things that excited them, while 62% almost never did. Although the percentages increased in talking about topics that worried kids to 33% several times a week, the surveys demonstrate a lack of communication among parents and children about issues that might affect their happiness and growth. [95] Were families sitting down to meals more frequently, the meal could once again serve as a needed forum for discussion and support of children's lives.

Furthermore, the sports participation of one child can contribute to conflict between that child and her siblings. The family meal becomes a battleground of resentment rather than a community building experience. In a study on high performance youth sports, 45% of the athletes were found to have sibling problems stemming from jealousy. The report included a story of, "One gymnast who reported, 'We never ate supper together, so my parents made a big fuss when I was home for dinner,' further alienating her from her siblings."[96]

In addition, the deterioration of the family meal ritual leaves American children lacking the manners developed in that context of politeness and socialization. As free time decreases, ". . . this means kids spend more hours on the soccer field and fewer listening to dinner-table criticisms about how bolting down those raw-meat sandwiches makes you look like a wild animal."[97] The growth of the convenience food industry has facilitated this loss of manners and the transformation of the family meal that sports require. In 1989, more than 70% of American households had microwave ovens in their homes. Microwavable meals allow the busy family to transform the kitchen into, " . . . a sort of filling station. Family members will pull in, push a few buttons, fill up and leave. We would receive freedom from social complexity."[98] Because it allows us to eat what we chose at the time that we chose to eat it, the microwave permits the family to avoid contact.

Furthermore, the fast food industry consumes an increasing share of the food dollars of overwrought, carpooling parents. Americans now spend 50% of their food dollars on ready prepared foods. Of this amount, a huge percentage goes to the restaurant business whose sales grew 234% to $239.3 billion between 1980 and 2002.[99] Half of these sales fed fast food establishments at which children less than 17 years of age eat four out of the five times they eat away from home.[100] Fast food meals, wrapped in their own "plates," meld right into the rhythm of the active family.

The personal choice available to fast food eaters, like those of the microwave meal, develops a strong sense of individualism in food preferences. Dr. Doherty warns that this personal agency creates children who refuse to eat meals at home, even if they like them, because they desired something else. "At these restaurants, children get precisely what they want, so why not at home?"[101] The individualism of convenience foods undermines the cooperation and humility learned in family meals.

Finally, proliferation of sports also impacts children who don't participate and who remain at home alone for the evening. As convenience foods proliferate, these children can independently feed themselves. However, a meal often deteriorates into grazing on "appetite-killing nibbles and munchies." Unsupervised children are left to eat foods which they can either "zap," or "unwrap." Unfortunately, these convenience foods eaten by both those on the go and those left behind lack essential nutrients, and thus our "healthily active" children counteract their athletics with deteriorating nutritional standards.[102]

As the amount of money that we spend on convenience foods increases, so does the caloric intake that they provide. Throughout the 20th century, "The most significant dietary changes have to do with the decline in whole foods and the rise in refined sweeteners and processed fats."[103] Families eating convenience foods refuel with these refined materials. Processing of convenience foods removes valuable nutrients. When artificially added back in, fats, salt and sugars accompany them. The lack of variety further exacerbates nutritional deficiencies of fast food menus. "Processed fats, extracted flour, sugar, and therefore calories, predominate: up to 40% of calories in fried and grilled items are from fat, while sodas' calories are 100% sugar."[104] Devoid of fiber, protein and sustainable energy, convenience products also suffer chemical additives such as colorings, flavorings and preservatives.

Studies show that a return to the family meal could reverse the deteriorating nutritional standards so common to the American child's diet. A study published by the American Medical Association showed that an increase in family dinners each week led to a higher intake of vitamins B_6, B_{12}, C and E, iron, calcium, fiber and folate as the child's odds of eating five servings of fruits and vegetables increased 45% over counterparts that ate less frequently in the home. Additionally, home eaters were less likely to consume fried foods and soda, and ate less saturated fat and refined sugars. Perhaps most importantly, the more families ate together, the more they discussed nutrition and related topics. Children who dined with their families ate a wider variety of whole and nutritional foods, and better understood the food pyramid.[105] Replacing the family meal with convenience foods threatens the health of future generations, yet leaves them ill equipped to understand the source of their problems.

"It just wasn't fun anymore."

In addition to contributing to the rise in consumption of convenience foods, changes in youth sports have paradoxically contributed to the decrease in activity level of American adolescents by restricting participation to those privileged with natural ability.

> One of the best things about youth sports [is] that they are participatory-children who play are actively involved. Yet even by the time children are nine or ten, there is a push toward the selection of the "best" athletes, who get the chance to keep playing, while the "not so good" athletes watch the good athletes. This tendency becomes stronger as children get older. By high school it becomes institutionalized.[106]

A system focused so heavily on talent development that it benches athletes, denying children the ability to learn new skills. Murphy argues that the need to build these new skills and experiences is essential to their continued interest in sports participation. Through his survey of 1,183 athletes, aged 11 to 18 years old, and 418 parents of children ages six through ten, Murphy found that 35% planned to quit their sports the following year.[107] A *Time* magazine article cites a study claiming that an incredible 73% of children quit their sport by age 13.[108]

The concentration of youth athletics into private clubs has exacerbated this exclusivity. Exorbitant dues restrict competitive activity to the middle class. Furthermore, as talented athletes bypass high school participation for year-round traveling squads, schools with limited budgets question the need to spend money on sports.[109] "Even school gym classes, which for generations forced even the laziest students to huff and puff at least once or twice a week, are becoming a thing of the past."[110] While in 1991, 41% of high school students attended daily physical education classes, by 1999 enrollment dropped to 29%.[111] Furthermore, the quality of exercise in existing classes is declining. In a study conducted by the Centers for Disease Control and Prevention, only 19% of enrolled high school students reported having been physically active for twenty minutes during their physical education classes.[112]

This organization of youth sports that discourages so many children from leading active lifestyles, along with consumption of convenience foods contributes to the increasing levels of childhood obesity rampant in contemporary America. Children who quit their sport may join the ranks of the, " . . . 13% of children aged 6 to 11 years and 14% of adolescents aged 12 to 19 years in the United States [who] were overweight."[113] The prevalence of obesity in adolescents has nearly tripled in the past twenty years, increasing childhood risks of heart disease, type-2 diabetes, high cholesterol and blood pressure and some forms of cancer.[114] Additionally, obese adolescents have a 70% chance of becoming overweight as adults, thus prolonging their exposure to these health risks.

The decline in mass participation in youth athletics proves unfortunate as a study done on environment, physical activity and children showed that, "Male and female sport team and exercise program participants during the past year were less likely to be in the overweight group."[115] Thus, if we truly wish to engender active lifestyles and restore the health of children growing up in a nation in which only one third of adults are active, we, "need to change our youth sports programs to align them with our goals and values."[116]

Thinner is faster, up to a point.
Hardly surprising, the extreme nature of youth sports has polarized consumption and weight problems at two extremes. Though organized sports have relegated many children to couches in American living rooms, subject to the onslaught of obesity, the emphasis on winning and changes in aesthetic standards in certain sports have also contributed to the growing number of eating disorders in the United States. Adolescent athletes, especially females participating in subjectively judged sports, sometimes sustain pressure to maintain a dangerously low weight to maximize performance.

The prevalence of anorexia nervosa and bulimia nervosa has surged over the past three decades, as media images predominantly attack adolescent females' self-worth. "Over the past 30 years, magazines and television programs have frequently, persistently, and increasingly glorified a tall, willowy, youthful 'look' and emphasized strict weight management while vilifying fat as unhealthy, ugly, and immoral."[117] In response to these pressures, girls are embracing either anorectic behaviors–fearing of weight gain and refusing to maintain weight over 85% of the norm through self-starvation–or bulimic cycles of bingeing and purging. A 1997 Commonwealth Fund Survey of the Health of Adolescent Girls reported that one in six girls between fifth and twelfth grade had binged and purged with 7% doing so regularly. Only 4% of high school boys reported regular disordered behavior.[118]

Young elite athletes show a higher rate of eating disorder incidence than the general population. A study of 695 female college athletes found that 39% met the criteria for bulimia nervosa.[119] In another done by the psychiatry and psychology divisions of the Toronto Hospital, 60% of the women suffering eating disorders had been involved in competitive athletics beyond intramural school competitions.[120] The prevalence of eating disorders in athletics stems from a number of factors including pressure from coaches and parents to succeed, the perfectionism and discipline characteristic of elite athletes, and the increasing emphasis on svelte bodies in aesthetic sports such as gymnastics, diving and dancing.

In studying the transformations of youth sports, Dr. Shane Murphy found that the longer athletes remain under the performance pressure to win, the more likely they were to develop disordered eating habits. "Increasing numbers of young people are seriously committed to highly competitive sports programs while coaches and athletes increasingly are aware of the advantage of reducing fatness for optimal athletic performance in almost all sports."[121] In most sports, weight over a healthy minimum may hinder speed, endurance or ability to jump higher and farther. The will and pressure to win by parents, coaches and children who have structured their lives and identities around their sports, provide strong incentives for athletes to engage in, "a naïve, desperate, and high risk attempt . . . to lower their body weight to achieve the highest possible level of performance."[122]

As the time that young athletes spend in training has increased, so has the impact of coaching attitudes. "The coach may be with the athlete more than the parents and may come to have even greater influence over the athlete than the parents."[123] Constructing their livelihood around the success of their athletes provides incentive for coaches to push for peak performance. By weighing, gossiping about others' bodies and restricting caloric intake, coaches can engender a negative image of food and its necessity for successful performance. Coupled with ignorance on nutrition and proper weight maintenance strategies, coaches who emphasize weight control increase their athletes' risk for developing eating disorders.

Coaches can also negatively impact self-esteem, further intensifying a common eating disorder risk factor.[124] Along with impacts on self-esteem, coaches working in a society that holds increasingly higher expectations for youth athletics encourage the perfectionism already common to many of the youth drawn to high intensity competition. A Southern Illinois University study comparing athletes and non-athletes found that the athletes consistently scored higher in perfectionism, a personality trait placing them at higher risk for the development of eating disorders.[125]

Finally, changes in the aesthetics emphasized in subjectively judged sports over the past three decades have promoted the rise in disordered eating. Women's gymnastics provides a clear example of this trend. In 1968, the Olympic gold medallist Vera Caslavska carried 121 pounds [55 kg] on her 26-year-old, 5 foot 3 inch [160 cm] frame. The sport underwent transformation beginning in 1972 when petite Olga Korbut's small 4 foot 11 inch [150 cm], 85-pound [38.5] body charmed television audiences. The sport became less an expression of artistic elegance and more of explosive combinations of difficult acrobatics for which smaller competitors can more easily manipulate the equipment to flip higher and faster.

Due to the change in performance expectations, the physique of gymnasts also changed. "In 1976, the six U.S. Olympic gymnasts were, on average, 17 and a half years old, stood 5 feet 3½ inches [161 cm] and weighed 106 pounds [48 kg]. By the 1992 Olympics in Barcelona, the average U.S. Olympic gymnast was 16 years old, stood 4 feet 9 inches [145 cm] and weighed 83 pounds [37.5 kg]–a year younger, 6½ inches [16.5 cm] shorter and 23 pounds [10.5 kg] lighter than her counterpart of 16 years before."[126] To maintain this frame, the girls trained eight hours each day on a 1,000-calorie diet. Though their level was more advanced than most, stories recounted by my national level teammates demonstrate a body-image obsession in all levels of youth athletics impacting how many young females view food.

Unfortunately, athletes sometimes sacrifice health to keep the window of success open. Female athletes working to maintain low body weight delay natural menarche. As a result, they may not develop sufficient bone density during the most productive years, the late teens. Furthermore, due to delayed menarche, some girls never experience their final growth spurt. Finally, ". . . it seems that the institutionalized preoccupation with body weight and slenderness that characterizes most female sports has consequences that reach beyond the competitive arena."[127] The Toronto study found that many of their subjects feared excessive weight gain as their career ended and began restricting their energy intake to account for output change.

Why not schedule family time?
As the intensification of time and skill level restructure youth sports to the detriment of the physical and emotional health of their children, parents search for ways to put their family life back on track. Some parents demand the reorganization of training and traveling schedules with sensitivity to family meals and holidays, while others simply refuse to allow their children to participate competitively.

Other parents, sports experts and psychologists, however, find the benefits of high intensity athletic participation too important to dismiss in the name of family time. Sports psychologist Shane Murphy believes that solutions to youth sports problems require encouragement of the activities rather than prohibition. He believes that correctly structured youth sports teach children the emotional skills needed to effectively compete, set and achieve goals, work on a team, and suffer loss. He attributes effective lifelong living to these skills and cites them as, "fundamental in providing children with a sense of self-esteem."[128] Parents also cite sports as keeping their children away from gangs, violence and the television. Furthermore, long hours carpooling and watching competitions may provide new opportunities for parent-child bonding. One father commented, "On the seventh hour of a road trip from western Pennsylvania you tend to hear a lot of things you wouldn't hear otherwise."[129]

Despite these benefits, parents cannot overlook the loss of social learning as the family meal is subsumed into hectic schedules. Nor can they overlook the body composition changes in their children who have been molded, either by rejection from or intensification of elite athletic training. The solution seems to lie in moderation of the time spent in sports and a return to a system that emphasizes enjoyment and development of lifelong participation. Yet, even with a concerted effort, parents will struggle to alter completely the structure of today's youth sports and so must find creative ways to emphasize the family togetherness. Though the family meal, "evolves and reinvents itself to meet current social demands and influences," the health of our nation's children depends on the ability of today's parents to balance extracurriculars with, " . . . the essential act of spending time each day with our family to share a meal, re-connect, and enjoy each other's company."[130]

References

BEASLEY, JOSEPH D., M.D., & SWIFT, JERRY. (1989). The Kellogg Report. Annandale-on Hudson, NY: The Institute of Health Policy and Practice, The Bard College Center

BLUM-KULKA, SHOSHANA. (1997). Dinner Talk: Cultural Patterns of Sociability and Socialization in Family Discourse. Mahwah, NJ: Lawrence Erlbaum Associates, Publishers.

BURCKES-MILLER, MARDIE, & BLACK, DAVID R. (Feb. 1988). Eating Disorders: A Problem in Athletics? Health Education, 22-25.

BURGE, FRANK. (2001, April 2). Kiss Family Dinner Goodbye. Electronic Engineering Times, p.125. Retrieved on March 26, 2002 from InfoTrac database (Expanded Academic ASAP) on the World Wide Web: http://eresources.lib.unc.edu/cgi-bin/external_database_auth?A=P|F=Y|ID=17|URL=http://infotrac.galegroup.com/itweb/unc_main

CAHILL, BERNARD R., PEARL, & ARTHUR J., Ed. (1993). Intensive Participation in Children's Sports. Champaign, IL: Human Kinetics Publishers.

COAKLEY, JAY. (2001). Sports In Society: Issues and Controversies. New York: McGraw Hill.

COSTELLO, DANIEL. (2002, April 19). The New Road Warriors. The Wall Street Journal, p. W12.

DAVIS, C., KENNEDY, S.H., RAVELSKI, E., & DIONNE, M. (1994). The Role of Physical Activity in the Development and Maintenance of Eating Disorders. Psychological Medicine, 24, 957-967.

USA TODAY Dning Together Strengthens Ties. (1998)., 126(2635), 4. Retrieved on March 28, 2002 from InfoTrac database (Expanded Academic ASAP) on the World Wide Web: ttp://eresources.lib.unc.edu/cgi in/external_database_auth?A=P|F=Y|ID=17|URL=http://infotrac.galegroup.com/itweb/unc_main

DOHERTY, WILLIAM J., Ph. D. (2001). Take Back Your Kids. Notre Dame, IN: Sorin Books.

DOWDA, MARSHA, et al. (2001). Environmental Influences, Physical Activity, and Weight Status in 8-16-Year-Olds. Archives of Pediatric Adolescent Medicine, 155, 711-717. Retrieved April 2, 2002, from the World Wide Web: http:// archpedi.ama-assn.org/issues/v155n6/rfull/poa00317.html

DOWELL, WILLIAM, et al. (1999, July 12). Inside the Crazy Culture of Kids Sports." Time, 154, 52-60.

ELMER-DEWITT, PHILIP. (1995, January 16). Fat Times. Time, 145(2), 58-65.

FIELDHOUSE, PAUL. (1996). Food and Nutrition: Customs and Culture. Cheltenham, England: Stanley Thornes Publishers Ltd.

GILLMAN, MATTHEW W. et al. (2000). Family Dinner and Diet Quality Among Older Children and Adolescents. Archives of Family Medicine, 9, 235-240.

INNESS, SHERRIE. (2001). Pilaf, Pozole, and Pad Thai: American Women and Ethnic Food. Amherst, MA: University of Massachusetts Press.

INSTITUTE FOR YOUTH DEVELOPMENT. (1999, June 3). New Analysis of National Data Reveal Risk, Protective Factors for Youth Violence and Other Risks. Retrieved on April 3, 2002 from the Institute for Youth Development Website, http://www.youthdevelopment.gov.

KANTROWITZ, BARBARA. (2000, July 17). Busy Around the Clock. Newsweek, 136(3), 49.

MEYERS, MIRIAM. (2001). A Bite Off Mama's Plate: Mothers' and Daughters' Connections through Food. Westport, CT: Bergin & Garvey.

MURPHY, SHANE, Ph. D. (1999). The Cheers and the Tears: A Healthy Alternative to The Dark Side of Youth Sports Today. San Francisco: Jossey-Bass Publishers.

OFFICE OF THE SURGEON GENERAL. (2002). Overweight in Children and Adolescents, [Data file]. Available from Office of the Surgeon General Web site,,http://www.surgeongeneral.gov/

PIRAN, NIVA, LEVINE, MICHAEL, & STEINER-ADAIR, CATHERINE, (Eds.). (1999). Preventing Eating Disorders: A Handbook of Interventions and Special Challenges. Ann Arbor, MI: Edwards Brothers.

ROBERT-MCCOMB, JACALYN. (2001). Eating Disorders in Women and Children: Prevention, Stress Management and Treatment. Boca Raton, FL: CRC Press.

RYAN, JOAN. (2000). Little Girls In Pretty Boxes: The Making and Breaking of Elite Gymnasts and Figure Skaters. New York: Warner Books.

SCHOEN, CATHY, et al. (1997). Risky Behaviors: Smoking, Drinking, Using Drugs, Eating Disorders, Lack of Exercise. The Commonwealth Fund Survey of the Health of Adolescent Girls. Retrieved March 28 2002, from the World Wide Web: www.cmwf.org/programs/women/adoleshl.asp#RISKY

SLATALLA, MICHELLE. (2000, July 24). Overscheduled? Here are Some Ways to Get Your Family off the Treadmill—and Still Keep the Kids' Piano Lessons." Time, 156,79.

STARK, ELLEN AND VISSER, MARGARET. (1989). A Meditation on the Microwave.Psychology Today, 23(12), pp. 38-40. Retrieved on March 28, 2002 from InfoTrac database (Expanded Academic ASAP) on the World Wide Web: http://eresources.lib.unc.edu/cgi-bin/external_database_auth?A=P|F=Y|ID=17|URL=http://infotrac.galegroup.com/itweb/unc_main

TAUBE, DIANE E., & BLINDE, ELAINE M. (1992). Eating Disorders Among Adolescent Female Athletes: Influence of Athletic Participation and Sport Team Membership. Adolescence, 27, 833-847.

SOCIETY, 32(2), 2-3. Two Parent Families, Shared Meals and Successful Learning. (1995). Retrieved on March 28, 2002 from InfoTrac database (Expanded Academic ASAP) on the World Wide Web:

ttp://eresources.lib.unc.edu/cgibin/external_database_auth?A=P|F=Y|ID=17|URL=http://infotrac.galegroup.com/itweb/unc_main

U.S. DEPARTMENT OF EDUCATION. (2000). Promoting Better Health for Young People Through Play Activity and Sports. Report to the President from the Secretary of Health and Human Services and the Secretary of Education, Fall 2000, 3. Retrieved on April 30, 2002 from Davis Library Microforms collection, University of North Carolina at Chapel Hill: ED1.310/2:447132.

U.S. DEPARTMENT OF HEALTH AND HUMAN RESOURCES. (1996). Physical Activity and Health: A Report of the Surgeon General Executive Summary. [Data file]. Available from the President's Council of Physical Fitness and Sports Web site, http://www.fitness.gov/

WOOD, ROY, C. (1995). The Sociology of the Meal. Edinburgh, Scotland: Edinburgh University Press.

Notes

1. Burge, 125.
2. Meyers, 28.
3. Doherty, 57.
4. Ibid, 57.
5. Blum-Kulka, 37.
6. Inness, 119.
7. Meyers, 110.
8. Blum-Kulka, 45.
9. Wood, 48.
10. "Two Parent Families . . .", 2.
11. Institute for Youth Development.
12. Doherty, 17.
13. Dowell, 54.
14. Murphy.
15. Ibid, 31.
16. Coakley, 112.
17. Murphy, 33.
18. Ibid, 35.
19. Coakley, 113.
20. Dowell, 55.
21. Costello, W12.
22. Dowell, 58.
23. Doherty, 18.
24. Ibid, 17.
25. Slatalla, 79.
26. Kantrowitz, 49.
27. Chadwick, 103-104.
28. Cahill, 103.
29. Slatalla, 79.
30. Stark and Visser, 40.
31. Stark and Visser, 38.
32. Fieldhouse, 208.
33. Doherty, 21.

34 Beasley, 148.
35 Ibid, 144.
36 Ibid, 148.
37 Gillman, et al., 235-236.
38 Murphy, 35.
39 Murphy, 19.
40 Dowell, 58.
41 Ibid, 59.
42 Elmer-Dewitt, 64.
43 U.S. Department of Education, 13.
44 U.S. Department of Health and Human Resources, www.fitness.gov/execsum.htm#5.
45 Office of the Surgeon General.
46 Office of the Surgeon General.
47 Dowda.
48 Murphy, 7.
49 Piran et al., 4.
50 Schoen, et al., www.cmwf.org/programs/women/adoleshl.asp#RISKY
51 Murphy, 21.
52 Davis, 964.
53 Burkes-Miller, 23.
54 Ibid, 24.
55 Piran, et fl., 246.
56 Ibid, 247.
57 Taube, 838.
58 Ryan, 65.
59 Davis, 964.
60 Murphy, 175.
61 Dowell, 56.
62 "Dining Together," 4.

Children's Cookery Books:
Nurturing Adults' Ideas About Society

Ursula Heinzelmann

At first glance children's cookery books seem to be concerned with introducing children to a new field of occupation and experience, with offering them new possibilities for self-expression that increase their independence from their parents. However, on closer examination it becomes clear that they also invariably serve the conscious or unconscious desire of adults to instil the next generation with their own social and ideological views. Through the analysis of four examples from the Germany of 1858 (the first "Dolls' Cookery Books" as the earliest such works in German were called appeared in 1854), 1912, 1961 and 1979 within the context of the author's personal experience this paper demonstrates how strongly the respective periods' social situation and dominant ideologies are expressed in children's cookery books.

Puppenköchin Anna by Henriette Davidis, a reprint of the original book from 1858.

Having been born in 1963 I don't, of course, have any memories of the time immediately after the Second World War or of that before the First World War, much less the end of the 19th century. However, through what my parents, grandparents and great-grandparents told me of their experiences during these periods they came to seem alive to me. When I read "The Dolls' Cook Anna"[1] from the successful German cookery book author Henriette Davidis published in Dortmund in 1858, I am immediately reminded of one of my maternal great-grandmothers. The distinguished, petite old lady with her white hair in a bun, who wore long silk dresses and crocheted shawls, lived with my maternal grandparents in the East Berlin suburb of Mahlsdorf, after having been bombed out of her home in the town of Eberswalde, 40 kilometres to the northeast of Berlin, during the Second World War. Apart from her bed, her small room contained a dresser of dark wood with little towers, and coloured glass windows and a red velvet sofa. It was a cosy retreat not only for her, but also for her grandchildren and great-grandchildren. She embodied the ideals of the Biedermeier period when the German middle classes withdrew from public life in favour of the company of circles of friends; a world reflected in the works of Carl Spitzweg, Annette Droste-Hülshoff, Eduard Mörike and Adalbert Stifter to name just a few. The destiny of women during this period lay in their role as housewife and mother, and young girls were expected and encouraged to play themselves into this role. It is this goal which Henriette Davidis deliberately pursues, however gentle her tone is:

This dolls' cookery book is intended for sweet and obedient little girls who like to learn to read, write and knit, and we hope that many of them who will be given it on their birthdays by the little Jesus or their mothers...

The "dolls' cookery books" of Christine Charlotte Riedl (1854, Lindau), Julie Bimbach (1854, Esslingen) and Henriette Davidis are the first cookery books explicitly intended for children published in Germany. During the reorientation of the Middle Classes towards the private sphere and a common emotional life within the family, which followed the failed revolution of 1848, the child's role was redefined. For the first time children were regarded as forming a distinct social group; a development which expressed itself in special clothing, in toys and in playrooms for children. No less important was the move away from children being born with a pre-determined destiny in adult life and towards the self-determination of their development as

Anna Wache, my maternal greatgrandmother with her daughter - my grandmother Gertrud - and her two granddaughters, the younger one being my mother, in 1942.

adults. In spite of this adults generally perceived the child's future social and economic success as depending in large part upon their care of it, and for this reason (in social classes with the necessary income) private teachers and trainers were frequently hired. It is in this context, that of the preparation of young girls for their adult role, that the "dolls' cookery books" are to be seen:

> First all the good little girls must make the effort to learn to read, in order to be able to use their cookery books, then come the hours of play, and when their mothers allow them, it's straight on to cooking. Oh, what a joy that will be!

The adults' concern for the child's future well-being did not preclude strictness. From the beginning a schoolmasterly voice with an admonishing tone can be heard, often through the idealized figure of the "dolls' cook" Anna, a real saint:

> Whoever receives this cookery book must follow what the dolls' cook Anna teaches. Listen carefully to what she says and observe what she does. She never pesters her mother to give her all kinds of good things to cook. Instead, she politely and thankfully accepts what is given to her…Altogether the dolls' cook Anna was such a satisfied little girl, even when her mother declined her request be allowed to cook on the dolls' stove and said, "not now, today we will prepare a dish for the doll without using the stove," then Anna quietly went and gathered leaves and flowers and made a wonderful dish from them…

Polite, thankful and satisfied…but not only that:

> She was always clean – clothes, face and hands – and her cooking utensils were also so clean and orderly. She never cooked without an apron in order to protect her clothes from stains. But she also sought to protect the apron; she never wiped her hands on it…Whilst cooking Anna was no less careful; she always strove to keep the stove clean, made sure that the pots did not boil over and if something was spilled, then she always mopped it up with the cloth intended for this purpose. Also she never made too many pots dirty…So the dolls' kitchen always remained nice and orderly…

Though Henriette Davidis speaks at the beginning of her book of joy, she not only seeks to bind this pleasure to a concern for cleanliness, modesty and economy, but also to instil in the child self-control over its own desires and inclinations:

> If she uses a piece of sugar or some raisins, then she does not lick it or chew them straight away as so many children do, nor does she taste what she is cooking more than is strictly necessary. Her observant mother once said to her, "dear Anna, in the kitchen one must get used to not tasting the sugar, raisins, almonds, fruit and whatever other ingredients one uses at all. Though it may be difficult don't follow your desire, then the denial will soon become a good habit" [my emphasis]

The last sentence is programmatic for the role of women during the Wilhelmine/Victorian period and was further underlined by the teachings of the church. The life of my great-grandmother, who was also called Anna, was completely orientated around her family and the church:

> As much as Anna was inclined secretly to eat a little of what she cooked, she strictly followed the instructions of her dear mother and held herself back every time…and that made both Anna and her mother so happy. More than this though – the dear infant Jesus, who only wants to have pious and obedient children, looked down upon Anna with approval…the infant Jesus loves the children, but also their mothers, whom he does not want to see troubled by their children…

Though the desire to instil model behaviour, economy and cleanliness stand in the foreground, the recipes show the professionalism of the successful author. A century after the first publication in 1844, Davidis' 'Practical Cookery Book' was in its 61st edition and is even today still regarded as a standard work in the German language. In contrast to the other "dolls' cookery books" of this period the recipes and cooking instructions are well adjusted to the age of the intended readership. The author takes no skills for granted, instead giving good basic instruction in a manner which is precise, yet easily comprehensible and friendly in tone regardless as to whether her subject is the cleaning and cooking of spinach or the preparation of a meat soup.

The strict tone of the work's introduction could be interpreted as having its roots in the view of the child as an inherently imperfect and unreasonable being which only through correct upbringing can be guided to salvation from original sin; the view that was the norm in Western Europe prior to the Enlightenment. However, elsewhere, Davidis adopts a policy of patient teaching that seems to grow out of the idea that nothing can be forced upon young children. Here the direct or, more probably, indirect influence of Rousseau's vision of the child as a pure, complete and deeply creative natural being seems to make itself felt. Well behaved as she is, Anna goes in for a surprising amount of playful improvisation and has a lively, creative imagination:

> a pear which is fried like an apple for apple pudding, but not as soft, can very well be your roast.

In the 'Flower Cuisine', where Anna uses grass and flowers as dishes for the dolls, serving them buttercups on chopped grass as fried eggs with spinach, we find Romanticism in full sail:

> Dear little girls, now I want to tell you one or two recipes from Anna's flower cuisine, though I don't have many to give you. Instead, I hope that you will make up some of your own, and will serve these according to your own idea, just as Anna did. For you know there is nothing to lose in flower cuisine as long as everything looks beautiful.

Although as a forthright advocate of natural cooking Helene Volchert belongs to this tradition, the tone of her 'Simplest Cookery Book for Scouts and Guides'[2] of 1912 is far removed from this kind of aesthetic mawkishness. Direct, sober and without a hint of extravagance, it is entirely in the mode of the "Reform" education movement of the time:

> Dear children! What advantages there are for you when you can cook for yourselves I hardly need to tell you. Particularly those of you who belong to the scouts or guides appreciate the value of being able to cook for yourselves whilst on hikes.

In 1902 the Swedish educationalist Ellen Key published her successful work 'The Century of the Child' about which Rainer Maria Rilke enthusiastically wrote that Ellen Key is

> the advocate and apostle of the child. She is dissatisfied with the present and hopes for the child which is the future.[3]

However, the world was changing not only with regard to educational methods and ideas. Nationalism was rampant on all sides, also in Volchert's introduction:

> Another thing. Foreign words for dishes for which there are good German words can still be found on menus. Out with the French and English words Sauce, Cotelette, Beefsteak, Roulade, Casserole! Instead of them we should say Tunke, Rippstück, Rindstück, Rollfleisch, Kochtopf, etc. So happily and courageously set to work!

The energetic cheerfulness of the last words express the same positive determination which my paternal grandmother possessed. Born in 1906, after schooling and a practical year working on a farm in Mecklenburg between Berlin and the Baltic Sea she began a horticultural apprenticeship; something most unusual for girls during the 1920s. "The boys were pretty astonished when without a second thought I turned up for work in trousers," she told me many times, "but they just had to get used to it." The 'Simplest Cookery Book' still treated boys and girls differently:

Elfriede Sprotte, my paternal grandmother, ca 1928, around 22 years old.

additionally it is best when cooking to tie a "Reform" apron over your dress, whilst the boys should wear a large leather apron.

But the English suffragettes did not take to the streets without effect and my grandmother never ceased to believe that the only thing which set her limits was the resolution with which she pursued her goals.

Nudism, vegetarianism and natural cuisine were all expressions of a new spirit which emphasized unspoilt, "pure" nature and which opposed the increasing mechanisation of food production (in 1898 an 'Address Book of Natural Healers and related Treatments: Kneipp Associations, Anti-Vaccination Associations and Vegetarian Associations'[4] was published in Berlin). Volchert also instructed her guides and scouts in this spirit:

The devaluation of foodstuffs. The latest results of scientific research in all civilized countries show that raw vegetable foodstuffs contain certain essential substances which are easily destroyed by heat during cooking. (Vetamins, Kompletins, nutrient salts, etc.) That is why one should not cook food any longer than is really necessary, otherwise it will be "over-cooked". For this reason, amongst others, certain dishes which we enjoy the taste of at home because we eat them as soon as they are ready, don't taste good in restaurants, because there they are kept warm on hot plates for hours after they are ready. This is also the reason that dishes which are heated twice during cooking, for example dumplings and desserts prepared from cooked dough, are less nutritious and can at best be considered tasty morsels. For this reason I strongly recommend that, whenever possible, you use fresh milk (or only let it cook very briefly) rather than use condensed milk from the tin.

The author of vegetarian and raw food cookery books[5] says bluntly,

Hot food is harmful. It ruins the teeth and stomach, (she insists), because the heat of cooking devalues foodstuffs. Ragnar Berg, the famous director of the laboratory (Dresden, [in the suburb of] Weisser Hirsch), also recommends in his book 'Daily Wonders'[6] the generous consumption of raw, ripe fruit (in easily digestible form) and tender fresh greens (lambs lettuce, watercress, all kinds of salad and lettuce) which are all rich in the afore mentioned substances.

Paradoxically, the nature fanatic Volchert also recommends one of the first convenience products, the liquid spice developed by Julius Maggi in 1886:

For 20 years I have found Maggi's spice convenient and practical. If a dish has turned out too bland, then by using a few drops of the liquid you can improve both the flavour and digestibility of the dish…A good little cook [male] or a practical little cook [female] must know that only genuinely tasty dishes are good for you. The palate is a good warning system. Though not everything which tastes good is digestible, you can certainly say that what does not taste good is indigestible.

Volchert's collection of recipes is no less pratical in its orientation than her tone so that her guide and scout readers probably ate rather well as a result. However, they did not have much time left to enjoy nature and cooking. Amongst the enormous losses of the First World War were the cheerful optimism and the belief that one could choose the course of one's own life which had characterized the middle and upper classes during the Belle Epoque. When in 1912 Volchert published a recipe for swedes:

Take 1 medium-large swede, 1 teaspoon flour, 1 dessertspoon fat (butter, palmin cooking fat, margarine), 1 pinch of ground marjoram, 1 teaspoon sugar (if posssible brown) or syrup, salt. Peel, wash and cut the swede in slices, then cut these in strips or cubes. Drop these together with the marjoram and fat in boiling water. As soon as the swede is cooked stir in the flour and season with the sugar.

She could not know that food would become so short in Germany during the First World War that even this vegetable went short during the so-called "swede-winter" of 1916-17 after the potato crop failed. The mere mention of swede was enough to make my great-grandmother and grandmothers shiver with repulsion.

During the following decades the "natural" and "Reform" movements got lost in exaggerated ideas and through the loss of self-criticism, and the Second World War followed the first. Only slowly was the chaos of Post-War Germany mastered. As Michael Wildt comments in his informative study of the eating habits of the Germans during the 1950s[7] the majority of the population longed,

> for a modern, democratic and prosperous society…[the Germans] had gone through an extreme experience. The desire for a return to "normality" determined the mentality of the late 1940s and 1950s in both West and East Germany.

By the early 1960s this goal had finally been achieved and by the years of my childhood in West Berlin the "bad times" belonged firmly to the past. However, the price for this was a

Dr. Oetker Kinderkochbuch from 1961

regression to the stereotypes of the late 19th century with the middle class family home idealized as the nest and the housewife as the guarantee for domestic perfection. Father goes to work to see to the financial side of things and mother stays at home to bring up the children. My first cookery book was the 'Children's cookery book' from the Dr. Oetker company of Bielefeld[8] whose coloured illustrations are populated by smart, well-behaved little girls – boys only appear when they are cooked for – who bear more than a passing resemblance to Davidis' "dolls' cook" Anna. One of the reasons that I later undertook a cook's apprenticeship was undoubtedly because I wanted to be part of this idealized world, so successfully had the adult generation at the time of my childhood passed on to me their longing for "normality" and the idea that the key to this lay in cooking and baking.

With six years of age and a fiery passion I set to work, not least because the book had been written for me:

> Ursula [my first name] wants to try it out too and bakes an apple cake…everyone is astonished, admires and praises her: "where did you learn this art ?" [they ask] "You can also try to bake the cake, for the recipe was written by DR. OETKER of Bielefeld," answers Ursula." — (my first name really belongs to my mother's generation and I share it with many of my friends' mothers, whereas I have never come across anyone else of my generation with this first name.)

It says something both for the recipes and for my mother's patience that none of the things I cooked or baked ever went really wrong. However, as it says in the introduction to this cookery book:

If you want to achieve a tasty result, then use the packs with the White Head logo! Always buy the DR. OETKER products if you want good results!

Ursula is baking an apple cake

That all of this served the education of a new generation of consumers for Dr. Oetker's packets, sachets and bottles –

> It's difficult to work hard and take a lot of trouble on an empty stomach. There's one thing one should never forget: he who wants to be strong must be a good eater! For he who does not eat well will become sick, then remains small and weak his whole life long. But to awaken the appetite everything must always be tasty and that's the reason you learn how to cook tasty dishes. It's a lot of fun and not difficult. Just read this book. It will help you. Here you will find precise instructions, according to DR. OETKER, as to how to prepare many wonderful things, which give children great pleasure. And now with a good start, a light heart and with DR. OETKER everything goes well –

was nothing particular. During this period of strong economic growth, unshakable belief in technical progress and urbanisation the name Dr. Oetker was synonymous with these products, just as paper handkerchiefs *were* Tempos and sticking tape *was* Tesa. It was only much later that I realized that vanilla sugar could be made with natural vanilla instead of vanillin, that girls do not always have to look smart, and can develop ambitions which extend far beyond the confines of the family home.

You only have to mention the names of Baader and Meinhof to understand why by 1979 the dream of an ideal world had become laughable. The 'Comic Cookery Book' by Evi and Hansjörg Langenfass[9] published in Reinbek near Hamburg that year, has comic strip type illustrations in black and white and calls every type of authority into question. Already in 1973 at Junior school I had read 'The Green Cloud' by A.S. Neill[10] a book full of fantastic images and unorthodox ideas, and in music lessons we sang revolutionary songs by Wolf Biermann and Franz-Josef Degenhardt. Every time I saw one of Rainer Maria Fassbinder's films I left the cinema in a disturbed state, but it was clear to me that his disillusioning portrayals of outsiders and fringe groups were somehow unavoidable. Demonstrations on the Kurfürstendamm, West Berlin's main thoroughfare, became an almost daily occurrence.

In the 'Comic Cookery Book' a cauliflower pudding is depicted as a riotous assembly of cauliflowers - the German word 'Auflauf' has the double meaning of crowd or assembly – faced by a badly organised group of policemen. Another pudding is given the shape of a bottom so that the headmaster can be bitten in the arse. A giant cucumber is turned into a Trojan Horse in order to topple a Central American military dictator. The Sun King Louis

XIV is portrayed as a despot and exploiter of the common people. In contrast to Davidis ("*don't follow your desires*") in the introduction the fundamental motivation for cooking is depicted to be hunger. Simultaneously with the concise and practical instruction on how to cook meat rissoles and spaghetti the 'Comic Cookery Book' seeks to develop a critical awareness of environmental politics and social issues in the mind of the reader. One example of this is the story of paradise in which tomatoes are discussed (they are also recommended "*as missiles to pelt boring public speakers and singers with*"):

> In the time when there were no cities, motorways or airplanes on earth, when all species of animal were still alive, when all rivers were drinking water, the clouds did not rain pollution, the seas were clean and full of fish…life was good in paradise…Eve went hunting and brought back deer, wild boar and other game. Whilst she was away Adam had cleaned the house, then he cooked. Sometimes it was the other way around.

It was quite a while before this influence took hold of me and I finally lost my longing for an ideal world full of smart little Dr. Oetker girls (a process which Germany as a whole is still in the middle of). By that time I was the first female apprentice in the kitchen of one of the best restaurants in Berlin. I was told that a restaurant kitchen is no place for girls, but the example of my paternal grandmother spurred me on. However, it has taken another generation before obedient and tidy little girls have turned more frequently into top female chefs.

If I attempt to draw a conclusion from this study of children's cookery books and I consider how much they have to say about the periods in which they were written, then it is rather astonishing what scant attention they have so far been given by food historians. The row of examples which I have presented could also be extended into the present by examining Dagmar von Cramm's 'Childrens' Cooking Alphabet'[11] of 2000. On the one hand the page long health warnings seem intended to further reduce readers' willingness to experiment and to be coloured by a paranoid fear of legal claims for damages, whilst on the other the complex lecturing on food science seems to show the influence of the deconstructivist cuisine of Ferran Adrià of Restaurant El Bulli and the research of Hervé This-Benckhard of the Collège de France.

Notes

1. Henriette Davidis, *Puppenköchin Anna. Ein praktisches Kochbuch für kleine, liebe Mädchen*, 2. vermehrte Auflage – [Nachdruck der Ausgabe] (Dortmund: Verlag von W. Joedecke 1858) (1. Auflage 1855/56, Groh, Dortmund) / Herausgeber Eckehard Methler. (Wetter: Evangelische Kirchengemeinde Volmarstein-Oberwengern, 1999=1858).
2. Helene Volchert, *Einfachstes Kochbuch für Kinder, Wandervögel und Pfadfinder*, Lehrmeister-Bücherei Nr. 211 – (Leipzig: Verlag Hachmeister & Thal, 1912).
3. Rainer Maria Rilke, *Das Jahrhundert des Kindes/* (Ellen Key) (1902). In: Ders.: Sämtliche Werke. Fünfter Band. Hrsg. vom Rilke-Archiv. (Frankfurt a.M., 1965), S. 584 – 592.
4. Adreßbuch der Naturheilvereine und verwandter Richtungen: als Kneipp-Vereine, Impfgegner-Vereine, Vegetarier-Vereine, approbierte Aerzte und ausübende Vetreter, Zeitschriften usw. - Ausg. November 1898, (Berlin: Möller, 1898).
5. Helene Volchert, *Receptbuch für vegetarische Rohkost* (nebst Anhang: Reformküche) *Notwendige Ergänzung zu allen Kochbüchern*, (Berlin: L. Volkmar, 1897).
6. Ragnar Berg, *Alltägliche Wunder, Etwas aus der neuzeitlichen Ernährungslehre*, 5. durchgesehene Auflage, (Dresden: Pahl, 1929).
7. Michael Wildt, Promise of More. The Rhetoric of Food Consumption in a Society Searching for Itself: West Germany in the 1950s in Food, Drink and Identity. Cooking, Eating and Drinking in Europe Since the Middle Ages, edited by Peter Scholliers, (Oxford and New York: Berg, 2001).
8. Dr. Oetker, *Kinder Kochbuch*, 2. veränd. Auflage, (Bielefeld: Ceres, 1964).
9. Evi und Hansjörg Langenfass, Comic-Kochbuch, Heiße und kalte Tips für Kochkönige und Katastrophenköche, (Reinbek: Rowohlt Taschenbuch, 1979).
10. Alexander Sutherland Neill, *Die grüne Wolke*, from the English: *The last Man alive*, (London: Herbert Jenkins, 1938).
11. Dagmar von Cramm, *Kinder-Koch-Alphabet: A-Z; Infos + Rezepte = Kochspaß'* (München: Gräfe und Unzer, 2002).

Slow Food, Slow School: Nurture and Education

Maurice Holt

The study of food and cookery ranges widely, since it deals with activities of central importance to our wellbeing and survival. Indeed, in this paper I want to argue that reflecting upon what we eat, and why, can be of immense advantage in analyzing a very different nurturing activity.

On the face of it, the slow food movement seems to have little to do with education, apart from the content of school lunches. This is to overlook its central thesis – that you are what you eat, and making judgments about food goes beyond gastronomic concerns to social and moral questions. This is a powerful insight, and it suggests that a similar proposition may be equally powerful – that you are what you learn.

For learning, too, goes beyond the primary issues of content and skill to social and moral questions concerning what it is good to know and do. In applying the approach of the slow food movement to schooling, I am arguing that nurture can usefully be extended to the practice of education – that the guiding metaphor, both in eating and learning, is one of self-nourishment in its widest sense.

To see education as a matter of nourishing the mind and spirit, rather than of absorbing a collection of facts and skills, may seem eminently reasonable but it is a proposal that directly challenges the current practice of schooling in the UK and the US. In both countries, utility prevails over humanity; the aim of school policy makers is to move all students forward in lock step, assimilating the same material, with a view to meeting the same externally-defined "standards" or "targets". I put these words in quotes because they are being used metaphorically to define the objective of the process, and metaphors are of great importance in shaping our conceptions. With repetition, they become conceptual furniture and pass unchallenged.

Assumptions about the ingredients and expedients implicit in the idea of fast food went largely unchallenged until the opening of MacDonald's in Rome led Carlo Petrini to ask, "Why not slow food?" Change the metaphor, and you change the frame of reference. What started out as a joke has turned into a worldwide movement, based on a new metaphor with very different implications.

This paper addresses the idea of slow food not for its gastronomic intentions but for the wider implications of its underlying beliefs. The founding manifesto of what was to become the slow-food movement declared: "A firm defence of quiet material pleasure is the only way to oppose the universal folly of Fast Life", and as the movement has grown, its main concerns have emerged. It is, "above all, a movement for cultural dignity", it is "a battle against a way of life based solely on speed and convenience", and it seeks to save "the cultural inheritance of humanity".

The metaphor of slowness is thus identified with culture, tradition and the good life, and one might use similar terms to describe the virtues of a humanistic approach to education. More specifically, the slow food movement identifies a definite *philosophical position* – that life is more than undigested experience; it draws upon *tradition* and *character* – eating well respects the past, its social context and its complex inheritance; and it recognises that *moral choices* must be made – some ways of rearing animals are preferable to others.

These attributes are themselves theoretical constructs, but they are a potent guide to very practical matters. They are about real people eating, arguing and legislating in ways that take account of specific issues and have regard for reasoned debate, tradition and character, moral choice and a sense of community. The ideals of slow food rest upon a form of action which embodies theory directly within practice; you learn as you cook as you eat. The end of the action is not predetermined; it emerges from the practical reasoning (to use Aristotle's term) that animates the process. And the results of such a process will not have universal application; they will depend upon the context within which it occurs.

All this makes a sharp contrast with fast food, where the preparation of a commercial burger, for example, begins not with a theory but with a hunch about what might be tasty and relieve hunger. Neither does its preparation draw upon tradition and character, as does that of *sole meunière* or a Genoese sponge-cake. On the contrary, it is designed to use unskilled labour, and the sourcing of ingredients is not a moral issue. The entire process is driven by a specified end result, from which a set of procedures is derived. The result tastes much the same in Paris and Moscow, and it is intended to.

There is certainly a place in the world for commercial fast food. And the fast food business model makes perfect sense, since the problem it addresses is uncomplicated and lends itself to a procedural solution. But the problem to be addressed is very different if one has in mind a meal – an eating event, one might say – that is at once eclectic, imaginative, and socially stimulating. Judgment, finesse, tradition and ambience all have a part to play, since taste is more important than indulgence, and chance is preferred to certainty.

To summarize, fast food is a deterministic exercise: given trained operatives and specified procedures, the product will emerge unvaryingly regardless of context. The process separates the end from the means. Given the means, the end is guaranteed. Slow food turns this on its head. The means will reflect both a particular place and time, and the views of the people who will prepare and eat the dish. The end will be known in general terms, as a certain kind of dish or a certain way of preparing some fish or fowl, but the essence of the process is that ends and means interact as it continues. An unusual herb comes to light, and so a different sauce is devised; the wood-fired oven is not as hot as expected, so there is discussion of how best to adapt the dish to these circumstances. And the eating of the dish is a shared experience in which all have taken part. The process requires that the means and ends interact, and that its context is respected.

Turning now to the case of education, I would suggest that a form of schooling based on externally-defined standards derives from the same deterministic thinking that governs mass-market fast food. What politicians esteem is a conception of educational practice that can be specified in terms of content and sequence and assessed in terms of agreed-upon ends capable of numerical expression. The engagement between teacher and learner must be as predictable as possible, even scripted if necessary (the UK government's "literacy strategy", for instance), and the efficacy of the operation can be measured by its results, which can be used to assess both students and their teachers.

The pre-packaged lesson, governed not by conversation and perception, but by perfunctory coverage of content according to some prescribed rubric, is strikingly burger-like in design and intent. But a lesson that encourages students to reflect upon a piece of historical evidence, or consider why Newton's idea of a force is both immensely useful yet completely abstract, is analogous to a meal where there is time to discuss flavours, methods of preparation, and to pursue whatever other matters arise from a social experience.

Slowing down shifts the emphasis from outcome to method, and favours the profound over the shallow. The pace will vary, to sustain engagement and allow for different responses, and certain kinds of learning may need a brisker approach – mastering the syntax of language, for example. The context of speed and efficiency, on the other hand, can rarely promote social enrichment and philosophical reflection. Just as a sense of community is inseparable from the notion of slow food, it is a vital aspect of what might be termed the slow school. Without it, learning becomes a solitary, sterile affair, of isolated students confined to texts and the occasional question. Change the metaphor and conversation becomes a prerequisite; discussion flows and a class becomes a community.

In short, a slow school aims to promote understanding rather than training. To make this happen, it is necessary to see the learning encounter not as a set of procedures but as a practical experience, illuminated by theory and itself capable of creating theory. If this sounds rather abstract, the analogy with slow food is helpful. It is not a matter of recipes but rather of bringing an informed understanding to particular actions, which in turn create new experiences and understandings. One might set out to make a particular dish, but what results is essentially contingent and not predetermined.

In the same way, a teacher in a slow school might set out to discuss the circumstances leading to the fate of Sir Thomas More, but be encouraged during discussion to step aside from this original end in view and examine, perhaps, More's interest in church reform. In doing so, teachers would draw upon their understanding of the period and revisit their understanding of how this topic can be handled. As in slow food, the teacher is a moral agent, deciding what it is good to do at this point in the process. Improvement is inherent in the interplay between theory and practice.

Since no theory guides or is generated by the practice of making burgers, it is inevitable that improving a burger can only be a matter of identifying "best practice". The process of improvement is reduced merely to the use of practice to improve on practice. Without an animating theory intrinsic to the process, there is no means for real improvement.

Precisely the same applies to the improvement of schooling based not on reasoned theory but on political dogma. The belief that education should be based on learning facts and skills makes no creative demands on the teacher; indeed, it deskills the talented teacher just as making burgers would deskill a talented chef.

The slow food movement, and indeed the study of gastronomy in general, is valuable in throwing light on education as a kindred form of practice – one that values what the philosopher Michael Oakeshott called "the idiom of the activity". Because eating is something we all have to do, studying it can have a transforming power that extends far beyond the kitchen. The notion of slow food, in particular, offers a model of the practical that can fruitfully be applied to many other activities, of which the formation and conduct of the school curriculum is one. The study of gastronomy and the culture of food should be seen not as an isolated province, but a field of inquiry that can contribute to life and society in a variety of ways.

References

DAVID AUERBACH, "Carol Petrini's digestive system". *Civilization,* February/March, (1998) p.27.

MAURICE HOLT, "It's time to start the slow-school movement". *Phi Delta Kappan,* September (1992) pp. 265-271.

MICHAEL OAKESHOTT, "Teaching and learning". In T. Fuller (ed.) *Michael Oakeshott on Education,* (New Haven: Yale University Press, 1989), p.62.

Food Guidance from my Grandparents

Philip Iddison

I do not have any analytical tools to determine whether my interest in food is the result of nature or nurture. I am aware that nurture did lay a valuable groundwork in my memory database and this is demonstrated in the appended memoir. On the other hand I wonder whether the genes developed in the generations of North Riding ancestors inculcated a respect for and interest in food. Practical and analytical skills have not only aided my engineering career but have also proved useful in food studies. Again I do not know whether these were those inherited in DNA or learnt at home and school.

Like many of my generation I was a relatively late starter to hands-on cooking. Thanks to a secure childhood in a Yorkshire home run by my mother as her full-time occupation there was no need to learn how to cook although I did observe a lot of cooking activity. Our food was very traditional, typical of early to mid 20th century British fare. It was mostly cooked at home and presented as three square meals each day[1]. Even our family holidays were self-catering and cannot have been much of a break for my mother. We did make frequent visits to my maternal grandparents' home, which had a very productive garden, a very traditional kitchen and where we enjoyed many Sunday lunches. My childhood food experiences were not contaminated by foreign food[2].

Three years in a hall of residence whilst studying engineering also presented little necessity to acquire serious cooking skills. Starting work in London and living in shared accommodation demanded a quick learning curve to pull my weight in the very basic kitchen of our house in Raynes Park. We did not have enough money to eat out on a regular basis and in 1971 there were few "ready meals" available[3]. Even convenience foods were limited to items like fish fingers and sausages. Like many others in this position I initially adopted some of my mother's standard meals before branching out into Indian and Italian cooking. Again this was quite typical for my generation.

Subsequent years of overseas work in the Middle and Far East ensured that my food horizons expanded continuously and encouraged detailed studies of other food cultures. These have necessarily concentrated on oriental food and have developed my understanding of the changes in those cultures in response to world development and in particular the pervasive development of the media and mass marketing in recent decades[4]. This in turn made me more aware of the changes that were happening to food in Britain.

The development of the skills required to obtain, cook and appreciate food was based on the groundwork that had been established in my childhood homes. I had watched my mother and grandmother select food in shops and subsequently cook it in their kitchens. Similarly I had watched my grandfather and father at work in their gardens as they produced fruit and vegetables for the family. I had also been exposed to the rearing of poultry and pigs. I had enjoyed food in our family meals and whilst it was the very traditional British food of it's period it was of consistently good quality.

In particular my grandparents taught me a lot about the production, processing, cooking, consumption and enjoyment of traditional British food. The broad spectrum of food handled at my grandparents and the fact that I had only intermittent access ensured that it all made a deep and lasting impression. I also learnt a great deal in my mother's kitchen in our home in Bradford.

I now appreciate that some of the learning was very subtle, almost subliminal. I became used to aspects of food which I would take for granted. For instance you can only learn to judge when a garden pea is ready to pick if you have a row of pea plants with which to experiment or be taught. It is no good waiting until the pea pod is bursting because the peas will be 'as tough as bullets' and really only good for drying or next years seed. On the other hand the pods start swelling before the peas develop and you can pick a pod of air containing peas that have not even reached the petit pois stage. The desired stage is in between these two extremes when the peas have their full flavour and succulence combined with substance. A simple skill learnt over a number of years in my grandparents garden and reinforced by sampling the peas as they were picked.

I was taught to plant and tend fruit and vegetables through a combination of helping and then doing the necessary tasks. I learnt to look after the poultry in a similar fashion and during my grandmother's absences had sole responsibility for the hens and bantams.

The quality of the food was exceptional, from the raw ingredients through to the finished dishes. Emphasis was placed on the flavour of these home produced foods and their freshness[5]. A standard had been set in my experience, which has acted as a benchmark for the rest of my culinary experiences even if these fall outside the ambit of the straightforward food of my childhood.

I learnt to appreciate particular styles of food such as the consumption of fruit jellies with meat, particularly poultry. These were principally redcurrant and blackcurrant jellies with the occasional pot of apple jelly. This is still a favourite taste and ensures that I will make my own jellies although I have now added quince jelly thanks to being extensively exposed to the fruit when I lived in Istanbul.

Another lasting taste is that of freshly baked pastry. Whether it was custard pies cooked in an enamel baking dish by my mother or the almond tarts at my grandmother's, they did not last long and were frequently consumed within a matter of hours. Whilst I was a little equivocal about the more highly baked edges of the pastry, the main body was delicious and fresh. This has resulted in a dislike of stale pastry, anything that is older than a day or so.

Opportunity or access is a key element in the nurture process. Had I not been given the responsibility of looking after the hens whilst also being made fully aware of their complete life cycle from egg to slaughter and consumption my whole appreciation of the part that poultry plays in our food would be substantially diminished. No visit to a pet zoo could provide the opportunity of this experience.

Similarly the frugal and simple lifestyle of my grandparents, which was largely followed by my parents, set a strong example for my own life. I still try to avoid food waste. The occasional tin or packet at the back of the storage cupboard, which has passed its use-by date, is a cause for minor angst.

Whether derived from nature or nurture, the memories, knowledge and skills laid down in my youth have served me well in my food odyssey.

∼

Memoir of Food at my Grandparent's Home in a South Yorkshire Coalfield Village (1956-1976)

Introduction

My maternal grandparents lived on the edge of the village of Carlton about 2½ miles north of Barnsley in the south Yorkshire coalfield. My grandfather, Wilfrid Gray, had been an electrician in the Warncliffe Woodmoor colliery in the village. He had retired due to ill health before or soon after I was born. My grandmother had entered domestic service as a teenager and after marriage became a housewife. Her given names were Eva May but she was called Nanan within the family.

Food guidance from my Grandparents

My recollections of their home started in about 1953 with sporadic visits as my parents lived in Hull at that time. My father bought a car in 1955 when we moved to Bradford and thereafter we visited Carlton as a family each alternate Sunday for many years until the late 60's. By the time I was 7 or 8 years old I was spending holidays at Easter and during the summer at my grandparents' home. I went with my elder sister on these visits of a week or two, though during the summer holidays my grandmother and sister would spend part of the holiday with relatives at Haxby, near York. My mother would then run the home and my father returned to work in Bradford during the week.

108, Wood Lane, Carlton

My grandparent's house was a simple redbrick detached two-storey home set in about a third of an acre of ground[6]. It was built in 1934 to my grandfather's design[7]. It was on the edge of the village and fronted onto a dirt road, Wood Lane, that gave access to arable farmland belonging to farms in the village[8]. A row of two-up, two-down miners' houses stood next to the plot. My grandparents had rented several of the homes in this row before they built their own home. Across Wood Lane there were extensive allotments dedicated to the growing of food and rearing of pigs, poultry and racing pigeons. A huge colliery waste tip dominated the land behind the house and in the stillness of the night the shot firing for the underground coal mining could be heard.

The house stood in one corner of the plot towards the back and was approached by a cinder drive flanked by privet hedges. Along the back edge of the plot stood a range of domestic buildings, which had all been constructed by my grandfather. These were separated from the house by a narrow concrete yard. From the corner nearest the house they were in sequence: garage and wash-house combined, with double doors and a boiling cauldron or set-pot built into a brick hearth in one corner: coal hole (store): second coal hole/store: my grandfather's workshop which also contained the boiler for the adjacent large greenhouse heating; the main greenhouse with three parallel growing beds and which was about thirty feet long: the small greenhouse about one third the size of its neighbour; a small boiler room for the small greenhouse; a boar shed and pigsty; two rooms which had been pigsties and which marked the corner of the plot but which were a general purpose store and hen shed latterly; the final building was a hen shed. All these buildings were brick built, with the obvious exception of the greenhouse superstructures. In the corner next to the pigsties was a complex of interconnecting wooden hen sheds, hen runs and a large general-purpose shed. At least two of the hen sheds had been shepherd's huts; these were mobile lodgings for the shepherds to be near their flocks, particularly during lambing. One still had the cast iron wheels on which it could be trundled around the country lanes from field to field. Ground adjacent to the hen houses was fenced in to a height of six feet with wire mesh to make separate hen runs for the hen houses. Near the greenhouse were three cold frames with large sliding glazed covers for plant propagation. A huge hawthorn hedge bordered the rest of the plot.

My grandparents received a regular ration of coal from the National Coal Board as part of their retirement benefits. As a result coal fires provided all heating in the house and greenhouses and much of the cooking also used this fuel[9].

The buildings and hen runs occupied perhaps one quarter of the ground. The remainder was devoted about equally to flower gardens and the production of fruit and vegetables. The flower areas were criss-crossed with paths edged in brick and had an extensive and somewhat eclectic collection of species[10].

The establishment had many of the characteristics of a country house estate, albeit in miniature. The combination of domestic buildings and substantial food production facilities created a measure of self-sufficiency and there was significant re-cycling of waste. From this brief description it is obvious that production, processing and storage of their own food were principal activities for my grandparents in their retirement.

Fruit and Vegetables

The vegetable sections of the garden were organised in four main blocks so that vegetables could be grown in rotation. Interspersed amongst them were fruit trees and soft fruit bushes including red, white and blackcurrants, raspberries and loganberries. There was a strawberry patch where individual fruit were protected for ripening by old glass jam jars. The fruit trees were Bramley and Lord Suffield[11] cooking apples, three eating apples which produced small tart fruit and which were, I believe, pippins, a greengage and a Victoria plum.

The vegetable selection was extensive; there was however always a preponderance of early and main crop potatoes to provide a full years supply for the household: King Edward's, Home Guard, Majestic and Redskins are varieties that I remember. If it was my job to go and lift a root or two of new potatoes, I would sift through the soil with the fork repeatedly to collect all the tiny potatoes, some only the size of a pea. These would be scrubbed and boiled and were a special treat.

Beetroot, carrots, parsnips, onions and to a lesser extent turnips dominated the root crops with occasional shallot, spring onion and radish crops. Dwarf French beans, broad beans,

Food guidance from my Grandparents

runner beans and garden peas[12] were the legume crops whilst the brassicas were spring cabbage, Tom Thumb hearted cabbage[13], Brussels sprouts and cauliflower. Webb's Wonderful and Little Gem were frequently planted lettuce, the main ingredient of any salad.

I remember the seedsmen's catalogues being studied in detail during the winter to select vegetables and flowers for the next season. In the 1950's Fogwill's and Toogood's catalogues were plain affairs, no colour printing was used for the vegetable sections and they resembled an abridged version of Vilmorin-Andrieux with many longstanding favourites available[14]. Some seed was collected from the mature plants, especially broad and runner beans and in some years seed potatoes were retained from the crop to be used the following year.

The greenhouses and cold frames enabled plants to be raised from seedlings. The seed was sown early in a box in the greenhouse and when the seedlings were starting their first true leaves they would be pricked out into new boxes to grow and harden off in the cold frames. I can remember pricking out 192 cabbage plants one year; my grandfather distributed the excess around the village. Brassicas and bedding plants such as marigolds, stocks and asters were propagated this way. Pea and bean seed was dibbed directly into the ground and root crops were sown into drills scored into the ground. The root crops germinated into thick hedges of vigorous plants, which would usually be thinned out to 6-9 inch centres to let the roots develop to maximum size. Nanan however did not space out the beetroot and carrots as she liked to eat the plants young and would effectively thin the rows by removing plants to cook as the crop developed.

Asparagus peas, Jerusalem artichokes, leeks, sprouting broccoli, marrow (not courgette!), and celery were all grown from time to time but not at the expense of the main eating crops which provided the bulk of the family's fresh food.

There were few herbs; a large parsley patch and mint are all that I can remember.

There was a substantial bed of rhubarb where young growth was forced in the spring under old galvanised buckets, which were no longer of any other use being perforated with rust holes. The tender young stalks, which grew in the late spring and early summer, went into the suet puddings or were stewed. I remember eating the very young stalks cut up raw with sugar for breakfast.

The greenhouses were devoted to tomato production during the summer and chrysanthemums during the winter. Red and yellow skinned tomatoes were grown, the latter being my favourite because they were not available commercially. Sometimes a few cherry tomato plants were included and there was always one cucumber plant which produced the traditional foot long fruit. Nanan sold some of the red tomatoes to people in the village; she used the stiff blue bags in which she bought sugar to package them for sale. In the autumn as the weather for ripening the tomatoes declined, any remaining green tomatoes were allowed to develop as much as possible before the plants were taken out of the greenhouse. These green tomatoes were carefully harvested, wrapped in tissue or newspaper and put into a drawer in the sideboard. Nanan would inspect these every few days to collect the ones that had ripened. Any excess green tomatoes were made into chutney.

Gardening was a family occupation and I was involved from an early age. When my Easter stay occurred late in April I would help with the potato planting. On weekend visits there was always some work to be done or some harvesting. During the summer I remember doing a lot of hedge trimming and weeding, seemingly never-ending tasks.

Pigs

Pig keeping stopped in the mid 50's, I remember being shown the boar and sow in their sties when I was very young[15]. The pigs were fed on pig cake, which was kept in a wooden bin in the yard. It was made by Leeds City Corporation from food waste and was formed into dried cakes. It had to be reconstituted with water to be fed to the pigs and the cake occasionally yielded cutlery, which was cleaned and put to good use.

The pig was killed in the autumn and on the appointed day the butcher came to help my grandfather. The pig was starved for at least a day beforehand. It took place on a Saturday when my grandfather would not be working and he would also be assisted by Jimmy Winter who also kept pigs on a larger scale on a small holding up Wood Lane. The butcher would stun the pig in the sty and it was then manhandled out of the sty and place on a tumbril, a wooden stretcher which had short legs about a foot long to keep it off the ground[16]. The throat was then slit and the blood collected. This was not processed by my grandparents but went to someone who specialised in making blood sausage. The pig killing and butchery were a community affair as many relatives and friends benefited by receiving part of the butchered pig. My father's mother received the chaps and skirting, generally known as the caul fat. She particularly appreciated these items and my father also remembers that the residue from the rendering of the caul was particularly delicious.

The carcass was then carried along to the washhouse where it was strung up the back legs to two hooks in the roof beams. The butcher removed the viscera and head for immediate consumption or distribution. The meat was left to cool and hang over the weekend and the butcher returned early the following week to joint the carcass. My grandparents kept the hams and bacon for home processing[17]; family and relatives in the village ate the remaining meat fresh. There was a large York stone slab in the washhouse under the window. My grandfather would spread a thick layer of salt on this and the hams and sides of bacon were put on the salt and it was rubbed in to the meat. This was repeated regularly until the meat was cured. It was then wrapped in muslin and hung in the washhouse for storage. As required the bacon or ham was taken into the kitchen to be sliced and cooked. My grandparents had the necessary knowledge and skills to achieve a good cure; meat was never lost by spoilage. My father does recall sometimes being able to discern a faint taste of the pig cake aroma in the meat, but nowhere near as bad as the fishmeal taste that permeated bacon when commercial pig farmers used that feed to excess. On this day the set-pot in the washhouse was filled with water and heated for cleaning the carcass.

The tumbrel and metal trays on which the pigs were killed and butchered were put to other uses in later years.

Poultry

The hens were kept on until the early seventies. There was a two-year rotation of the flock. A dozen day-old chicks were bought from the hatchery each year and were raised primarily as egg producers although they all ended up being eaten for Sunday lunch after about two years. The chicks were transported in a cardboard box with large circular holes in the side. Any weak chicks were kept in the box next to the kitchen hearth to be fed regularly until they were strong enough to join the rest, who had been put in a special small portable run inside one of the hen runs[18]. A few cock chicks were often included as extras and were not wasted, meeting an earlier fate than the laying hens. I remember that my grandmother watched out for the birds that were not laying well and these were selected for early consumption. Rhode Island Red, Buff Rock and White Leghorn were the breeds chosen, hybrids only started to be available in later years. My grandmother also usually had a few bantams, which were smaller than the hens and whose eggs were slightly smaller than the smallest grade of commercial eggs available these days[19]. Ducks, geese and guinea fowl were reared from time to time but never in large numbers.

Whilst I was on holiday at Wood Lane I became responsible for feeding, watering, cleaning[20] and egg collecting duties. It took a little subterfuge and my jersey pulled over my hand to be able to rummage under a broody hen that was insisting on sitting on the eggs, a right defended with a sharp beak[21]. Most of the feed came in half-hundredweight bags from the Barnsley British Cooperative Society, ordered on visits to town and delivered to Wood Lane. It was stored in large metal bins in the workshop; mice were a serious pest and were regularly caught alive in a patent trap[22] Pellets, meal and maize, which was called Indian corn, were fed to the hens. During the winter, vegetable scraps from the kitchen were boiled up, mashed and mixed with meal for the morning feed.

My grandfather would kill the chicken which had been selected for Sunday lunch several days in advance. Its throat was cut and the bird was bled[23]. It was hung up from a roof beam in the workshop with the head tied up in a piece of newspaper. A pail would be to hand; anybody passing by took a hand in plucking the carcass. My grandmother would draw the bird the night before it was to be eaten, an operation I watched with fascination[24]. All edible portions were used; my grandmother seemed to be particularly fond of boiled gizzard. The birds were often layers and the partially developed yolks in the ovary were carefully reserved for baking. The cleaned carcass was trussed for roasting the following morning.

My parents received a large part of their egg supply from Wood Lane. Some eggs were also sold or given to relatives and friends in the village. Double-yolk eggs were a regular occurrence, they could be identified by their extended length. At peak laying time there was an excess of eggs and these were put down in an enamel pail in a waterglass[25] solution. The pail was kept in the washhouse and the eggs could be kept for several months. They could be removed as required: the waterglass had formed a jelly like coat to the shell, which had to be removed. They were only used for baking.

My grandmother would go gleaning in the local fields after the corn had been cut. Many women from the village did this as most people kept hens on their allotments and the ears of wheat, barley or rye would supplement the poultry feed.

The Kitchen

The kitchen was the core of the home and occupied half the ground floor. It was invariably the point of entry into the home; a small lobby led directly from the back door, the front door of the house was rarely used.

A large central table and a Yorkshire range built into the gable wall dominated the room. To the left of the range, tucked into the corner, was a large rectangular pottery sink[26] with a wooden draining board and small stone work surface which supported a two ring gas burner. Above the sink a small window gave a view past the greenhouses and towards the hen runs.

The Yorkshire range had a fire hearth with drop bar and two trivets to support pots that could be swung over the fire. Generally only one trivet was installed and it served to keep pots warm during the cooking of a meal. The drop bar was a grate at the front of the fire hearth that could be rotated from a vertical position to the horizontal to expose more of the coal fire. This could be used to keep small pots warm and was essential if you wanted to make toast with a toasting fork. The oven was to the left of the hearth with two perforated steel shelves and a heavy door. Above the oven was a hot box with a separate drop down door. Food could be kept warm and my grandmother used to dry citrus peel in it for use as firelighters. A damper controlled the flow of hot air from the hearth around the oven and was the only means of regulating the oven temperature apart from physically raking the coals to one side away from the oven side. A fireback boiler provided hot water to the kitchen sink and upstairs bathroom.

In early years the range was a cast iron or steel model which was cleaned and blackleaded every Friday, an operation which started before breakfast. It was replaced after a few years with a practically identical model in green enamel. The reduction in cleaning effort required was the reason for the change.

Nanan's skill in working with these cooking ranges is now difficult to appreciate. The gas burners next to the sink were only used to boil vegetables and finish gravy or make sauce. Roast meats, roast vegetables, Yorkshire pudding, pastry, breads and cakes were all produced in an oven with no calibrated temperature control. The heat from the fire would vary with the quality of the coal, the wind's effect on the draught produced by the chimney and how well it was stoked and tended. The stoking and tending of the fire were continuous operations if there was cooking to be done. Baking in summer meant having a roaring fire and all the windows open.

Continuing around the room in an anti-clockwise direction there was a built-in cupboard above three drawers where crockery, table linen etc. were stored[27]. A rocking chair stood in the corner and between this and the door to the front room there was a long sideboard. It contained the sterling silver forks and spoons which Nanan had inherited or been given by the Barber sisters for whom she had worked in service. These fascinated me as a child with a variety of engraved monograms, initials and hallmarks.

The door to the front room was in the corner of the room opposite the sink and on the adjacent wall there was the door to the pantry. This extended partly under the stairs and the ceiling sloped down on that side. The part under the stairs was at a lower level down a substantial step, partially below ground level to keep temperatures even. There were two stone slabs built into the fabric of the walls which acted as large storage shelves at waist height. They also acted as simple temperature control features and milk, butter and cheese were stored on them[28]. There was a tiny window and a bare bulb for light at night. The first refrigerator arrived in the mid 60's. Open wooden shelves held the rest of the grocery provisions.

A storage lobby filled the space between the pantry and back door lobby on this wall. There were always two buckets full of coal in the store, and one of my chores on visits was to replenish these. The last wall of the room had a large window overlooking the backyard. Under the window there was a white enamel worktop on a wooden chest of drawers. This was where Nanan worked and cooked, rolling out pastry and hand beating cake mixes. There were no kitchen appliances and the batterie de cuisine was simple, a balance scale with a set of brass and iron weights, plain steel knives, enamelware, tinned bakeware, a conical sieve which was the bane of my mother's life when it had to be cleaned, mainly aluminium pans for boiling, an iron frying pan and the usual pottery bowls, jugs and plates.

The central deal table folded in two and rotated to halve its size. It was generally folded and covered with a blanket, being deployed for the family meals. Under the top was a storage area with a large silver ladle that was rarely used and a treasure trove of old newspapers including a Lloyd's Weekly News supplement titled 'The Deathless Story of the Titanic' and a Daily Sketch of 12th December 1936 headlined "Ex-King's Farewell Broadcast to Empire". The table was used as the family dining table and we sat on bentwood chairs.

Food guidance from my Grandparents

Sunday Lunches

Nanan cooked the Sunday lunch for the family using the Yorkshire range and the two-ring gas burner. Although in later years an electric cooker was installed in the kitchen she did not use it for this meal.

Our Sunday lunches were quite formal affairs. Once the preparation was finished we all sat around the kitchen table, which was covered with a white linen tablecloth. The best china and the silver cutlery were used and we all had linen napkins. It was always a roast meat meal in winter, often their own chicken, otherwise beef or on rare occasions goose. If we were to have beef the Yorkshire pudding[29] would be sliced up and served first with gravy. The chicken from the bird's leg and thigh was always quite dark meat and substantial, unlike modern chickens. Nanan would have the 'oyster bits' from the bird's back. The gravy that was made from the chicken dripping was always very pale in colour. No gravy browning was used and despite its anaemic appearance it was very tasty.

Puddings were usually steamed sponges, sultana or treacle with ginger during the winter. Christmas puddings were made and were consumed on and after Christmas day. Suet crusted steamed apple and rhubarb puddings were also on the menu. There was usually a choice of sweet white sauce or custard. During the summer coconut or almond tarts and 'honeycomb mould' were the choices. This pudding was made from gelatine, eggs and milk and always separated into two layers, one solid and jelly-like and one with quite a fluffy consistency. It was made in an aluminium mould and was turned onto a plate to be served.

Other Food

My grandmother cooked only traditional food. Apart from the roast dinners she was particularly adept at baking bread, cakes and pastry.

Monday was washing day and the lunch was usually cold meat, potatoes and vegetables, which was not a favourite meal for my sister. Meat pie made from shin beef and kidney was a mid week lunch special.

Nanan baked all her own bread in the early years of my visits. Only fresh yeast was used and this was bought at Hinchcliffes in Barnsley. The bread was predominantly white; brown bread was purchased in later years. Nanan would reserve a little of the dough when I was staying to make a hand of bread fingers for me to consume hot from the oven. I was always told that eating fresh bread would give me indigestion but it did not deter me from pleasure of hot fresh bread. Teacakes, plain or with currants, scones and hot cross buns at Easter were also produced.

Food guidance from my Grandparents

Nanan's particular speciality was simnel cake. This was a particular treat and one of my favourite cakes, vying with Christmas cake for the top spot. The cake crumb was light, pale cream and laced with currants. Through the centre of the cake there was a layer of almond paste, loaded with flavour and a good half-inch thick. The announcement that there was simnel cake for tea always created a frisson of expectation, which was always satisfied at tea. Very rarely the cake would also have a marzipan top with 12 small balls of marzipan representing the apostles. My mother inherited Nanan's culinary skills and in particular the baking of simnel cake.

Another of her specialities was almond macaroons, baked on rice paper and laboriously decorated with an almond which my sister had often blanched, skinned and split. Another baked speciality was almond and coconut tarts. These had a pastry base, a layer of plum jam and then a moist and firm almond or coconut sponge filling decorated with pastry strips. We always ate these freshly baked and they were succulent and full of flavour with excellent pastry.

When Nanan made plum jam with the Victoria plums, she left the plum stones in the jam. After a year or two of storage in the pot, the area around the stone would be suffused with the taste of almond from the kernel. Raspberry jam and jellies of redcurrant, blackcurrant and apple were also produced, the latter largely for consumption with poultry. Quite a lot of the jam was used in baking.

Nanan made raspberry vinegar by filling a bottle with fresh raspberries and then covering them with vinegar and a little sugar. She would use the vinegar as a condiment on cold Yorkshire pudding.

In the early years milk was collected in a lidded aluminium can from Brown's farm in the village. When bottle deliveries started to be made they were deposited in a box perched on the wall that divided 108 from the row of miner's houses. The box also had a covered section for the mail.

Nanan would drink the water in which green vegetables had been boiled when it had cooled. Only puddings were steamed in those days, steaming vegetables was unheard of.

Ringtons tea and coffee was delivered by a travelling salesman who drove a Morris Minor van, which had a very smart livery of olive green bodywork and gold lettering. The tea and coffee came in yellow paper cylindrical packages. Coffee was a rarity; I cannot remember it being drunk and can only assume that the relatively small quantities purchased were used in baking.

Food guidance from my Grandparents

Nanan referred to young hawthorn leaves[30] as 'bread and cheese' as they were edible. My sister remembers trying them and not being impressed with them as a source of food. Nanan did make rose hip syrup but I cannot remember the elder flowers and berries, which grew abundantly in Wood Lane, being put to any use. Similarly I have no recollection of blackberries being collected, probably because of the abundance of other soft fruit in the garden.

Recycling
Several forms of recycling have been mentioned already. Recycling has become very fashionable but is not a modern invention; re-use of anything with a residual value was a natural part of life in the 50's and 60's. All non-woody garden waste that was not contaminated with serious weed such as columbine or couch grass was put on the large compost heap to rot down for manure. Woody garden waste was burnt and the ash distributed on the garden. The family cat and dog[31] were largely fed on kitchen scraps. Waste from vegetables was given to the pigs or cooked for the hens.

The recycling included some unusual items. The house had a toilet but this was on the ground floor next to the back door. The house had been built for a working man's family and this dictated the location of the toilet. The upstairs bathroom did not have a toilet; instead under every bed there was a chamber pot for use at night. Any urine was collected in the morning in a bucket covered with a cloth and was used on the garden.

My grandfather had a reputation in the village for being able to fix almost anything in that pre-electronic age. His workshop had a wide range of tools and also an extensive selection of new and salvaged pieces of ironmongery, fixings and raw materials. I am sure that the experience of seeing him working with those tools and subsequently having access to them as I grew up was a strong influence in my subsequent career choice of engineer.

Nanan used goose fat as a hand moisturiser and my grandfather used it to grease tools for storage. The pinion feathers of the goose were used as a duster for the corners of windows and other inaccessible spots.

Two cast iron baths collected all the rainwater from the gutters of the domestic buildings and were the water supply for the garden. There was an outside tap and hose but it was rarely used. After many years of cultivation the vegetable garden soil was rich in humus to the depth of the double digging required for potato cultivation and hence retained moisture efficiently.

The soil in the greenhouse beds was not renewed with material from outside the garden. It was either laboriously searched by hand each spring for pests, or sterilized by heating on a large iron plate above one of the greenhouse furnaces. Compost was similarly treated before use in the greenhouse. Very few pesticides were used, in the greenhouse there were always some African marigold plants to deter insects. All crops were regularly planted in rotation around the garden and pyrethrums were also common in the garden.

Medicinals

Nanan generally had robust health, which was in stark contrast to my grandfather, who was an invalid in varying degrees for the last 17 years of his life. She had inherited a certain number of traditional country medicinal cures. As a boy these did not interest me and I took very little note of them.

My sister does remember being given camomile tea for her adolescent spots. The whole dried camomile flower heads were steeped in boiling water overnight, strained and then drunk, a foul tasting brew according to my sister.

Nanan did have a small bottle of olive oil purchased at Boots the chemists. It was labelled BP[32] and was used for medicinal purposes only.

Bibliography

EVELEIGH, DAVID J, *Firegrates and Kitchen Ranges,* Shire Album 99, (Aylesbury: Shire Publications,1983).
VILMORIN-ANDRIEUX ET CIE, *The Vegetable Garden,* (London: John Murray,1885).

Notes

1. The only non-traditional element that had a major role was the packet cereal which was a breakfast staple by the late 1950's. My favourite was Kellogg's Rice Krispies but Cornflakes and Frosties made regular appearances. Most of the bread was purchased at a local bread shop but none was pre-sliced or pre-packed.
2. My parents and grandparents made few changes to their culinary regime throughout their lives; if anything did change it was to introduce a new recipe version or make the food simpler. I was therefore able to enjoy the food of my upbringing each time I returned to my parents' home.
3. Dehydrated Vesta meals, which were usually curries and early boil-in-the-bag fish with various sauces, come to mind.
4. My paper to a Folklore Conference in Al Ain in 2000 reviewed the changes in the food culture of the United Arab Emirates and the important role that it plays in the complex composition of heritage and folklore.
5. I remember being instructed to collect carrots on the morning that they were to be served for lunch. I would loosen them from the ground with a fork, pull them out by the tops, wash the roots in the rainwater bath outside the greenhouse and twist off the tops which released a strong carrot aroma.

Food guidance from my Grandparents

6. I measured the size of the plot when a section of it was sold towards the end of my grandmothers life. The productive area was probably a little below the quarter acre generally considered adequate for a family's food self-sufficiency.
7. I have a receipt for the payment of £200 on account for the construction of 108, Wood Lane dated 11th April 1934.
8. During my visits to Wood Lane I observed the immediate post war development of the arable farming industry. The fields were chiefly sown with wheat, barley and occasionally rye. At harvest the crop was cut with a reaper and binder drawn by a tractor, I do not remember any horse drawn equipment. The sheaves were made into stooks to dry in the field and then were threshed in the field. There was great excitement one day when a steam traction engine passed the house hauling a threshing machine up the lane to the fields. This was when I was very young, more often my trips up the lane to walk the dog would reveal a threshing machine being powered by a farm tractor. The straw was often stored in ricks in the field, which were roughly thatched with straw to keep them dry. There was a little dairy farming and this seemed to increase in later years.
9. The coal was delivered loose by a lorry each month which would back into the yard and tip the allotted amount, I think that it was half a ton, onto the concrete. I frequently shovelled this into the coal store, quite a task as the door sill was about three feet above the concrete surface.
10. I remember a southernwood bush (*Artemisia abrotanum*) which had a very strong smell when bruised between fingers, old English floribunda roses, a double white lilac tree which was Nanan's favourite amongst quite a collection of lilacs, a huge patch of lily-of-the-valley, Soloman's seal, aquilegias, an extensive collection of delphiniums, magnificent oriental poppies and a collection of classic chrysanthemums.
11. This variety is first recorded in 1836: the fruit cooks to a mousse.
12. Kelvedon Wonder was a frequent choice being a good cropper and the best first early pea.
13. This was the smallest variety of Savoy cabbage available.
14. Reading through these two seedsmen's catalogues at the Royal Horticultural Society Lindley Library was a trip down memory lane. Reviewing catalogues from the twenties to the sixties incidentally revealed the steady decline in commercially available varieties as the years passed: 72 pea varieties available in 1928 from Toogoods had dwindled to 27 by 1966; potato from 49 down to 20.
15. I rely on the recollections of my father, Frank Iddison, who was present on pig killing days and who not only observed the ensuing food processing but also enjoyed the end products.
16. Entering the sty to feed or clean them at maturity was a hazardous operation. It would take the efforts of three or four men to move the stunned body.
17. My paternal great grandfather was a carter by trade and lived in the village of Wath near Ripon in North Yorkshire. He also kept a family pig and my father remembers that the family did not keep the hams. One was sold to the vicar and the other to the doctor, they had standing orders. The money raised helped to purchase the piglet to raise to maturity over the next year. The sides of bacon were stored in the kitchen, hanging from the upper floor beams; my father remembers the salt crystals on the surface glistening in the light.
18. Foxes were a problem and one of the rituals of life at Wood Lane was the locking up of the hens into the henhouses in the evening. On light summer evenings this could involve chasing the hens around the run until they had all safely hopped through the bob-hole into the hen house where they would be secure for the night. Conversely the first job before breakfast was to feed and let out the hens.

Food guidance from my Grandparents

19 A distant relative, who lived in the Manor House at Haxby near York, kept bantams to show and my father found them perched on the clothes horse in front of the open fire one Friday evening. They were drying out after being given a wash. They were going to a show the following day.

20 Cleaning required the dropping boards under the roosting rails to be scraped clean every morning with a semi-circular metal tool which my grandfather had made, the hen droppings thus collected were put in an area of the compost heap to weather before they could be used on the garden. All water bowls were cleaned out regularly and at least once a year the straw and litter in the hen sheds was replaced.

21 There were nesting boxes in the hen sheds and in each box there was a pot egg to encourage the hens to use the nest boxes and not lay the eggs in other places. I became adept at telling the difference between real and pot eggs when rummaging under the breast feathers of a broody bird. Sometimes a bird laid its egg whilst it was roosting, the egg was sometimes intact and recoverable. As well as feed, the hens were supplied with a bowl of grit to ensure that the egg shells were strong.

22 My grandfather had purchased the trap by mail order and it was very effective, frequently catching more than one mouse when baited with a small piece of cheese. The trap was humane but the mice went to feed the garden cat! My grandfather would stand a metal pail in the centre of the yard and empty the trap into it. The cat waited for the mice to scramble out of the pail.

23 The selected bird was separated from the flock for a few days in a small coop, presumably its laying capacity could be checked and it was probably starved for a day or so. The actual slaughter was carried out over the compost heap so that the blood would not be wasted. Unlike pig's blood, which was valued, chicken blood was not used for human consumption.

24 It has to be said that the operation was quite smelly: the hanging for several days had initiated biochemical changes, which contributed to this. These had also presumably helped with the flavour and tenderness of the finished product. The hens led an active life with opportunities to run and scratch around and even fly a little. Without careful processing the end result could be very tough indeed as witnessed by my father when he killed a family chicken soon after the war. Clara was about four years old and no amount of cooking would make her meat tender.

25 Waterglass is the common name for a solution of sodium silicate which precipitates out as a gel to coat the porous eggshell and prevent spoilage.

26 Otherwise known as a Belfast sink.

27 The bottom drawer contained our children's toys.

28 In the summer the milk was kept in a pail of cold water in the washhouse to make use of natural evaporative cooling.

29 The Yorkshire pudding was cooked in the beef dripping in the tin in which the beef had been roasted, it was therefore a single pudding and although the edges might be crisp, the centre was luscious folds of soft cooked batter coated lightly with beef dripping. With the beef gravy it was delicious. The only better specimens that I have encountered were cooked by our summer holiday landlady, Mrs Crane at Filey. All the Yorkshire puddings that I have eaten since my childhood have been individual brittle travesties of these memories.

30 Craetagus monogyna.

31 The cat was semi-wild and never came in the house; its food was put in a saucer on the back window ledge. The dog was a guard dog and was kept on a long chain outside the backdoor with a large wooden kennel for it to sleep in. It was taken for three walks each day up Wood Lane and around the surrounding fields and allotments.

32 Standing for British Pharmacopoeia confirming that it had been prepared according to a pharmaceutical standard.

Nurturing a Holiday:
Christmas Foods in 18th and 19th Century America

Cathy K Kaufman

Christmas conjures certain images in the American mind: Santa and his reindeer, evergreens embracing gaily wrapped packages, and a great bird roasted to bronze perfection crowning the family dinner table. So well entrenched are these icons that they seem part of an immutable tradition. Yet these indicia of Christmas, by and large, are products of the 19th century, a time when, according to historians Stephen Nissenbaum and Penne Restad, a culturally disparate America, rent by regionalism, slavery, economic dislocations and burgeoning industrialization, seized upon the most nostalgic elements of its various ethnic traditions and massaged them into a family-oriented holiday suited for the modern market economy.[1] This American "melting pot" holiday blended bits of English, Dutch and German folk culture, and added a dollop of creative romanticism, seen especially in the literature of Washington Irving and Charles Dickens. By the mid 19th century, Christmas was developing a distinctly American flavor with a plump Santa Claus bringing joy to families at their hearths, the universal locus of domesticity. As the country descended into civil war, the newly minted American Christmas provided a glimmer of cultural cohesion, uniting the celebrants in a common tradition that exploded into a national holiday in the 1870s. It was at this mid century point that Christmas dinner connoted several specific dishes, turning the dinner into a formulary that was to last in America through the first World War and was a measure of immigrants' acculturation.

Christmas before Santa Claus

Christmas has always been surrounded by self-conscious invention. Nothing in the Gospels hints at the actual date of Christ's birth, and, contrary to the *agapes* of the earliest Church, there is limited evidence of feasts to celebrate Christ's birth prior to the reign of Constantine. Conventional wisdom places the fourth century choice of the December 25 date for the Feast of the Nativity as calculated to offer a Christian alternative to the pagan Saturnalia, a period of raucous partying, gifting, and social role reversal during the last week or so of December. Masters feted slaves, open gambling was permitted and public feasting and drunkenness abounded. Once the Eastern Church established Epiphany at January 6, the date for the Nativity was a foregone conclusion, requiring the Church to co-opt the well-entrenched Roman holiday, donning it with a veneer of piety in an effort to adapt local customs to a changing power structure.

Centuries later, some Protestants would use this weak Scriptural foundation to argue that Christ did not intend for his followers to celebrate the anniversary of his birth. Puritans, Quakers, and others brought their anti-popish practices to American shores from England and Germany. From the early 17th through most of the 19th century, there were limited, but notorious Christian pockets in America that actively disapproved of the religious or secular celebration of Christmas. Some viewed the fashionable parties fed by terrapin, champagne and blancmanges as profligate excess, harmful to family welfare. Others feared the creeping influence of a dogmatic Catholicism. As late as 1874, the Plymouth Congregationalist minister and reformer Henry Ward Beecher wrote that Christmas had always seemed foreign to him; he understood it as a holiday only because the Episcopalians in his town brought evergreens into their church, emulating the "Romish Church." Not surprisingly, there is no mention of Christmas foods or celebrations in the cookbooks and household manuals written by his prolific sister, Catharine Beecher.

St Nicholas, who, under the skillful pens of Washington Irving's *Knickerbocker History of New York* (1809) and Clement C. Moore's *A Visit from St Nicholas* (1823)[2] would morph into the modern-day Santa Claus, occupies popular imagination as the Dutch contribution to the Christmas season. While it is certainly possible that St Nicholas lurked in homespun observances, New Year's was the most widely documented Dutch holiday, and most scholars have found little for evidence of the colonial celebration of St Nicholas's Day (generally identified as December 6) in the 17th and 18th centuries. Amsterdam's Reformation Government had heard reports of public rowdiness on St Nicholas Eve that it linked to "the superstition and fables of the papacy," and responded by issuing a bylaw banning New Amsterdam colonists from assembling "on the Dam or any other places and streets within this town with any kind of candy, eatables or other merchandise . . ."[3] The fact that Amsterdam was moved to legislate from afar suggests that there was some public disturbance associated with St Nicholas, but these cannot have been very great, as no prosecutions were reported under the law. Although food historian Peter Rose points to records of the Dutch Reformed Church in New Netherland that document Christmas services, and believes that St Nicholas Day was commonly observed with gifts of candy to children,[4] there were no mentions of St Nicholas celebrations in gazettes or periodicals until the 1770s. Even then, only scant handfuls emerge, and these had a decidedly anti-British political tone in the superheated pre-Revolutionary War air.[5] Given the religious and cultural diversity found in early America (Restad states that 18 different languages were spoken among the 500 or so Dutch colonists in New Amsterdam alone), it seems fair to conclude that colonial Christmases, when and where they were celebrated, were anything but homogeneous.

So what happened on and around December 25 in 17th and 18th century America? For some, it was business as usual: schools and businesses open, churches closed (unless the day fell on a Sunday), with no feting whatsoever tolerated. In a famous passage from the diary of William Bradford, Plymouth Colony's governor in 1621, Bradford relates chastising some recent arrivals who had begged off work detail as against their conscience because of the holiday. When Bradford returned at noon, he found these fellows engaged in all sorts of games and merrymaking, at which Bradford bellowed that it was against *his* conscience that they should play while others worked. He proudly reported that no public Christmas revels took place thereafter.

For others, some notice of the day was taken, with a modest break in routine, but nothing that compares with the anticipation and virtual standstill that grips contemporary America around the holiday. Philip Fithian, the tutor to the very wealthy Robert Carter family in Virginia enjoyed an elegant Christmas dinner, but commented that it "was no otherwise than common" considering the standard of the household. Fithian's charges had a few days' respite from their studies, but Mr. Carter, who had breakfasted late, did not even come down to dinner, leaving Fithian to carve the roasts for the mistress and her children. While he attended several parties, the only special food noted was a "large Pye cut to signify the Conclusion of the Holidays" on December 29.[6] Similarly, Martha Ballard, a middle class housewife in Maine, baked cakes and "Mins pies" throughout the late 18th and early 19th centuries during late December. These goodies were sometimes prepared after Christmas for the more important New Year's dinner. Mrs. Ballard performed routine housekeeping chores, such as polishing pewter or knitting on December 25 and only sporadically referred to the day as "Christmas" in her diary.[7]

Further evidence of the relative unimportance of Christmas as a time for special foods at the turn of the 19th century comes from the 1805 American edition of Hannah Glasse's *The Art of Cookery Made Plain and Easy* (Alexandria, Virginia). Although Mrs. Ballard would have found therein general recipes for mince pies, the edition omits the two recipes specially denominated for Christmas in the original 1747 English edition, the Yorkshire Christmas Pie and the Plum Porridge for Christmas. Other regional recipes, such as the Cheshire Pie, made it into the American edition, so it is not merely a case of dropping regionalisms. Nor does it seem to be a question of updating or simplifying the book. Many complex, very old-fashioned recipes, such as the intricate Goose Pie, permeate the American edition. Most tellingly, both the Yorkshire Christmas Pie and the Christmas Plum Porridge appear in the 1803 London edition, the last version I am aware of published before the American edition. The exclusion of specific recipes for Christmas might have been part of an after-the-fact patriotic retooling of the work for the American audience, as Christmas in 18th century America tended to be celebrated by those culturally and politically sympathetic to England.[8]

Those who celebrated Christmas often did so with gusto, even in the face of frontier hardships. New England sea captain Robert Gray, exploring the coast off what is now Vancouver, held a special dinner to mark the day. The ship's mariner, John Boit, described preparations for the Christmas dinner of 1791:

> This day was kept in mirth and festivity by all the Columbia's Crew, and the principall Chiefs of the Sound by invitation din'd on board ship. The Natives took a walk around the work shops on shore, they was supprized at seeing three tier of wild fowl roasting at one of the houses—indeed, we was a little supprised at the novelty of the sight ourselves, for at least there was 20 Geese roasting at one immense fire, and the Ships Crew appear'd very happy, most of them being on shore. The Indians cou'd not understand why the Ship and houses was decorated with spruce bows. At 12 Clock fir'd a federall Salute, and ended the day toasting our sweethearts and wifes.[9]

The unusual circumstances of the *Columbia* surely influenced the guest list, but not the holiday's general outline: for those who celebrated Christmas in the 18th and early 19th centuries, it was a bountiful dinner with noisemaking and drinking.

The noisemaking had a darker side, rooted in European traditions. Periods of public "Misrule" marked the close of the harvest season and the slaughtering of animals for the winter. Fresh meat was abundant and little agricultural work needed to be performed, so that ordinary behavior was cast aside and gluttonous gorging was the rule. For a series of complex reasons, some tracing back to the Saturnalian social inversions of the Roman Empire, all sorts of public antics took place. Cross-dressing, mumming and caroling, and parading in disguises (including blackface) were common folk celebrations, punctuated by begging for food, drink and money. Sanctioned as a social safety valve, part of these festivities was essentially a bribe: those lower on the socio-economic ladder demanded and received gifts from those above, in exchange for relative peace and tranquility throughout the rest of the year.[10] Before Oliver Cromwell's suppression of Christmas in mid 17th century England, Elizabeth I and James I had encouraged members of the gentry to return to their country estates to offer up ritualized Christmas feasts to the extended community.

The annual Christmas period of license was easily transplanted to the American Old South, with its slave holidays and widely-lauded hospitality. The season was remembered fondly by many, including some of the slave population, although others saw it for the exploitation inherent in these brief Saturnalia.[11] Locked in the landed plantation system, many slave-owning Masters consciously mimicked the "Merrie Old English" tradition of feudal lords hosting great midwinter feasts for all of the dependents by feasting not only the immediate and extended family members who lived in the Big House, but also the overseers, laborers and slaves, who formed the economic unit of the plantation.

By the early 19th century, changes in the social and economic structure of both England and America made the vision of a *paterfamilias* bestowing largess on the extended dependents of the household increasingly inapt. With the pressures of urbanization and nascent industrialization, bands of roving, rowdy beggars conjuring up the Lord of Misrule, carousing publicly and noisily, seemed especially threatening to proper bourgeois society.[12] What had evolved as a limited respite for seasonally unemployed agrarian workers now was menacing to the general order, as concentrations of underemployed youths gather in cities and towns, eroding the ties that had bound pre-industrial societies together and tolerated, if not expressly sanctioned, the raucous Christmas festivities. By the 1820s, nostalgic antiquarians catalogued the traditions of Christmases past, that "[i] n London, as in all great cities, particularly in those which are commercial, where strangers continually arrive, and new customs are daily introduced, observances of a nature similar to those formerly kept at Christmas must soon be lost." (The author assumed, however, that plum puddings and mince pies would survive the onslaught of modernism "on the score of their intrinsic value to gastronomists.")[13] An American diarist in the 1840s, seeing the increasing domestication of Christmas, similarly concluded that the raucous public displays were "fast disappearing . . . giving way to American tastes and American amusements, much to the benefit of morality."[14]

Washington Irving subtly underscored some of the difficult issues in taming the holiday in his *Sketch Book of Geoffrey Crayon* (1819), where he devotes five short chapters to his fictitious vision of a traditional English Christmas. Set in the mythical country manse owned by Squire Bracebridge, these particular vignettes were enduringly popular and finally published in 1875, after the American Civil War, as a separate holiday gift volume under the title *Old Christmas*. Irving's Squire Bracebridge opens Christmas day by "inviting the decent part of the neighbouring peasantry to call at the Hall on Christmas day, and distributing beef, and bread, and ale, among the poor that they might make merry in their own dwellings." The participants dance and frolic, although there is an ominous undercurrent in Irving's fiction. The narrator relates that several years earlier, the Squire had invited all of the local country folk to Bracebridge Hall in an effort to revive the traditional celebration:

Such was the good Squire's project for mitigating public discontent; and indeed, he had once attempted to put his doctrine in practice, and a few years before had kept open house during the holidays in the old style. The country people, however, did not understand how to play their parts in the scene of hospitality; many uncouth circumstances occurred; the manor was overrun by all the vagrants of the country, and more beggars drawn into the neighbourhood in one week than the parish officers could get rid of in a year.

Thus the Squire invited only the "decent part" for the public beef and ale dinner. The day culminates with family and social peers enjoying a mythologized Tudor-style banquet, replete with a boar's head garnished with rosemary and the medieval favorite peacock pie, made with pheasant because the kindly Squire could not bear to kill one of the beautiful birds. The meal ceremoniously concludes with a tremendous silver vessel carrying wassail that the Squire mixes himself, "alleging that it was too abstruse and complex for the comprehension of an ordinary servant."[15] Antebellum plantation owners, too, personally prepared eggnog, refusing to delegate the delicate flavoring to anyone. Not only were family and guests given a stiff shot as the Christmas morning eye-opener, but the contents of the common bowl were sometimes ceremoniously distributed to the slaves; coming to partake of the alcoholic nip prepared by the Master's hand would likely be the only time during the year that the field workers were permitted to penetrate the precincts of the Big House.

Christmas Dinner in Santa's Heyday
By the second quarter of the 19th century, the image of Santa Claus, although not yet fixed in his portly red suit, was rapidly growing as a beneficent giver of candies and toys to children. But the final, critical image in nurturing the American holiday came with Charles Dickens,

who created a relevant image of Christmas that resonated in a populace trying to make sense of the emerging industrial world, especially the new economic relationships among members of the expanding and vaguely defined middle classes. *A Christmas Carol*, published just before Christmas in 1843, sold out its first full edition in London of 6,000 copies in one day and was rapidly devoured by Americans in pirated serializations and then legitimate copies, outselling the Bible in the 1840s.[16] Dickens' tale of redemption against the backdrop of industrialization appealed to a wide audience, from young children mesmerized by the ghost story to sophisticates such as Phillip Hone, a former Mayor of New York City, who was completely seduced in January, 1844:

Dickens has been writing a little thing called "Christmas Carols," which is published by the Harpers in a pamphlet, price six cents, and in the *Sun* newspaper, with plenty of other matter, for three cents, For its intrinsic merit it is worth as many dollars. It is a perfect jewel, an opal with light beaming from every part; one of those quaint, simple, affecting things which make you laugh and cry to your heart's content, and then wonder how you could laugh and cry so much over thirty pages of nothing at all.[17]

Although pastoral Bracebridge Hall and the shabby four room Cratchit house in London form contrasting stages for idealized notions of Christmas, both stories rely on Christmas dinner to point up larger issues. Like Squire Bracebridge, the Spirit of Christmas Past reminds Scrooge of the joy he felt at the party hosted by his first employer, Old Fezziwig. An urban version of the rural gentry's party, Fezziwig hosts his cavorting employees, his cook, the local baker, milkman and neighbors to a party including cold roast and boiled meats, mince pies and beer. But the most detailed and poignant dinner description, voyeuristically seen through the Spirit of Christmas Present, is the modest repast that Mrs. Cratchit proudly brings to the table, a dinner that cost the family a week of Bob's puny wages. Starting with a goose (that had been cooked at the local bakeshop, as the Cratchits, on the lowest rung of the middle classes, lacked an oven), the meal was "eked out" by gravy made in advance by Mrs. Cratchit (with the goose roasting at the local bakeshop, it is a bit perplexing how she made the gravy "ready beforehand in a little pot"), applesauce, mashed potatoes and sage and onion stuffing. The *pièce de résistance* was the boiled plum pudding flaming with brandy and bedecked with holly. Like Bracebridge Hall, the meal concludes with a strong potion made by Bob himself. But the Cratchit drink is not traditional wassail; instead, the moralizing Dickens pulls the story back from the brink of saccharine overkill, putting into sympathetic Bob's hands the workingman's bane, gin, and a few precious lemons. The potion is served in "the family display of glass; two tumblers, and a custard cup without a handle."[18] There is, of course, not even a hint that the Bob the clerk drowns his miseries in proletarian gin, but Dickens cannot resist this detail in the archetypical meal that readers would have recognized as a jab at the evils suffered by the working classes in industrializing England.

In the happy conclusion of *A Christmas Carol* Scrooge repents, sends the Cratchit family the biggest turkey (much more luxurious and expensive than goose in the 19th century) in the poulterer's shop (although we learn nothing else about the meal that actually takes place), and raises Bob's salary. Although a few contemporaneous English critics found the story patronizing and lacking in a promise of real economic reform, the story was instantly seared into the mindset of the Anglophone world.[19]

If imitation is the sincerest form of flattery, then the Cratchit turkey dinner became one of the most widely admired meals in America, defining critical elements of a proper Christmas dinner. Prior to that time, scores of early to mid 19th century American accounts describe Christmas fare ranging from oysters, beef, and ham to eggnog and mince pies, with turkey as but one of the offerings. Mayor Hone himself, commenting on the offerings of New York City's Fulton Market a few days before Christmas in 1842, "wondered where mouths could be found for the turkeys, geese, ducks and chickens which a saw there, and today, when walking up Broadway, I was tempted to exclaim 'Where can ducks and chickens, turkeys and geese, be found to fill all these mouths?'"[20] Dickens, of course, does not invent turkey at Christmas; roast turkey appears as one of many dishes in Robert May's menu for Christmas dinner found in *The Accomplisht Cook* (facsimile ed., 1685), and the bird was a luxury item in England and Europe in the 18th and 19th centuries, often crammed with black winter truffles to gild the lily on wealthy tables. Wild and domesticated turkeys were American options that regularly appeared on tables, and early 20th century mythology, much like that surrounding Thanksgiving, claims that starving colonists happened upon turkeys to break their meager diet just in time for the holiday, with Americans never deviating from that custom.[21]

But the specific association of turkey as the focus of Christmas dinner became ever greater after publication of *A Christmas Carol* and grew to a crescendo during and after the Civil War, regardless of the exorbitant prices that turkeys commanded in the blockaded South. One Southern matron sorrowfully watched as Union soldiers plundered her pantry of the cakes and rusks she had specially baked. But nothing raised her dander more than the soldier carrying off the dressed turkey she had purchased at great sacrifice, having "spent six dollars, and sent a man miles on horseback to get it rather than have nothing good and pleasant for our Christmas dinner."[22] Soldiers on both sides of the conflict wrote letters home detailing their Christmas meals. Not only does turkey appear with surprising frequency, given the uncertainties of wartime, but it is the one item that is frequently prefaced by the term "Christmas;" that is, fortunate soldiers describe enjoying Christmas turkey. They may complain about turkeys "selling at $11 each," or being affordable only if the rest of Christmas dinner "was accompanied simply with potatoes and cornbread," yet the decision to splurge on the turkey and forego the other "traditional" trimmings suggests the iconic status as the centerpiece of Christmas dinner that Scrooge's gift was assuming.[23]

Life continued to imitate art, at least when it came to Christmas dinner. On Dickens' second tour to American, in 1867, he gave an interpretive reading of *A Christmas Carol* on Christmas Eve in Boston. A Vermont factory owner attended, who had always subscribed to the Puritanical disregard of Christmas. After hearing the story, he took the unprecedented step of closing the factory the next day for the holiday; the following year, he instituted the tradition of giving each factory worker a turkey for his Christmas dinner.[24] The beneficent celebration has moved from a rowdy public feast given to the dependents by their economic superiors to one in which each family celebrates independently and intimately.

Cookery writers pitched in to tame other aspects of Christmas dinner in the mid-19th century. Sarah Josepha Hale, writing in *The Good Housekeeper*, rued the tradition of serving mince pies at Christmas, one that she claimed "was too firmly rooted [even] for the 'Pilgrim fathers' to abolish." (Puritans had allegedly railed against mince pies as "idolatry in a crust" because of the association of the spices in the pies with the gifts that the Magi brought to the Christ Child.) She believed them so difficult of digestion that "for children they should be forbidden food; so tempting is the taste, that the only security consists in not tasting. So the 'good housekeeper' will be careful not to place temptation too often before her family."[25] Eliza Leslie similarly found fault with certain mince pies, although on the grounds of elegance, rather than digestibility. She critiqued "The foolish custom of setting the pies on fire after they come to the table and causing a blue blaze to issue from the liquor that is in them, is now obsolete, and considered ungenteel and tavern-like."[26] In other words, flaming pies might have been tolerated for rowdy public celebrations, but they were inappropriate for the domesticated holiday. Although mince pies continue to appear at Christmas dinner (Miss Leslie's own proposed menus for Christmas and New Year's dinners in her 1854 *New*

Receipts for Cooking list mince pie as one of the desserts), they are now associated exclusively with "traditional" holiday fare and seldom appear outside of a Thanksgiving or Christmas dinner.

The most revealing statement of the changing role of Christmas comes from Mrs. Hale's *Manners, or Happy Homes and Good Society All the Year Round* (1868). Seeing Christmas dinner and related celebrations as one way to "keep up the feelings of patriotism and the memories of home," Mrs. Hale devotes Christmas to the "children and the childlike." She warns mothers against decorating the now-common Christmas tree with "*sugar candies now 'made to sell,'*" looking after the health of her brood.[27] These 19th century candies adorning the domestic holiday are a far cry from the raucous public mischief practiced by New Amsterdamers assembling on the dam and in the streets with candy and eatables.

References

1. For a general cultural overview of the evolution of Christmas in America, see Stephen Nissenbaum, *The Battle For Christmas,* New York: Random House (1996); Penne Restad, *Christmas in America*, New York & London: Oxford University Press (1995); Karal Ann Marling, *Merry Christmas! Celebrating America's Greatest Holiday*, Cambridge, MA: Harvard University Press (2000); James A. Barnett, *The American Christmas: A Study in National Culture*, New York: Macmillan Company (1954).
2. Recent scholarship casts doubt on Moore's authorship of the famous poem. See Don Foster, *Author Unknown*, New York: Henry Holt & Co. (2000).
3. Quoted in Charles W. Jones, "Knickerbocker Santa Claus," *The New-York Historical Society Quarterly*, 38:357, 362-63 (October 1954).
4. Donna R. Barnes and Peter G. Rose, *Matters of Taste: Food and Drink in Seventeenth-Century Dutch Art and Life*, Albany Institute of History and Art (2002).
5. Jones, pp. 363-67.
6. John Rogers Williams, ed., *The Journal and Letters of Philip Vickers Fithian, 1767-1774*, Princeton Historical Association, vol. 1 (1900).
7. Nissenbaum, pp. 28-30.
8. J.M. Golby and A.W. Purdue, *The Making of the Modern Christmas*, London: B.T. Batsford (1986), p. 37.
9. John Boit, *A New Log of the Columbia* (Edmond S. Meany, ed.), Seattle: University of Washington Press, 1921, p. 20, quoted in John E. Baur, *Christmas on the American Frontier, 1800-1900*, Caldwell, OH: Caxton Printers, Ltd. (1961), p. 74.
10. *See generally* Nissenbaum, pp. 3-11; 90-107.
11. Shauna Bigham and Robert E. May, "The Time O' All Times? Masters, Slaves, and Christmas in the Old South," *Journal of the Early Republic*, 18: 263-88 (1998).
12. Susan G. Davis, "'Making Night Hideous': Christmas Revelry and Public Order in Nineteenth-Century Philadelphia," *American Quarterly*, 34:185-99 (1982).
13. "Christmas-Keeping," *The New Monthly Magazine and Literary Journal,* (London), 2: 609-14 (1821).
14. Harnett T. Kane, *The Southern Christmas Book*, New York: David McKay Co. (1958), p. 137, quoting the Presbyterian Bishop Henry B. Whipple on a visit to Florida in the 1840s.

15. Washington Irving, *Old Christmas* [1894 facsimile ed.], London: Macmillan & Co. (1979), pp. 110, 133.
16. Marling, *Merry Christmas*, 150.
17. *The Diary of Philip Hone,* Allan Nevins, ed., New York: Dodd, Mead & Co. (1927). Entry for January 27, 1844.
18. Michael Patrick Hearn, *The Annotated Christmas Carol by Charles Dickens*, New York: Charles N. Potter (1976), pp. 98, 121-124.
19. Hearn, p.166.
20. Hone diaries, December 26, 1842 entry.
21. Horace Vose, *Turkey Secrets*, Philadelphia: Wilmer Atkinson Co. (1912).
22. Gwen, ed., *Cornelia Peake McDonald, A Woman's Civil War—A Diary*, University of Wisconsin Press (1992), quoted in Kevin Rawlings, *We Were Marching on Christmas Day*, Baltimore, MD: Toomey Press (1995), p.83.
23. Rawlings, pp. 76, 84, 94, 65.
24. Golby and Purdue, p. 48.
25. Sarah Josepha Hale, *The Good Housekeeper* [6th ed., 1841], Jan Longone, intro., Dover Reprint (1996), p. 85.
26. Eliza Leslie, *New Cookery Book*, Philadelphia: T. B. Peterson and Brothers (1857), pp. 160-61.
27. Sarah Josepha Hale, *Manners, or Happy Homes and Good Society All the Year Round*, Boston: J. E. Tilton (1868), pp. 361-71.

The Flavour Continuum

Samantha Kilgour

Introduction

What is the ideal way to nurture a child's relationship with food? How best can a healthy relationship to food and eating be achieved? This paper aims to explore the path of learning that nature may have intended for eating from the womb through to early childhood. From the vantage point of our industrial society we would probably call it a primitive approach, but if we were nurturing our children instinctively and without interference how would the process look? Here I will attempt to map the journey of taste from the uterus to weaning. Given the complex interaction between mother and child in the early stages of life the process might best be viewed as one which provides a 'flavour continuum', an ongoing blueprint unique to each individual that helps us to map out which foods we like and dislike as well as to accustom us to the foods we are likely to encounter in our early years.

In Utero

It seems odd to think that an unborn child is capable of making fine distinctions in the smells and tastes that it encounters in the womb, but the olfactory and tasting systems of the unborn foetus begin to develop at some point between 11 and 15 weeks gestation. Until recently, it was thought that babies could not detect smells in the womb and that the olfactory system could not function in the absence of air and breathing. However, we now know that the olfactory system and the taste buds are highly sensitive in the unborn child.

> The structures needed for tasting develop at around the same time as the olfactory system and experts believe that tasting begins at that time. Tests show that swallowing increases with sweet tastes and decreases with bitter and sour tastes. In the liquid womb space, a range of tastes are presented including lactic, pyruvic, and citric acids, creatinine, urea, amino acids, proteins and salts. Tests made at birth reveal exquisite taste discrimination and definite preferences.[1]

The foetus is capable of distinguishing between many odours and flavours. Research has shown that around 120 compounds are detectable in amniotic fluid[2]. Chemicals from the mother's bloodstream cross the placenta and become part of the amniotic fluid, thus exposing the foetus to a variety of tastes and smells unique to its own prenatal environment. Foods eaten by the mother will leave their mark on the child's developing palate. Odiferous associations formed in utero alter subsequent foetal behaviour and are retained into postnatal life. One experiment showed changes to foetal heart rate and breathing when their mothers drank coffee[3]. Several studies demonstrate olfactory responsiveness post-birth to substances that the mother has consumed. Particular likes and dislikes occur with strong tasting and smelling foods such as garlic or aniseed. After birth, babies exposed to the smell of anise will react positively or negatively depending on whether or not their mother ingested foods with the smell and taste of anise during pregnancy[4]

The sensory bombardment experienced by the foetus must surely leave permanent marks on the way in which the baby will relate to certain tastes. Even in the womb the child is already being programmed to accept its mother's milk after birth. The exposure to the common flavours of the culture in which the child is to be raised begins long before any taste of solid food passes the lips. Both amniotic fluid and breast milk uniquely reflect the preferred foods of the mother and help shape the child's later reactions to the foods it will encounter[5].

In the environment of the womb nature and nurture are inseparable, for inside its mother the baby has all its nutritional needs met automatically. In the 'flavour continuum' it will be the mother who continues to provide nutrition and nurturing after birth. From an evolutionary point of view this shaping of an child's palate makes perfect sense. The natural processes of development in the womb condition the child to respond positively to the foods available to its mother, meaning that it can readily adapt to the taste of breast milk and later still to family foods.

After birth
Learning to eat is the first skill a baby will master. A newborn is capable of crawling up his mother's abdomen in the moments immediately following birth to reach his first source of nourishment, the breast[6]. It is only after birth that the newborn infant experiences hunger for the first time, and considering the prenatal influence of smells and tastes in the amniotic fluid it seems that the infant will recognize the smell and taste of his mother's milk.

In most non-industrial societies the baby will be carried by its mother and fed whenever it expresses an interest in suckling. This ensures both physical and emotional nurturing, conveniently packaged into one. Here in the West many babies are nourished differently. They are fed artificial milk from plastic bottles with silicon teats. The act of eating is thus not quite the same sensual experience. Warm flesh and the constantly changing taste of breast milk are replaced by bland-tasting formula and usually a lack of skin-to-skin contact.

The first milk is colostrum and is present immediately after birth. It is a vital first food and contains essential fluids, vitamins, minerals and antibodies that nourish the baby until mature milk comes in several days after birth. As colostrum is a concentrated food perhaps it has more intensely familiar cues for the newborn to respond to as learned in the womb. Following the idea of an uninterrupted flavour blueprint, let us assume that the gradual alteration from colostrum to milk serves some purpose in accustoming the newborn to liquid food.

Breast milk also changes in consistency during a single feed; initially the baby receives foremilk, a thirst-quenching liquid that gradually changes into hindmilk, which is richer and thicker and satisfies hunger. Breast milk also alters in volume and consistency according to the child's needs and appetite. In addition, it contains antibodies to germs and viruses that the mother has encountered, thus providing her child with tailor-made preventative medicine.

There is, of course, another side to breastfeeding: the nurturing of an intense physical and emotional relationship between the mother and child. Since the baby is, theoretically at least, entirely dependent upon its mother for nourishment, an intense attachment is needed to ensure its survival. This mutual relationship grows and develops over the years. The physical aspect of nursing, the familiar scent and taste of the mother, the one-on-one bond of trust, all contribute to the child's relationship to food and eating. The act of eating is not simply one of physical sustenance, it is also an emotional experience which provides comfort and reassurance. Breastfeeding is the earliest source of pleasure and comfort.

How does this affect the palate? Will being breastfed have a long-term effect on the tastes and textures and infant prefers as it grows? Breast milk, like amniotic fluid, contains traces of the flavour of foods that the mother has consumed. Therefore babies are exposed to a variety of flavours, as each feed will taste subtly different. Research shows that breastfeeding does have an effect on the way an infant reacts to solid foods during weaning.

Weaning

There are many different definitions of weaning, but here we will assume that the process culminates with total withdrawal of breast milk. The current Western practice is to introduce solid food at around four months and withdraw breast milk at about the same time or soon after. However, the World Health Organization guidelines state that breast milk should be a child's exclusive food for at least the first six months and that breastfeeding should continue until at least two years of age. Breastfed babies need no other food or liquid for the first year of life.

How long would babies nurse for if the natural process of weaning were uninterrupted? K. Granju suggests in *Attachment Parenting* that in most parts of the world babies are breastfed for at least two to four years and that weaning children before one year of age, or not nursing them at all (as is common in Western society), is a 'marked exception to the rule'[7]. Research would suggest that the natural weaning age of a human infant is somewhere between three and seven years[8] It is during this period that children begin to lose their milk teeth and the mature teeth come through. Perhaps this is why they were described as milk teeth in the first place. Their loss coincides with the end of the breastfeeding window.

Following the 'flavour continuum' would therefore have a gradual introduction to solid food and weaning which would be a process that lasted for years, not months. When breast milk is continued alongside the introduction of other foods, the child has a chance to become accustomed to the taste through milk. New flavours can be explored before the child has even taken a single bite of a food.

When the time does come for real food, the breastfed infant will already have at least some predetermined likes and dislikes. In one study, babies whose mothers drank carrot juice reacted more positively to carrots than those babies whose mothers did not[9]. From an evolutionary standpoint it would seem logical that a child be favourably predisposed to foods consumed by the mother as these foods are likely to be the ones available.

Does the timing and manner of weaning also affect the process? Babies who begin their introduction to solid food after the age of six months will usually be able to sit up unaided and chew properly, which allows them to interact with other members of the family at mealtimes. For babies who are introduced to food at the family table, the process of supplementing their diet with solid food must be very different from those immobile babies who are spoon-fed whilst semi-reclining. Older babies can eat most of the foods consumed by their families, so long as simple guidelines are followed. Eating with other siblings or the whole family allows the social aspect of feeding begun during breastfeeding to continue and a breastfed infant is already used to the taste of the foods eaten regularly by the family. Food and eating can then be an integral part of the child's life, in more than just a physical way.

From an emotional or developmental standpoint, allowing a child to self-wean means that the child has decided for herself that she is ready to move on and leave the long process of weaning behind. The decision to stop nursing is a very personal one for each individual nursing pair. Many mothers will decide when they wish to end the breastfeeding relationship but for others it is a mutual decision made when the child is ready. Because the breastfeeding relationship is about more than just the physical act of eating it is likely that there are many more emotional and physical factors affecting the child that we are unaware of. The consequences of weaning a child before they themselves are ready are unknown.

The way most people do it

Having looked at the path from the prenatal environment to total weaning from breast milk, and having seen that it is a process that can take years, not months, let us look at the more typical Western approach to nurturing babies. It is quite different to the continuum that nature seems to have intended.

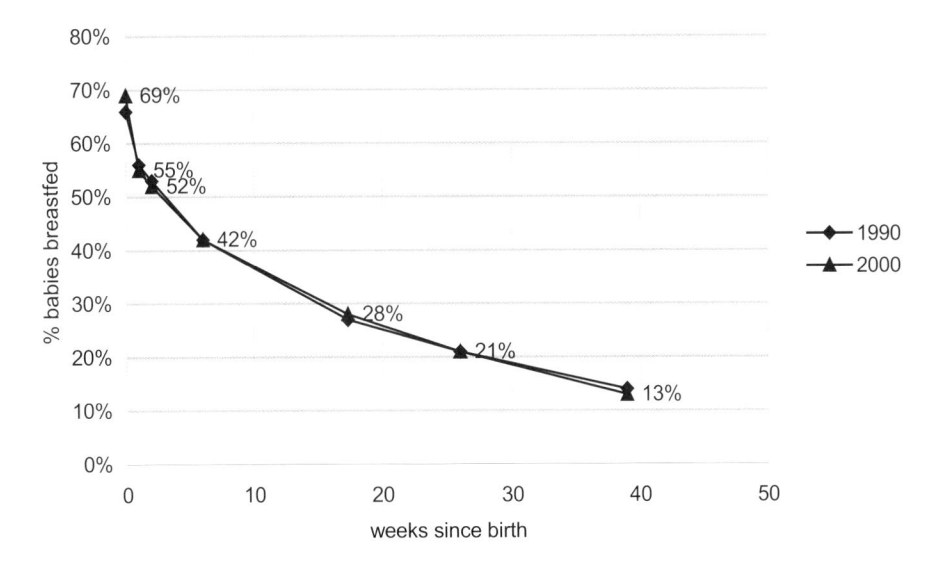

UK Breastfeeding rates 1990 & 2000, [UK Department of Health, Infant Feeding Report 200010]

A Department of Health report into breastfeeding rates in Britain has demonstrated that by the age of six weeks fewer than half of all British babies are still being breastfed. Around thirty percent of babies never taste their mother's milk at all.

Mothers are often advised by health visitors to introduce solid foods at around four months, even if they are breastfeeding, although government guidelines state that breast milk should be the child's sole source of nutrition until the age of six months. In the UK only one in five babies was still breastfed at the six month mark in 2000.

If a breastfed infant is 'programmed' to react favourably to the foods available to its mother, what about the artificially fed infant? Will the conditioning from the womb still be present and affect the foods that are accepted or rejected during weaning? If not, what then? Does the child have a blank canvas to work with? It would seem from several studies that the 'blank canvas' of the artificially fed infant is not blank but bland. Formula milk tastes exactly the same at each feed, and should always be the same texture if it has been reconstituted correctly. The baby is not exposed to variations in taste or viscosity in the same way a breastfed baby is. Therefore new foods and textures are perhaps more likely to be met with suspicion.

How does this interruption to the natural programming of the palate affect the way these babies relate to food and eating? The answer is that we simply don't know. Unfortunately no research seems yet to have looked at the possible effects of breaking the 'flavour continuum'

It is difficult to enter into any discussion of breastfeeding and artificial feeding without causing offence. For many the advent of reliable infant formulas will have been literally a lifesaver. Babies can now be safely fed when breast milk is not available. Mothers who cannot breastfeed for medical reasons, or who choose not to for personal reasons, have a safe and reliable means of nourishing their children. Alternative milks are available for those babies with allergies to cows milk and ordinary formula now contains additional ingredients designed to provide more of the substances found in breast milk, such as long-chain fatty acids.

The issues surrounding the manufacture and promotion of artificial milks and baby foods are complex. The ban on advertising artificial milks for newborns has spawned the 'follow-on milk' industry. Now, manufacturers concentrate on promoting their milks suitable for children six months of age and over, and their ranges of 'baby food' in jars and packets. Manufacturers, supermarkets and the media make it seem normal to feed babies powdered milk and mush. For the time-pushed parent this packaged approach might be a godsend, but what does it say about our culture's attitude to food that we believe children need to be fed a specialized and heavily processed diet? What happened to the idea that mealtimes are a social as well as a physical occasion? Why do we no longer value the nurturing aspect of eating together as a family? Modern lifestyles are surely partly to blame, but what are parents to think when leading supermarkets repackage food, add vitamins and label them 'designed for children'? Isn't it quicker in the long run to feed our babies the same food we feed ourselves? Some people must doubt their ability to feed their children adequately through their own efforts and given the shocking state of food education and awareness in schools it is highly likely that many new parents don't even know how to feed themselves.

At nine or ten months of age a baby sitting at the family table is old enough to exercise choice as to which foods she would like to try, to feed herself finger foods and possibly use a spoon. How much more pleasant than to sit in an infant seat being stuffed with something that no-one else is eating.

How things have changed

The first part of this paper briefly explored the physical intricacies of the mother-child relationship in so far as it concerns food and eating. There was no mention of Dad, for unless he can breastfeed too he is a little out of the picture. It isn't very politically correct, but one may assume that in the survival blueprint he is out hunting or gathering in manly style.

In the days before infant formula became available there was no choice but to breastfeed a baby for at least several months. Wet-nursing was the only viable alternative if infant survival was to be achieved, although many babies did survive on pap or gruel albeit with serious health consequences. This does mean that the bond between a mother and her child really was essential to the survival of the baby. It also meant that women were restricted in that they could not leave the child for more than a few hours at a time. Nowadays women have the choice of expressing milk to be given in their absence, or they can decide to offer substitute milk instead. Fathers can also be involved in giving milk to their children.

In many tribal cultures, such as the !Kung San¡ in Africa, babies are always with, and usually carried by, their mother, but other women help to share the burden of raising children and babies are nursed communally when necessary. Children are rarely weaned before the age of two and a half and it is not unusual for breastfeeding to continue until the age of five. Imagine sending a child to school in Britain if they were still part of a nursing relationship. It would probably shock most people and an investigation by Social Services would perhaps be inevitable.

Other things have changed too. The way in which families eat together has altered drastically in the last century. Mealtimes are for many families no longer a time to meet and share together but often a rushed or solitary occasion where the sound effects are likely to be provided by the microwave or TV rather than the buzz of conversation.

Eating disorders and obesity are on the rise. This is perhaps partly due to the surplus of food now available to many in the West, but is it possible that the interrupted programming of our relationship to food is also to blame? Bottle-fed babies are known to be more likely to suffer from obesity in later life than breastfed babies. Could this be due to the fact that a breastfeeding baby learns to self-regulate its intake of food from birth? Is it possible that bottle-fed babies are more likely to develop problems with their relationship to food and therefore use food and eating as a means of controlling their world? Does early weaning interrupt the natural progression of the relationship between mother and child?

No one as yet knows the answers to these questions. We do know that there will always be bottle-fed babies who will eat happily and with vigour and perhaps become gourmets, just as there will also be breastfed babies who are especially fussy and have a difficult time with food and eating. There are many social, physical and psychological factors to consider in each individual case. More research is needed to see exactly how early childhood eating patterns affect long-term relationships with food and eating. The Victorians certainly believed that breastfeeding had a long-term effect on the individual. 'During the time a child receives nourishment at its mother's breast the earliest bond of sympathy, destined to influence a lifetime, of parent and child, is mutually formed'.[11] They also advocated an approach to adding solid food into the diet that is similar to the one being reintroduced in Britain. 'As a general rule the appearance of the different kinds of teeth may be taken as an indication of the description of nourishment most suitable to the growing frame. Thus, till about the age of from five to eight months – i.e., while the gums are in a toothless state - milk should constitute the food of a healthy babe. Between the tenth and 16th month the teeth next the front, and also the first double teeth, are generally cut. At twelve months old, if the child be healthy, an evident want of some sort of animal food will generally be apparent.'[12] In the space of a century the advice has come full circle.

Conclusion

We have looked at the way in which the process of learning to eat begins even before we are born. The 'flavour continuum' seems designed to support a child in its first experiences of food. From learning to swallow and recognise flavours in the uterus the baby is able instinctively to search for and suckle at the mother's breast. The exposure to familiar tastes continues throughout breastfeeding and serves to prepare the baby for learning to accept foods during the weaning process. The customized tasting training helps to ensure the best possible start for the baby and assist with acceptance of the foods available . New foods are less likely to be rejected if the substance is one that the mother is also consuming or has consumed.

What we do not know is what effect any interruption to this process has. More research is needed to determine, if possible, the implications of altering our flavour continuum in infancy and early childhood. We do know that the palate can be retrained. People can learn to eat and enjoy foods that once repelled them, or sample foods that are unfamiliar to them, perhaps from other cultures. Adapting to new tastes is a learning process that continues throughout life as we try new foods and flavours and decide whether or not we like them. Each individual has the ultimate choice about what they choose to like and dislike.

The other factors relating to the 'flavour continuum' are less measurable. Food and eating are intertwined with our early relationship with our parents, and also with their relationship to food and eating. For the breastfed baby eating is an intensely nurturing experience encompassing many physical and emotional factors as well as the simple act of receiving nourishment.

Perhaps a more detailed understanding of the way in which our early environment influences our later relationship to food could pave the way for improvements in the way our society feeds its children, and the attitude it takes to the way in which they are fed. Research may reveal new knowledge which would help us to ensure that our children are less at risk from eating disorders or other problems with food and eating, and help to guide us in finding a positive route to ensuring a happy attitude to food throughout life.

Notes

1. The Fetal Senses by David B. Chamberlain, Ph.D. 2000
2. Schaal, B., Orgeur, P., and Rognon, C. (1995). Odor Sensing in the Human Fetus: Anatomical, Functional, and Chemeo-ecological Bases. In: Fetal Development: A Psychobiological Perspective, J-P. Lecanuet, W. P. Fifer, N. A., Krasnegor, and W. P. Smotherman (Eds.) pp. 205-237. Hillsdale, NJ: Lawrence Erlbaum Associates
3. ibid
4. Benoist Schaal, Luc Marlier and Robert Soussignan. Human Foetuses Learn Odours from their Pregnant Mother's Diet Chem. Senses 25: 729-737, 2000. Oxford University Press
5. Menella J, Jagnow C, Beauchamp G. Prenatal and postnatal flavour learning by human infants. Pediatrics Vol. 107 No. 6 June 2001, p. e88
6. Marshall H. Klaus, Phyllis H. Klaus, Your Amazing Newborn, (Reading, Mass.: Perseus Books, 1998).
7. Granju, K.A. Attachment Parenting, (New York: Pocket Books, 1999).
8. Dr Katherine Dettwyler.
9. Menella J, Jagnow C, Beauchamp G. Prenatal and postnatal flavour learning by human infants. . Pediatrics Vol. 107 No. 6 June 2001.
10. Hamlyn B, Brooker S, Oleiniokova K, Wands S. Infant Feeding 2000, (London: The Stationery Office, 2002).www.doh.gov.uk/public/infantfeedingreport.htm
11. Victorian London - Publications - Etiquette and Household Advice Manuals – Cassell's Household Guide, New and Revised Edition (4 Vol.) [18731874] - The Rearing and Management of Children - (5) Food in Infancy. www.victorianlondon.org
12. bid

Picnics and Fairy Tales: or, Let them Eat Cake Satisfy the Psyche and Starve the Child

Walter Levy

Children's stories, fairy tales and folk tales often explore complex themes of love, anger, anxiety, sibling rivalry, and parental love and make them accessible to children in "simple" ways. A good story can help children to make some reasonable sense of the anxiety, fear, uncertainty of the adult world, and overcome it. Bruno Bettelheim has deep meaning sought out in fairy tales in *The Uses of Enchantment* (1976), and I agree with his suggestion: "For a story to truly hold the child's attention, it must entertain him and arouse his curiosity. But to enrich his life, it must stimulate his imagination." Though I suspect that Bettelheim's probing for deep meaning in fairy tales rubs off the patina of the child's wonder, there is a risk of robbing the sense of wonder for a psychoanalytical exegesis.

More literary than psychoanalytical, Maria Tatar's *Off With their Heads!* (1992) is a study that favors story character and action. Taking its title from Lewis Carroll's termagant, the Queen of Hearts, Tatar's inclination, unlike Carroll's, is to follow the dark side of fairy tales, where there are no picnics. Tatar works from the assumption that "From its inception, children's literature had in it an unusually cruel and coercive streak—one which produced books that relied on brutal intimidation to frighten children into complying with parental demands." Tatar says that the literature displays two kinds of intimidation—making children miserable or death.

With such a dispiriting premise, it is a pleasure to step into the light of children's picnic stories that are based on the premise of enjoyment. Jack Zipes's commentary in *When Dreams Come True* (1999) begins with the oral tradition of fairy tales, in which he observes the protagonist is mostly successful, receiving for his or her trials marriage, riches, survival and wisdom –or any combination thereof. Generally, the oral tales end happily, though there is no surety. The shift from the oral to the literary tale began in mid 16th century Milan. These tales, meant for adults, were amusing, satiric short stories concerned with such subjects as social conduct, morality, and sexual and ethical codes of behavior. Later, French writers of the late 17th century Paris invented the *conte de fée,* again tales meant for adults.

Picnics and Fairy Tales

The most important of the fairy tale authors, Catherine D'Aulnoy (*Les contes des fées, Fairy Tales,* 1697-98) and Charles Perrault (*Histoires ou contes du temps passé,* 1697) keep to the oral tradition of the happy ending, although D'Aulnoy seems to have tortured her protagonists in some stories, and Perrault gets a bit dicey in "Donkey-Skin" (1694) and "Tom Thumb" (1697).

Fairy Tales hit their stride in the 18th and 19th centuries, when the genre was perfected and many of the tales we still treasure appeared: Marie Le Prince de Beaumont's "Beauty and the Beast." (*Children's Magazine* 1756), Wilhelm and Jacob Grimm's *Children's and Household Tales* (1812-13), E.T.A. Hoffmann's *Tales of Fantasy* (1814-15), Charles Dickens's *A Christmas Carol* (1843), Hans Christian Andersen's *Wonderful Stories for Children* (1846), Lewis Carroll's *Alice's Adventures in Wonderland* (1865), and Oscar Wilde's *The Happy Prince and Other Tales* (1888).

Lewis Carroll. *Alice in Wonderland.* Illustrated by John Tenniel (1865)

Picnics and Fairy Tales

Picnic Stories and Wonder

Picnics stories, like their fairy tale forebears, are full of wonder, fantasy, and magic. Literary picnickers are as often human as animal, and the two interact without noticing that there is a difference. Lewis Carroll's Alice in Wonderland (1865) mixes humans, animals, and creatures in a fantastic / miraculous world somewhere down the rabbit hole. At the Mad Tea-Party, an al fresco picnic, (Chapter 7) Alice encounters the Mad Hatter, Doormouse, and the White Rabbit. Alice's appearance is not remarkable, since she has nibbled a bit of mushroom and is about two feet tall, the size of the Hatter and the Hare. The setting is a garden where a large table is set under a tree at which the Mad Hatter, March Hare, and Doormouse are sitting closely packed at one corner. When Alice approaches they shout, "No room! No room!" Alice indignantly replies, "There's plenty of room!" and she sits down in a large arm-chair at one end of the table." (According to Arthur Rackham, it's set for twelve.) Alice is offered wine (but there isn't any), there is tea (but Alice isn't offered any), and there is a milk jug (but Alice isn't offered any). When the March Hare tells her, "Take some more tea," Alice replies, "I've had nothing yet, so I can't take more." The Hatter corrects her, "You mean you can't take less" . . . it's very easy to take more than nothing." At last, overcome with hunger, the girl helps herself to some tea and bread-and-butter. Deeply annoyed, Alice leaves and says to any that might hear her: "At any rate, I'll never go there again! . . . It's the stupidest tea-party I ever was at in all my life!" Still hungry, Alice nibbles her mushroom until she is about a foot high and then wanders into the garden of the Queen of Hearts.

L. Frank Baum's *The Wizard of Oz* (1900) tells the fantastic story of Dorothy Gale, who has been transported from Kansas by cyclone, unhurt, to the Land of Oz. Dorothy's adventures, which Baum facetiously calls "modernized fairy tale, in which the wonderment and joy are retained and the heartaches and nightmares left out" has its share of frightening and gruesome moments. Baum likes to exaggerate his story's lack of violence, but despite the violence of the attack of the Winged-Monkeys, the fighting trees, the poppy field, the Wizard's request that Dorothy commit murder, Dorothy's quest ends well. You know the story, but perhaps have missed Dorothy's picnic, which occurs in Chapter III, not long after Dorothy, in her blue and white checkered dress and silver shoes, rescues the Scarecrow from his perch in the cornfield. Scarecrow joins Dorothy for the walk, and after a time, Dorothy rests beside the road near a little brook. There, at ease, she opens her basket and takes out some bread. She offers some to the Scarecrow, but he refuses, telling her, "I am never hungry," he said, "and it is a lucky thing I am not. For my mouth is only painted, and if I should cut a hole in it so I could eat, the straw I am stuffed with would come out, and that would spoil the shape of my head." (44)

W. W. Denslow's illustration for Dorothy's picnic follows the text; there is a stream with cattails, a patch of grass, and a convenient bank of earth to sit on. Dorothy and the Scarecrow sit side-by-side, while Toto hungrily eyes the bread in Dorothy's hands. A picnic lunch of bread only is not a feast, but Dorothy eats and does not complain. Typically, the food Baum provides for his heroine is high carbohydrate, a typical food choice for too many children's picnics. The picnic lunch leads to the Emerald City, Oz, and the way home, where Dorothy awakens to a newly rebuilt farm and Toto barks joyously.

L. Frank Baum. The Wonderful Wizard of Oz. Illustrations by W. W. Denslow (1900)

Ian Fleming's Chitty-Chitty-Bang-Bang (1964) is the story of a magical automobile (a thinking car-boat-airplane) that begins with an ordinary family outing (another name for a picnic) one hot Sunday morning in August when Commander Caractacus Pott, the father, makes an announcement to Mimsie (the mother) and Jemima and Jeremy (the eight-year old twins):"Today," he said, "is going to be a roaster, a scorcher. There's only one thing to do, and that's for us to take a delicious picnic and climb into Chitty-Chitty-Bang-Bang [sic] and dash down the Dover Road to the sea." Everyone is delighted with the idea, of course, and keeping to the essential patterns of the picnic, and in true Fleming tradition, the family eats well: "Mimsie [the mother] filled a basket with hard-boiled eggs, cold sausages, bread-and-butter sandwiches, jam puffs (with, of course like all good jam puffs, more jam than puff), and bottles and bottles of the best fizzy lemonade and orange soda." (26) Even Chitty-Chitty-Bang-Bang is well provisioned; Pott fills her with gas, checks the water in the radiator, the oil, tire pressures, cleans the windshield, dusts the body, and polishes the chrome.

The magic begins when Chitty-Chitty takes to the air, and it's a driver's dream come true as the car leaves the jammed traffic below and begins to fly to the beach. When the family is sated with food and has finished swimming and playing, they fall sleep and forget about the tide. Just when the situation is nearly dire, and the tide is rising furiously, Chitty-Chitty awakens the Potts and flies them off to the coast of France, for another adventure that ends well.

Faith Ringgold's *Tar Beach* (1991) tells a night-picnic story as a pretext for magic realism. The picnic takes place on a rooftop of an apartment house in New York City that is affectionately referred to as tar beach. Here Cassie, the heroine, and her family enjoy a night out under the stars. While the parents and friends assemble the fried chicken, watermelon, cakes, cookies, and iced drinks, Cassie literally takes off and flies in the starry sky. She leaves her parents and neighbors below, soaring high over neighborhood buildings and the George Washington Bridge before returning to eat. Ringgold's picnic suggests more than whimsy, for she intends Cassie to symbolize the freedom of youth and the ability to overcome the nagging harshness of racism and the confines of big city living. Bringing her brother BeBe along, Cassie says, "I have told him it's very easy, any one can fly. All you need is somewhere to go that you can't get to any other way. The next thing you know, you're flying among the stars."

Picnic Stories, Food and Happiness

The wonder and magic inherent in picnic stories iterates the literary fairy tale. Stories for both are concerned with broad issues of adventure, happiness and success, social communion, and bringing families and friends together. But unlike their fairy tale forbearers, picnic stories always include food and the rituals of eating meals together. Picnic authors know that a satisfying story for children must have food. It might be surmised that stories dedicated to happy endings and uplifted spirits might aim to provide a wholesome and nutritionally balanced diet. Alas, this is not to be, and with some exceptions, children's picnic stories are built on the patterns of happy action and eating nutritionally poor sweet and fatty foods. It is as if picnic authors write by the mantra: "Satisfy the psyche but starve the child."

This is not a contemporary issue; in fact, the unbalanced picnic menu seems to have been established with the rise of picnic literature in the early 19th century, and the anonymous ballad *Cock Robin and Jenny Wren; The Happy Courtship; Merry Marriage, and Pic-Nic Dinner of Cock Robin. To Which is Added Alas! The Doleful Death of the Bridegroom* (1806) includes a menu served at the love birds' *al fresco* wedding feast to which each guest contributes a share of the food. What they bring sets the pattern of what is to come: Robin brings cherry pie; Owl brings wheat; Raven brings walnuts; Magpie brings cheese, Pigeon brings tares; Magpie brings nuts, and Little May, a girl, brings cheese, apples, bacon, and plums. Inexplicably, Sheep brings wool to the luncheon, and Robin also brings currant wine. The inclusion of wine on the menu is a bit startling for a children's story, but it is a rather adult story to begin with.

A more realistic children's story is Stella Austin's *Stumps* (1845) that tells the story of a devil-may-care girl of four, the eponymous Stumps, who is the child of an upper-middle-class family. The children's picnic hamper, packed by the housekeeper, is filled with apple tarts, plum cake, shortbread, mulberry tart, sponge cake, bread and butter, hard-boiled eggs, plums, pears, and greengages, and macaroons. Though this feast may be enough for some, Stumps complains because there is no "trawberry' jam." The fun of the picnic is offset by a disturbing event when Stumps runs off and climbs a steep hillside. Seeing the danger Tom, a foundling boy spending time with the family, rushes to save her. But the rescue ends badly when he falls and is critically injured looses his ability to walk. Stumps is distressed, of course, and the episode becomes a lesson in humility, but life goes on, there will be more picnics -- and the boy is, after all, not upper class. The ending of this extremely popular Victorian tale is a hard-edged reminder of how class and social mores intrude in our literature.

Mark Twain's picnic in *The Adventures of Tom Sawyer* (1876) is a humorous satire of American life in the South. But the gist of the picnic episode, which begins the long climax of the novel, is that fairy tales end happily. So when picnicking with friends along the Mississippi River, Tom Sawyer and Becky Thatcher get lost in McDougal's Cave. Upset but not desperate, Tom assumes the role of the gallant knight, while Becky plays damsel in distress. At all times, Tom is a gentleman at Becky's service, offering her what food there is – cake:

"Tom, I'm so hungry!"

Tom took something out of his pocket.

"Do you remember this," said he.

Becky almost smiled.

"It's our wedding cake, Tom."

"Yes—I wish it was as big as a barrel, for it's all we've got."

"I saved it from the pic-nic for us to dream on Tom, the way grown up people do with wedding cake—but it'll be our–"

She dropped the sentence where it was. Tom divided the cake and Becky ate with good appetite, while Tom nibbled at his moiety. There was abundance of cold water to finish the feast with."

Why Tom kept cake in his pocket is a bit of Twain's whimsy. Of course, it isn't a funeral cake, or for that matter a wedding cake. But it is cake, and it demonstrates again that picnic food for children and juveniles is mainly a matter of carbohydrates. After three days, Tom, made confident by a kiss, finds a way out. They return home tired but overjoyed. At first glance, the cake for Tom and Becky is a small detail until one begins to notice that the pattern of food choices in children's picnics runs to high carbohydrates and fats. Why this should be the case is a puzzle, though such foods seem to be an indulgent adult attitude for providing children with what they typically want most.

Canvassing other children's picnic meals is delightful but not for dieters. So for the abstemious, it is best to avoid Rat's riverbank picnic in Kenneth Grahame's *The Wind in the Willows* (1908). Chapter one, "The River Bank," begins when the Mole gives up his spring-cleaning and wanders down to the river where he meets Rat. After a short ride, Mole's first, they row down the river for a picnic. Rat has packed a "fat, wicker luncheon basket" that he breathlessly tells Mole is filled with "cold chicken inside it . . . . coldtongue coldhamcoldbeefpickledgherkinssaladfrenchrollscressandwidgespottedmeatgingerbeerlemon sodawater." Rat's response, by the way, is appropriate for a picnic meal because picnic food is always served all at the same time, unlike a home or restaurant meal, which is served in courses. The picnic is eaten on a green patch of turf just beside the river: "The Mole begged as a favour to be allowed to unpack it all by himself; and Rat was very pleased to indulge him, and to sprawl at full length on the grass and rest, while his excited friend shook out the table cloth and spread it, took out the mysterious packets one by one and arranged their contents in due order gasping, "O my! O my!" at each fresh revelation."

A. A. Milne's *Winnie-the-Pooh* (1926) includes a picnic grounds, and Christopher Robin's map shows "Nice place for Piknicks" just above the "Sandy Pit where Roo Plays." Presumably this is where Christopher Robin hosts an alfresco luncheon for Pooh, Owl, Piglet, Kanga, and Eeyore. The menu is not described but Pooh agrees to come along, even though the party is for him, because he is assured that he will be served "little cake things" covered with pink sugar icing.

Picnics are restorative, contrary to other dire tales for children. Francis Hodgson Burnet's *The Secret Garden* (1911) is filled with clandestine picnics. The cousins, Colin Craven, a fearful make believe invalid, and Mary Lennox, a yellow-faced, sickly, and wretched girl, have picnics in the secret garden where mystery and magic nurture the body and the soul. At first, Susan Sowerby, an estate servant, provides them fresh milk, crusty cottage loaf and currant buns, folded in a white and blue napkin. Later the children build an oven of stones, and with supplies purchased for them by kind-hearted Susan, they roast eggs and potatoes, garnished with butter and salt. In this instance, there is an inverse relationship to poor health and eating poorly: contrary to expectation, the carbohydrates, the cholesterol, and the fatty butter work to make the youngsters happy, laughing, and feeling spiritually well fed.

Some authors of children's picnic stories develop variations on the food theme. Jimmy Kennedy's lyric for "The Teddy Bears' Picnic," (1932), based on a 1907 tune by John W. Barton, makes no mention of food. The bears play games, sing and dance, but they do not eat anything. Of course, the song has nurtured the collective psyches of us all, but it inadvertently separates us from nourishing picnic food. However, as illustrated by Alexandra Day, "The Teddy Bears' Picnic" (1983) the picnic is a food feast of the usual children's foods: honey, bananas, pears, oranges, cake, soda, jellybeans, marshmellows and chips. Inexplicably hanging nearby are garlands of red peppers and garlic. Cookbook authors Suzanne Barchers and Peter Rauen's *Storybook Stew* (1996) use the *Teddy Bears' Picnic* as the basis for encouraging children to make "Teddy Refrigerator Cookies."

A rigid menu of carbohydrates and fatty foods is offered in Astrid Lindrgen's Pippi's Extraordinary Ordinary Day (1950). Pippi Longstocking, a brash, energetic, good-natured girl of nine, who explains that she learned to cook on her father's ship, selects the picnic meal. After zipping through some household chores, Pippi takes her friends on a picnic where they sit on the grass next to a nice sunny rock, eating sandwiches with meatballs and ham, sugared pancakes, brown sausages, and pineapple puddings. When the picnic is over, the happy group wanders home, Pippi loudly singing:

> In the happy summertime
>
> Through field and wood we make our way.
>
> Nobody's sad, everyone's gay.
>
> We sing as we go, ho-lá, ho-ló!
>
> You who are young,
>
> Come join in our song.
>
> Don't sit home moping all the day long.
>
> We sing as we go, ho-lá, ho-ló!

Jane Werner's *Walt Disney's Mickey Mouse's Picnic* (1950) begins when Mickey Mouse arrives at Minnie Mouse's house on the way to a picnic in the country. The story's plot demonstrates that eating outdoors and being with friends away from the ordinary life in town is fun. The story's subtle pedagogical message is that correct social behavior, the common decency of inviting all of your close friends to a picnic and not excluding anyone who you think is trouble. With high spirits, Pluto, Goofy, and Clarabelle Cow, crowd into Mickey's red convertible. Donald Duck is conspicuously missing. When his absence is noted, Mickey says, "Yes, but there is always trouble when Donald is along." As they drive away, Donald observes them, full of rage. The picnic is held in the country under a great shady tree where they spread a red and white checkerboard pattern blanket. The fun includes swimming, but when the group returns, the lunch basket is gone. Just when they are distressed enough, up strolls Donald, who suggests that his friends share his picnic lunch –a selection of carbohydrates: "peanut and jelly sandwiches and cold meat sandwiches and devilled eggs and potato salad, radishes and onions and pink lemonade, and a great big chocolate cake!" The radishes and onions are a nice touch, but the rest of the salad is missing. Finally, Mickey says, "I guess we misjudged you, Donald, old boy." But Minnie finally decides to force the issue and Donald is exposed as the picnic basket lunch thief. Chagrined, Donald admits his theft. They laugh, and Mickey says that they have all learned a lesson. Next time all the friends, including Donald, will be invited to the picnic. They drive back to the city singing:

> What a beautiful day for a picnic,

What a practical day for a lark!
We will frolic all day
In the happiest way,
And we won't get back home until dark!

Selected Picnic Menus

The menus in picnic stories suggest that authors have a single mind–that the foods selected to satisfy children's palettes is a collection of sweets and fats. Evidently, authors give in to simplicity and prefer not to extend eating experience or inculcate balanced dieting. It's as if there is a head-to-tail mentality when it comes to the food served at a picnic. For good or ill, what I have to report is that with few exceptions the child's picnic menu is a remarkably fixed combination of sweets and fats. For the sake of scale, and some variety, here is a select survey of texts and menus from 1958 through 1997.

* Marmalade! Michael Bond's picnic, *An Adventure at the Seaside* (1958) is about Paddington, the Peruvian bear named for the train station, who is content to munch marmalade sandwiches while others eat ice cream.

* Margaret Gordon's *Wilberforce* (1982) is about the eponymous bear whose grandmother packs a robust basket that is filled with a raisin cake, a rolled cake with filling, a pie, sandwich cookies, a jar of jelly, a pile of sandwiches (fillings unknown), a salt or sugar cellar, apples, bananas, and drinks. It's no wonder that Wilberforce is tired at the end of the day.

* Eric Hill's *Spot's First Picnic* (1987), provides two picnics. For the first picnic, Spot helps Mom to prepare the bread and jam and cheese sandwiches, which he packs along with a bone and a canteen, contents unknown. The second picnic is a blanket spread on the parlor floor where Spot and friends eat more jam sandwiches, cookies, tomatoes, oranges, and bananas.

* Jack Harris' humorous *Garfield's Picnic Adventure* (1988) supplies a picnic basket stuffed with fried chicken, hot dogs, mustard, Swiss cheese, and cookies.

* Jacqueline Woodson's *We Had a Picnic This Sunday Past* (1997) is the story of a traditional picnic in an urban park, where the family brings sweet corn, cinnamon bread, cranberry muffins, sweet potato pie, peach cobbler, yams, potato salad, salad, a big old ham, cornbread, homemade ice cream and a store-bought cake. Grandma gets up at four in the morning to fry the chicken and bake biscuits. *We Had a Picnic* may not provide a

well-balanced nutritious meal but it does show us a family exuding good will and fellowship at a picnic.

Among the exceptions to the picnic-menu-rule is Michael Muntean's *Look What I Found* (1981) a picnic story in which the Sesame Street Muppets travel to a woodsy locale for a *déjeuner sur l'herbe*. The gang here spreads a blanket on which to eat peanut butter sandwiches, grapes, bananas, and drinks (unknown contents) from a thermos. Edward Knapp's *What! No Spinach?* (1983) is about a picnic on a dock where Olive Oyl has perversely prepared two picnic baskets packed with salami, fresh rye bread, pickles, root beer, and lemonade. The meal is graciously declined by Popeye, an unlikely gourmet, who demurs, "No, thanks, Olive, I'd rather have spinach." The real surprise is the vegan picnic in Laurent de Brunhoff's *Barbar's Picnic* (1965) at which is served bananas, pears, apples, grapes and a sandwich (filling unknown).

With these inevitable exceptions, it is usual for children to cram carbs and fats with gusto. Beverages are gulped though the range seems confined to lemonade or unnamed soft drinks.

Picnic Cookbooks for Children

Food in real life and in adult picnic stories ranges in quantity and quality—but for children, it's always cuisine prepared on the quick and eaten on the run, so to speak, even when they are at rest on a picnic blanket. Children are gourmands demanding speedy preparation, speedy cooking, and speedy eating. Cleanup, if any, is usually left to the grown-ups. Surprisingly, modern authors pretend not to notice real-life preferences for fast foods. Picnic authors avoid mentioning foods purchased from fast food outlets, and none as yet, to my knowledge, has portrayed a literary picnic of chicken nuggets, cheese pizzas, and Jamaican beef patties, judged the favorite foods of New York City school lunchrooms.

Picnic storybook and cookbook authors suggest similar menus. As a group, they tend to play up the notion, perhaps inadvertently, that some foods, more than others, are fun to eat, and so place more emphasis on the so-called fun-food –carbohydrates and fats. Proteins get less emphasis, and the balanced meal is something that doesn't sell books. Jan Longone, a food historian, points out that from 1870s to the 1920s American cookbooks for children tend to be more concerned with etiquette and less with cooking or eating. In "As Worthless as Savorless Salt"? Teaching Children to Cook, Clean, (and Often) Conform," (*Gastronomica*, Spring 2003), Langone says that the Victorian ethos prevailed and children were encouraged to behave while they have fun, but they were not expected to cook or take part in the preparations.

Some cookbook authors do offer good advice about eating for good health and taste, and contemporary cookbooks now include children in the preparation (but not the planning) of a menu. Linda White's *Cooking on a Stick: Campfire Recipes for Kids* (1996) is cookbook like picnic literature that favors carbohydrates and sugars. White's menu has variety cutesy names for foods like Snail on a Limb (biscuit dough coiled around a stick), Veggie Herd (vegetables in a pouch), Bird's Nest Breakfast (ham, potatoes, and eggs in an orange shell), and Moose Lips (apple, peanut butter, and marshmellows). Sunset Books' *Best Kids Cook Book* (1992) includes a recipe for a "Rainy Day Picnic" that provides instructions for making a tent at home (take two chairs and cover with a blanket, use another blanket for the floor, eat by flashlight). The menu suggests a variety of foods, provides nutritional analysis, and it is as balanced a meal as one finds on a children's picnic: Already Ready Soup; Tuna-stuffed Pockets; Pass the Peanut Butter cookies: and Really Strawberry Shake. Whether the public is ready for a children's cookbook that scants sweets and fats is something for the future. Similarly, whether the reading public is ready for picnic stories in which the children are not sweet-starved is moot.

The Happy Child or Let Them Eat Cake

Looking over the literature, it is evident that picnic foods in children's stories do not encourage good eating habits. Picnic authors (their agents, editors, and publishers) all implicitly contend that sweets and fats make children happy, and the children in their stories never argue with what is offered to eat. The public seems to agree; children *are* starved for sweets, and the picnic menu is appropriate because the children devouring picnic foods are contented and happy. And who is to argue if the picnic world children inhabit is a happy place? Who cares to count carbohydrates when childhood's spirit and imagination are well-fed on cakes-cookies-sandwiches-and-lemonade? Let's face it, the children's picnic world is a wonderful world, the weather is almost always a perfect summer day and though it might rain, there is never enough to ruin the day. Fairy tales may often begin with the phrase "Once upon a time," but picnic stories begin with the announcement: "It is a great day for a picnic!"

Selected Bibliography

ANONYMOUS. (1806) Cock Robin and Jenny Wren; the Happy Courtship; Merry Marriage, and Pic-Nic Dinner of Cock Robin. To Which Is Added Alas! The Doleful Death of the Bridegroom. London, J. Harris.

BAUM, L. FRANK. The Wonderful Wizard of Oz. Illustrated by W. W. Denslow. New York: Dover Publications, Inc., 1900. Reprint, 1960.

BETTELHEIM, BRUNO. (1976). The Uses of Enchantment: The Meaning of and Importance of Fairy Tales. New York, Random House.

BOND, MICHAEL. (1958). "Adventure at the Seaside." A Paddington Treasury. Boston, Houghton Mifflin Company.

BRUNOFF, LAURENT DE. (1965). Barbar's Picnic [Pique - Nique Chez Babar]. Translated from the French by Merle Haas. New York, Random House.

CARROLL, LEWIS [Charles Lutwidge Dodgson]. (1865). Alice in Wonderland. Illustrated by John Tenniel. Arthur Rackham's illustration of the "Mad Tea Party." In Alice's Adventures in Wonderland. London, William Heinemann. London. 1907.

CHITTY-CHITTY-BANG-BANG. (1968). Directed by Ken Hughes, written by Roald Dahl and Ken Hughes. United Artists/Warfield/DFI/Albert Broccoli. 1968. Based on Ian Fleming, Chitty-Chitty-Bang-Bang: The Magical Car. New York, Random House, Inc. 1964.

DISNEY, WALT. (1965). Walt Disney's Mickey Mouse Book. Racine. WI, Western Publishing Company.

GRAHAME, KENNETH. (1908). The Wind in the Willows. Illustrated by Arthur Rackham. New York: The Heritage Press, 1940. Also an edition illustrated by Mary Jane Begin. New York, SeaStar Books. 2002.

HARRIS, JACK C. (1988). Garfield's Picnic Adventure, Created by Jim Davis. Racine, WI, Western Publishing Company.

HILL, ERIC. (1987). Spot's First Picnic. New York, G. P. Putnam's Sons.

KENNEDY, JIMMY. (1907). "The Teddy Bear's Picnic," Illustrated by Alexandra Day. New York, Aladdin Paperbacks. 2000.

LINDGREN, ASTRID, (1950). Pippi's Extraordinary Ordinary Day. Illustrated by Michael Chesworth, New York, Viking Press, Inc.

LONGONE, JAN. (2003). "As Worthless as Savorless Salt"? Teaching Children to Cook, Clean, (and Often) Conform," Gastronomica. 3 (2): 104-110.

MILNE, A. A. (1926). Winnie-the-Pooh. Illustrated by Ernest H. Shepard. New York: E.P. Dutton & Co.

MUNTEAN, MICHAEL. (1981). Look what I Found!: Featuring Jim Henson's Sesame Street Muppets. Racine, WI, Western Publishing Company in conjunction with the Children's Television Network.

PERLE, RUTH LERNER. (1991). The Rainy-Day Picnic. Produced by Kroha Associates, Inc. Middletown, CT ed: The Walt Disney Company, 1991.

RINGGOLD, FAITH. (1991). Tar Beach, New York, Crown Publishers.

TATAR, MARIA. (1992). Off With Their Heads! Fairy Tales and the Culture of Childhood. Princeton, Princeton University Press.

WERNER, JANE. (1950). Walt Disney's Mickey Mouse's Picnic. Racine, WI, Western Publishing Company.

WOODSON, JACQUELINE. (1997). We Had a Picnic This Sunday Past. Illustrated by Diane Greenseid. New York, Hyperion Books.

ZIPES, JACK. (1999) When Dreams Came True: Classical Fairy Tales and Their Tradition. New York: Routeledge.

The Business of Food: Preserving Culinary Traditions Keeps the Family Fed in the Philippines

Pia Lim-Castillo

Introduction – Filipino society is basically matriarchal

Many of our food memories and culinary learning experiences are connected with our mothers. Mothers determine our food culture. They not only decide on the food we eat, but by cooking it, decide on its particular nuances or register of taste. It is their example of daily unspoken devotion that becomes the model for their daughters – and indirectly for their son's wives.

Our ideas of taste and value; of nutrition and menus; of like and dislike; of time and occasion; of cooking and homemaking; of the ordinary and the special, are influenced by our mothers. The heritage of skills and secrets are passed on by mothers to daughters and sons. It is their role in shaping, preserving and transmitting food culture (Fernandez, 1994, 75-78).

In a third world country such as the Philippines, women augment the family income through trades involving food. This provides an additional if not the main source of income for their families at the same time allowing them to watch over their growing family. With social conditions such as an average of more than two offspring to a family and fathers not earning enough to feed, clothe and shelter their children, the women contribute to the family income by cooking foods at home and selling them.

Cooking and selling are generally trades taught to women. Foods are prepared at home or in community centers where women can take care of their children and at the same time eke out a living. In most cases, food preparation and sales are either family or community activities where tasks are shared. Although profits are marginal, women subsist on the income since a steady demand for cooked traditional foods exists.

All over the country, it is common to find women working together preparing foods for sale while keeping a watchful eye on the toddlers nearby. It is like a day care center and kitchen rolled into one. There is division of labor and each one is assigned a specific task and the income is divided equally or is used to provide for the family's needs.

A common thread ran though all my interviews. Admirable women are keeping Filipino culinary traditions alive by preparing dishes using traditional techniques and ingredients. Now becoming a rarity, these recipes and methods need to be archived as they form part of our culinary culture. In most cases, women learn their cooking ways from their parents and grandparents and continue to make a living out of it in order to raise their families.

Children are not left scot free to play. Once they are old enough, they are given tasks commensurate with their abilities until they reach an apprenticeship period in learning a livelihood that would hopefully survive several generations. In a paper entitled Food History and the Death of Memory presented at this symposium in 2000 by Gerald and Valerie Mars, they spoke of traditional forms of teaching and learning cooking via "the habit of hands", a way of relating to objects and processes such as learning to cook a traditional cuisine which also involves verbal instruction (Mars, 2001, 158). All the cases presented have used this learning method to impart skills to their children.

The information for this research is based on interviews of women at work. To capture the essence of the communal activity, a video of the whole process was indispensable as techniques are best described and learned when watched. Four women have created niches for local food products in the provinces of Negros Oriental and Iloilo, two islands in the Visayas. These examples are meant to showcase how families have been nurtured through food, the involvement and early apprenticeship of children and finally how values formation and food history are being preserved through their efforts.

Dumaguete and its *Budbud*

Dumaguete, the capital city of Negros Oriental, is known for its *budbud kabug,* a banana leaf wrapped snack made of millet cooked in coconut milk and sweetened with sugar. The color is pale yellow akin to corn with a very fine taste and texture. Millet is not one of our native crops so it seems surprising that the people of Dumaguete would end up cooking it using traditional methods of cooking snacks, which is with coconut milk. Dumagueteños say that they have been making *budbud kabug* for over 100 years, and millet is grown in the areas of Valencia and Siaton.

In Dumaguete, several families make this snack as the city is known for this delicacy. Women and their families have been making *budbud kabug* and recipes and techniques have been handed down for generations. These are well-guarded secrets that are not given out as their livelihood depends on it.

Millet is one of the oldest foods know to humans and possibly the first cereal grain to be used for domestic purposes. Millet has been used in Africa and India as a staple food for thousands of years and it was grown as early as 2700 BC in China where it was the prevalent grain before rice became the dominant staple (Ward, 1997, 43). It seems plausible that this grain was transported via Chinese trading junk boats or Spanish galleons and then planted in the south where the first Spanish colonizers settled. Exactly when this food came to be considered as local food fare is not known but older people in Dumaguete claim memories of *budbud kabug* for at least a hundred years.

Josefina Lagahid learned how to make *budbud kabug* from her mother. At six years old, she was already helping out in the kitchen cutting up the pieces of banana leaves or grating the coconut or cleaning the cut up banana leaves with the residue of the grated coconut after the milk has been extracted. As she grew older, more tasks were given to her in the kitchen. She was only able to reach 5th grade, when she had to stop studying to help out further in order to meet the burgeoning needs of the family. For over 70 years, their family has had a stall in the market. The stalls where *budbud,* coffee and hot chocolate are served is called *painitan* (warm up place, that is, a café). Josefina's mother used to make different kinds of *budbud* for their market stall while the older sisters of Josefina would work in the market selling *budbud* and chocolate made from cacao grown in Negros Oriental and the neighboring island of Siquijor. While Josefina busied herself making *budbud,* her sisters roasted the cacao beans and pounded them into *tabliya* for next day's sales. At the crack of dawn, one of her brothers would bring all the products to the market so that people could have them for breakfast.

Budbud preparation starts right after lunch. Josefina begins by extracting the milk from the coconut and after all the milk has been extracted, she brings this to a boil in a large cooking vat or *taliasi* to which she adds a tablespoon of salt. Her husband assists her by washing two kilograms of millet and draining it to be added to the coconut milk mixture when it comes to a boil.

Millet is like rice where the amount of liquid needed to cook it depends on the moisture level of the grain. Feel for the grain is learned from experience and never in terms of exact amounts of liquid to be used. It is stirred constantly until it is half cooked before adding sugar and must be stirred until coconut oil appears on the sides of the vat. The millet must be stirred in a uniform direction so as not to break the millet. This process can drain the energy from the cook if working alone. In Josefina's case, she works in tandem with her husband and son. While husband and wife are busy in the kitchen, the son is given other tasks.

When the millet is finally cooked, it is transferred to a container ready to be wrapped in banana leaves. They are shaped into long fingers, rolled and folded, then bunched into 5 pieces and tied with short strips of banana leaves. Once all the cooked millet is wrapped and tied together, they are put in a steamer where they are steamed for two hours before they can be eaten. The steaming softens the millet further, fully cooks the coconut milk and allows the flavor of the banana leaf to meld with the millet and coconut. The whole process takes at least five hours from beginning to end, where it is cooled in the vat up to the following morning.

Although bottled petroleum gas is available to them, they still prefer to cook using firewood as this was how they learned to do it and cooking with firewood gives a distinct flavor which you cannot obtain when using gas. Furthermore, firewood is free and is collected from the dried twigs and branches found around their homes.

Most of us would rather buy *budbud* than make it because it takes several hours from start to finish. Josefina and her husband, Icoy, have chosen to spend whole afternoons making about 200 to 300 pieces daily to sell in the market. This is what Josefina has learned from her mother and she continues to do so because she has seen how her family has survived on this business. Through her efforts, Josefina and her family are keeping culinary tradition alive making *budbud kabug* daily with hardly any changes in methods.

The city of Tanjay in Dumaguete is known for another specialty, it is *Budbud sa Tanjay*. The difference between *budbud kabug* and *budbud sa Tanjay* is in the main ingredient used. The latter takes its name from the city of *Tanjay* and the basic ingredient is glutinous rice. During fiestas, they have a *budbud* contest to judge the best *budbud sa Tanjay*. Three ladies, the third generation of a family of *budbud sa Tanjay* makers are Emma and Arsenia Girasol and Didi Guevarra. They are all first cousins who remember their grandmother and their mothers teaching them how to make it.

The process of making *budbud sa Tanjay* is similar to *budbud kabug* except for two things. One, pearly white long grain glutinous rice is used and second, the final method of cooking is boiling instead of steaming. The quality of this *budbud* is dependent on the glutinous rice which must be totally unadulterated by regular rice which is cheaper. Glutinous rice takes longer to cook than regular rice and the textures are very different. If one uses a combination, the resultant *budbud* leaves some rice grains undercooked, shortening the shelf life of the final product. The process of cooking the rice with the coconut milk is the same as the *budbud kabug*.

For variety, they have a *budbud* called *balintawak* where 1/3rd of the cooked rice is mixed with chocolate *tabliya*. These are rolled separately then intertwined creating a spiral design like a candy cane before they are wrapped in banana leaves. Wrapping them tight is essential to ensure that the flavor of the *budbud* will not be adulterated during the last stage of boiling.

Once the *budbud* are wrapped, they are transferred to a casserole filled with shredded pieces of banana leaves to protect the *budbud* from getting burned. It is then boiled until the crackling sound of frying oil is heard - the point where the coconut milk and rice are thoroughly cooked. Properly and patiently cooked with no shortcuts, *budbud sa Tanjay* is chewy, completely moist and will last a whole week without refrigeration because the antibacterial and antifungal properties of coconut oil and the cooked banana leaves protect it.

All these four women prepare their specialties instinctively. It would be difficult to try to make them standardize their recipes as they have been taught to feel and be flexible and to judge based on their senses of smell, taste, feel and sight. A common practice in the provinces in terms of measurement is to use implements that are available be it empty tin cans or ladles - in terms of wholes or fractions of it. Measurements were not that important, since native cooks improvise, are flexible and measure by instinct (Fernandez, 1994, 108). In the case of the cooking of *budbud kabug* and *budbud sa Tanjay*, the ladies who make them used cans of yeast, milk, glasses in attempts to standardize their recipes. There is no such thing as standardized weights and measures. For an outsider to learn these foods, it is important to assimilate their methods and to try standardizing it elsewhere.

Iloilo

Women who cook foods at home for sale usually work in tandem with other women to do the selling. People who sell food are called "*Manug-libud*" by the Ilongos. Literally, this means "the ones going around". One person or group takes care of the production of different delicacies while someone else (the *Manug-libud*) picks them up and takes care of distributing them to markets and other selling areas. Usually a "*Manug-libud*" will order foods from one or more women for pick up early in the morning and then comes back to pay for the products at the end of the day. Orders for the following day are taken by the supplier when they pick up their daily orders. One will find *manug-libud* in markets, outside schools, hospitals and churches, in the town plaza and in other strategic locations where there is a market for these foods.

Manug-libud women survive to this day because the foods they sell are local fare favorites that are excellent, inexpensive and not everyone has the time to make them at home and in large quantities. One would expect to find a *Manug-libud* selling a minimum of five different snacks composed of savory or sweet items such as *panara* (a fried turnover made with mung beans, pork and shrimps), *bitso-bitso* (ground glutinous rice shaped in twists, fried and glazed with muscovado syrup and toasted sesame seeds), *mwasi* (ground glutinous rice that is boiled and covered with freshly grated coconut and eaten with muscovado and toasted sesame seeds), *arroz valenciana* (glutinous rice with pork, chicken and peas cooked with turmeric powder and wrapped in banana leaves). All these foods will at least take half a day to prepare and people who do not have the time to prepare these dishes would rather buy them.

Admittedly, although there are still several *manug-libud* in the Visayan provinces, changing tastes and food trends as well as lack of time are forcing producers to prepare foods like hotdog sandwiches and spaghetti. The number of manug-libud selling traditional foods are dwindling. Those that still make them have earned their market niche and clientele, allowing them to continue with their craft.

One such woman is Suping Emberso, a mother of six who has been a supplier of *manug-libud* for over forty years. In this business, she found that she could be home to raise her family and at the same time augment their income to be able to send all of her children through college.

Suping would start by going to market before dawn to buy her ingredients for different kinds of foods. By 7 am, the *manug-libud* would go to her house and pick up their orders of different products. After the *manug-libud* picks up all of Suping's products, she moves on to cook lunch for the family and then prepares for the afternoon snack fare that the same person would pick up. These are picked up by 3 pm and sold again. She only gets to rest by 4 pm but in a few hours, she will be preparing dinner for her family. This daily routine of hard work provided her with a stable income to raise her family that when the business peaked, even her husband left his job to assist her. Suping's life revolved around the market, kitchen and her family. At the age of 67, she takes pride in being the best supplier of the *manug-libud* in the whole of Jaro. In her retirement, she continues to cook for special orders, caterings and fiesta. Blessed with a decent livelihood learned from her mother, Suping was able to raise a family through cooking. She has also passed on this craft to her children who have learned to make them as a fallback should their chosen careers fail.

Last but not the least of examples is a bakery business in the city of Molo, Iloilo which was started in the late 1800's by women. *Panaderia de Molo* (bakery of Molo) was an offshoot of a church construction. Because cement was not yet in use in the islands, eggwhites and lime were mixed to produce the mortar for the adobe walls of the Church of Molo. Hundreds of thousands of egg whites were needed to build the adobe skirt around the church structure (Gonzalez, 1993, 114). Throwing away all those egg yolks would have been extremely wasteful so the Spaniards taught women in Molo how to use the egg yolks to make biscuits and encouraged the womenfolk to find ways and means to use the egg yolks. It is not only in Molo where women made use of egg yolks but all over the country where the Spaniards were building churches. Recipes such as *leche flan* (a baked custard similar to crème brûlée), *yema* (egg candies made with egg yolks and sugar coated with caramel syrup), *tocino del cielo* (crème caramel made with butter, egg yolks and sugar) became fashionable desserts created from architectural waste products.

Panaderia de Molo was started by three spinster sisters as a cottage industry. It was a good business that had a daily inflow of cash from sales. After 30 years of running the business, the spinsters turned it over to their niece, Luisa Jason, in 1920. Early in life, Luisa was apprenticed for making the biscuits when she was only 14 years old, to prepare her to handle the business later on. Luisa had 7 children 5 daughters and 2 sons. Through the *panaderia*, she and her husband, were able to educate and raise their children. The family survived the war because they had cash to buy their necessities from daily sales. Just like her, she made sure that her children would be apprenticed to the business. In the 60's, Luisa retired and turned it over to her children (the 3rd generation). It was during this period when they started to mechanize some of the procedures as the business was booming and they could not cope with the demand for their products without mechanization. Kneading was now partially mechanized using machines similar to pasta makers and mixing was no longer a manual process. Following in the footsteps of their parents and with the old matriarch alive, even the granddaughters were made to work on Sundays to learn the trade. Having survived over a century with women running the business, they felt that their children should also learn the trade to be able to take over with the smoothest of transitions.

To this very day, despite mechanization of some processes, one will still find large wooden kneading tables from the early 1920's and wood fired ovens. In one corner, fat is rendered on a weekly basis for use as shortening. The label has not changed through the years and the employees working there are children of former employees. With the church no longer in need of egg whites, the family came up with recipes using egg whites rather than throwing them away. In addition to their line of egg yolk based biscuits, they now have several meringue products.

After three generations of family apprenticing and handling the business, five entrepreneurial grandchildren of Luisa (not spared from the apprenticeship procedure) now run the *panaderia*. Las Nietas de Luisa (granddaughters of Luisa in Spanish) understand their legacy and their humble beginnings and have seen how the older generations have survived through the years with a learned trade. Their processes have changed very little allowing technology only to speed up certain tasks but not to change the character and nuances of their products. They have been flexible to adjust when necessary but have kept to tradition whenever possible. This is what they know and it has sustained them well.

This last example is by far one of the longest existing family run food businesses in the country spanning four generations and several regimes. At the very core of its existence is family not only by blood but also of its employees. It is with a sense of pride that they are keeping a culinary tradition alive in the province of Iloilo. Anyone who comes to visit Iloilo would have heard of the famous biscuits of *Panaderia de Molo*.

Conclusions and Valuable Lessons Learned

Education is more than just going to school and learning to read and write. What we learn is based on exposure given to us by our families. A child is brought to the market to learn what and how to buy basic ingredients such as rice, coconuts, millet, eggs, meat, vegetables and fish. Although learning to cook is taught when the children are much older and more capable, they are made aware of the intricacies of basic ingredients at a young age. When it is time to learn cooking, it is mostly women that are taught as in traditional societies. Women are made to learn trades as fallback positions but they are also expected to raise their families. Once the girls are old enough, they go through an apprenticeship process where they also learn trades but also form values in terms of discipline and hard work.

Not all the food products mentioned in this paper are indigenous Filipino food but have become local fare in the provinces through the years. *Budbud kabug* came to be considered local fare in Dumaguete because the way it was cooked in coconut milk was highly acceptable to the townsfolk. The *Arroz Valenciana* is a Spanish dish but the version made by

Suping is flavored with turmeric rather than saffron and the sausage used is Chinese sausage rather than Spanish *chorizo,* showing influences of Spanish and Chinese cuisines. The biscuits of *Panaderia de Molo* arose from finding ways to make use of egg yolks. All these food products began as regional cooking habits with ingredients limited by the natural environment or they were open to local exchanges of influence and modification by such new products as can be accommodated in a regional tradition (Fernandez-Armesto, 2001, 155).

The concept of the *manug-libud* and food preparations done at home for sale are slowly losing ground to fast food chains and changes in diets and food preferences of the local folk. The high cost of living makes it difficult to spend five hours in the kitchen for just marginal profit gains from their labor. Women are tempted to cook easier dishes or are shortening the processes or even adulterating them for profit. The women that still do them traditionally continue because it is what they know how to do well. What they sell is part of the indigenous and indigenized cuisine that steadily supplies the town and city markets, the tables of the poor and the lower middle class who constitute 90% of the Philippine population. It is the indigenous cuisine that will not get much updated technology, standardization of sourcing, or stabilization of supply routes. Native food will not get written up in too many cookbooks and magazines, or featured on television. But these uncolonized foodways will steadily confirm the culture, provide documentation of what is Filipino for generations of anthropologists and researchers, and assert the national identity (Fernandez, 1994, 229).

Many traditional recipes are fast disappearing or have been totally lost. A lot of mothers, grandmothers, and cooks have passed away without writing down their recipes or without passing them to children or grandchildren. I hear stories of women who wish to pass them on and have found no takers because their children or grandchildren are at their offices, computers or businesses and have no time for the kitchen. A lot of our history will be lost if we don't learn, document and patronize these foods of the past.

These women have stuck it out preparing dishes that speak of our culinary culture for people to appreciate. As consumers, if we want to preserve these traditional foods, we have to understand how they are prepared, how much time goes into them and allow the makers to earn better. They have not only been preserving a culinary tradition but also a way of life and educating their families with forthright values needed in our society.

References

Fernandez, Doreen G., *Tikim: Essays of Philippine Food and Culture,* (Metro Manila: Anvil Publishing, 1994).

Fernandez-Armesto, Felipe., *Food: A History*, (London: Pan Macmillan Ltd., 2001).

Gonzalez, Gene R. *Cocina Sulipeña*, (Makati: Bookmark, Inc., 1993).

Mars, Gerald & Valerie. Food History and the Death of Memory, in Food and the Memory, Proceedings, 2000, Prospect Books, Blackawton, Totnes, Devon, 2001, pp. 157-162.

Ward, Susie, Clifton and Stacey. *The Gourmet Atlas*. London: Quarto Publishing PLC, 1997

Mentoring: a model for the future nurturing of Culinary Talent

Máirtín Mac Con Iomaire

Introduction

Should time be invested in nurturing the next generation of Culinarians in order to improve the profession? Is fear and intimidation acceptable in a professional kitchen? Can we identify the reasons behind the high levels of staff turnover? What is mentoring? In this paper I hope to address these questions, and to discuss mentoring as a model for nurturing culinary talent. I draw upon both personal experiences and those of students who have experienced mentoring as part of the Professional Internship Module of the BA in Culinary Arts in the Dublin Institute of Technology to support my position.

This paper is written in the context of exceptional growth, labour shortages and high staff turnover within the Irish hospitality industry (Keating and McMahon, 2000, Bord-Fáilte, 2001). Labour shortages and high staff turnover within the hospitality business is not only an Irish problem but also an international one (Hoque, 2000). A recent employment survey (CERT 2002) forecasted the need for 125,000 new employees in the Irish catering industry in the five years up to 2007. Of this number 100,000 would be due to labour turnover. The report identifies the areas of restaurant service and kitchen as areas with particularly high levels of labour turnover.

It is difficult to see the forecasted numbers being achieved unless all of the factors responsible for high staff turnover are clearly identified and addressed. CERT, the state tourism training agency, has carried out a number of 'where are they now?' research reports covering the period from 1966 – 1998. The main reasons given by respondents for leaving the industry were better pay elsewhere (22%) followed by irregular (17%) or long (15%) hours in the tourism industry. The majority of respondents (56%) had worked in between three and eight different establishments since graduating.

The Culinary Underbelly

The deeper issues of bullying and kitchen violence seem to have been either ignored or sanitised from official reports. My second work-placement during college was in a gourmet restaurant. This was my first experience of split shifts and the culture in this kitchen was one of fear and intimidation. The head chef was prone to violent outbursts and had a propensity to smash the odd plate off the wall for dramatic effect. I dreaded going back to work in the afternoons, repeated ridiculing had undermined my self-confidence, and this often led to my falling behind in my work. I began to come back to work an hour earlier to keep ahead, and my fortunes changed for the better. The following year I worked with a similarly volatile chef, who happened to be French. I learned a great deal about food in these two establishments but I also concluded that although they were both excellent cooks, their behaviour disqualified them from being considered professionals in the accepted use of that term. In my opinion violence or abusive behaviour have no place in a kitchen. A really good chef is well organised and instils confidence in his/her brigade. Like many a good teacher or parent, the good chef would only have to give a disapproving look to make one shape up! A.A. Gill, the critic, once generalised that chefs as a breed are socially inept and not very clever, and whilst arrogant in their kitchens, they are hopelessly gauche outside. Galvin (2003) refutes this and states that most good chefs are amazingly bright, generous, energetic individuals whose work is fiercely demanding. He explains what Gill considers gauche as merely not suffering fools easily.

Kitchens are run on an authoritarian hierarchical model. The word chef means chief, and there can only be one chief in a kitchen. Anthony Bourdain (2000) clearly states his perceptions of what he expected when joining the hospitality industry: apprenticeship in France, evil drunk chefs, crackpot owners, low pay and terrible working conditions. Johns and Menzel (1999) acknowledge kitchens as stressful places, because of the variable demand and the tight specifications placed upon the product: workload surges at peak times leave kitchens temporarily understaffed and a high turnover of employees means that the available staff may lack necessary skills. Another interesting source of stress identified in the research, particularly among leading restaurants, is the 'constant scrutiny' by Michelin inspectors, which in turn could precipitate violence. Johns and Menzel (1999) conclude that the acceptance of violence in top class kitchens is linked with the cult of the individual and artistic temperament.

There seems to be a deep seated cultural acceptance of violence as part of the striving of a perfectionist or the legitimised whim of iconised individuality.

I strongly condemn such violence. I am concerned that novices in the field learn that such behaviour is unacceptable. My aim is to prevent the novices from perpetuating the myth, modelling themselves on violent chefs, thereby maintaining a vicious circle of bullying.

Chefs historically were known to drink because of the unbearable heat and a culture where wine seemed as available as water. Up until recently a leading Dublin hotel had a 'sweat pint' system as part of the chef's terms and conditions of employment (Field notes 26 April 2003,p.3). This system and culture resulted in high levels of alcoholism among chefs. It has long been mooted that as long as there were hungry waiters, there would never be a thirsty chef. This inadvertently led to the invention of the Irish Coffee. The chef received his whiskey camouflaged in coffee topped with cream. On being found out the chef said he was inventing a new dish, an explanation that the management were keen to exploit. Mars and Nicod (1984) identified an institutionalised acceptance of 'fiddling' or 'the informal rewards system' among waiters, and state that those who benefit do so with the collusion of management. Gerry Galvin, former restaurateur and consultant chef describes hotel managers as culinary voyeurs, somewhat like the literary critics Brendan Behan described as eunuchs, who knew how the job was done, but could not do it themselves. Chivers (1973) describes chefs as having declined in terms of skill and in terms of status. Mennell (1996:199) agrees with this assessment and suggests that the dominance of management, with its disdain for the craft of cooking, has contributed to this decline in ascribed status.

The genre of the 'celebrity chef' is a fairly recent phenomenon. Many young people are drawn to the industry by the glamour and fame of these 'celebrity chefs'. The reality of the industry can soon cause them to change their mind. Professor David Foskett claimed in *Caterer & Hotelkeeper* magazine that 'Jamie's Kitchen', a celebrity chef reality television programme, has set the public's perception of professional cookery education back 50 years. Mennell (1996:197) suggests that although much has been written about the famous individual chefs throughout history, the vast majority of practitioners worked extremely hard, under difficult conditions for average remuneration. In hard times it was considered a good job. A colleague once recalled how his mother advised him to become a chef because he would be fed well and be in out of the rain. Conditions have vastly improved since the days of the coal fired range, where there was no controlling the heat in the kitchen. Frank

Farren, a retired chef (aged 77) recalls the war years when coal was in short supply: '*a ladle of oil under a stockpot would coax it to a fast boil but also fill the kitchen with black smoke*' (field notes 28 May 2003 p.4). Marie-Antoine Carême is said to have died at 48, burned out as much by the fumes of his ranges as by the flame of his genius. Technological advances have helped improve working conditions, but unfortunately some aspects of kitchen culture seem to have remained stagnant and escaped serious critique. George Orwell's (1933) description of scurrying waiters and shouting, ill-mannered chefs still has a resonance in some of today's kitchens.

Motivation and Nurture

So what are the factors that motivate chefs to continue working in this industry? Mullins (1999) explains the underlying concept of motivation as some driving force within individuals by which they attempt to achieve some goal in order to fulfil some need or expectation. These needs may be:

- Extrinsic (pay, security etc.)
- Intrinsic (job satisfaction, personal growth and development etc.) or
- Social (friendship, relationships, desire for status or dependency).

Armstrong (1996) outlines how extrinsic motivators can have an immediate and powerful effect, but that it does not necessarily last long. Intrinsic motivators, which are concerned with the 'quality of working life', are likely to have a deeper and longer-term effect because they are inherent in individuals and not imposed from outside.

A certain minority of culinary students however, working in temperamental, stressful up-market gourmet restaurant kitchens would appear to disprove Maslow's hierarchy of needs theory, since they are willing to trade both physiological and safety needs for the perceived social need of being accepted among their peers. But only a minority are willing to make this trade off. In my research, I asked head chefs involved in mentoring the BA Culinary Arts students the question 'what motivates your staff?' The response was as follows:

Training / Learning	54%
Teamwork and Co-operation	42%
Good atmosphere	54%

Mentoring

Good Communication	36%
Social aspect (parties, socializing, sport club, football etc.)	48%
Good Wages	36%
Leadership from top down	30%
Respect	18%
A good Appraisal System	18%
Good Hours	12%

The hospitality industry is a low paid industry but social aspects and teamwork can motivate. Eleanor Walsh from Eden Restaurant explains:

> We bring the staff out three times a year (social), have staff meetings once a month, run competitions. When you are buzzing the staff buzz off you.

Paul Keogh from Brasserie na Mara believes his staff are motivated by their ability to learn, and influence what goes on the menu:

> We help build a career for good staff and when they eventually decide to move on we help them in choosing their next job. We develop career chefs not industry fodder.

A chef must be responsible not just for the selection, preparation, cooking and presentation of food, but also for managing manpower, machinery and materials within a tight budget. Chefs today are measured as much by their profit margins as they are by satisfied customers. The following three factors, in my opinion, contribute to making it an even more stressful occupation:

Most chefs have received little or no management training. In 1996 I was executive head chef for a catering company, with 26 staff under my command and a turnover of £11 million. What had prepared me for this? What training had I received in managing people? Although I had attended advanced cookery courses since graduating from the professional cookery course it was clear that I would have benefited from more knowledge of organisational behaviour, and management studies.

Communication skills are essential in a kitchen but again formal communication training is very often ineffective. I illustrate this point to my students each year by recalling the tale (which I'm sure is universal) of the chef who asked a new kitchen porter to drain a pot of beef stock. When he returns to see a pot of bones waiting for him he explodes with anger on finding that the porter had poured the liquid (8 hours of gentle alchemy) down the drain. Had he clearly communicated that he wanted the stock kept and the bones discarded this situation would not have occurred.

One of the chefs' greatest challenges is the deep-rooted culture in catering that the show must go on regardless. This can lead to brigades trying to operate at peak performance whilst understaffed or with broken equipment. Frank Farren recalls the extreme dedication of a Miss Mullins, the manageress of the Central Hotel in Dublin in 1944, who on the very day she died had had to be restrained from getting out of bed to attend to the Board of Directors meeting that morning (Field notes 28 May 2003, p.2).

Erraught (1998) identified the gap in the training and education provision for head chefs. Head chefs have not been equipped in their college training with the management skills necessary to function as effective managers. The most popular chefs' course in Ireland taken either full time or by part-time 'day release', culminating in a Certificate in Professional Cookery, has been a second level training programme run by CERT and offered in various colleges throughout the country. Research in the mid 1990's culminated in the development of an honours degree in Culinary Arts in the Dublin Institute of Technology. This research engaged with the concepts of both mentoring and work-based learning. The literature shows overwhelming agreement on the importance of internships in hospitality education but also highlights the fact that little research has attempted to identify the elements that contribute to a satisfactory internship by collecting first hand reports from hospitality interns (Nelson, 1997). It was decided that with the development of this new degree course, a new model for professional internship also needed to be developed. It was proposed that the students would be assigned mentors with established positive reputations within the industry.

> The internship is one of the key integrating elements of the degree in culinary arts. It is a work based learning programme in a culinary arts professional environment and is a major contributor to the student's personal and professional development. (Course-Document, 1998)

Mentoring and Nurture

But what are the origins of mentoring? The term 'mentor' is over 3,000 years old and has its origins in Greek Mythology. When Odysseus went off to fight the Trojans, he left his trusted friend Mentor in charge of his household and his son's education. Mentor's name has been attached to the process of education and care by an older, experienced person. Mentors have been defined as high ranking, influential senior organisation members with advance experience and knowledge, who are committed to providing upward mobility and support to a protégé's professional career (Roche, 1979, Kram, 1995, Collins, 1983). Murray (1991) defines mentoring as

> a deliberate pairing of a more skilled or experienced person with a lesser skilled or experienced one, with the agreed-upon goal of having the lesser skilled person grow and develop specific competencies.

This mentoring relationship can be defined as an intense, lasting and professionally beneficial relationship between two individuals. In this relationship the more experienced and powerful individual, the mentor, guides, advises, and contributes in any number of ways the career of the less experienced, often younger, upwardly mobile protégé. Given this definition, it is not surprising that mentoring is not a common experience. The relationship requires a long-term reciprocal commitment of energy and time. It requires two people who come together in a mutually opportune time and who respect and enjoy one another enough to spend significant amounts of time together. It requires nurturing.

BA Culinary Arts

The BA Culinary Arts, initiated in the 1999/2000 academic year in the School of Culinary Arts and Food Technology, differed drastically from the second level certificate program previously in place. The guiding philosophy of the BA in Culinary Arts is to move beyond the utilitarian and traditional craft-based apprenticeship training in professional cookery towards an academic and scholarly form, which reflects high status knowledge thereby improving culinary arts education (Interim-Report, 1998). Hegarty (2001) explains that this new degree is

> aimed to *develop the intellectual capacity of the individual rather than the wrist-to-fingertip drills of the traditional apprenticeship and to maximise the potential of each individual student. Such philosophy has considerable potential advantages for it would enable culinary arts to stake a place for itself in higher education, where culinary arts teachers, for the first time would be taught and trained*

The programme has a strong student focus based on active student participation and exposure to a variety of teaching and learning opportunities. The aim is to move from the concept of teachers thinking of themselves as 'subject teachers' to becoming facilitators of student learning pursued through the medium of culinary arts (Hegarty, 2001). A programme in culinary arts needs to be a holistic educational experience for the student and not merely focused on the staffing needs of industry (Fuller, 1983). The following quote from Cleminson and Bradshaw (1996) mirrors the professional internship program's philosophy:

> In the first place, learning in the workplace must engage the interest and curiosity of the aspiring professional who must bring to the workplace a body of knowledge which can be challenged and reinterpreted in the workplace through practice and observation of practice.

The participating establishments are chosen carefully for the quality of the mentoring available rather than the size or status of the establishment. The goal of the programme is to facilitate accelerated learning (McKee, 1999), experiential learning (Kolb, 1984, Boud et al., 1993) and reflective practice (Schon, 1983).

Students on the first two years of the course spend six weeks annually on internship in Ireland. Some second year students choose to spend their internship in food related non-kitchen placements. Third year students spend eight weeks on an international internship. Students are required to keep a reflective/learning journal whilst on placement, and have regular meetings with their mentor to discuss progress. At a workshop for new mentors for the second cohort of the Internship programme the Head of School, Mr Joseph Hegarty, explained that the professional internship differed drastically from previous industry placement:

> We have changed the notion of industrial placement entirely... what happened is that students were taken and put into industry, nobody gave a care about them, then they came back, wrote a report that was usually a collection of brochures about the place, there was no critical assessment, there was no contribution and really and truly there has been no genuine contribution from this industry for the last seventy years.
> (JH 23/10/00)

In the early meetings with industry representatives (potential mentors) it took a while to convince some of them to move away from the short term 'what's in it for me now?' attitude to a more long-term strategic vision of increasing the pool of highly educated talented individuals that could help raise standards within the whole industry. Students were placed on a six week unpaid placement in many of the top establishments around the country. The mentors were asked to pay them not in monetary terms but by investing time in the students' learning. Research (Mac Con Iomaire 2001a) from the first two iterations highlighted the importance of students meeting their mentors, building a rapport prior to commencing the internship, and also the importance of receiving a proper induction. Induction involves the introduction of a new member of staff to the culture and environment, its policies, practices and to other members of staff. Mullins (1996 p.691) writes:

> A warm welcome, initial introductions, and a properly planned and designed induction programme will do much to reassure members, and aid their motivation and attitudes to their work performance.

The Ritz-Carlton group place great importance on the period of induction viewing the first few days as critical, as newly hired workers -'are like sponges'- will absorb good and bad practice.

Similar research (Mac Con Iomaire, 2001b) suggests that this internship programme causes industry participants to re-think how they treat existing staff and how their organisations might benefit from engaging with mentoring programmes. Also, this research showed that even in a climate of labour shortages, nearly all establishments involved in mentoring our students had good loyal staff and remarkably low levels of staff turnover. Zey (1984) confirms these findings concerning mentoring programmes and states that the result of the mentoring relationship can benefit the protégé, the mentor and the organisation. The protégé receives knowledge and skills, support, protection and promotion. The mentor may realise assistance on the job, prestige and loyalty. The organisation achieves development of employees, managerial success, reduces staff turnover, and increased productivity. Dr. Linda Phillips-Jones highlights some of the benefits of mentoring as follows;

> Organisations that want to attract high performers are offering (along with high salaries) other perks including formal mentoring opportunities. High potential candidates want to know they'll be developed by their new employers.

> Formalised mentoring shortens mentees learning curves. Mentees become more productive sooner because they gain knowledge, skills, and core values more quickly from mentor-guided experiences than from longer-term, traditional methods.'
> (Phillips-Jones, 2000)

Student Feedback

During my research I asked students to describe what the highlight of their internship was in order to identify the benefit of the internship from the students' perspective. The main themes emerging from this question were:

1. Gaining confidence and a sense of achievement particularly when given feedback or thanked for the job done.
2. The excitement of doing something for the first time.
3. Being challenged and rising to the challenge.

There were many comparisons between the highlights of the first and second iteration particularly learning new things and new ways of learning. The students really enjoyed the sense of teamwork in professional practice and the experience of working in a real live professional environment.

Students were also asked to comment on the lowlight of the internship. The main themes emerging from this question were:

1. The lack of pay.
2. The lack of time for learning.
3. Monotony of the work or insufficient work.
4. Feeling lonely, finding the work and environment tough, extremely tiring sometimes leading to tears.

Since fine-tuning certain aspects of the internship based on feedback from the first two iterations, our programme at the DIT is running extremely well. Mentors have become more comfortable in their roles and we are continuously attracting new mentors to the programme as it develops. Students have benefited also as the following excerpts from a student's reflective diary illustrate how the learning progressed:

Day 1

Today is my first day. I was nervous but not as bad as last year. One of the most crucial aspects that I want to receive from work experience is to increase my confidence. The head chef approached me at the end of my shift and asked me what exactly I would like to learn…he is very nice in that he doesn't want me doing too much as he doesn't want to exploit me, which I thought was very thoughtful.

Day 2

I am slowly beginning to learn the lunch menu by observing. The layout of the kitchen is a bit annoying; but I am going to try staying positive at all times. I like working here but cannot see myself staying for the summer, that is if I was asked.

Day 3

I feel a lot more easy now; I'm getting familiar with the lunch menu. Hopefully next week I will feel a lot more settled.

Week 3

This week has been going very fast. I am given more responsibility. I am getting to do the vegetarian and potatoes on my own. I am happy I am fitting in well. I believe I am learning a lot, I can see an improvement in my knife skills.

Week 4

I feel really good when I am given the responsibility to do so many tasks, it makes me feel part of the team and that they depend on me. I am getting more confident in myself and in the work I do.

Week 5

I got to do two new tasks today. I find everything takes twice as long when you don't know what you are doing. I had to even ask them to show me examples, but it has to be done, I would rather ask them than do the job wrong. Tomorrow we have a busy lunch. I feel part of the team

Week 6

Today was a good day for me. I got the responsibility of doing pasta to make noodle cakes. I am feeling more confident and I am enjoying myself as well. It was a slow process starting off but looking back I believe that I have gained a great deal and learned not just about my ability but also what it is like in a new environment. It has been a valuable lesson in my course.

This student was asked to stay on for the summer at the end of the professional internship period and accepted the offer.

During the first year of the programme 80% of students enjoyed their internship and 90% of industry found their role as mentor fulfilling. One industry respondent didn't find the role fulfilling because he wasn't sure that he was making any headway with the student. The number of students who enjoyed the internship had risen to 90% in the second iteration and this number has risen to 96% among the fourth and most recent cohort. The general mood is summed up by the following comments:

It was a blast, I love the place, the people, the work everything.

I learned an extreme amount and got on well with everyone.

The weeks have flown by. The staff were very friendly and encouraging. There was one night that was very busy and the buzz from the kitchen and service was brilliant.

Of the few who didn't enjoy their internship the reasons are explained in their comments:

Kind of in-between: I got to see an actual kitchen at work but I sometimes felt like I didn't have a clue. I like to know what I am doing.

Low standard of food, I did the same thing every day.

I felt he didn't want me to learn his tricks of the trade as I wasn't going to be there long term.

This last comment shows there are still some of the old style chefs around who feel that to have knowledge is to have power. I would suggest that sharing knowledge is much more empowering.

Conclusion

In conclusion time invested in nurturing culinary talent, in my opinion, is time well spent. The philosophy of mentoring needs to be generalised into the wider culinary arts community in order to transform the nature of the kitchen into a nurturing environment. This is not going to be completed overnight. Let me make it clear, there is no place for violence or bullying in any kitchen. Through my research I have identified that establishments that provide good learning and working environments have little difficulty in recruiting and retaining staff. The experience gained from mentoring students from the BA Culinary Arts has caused employers to reflect on how they treat existing staff. Successful mentoring does take time and depends on matching the right mentor with the right mentee. We have begun to encourage industry away from the short term 'what's in it for me?' mindset to a more long-term vision of making the industry more professional. This year's graduates are the mentors of the future. Lets hope nurture will continue to influence nature for the better.

Bibliography

ARMSTRONG, M. (1996) *Personnel Management Practice,* (London: Kogan Page).

BORD-FÁILTE (2001) *Tourism Facts 2000,* (Dublin: Bord Fáilte).

BOUD, D., COHEN, R. AND WALKER, D. (Eds.) (1993) *Using Experience for Learning,* (Buckingham: Society for Research into Higher Education & Open University Press).

BOURDAIN, A. (2000) *Kitchen Confidential.* (London: Bloomsbury Publishing).

CERT (2002) *125,000 New Recruits Required by Tourism Industry*, CERT, Dublin. Available from www.cert.ie/about_cert/press_releases [Accessed 29 May 2003]

CHIVERS, T.S. (1973) The Proletarianisation of a Service Worker, *Sociological Review*, Vol. 21 pp.633-656

CLEMINSON, A. AND BRADFORD, S. (1996) Professional Education: the relationship between 'academic' and experiential learning, *Journal of Vocational Education and Training,* 48, 3 249-259.

COURSE-DOCUMENT (1998) Document in support of an application to academic council, Dublin Institute of Technology for a Bachelor of Arts Degree in Culinary Arts.

COLLINS, N. W. (1983) *Professional women and their mentors,* (Englewood Cliffs, New Jersey: Prentice Hall).

ERRAUGHT, E. (1998) Recognition of The Gap in The Training and Education Provision for Head Chefs, Masters Thesis, Dublin City University.

FULLER, J. (1983) Hotel Management Education In *The Management of Hospitality* (Eds, Cassee, E. and Reuland, R.),(Oxford: Pergamon Press).

GALVIN, G. (2003) Gerry Galvin's Stockpot, *Food and Wine Magazine* (June edition), Dublin: Smurfit Publishing, p.52.

HEGARTY, J. (2001) Standing the Heat, *Unpublished Ed.D Thesis,* University of Sheffield.

HOQUE, K. (2000) Human Resource Management in the Hotel Industry: Strategy, innovation and performance, (London: Routledge).

JOHNS, N. & MENZEL, P. (1999) 'If you can't stand the heat…Kitchen Violence and Culinary Art. *International Journal of Hospitality Management*, 18, 99-109

KEATING, M. AND MCMAHON, L. (2000) Human Resource Management Practice in the Irish Hotel Industry In *Irish Academy of Management Conference.*

KOLB, D. A. (1984) Experiential Learning: experience as a source of learning and development, (Englewood Cliffs, New Jersey: Prentice Hall).

KRAM, K. E. (1995) Mentoring at work: Developmental relationships in organisational life, (Glenview, IL: Scott Foresman).

MAC CON IOMAIRE, M. (2001a) An Evaluation of the Professional Internship component in the BA Culinary Arts. *An Action Research study of the first and second iterations of the Professional Internship in order to improve practice* (Unpublished Thesis) Dublin Institute of Technology.

MAC CON IOMAIRE, M. (2001b) To investigate what effects (if any) the mentoring programme within the B.A. Culinary Arts Professional Internship, is having on the culture of the participating establishments (Unpublished HRM research paper).

MCKEE, L. (1999) Accelerated Learning In *Gower Handbook of Training and Development* (Ed, Landale, A.), (Aldershot: Gower).

MARS, G. AND NICOD, M. (1984) *The World of Waiters*, (London: George Allen & Unwin).

MENNELL, STEPHEN (1996) *All Manners of Food*, (Chicago: University of Illinois Press).

MULLINS, L. J. (1999) *Management and Organisational Behaviour,* (London: Pitman Publishing).

MURRAY, M. (1991) *Beyond the Myths and Magic of Mentoring,* (San Francisco: Jossey-Bass Publisher).

NELSON, A. A. (1997) Hospitality Internships: the Effects of job dimensions on student satisfaction, CHRIE Conference Proceedings, Rhode Island.

ORWELL, G. (1933) *Down and Out in Paris and London,* (Harmondsworth: Penguin).

PHILLIPS-JONES, D. L. (2000) Why mentoring in these economic times? [Online], Available: www.mentoringgroup.com/ideas.html [2000,May 16]

ROCHE, G. R. (1979) Much ado about mentors, *Harvard Business Review,* 57,14-28.

SCHON, D. (1983) The Reflective Practitioner: How Professionals Think in Action, (New York: Basic Books).

ZEY, M. G. (1984) *The Mentor Connection,* (Homewood, IL: Dow Jones-Irwin).

The Earth's golden oil: the shelf-life of Nurture
A vertical tasting of Manni extra virgin olive oil 2001 and 2002

Armando Manni

Extra virgin olive oil is a fruit juice

Extra virgin olive oil is simply a centrifuged fruit juice. Because of this it has a wonderful taste and beneficial effects on human health, but it is also very fragile.

The extract consists almost entirely of lipids, but while the major part of extra virgin olive oil consists of fatty acids (>95%) bound to glycerol, a large number of components are present only in small amounts [1] These so-called minor compounds can be subdivided into phenols, tocopherols, flavour compounds, hydrocarbons and sterols, and are of great importance. Some of them have been reported to be beneficial to human health by preventing such injurious or deleterious processes as oxygen free-radical induction of lipid oxidation; [2] others improve the stability and are responsible for the unique flavour of the extra virgin olive oil. More than 70 compounds are believed to contribute to the unique flavour and taste of olives and extra virgin olive oil.

The oil, a potent antioxidant

The phenols in extra virgin olive oil act as potent antioxidants in our blood[3], more potent than vitamin E, which, in any case, extra virgin olive oil contains. This is essential for human health because the uncontrolled oxidative processes that produce free radicals[4] contribute to the development of heart and circulatory disease[5] Phenols also possess anti-inflammatory and immunostimulant properties that have a preventive action against some carcinomas, such as those of the breast, colon and digestive tract and those related to hormonal causes[6].

Today, researchers conclude that many of the cardioprotective and anti-cancer effects of the Mediterranean diet are due to the use of extra virgin olive oil - especially the antioxidant activity of the phenols[7]. The oil protects against much more than coronary heart disease, hypertension, thrombosis, carcinomas, diabetes, rheumatoid arthritis, obesity and the rest[8].

The elevated content of antioxidants contributes, in fact, to counteracting cognitive problems related to cerebral aging and also to longevity. In Italy and Greece life expectancy is greater than in the countries of northern Europe despite the continuing greater percentage of smokers[9].

The fragility of the oil: what are the enemies?

Research indicates it is important to consume extra virgin olive oil that contains a high level of phenols. Even more important, these phenols must be intact and alive[10]. This means that we need to improve research on how extra virgin olive oil is extracted and, at the same time, devote all the attention we can to improving preservation of the oil[11]. This will give us an extra virgin olive oil with great taste, great longevity and great health benefits[12].

The scientific community has long known that the life of an extra virgin olive oil is marked by two events: hydrolysis and oxidation. These phenomena can occur naturally in the fruit from enzymes[13] and then, after the extraction of the oil, can be increased by external factors, such as light and oxygen[14].

In fact, the level of minor compounds in extra virgin olive oil, higher after extraction, drops over time. But, as the Israeli researcher T. Gutfinger[16] showed in 1981, oxidative stability depends directly on the presence of phenols. So, we need to preserve them.

Light, temperature, and oxygen contribute to the degradation of phenols

Gordon and others[17] found changes in oil quality with the presence of oxygen in the bottles (alpha tocopherol was reduced 20% after 2 months and 92% after 12 months). As the level of antioxidants decreased, the concentration of polyunsaturated fatty acids started oxidation (after 8 months). Okogeri[18] studied the changes in the concentrations of tocopherols, total phenols, and complex phenols owing to environmental conditions. Under diffused light, 45% of the phenols were lost in 4 months, whereas tocopherols were decomposed by 79% during the same period. The total phenol count was reduced 57-63% in 6 months. When the oil was stored in the dark, tocopherols and total phenols exhibited similar profiles of degradation, reducing by 39-45% in the first 6 months and 50-62% in 12 months. The levels of the above antioxidants were further related to peroxide formation. Remaining levels of these compounds, at Peroxide Value = 20 meq/kg, ranged between 50% and 73% under diffused light and between 40% and 62% in the dark. Psomiadou and colleagues observed changes in polar phenols in relation to the presence of oxygen recommending an urgent change in the practice of packaging.

The Quality of packaged olive oil depends on temperature, packaging, oxygen permeability and light transmittance

Ultraviolet radiation (UV rays) is particularly damaging[19] since it contributes to starting self-replicating alteration processes (by formation of peroxides). Several studies show how light increases the oxidation process (as early as the second month after bottling) and suggest keeping the oil in the dark. Kanavouras and Hernandez (2002) found that the quality of packaged olive oil depends on temperature, packaging, oxygen permeability and light transmittance. Extra virgin olive oil packaged in ½Lt glass, PET, and PVC bottles was stored at 15°C, 30°C, 40°C under light or dark conditions for one year and were withdrawn every two months. Olive oil flavour compounds, peroxide index (PI) and the UV spectrophotometric extinction coefficient at 232 nm (K232) were recorded. Olive oil stored in glass, in the dark, and at 15°C showed very low oxidation indexes and essentially maintained its original flavour profile for at least 10 months. Olive oil packaged in PET or PVC bottles at 15°C was altered after 6 months. Higher temperature and the presence of light increased oxidation and chemically altered the oil. The beneficial high content of minor compounds in the extra virgin olive oil can be maintained by keeping it in a cool, dark place, away from oxygen[20].

Keeping the oil intact and alive

Ultraviolet Rays: Bottles of oil are usually stored under light in stores and at home, and unfortunately it is a marketing strategy of most producers to use transparent glass for bottling (instead of using a dark highly protective glass), even if it allows the light to shorten the "life" of minor compounds, therefore, shortening the "life" of extra virgin olive oil. This is because consumers want to see the green colour of the olive oil. Additionally, although it is illegal, producers can alter the colour of the oil with the addition of chlorophyll. We have been able to guarantee (through a complete process of protection) the absence of contact between oil and light, preventing the formation of peroxides, and in the end keeping the oil "alive" by a protection of 99.99% against UV rays.

Oxygen

The oil's other great enemy is oxygen. The oxidation process begins during the pressing of the fruit in the mixing chamber and continues in the bottle where the oil is stored for a long time. For this reason, researchers indicate that the best way to manage the oxidation process of extra virgin olive oil is to decrease the oxidation process in the bottle. One must do this by removing any oxygen in the bottle and preventing oxygen from re-entering once the bottling process is complete. In collaboration with the University we have done this. The results are a stable extra virgin olive oil with a long shelf life (complete results are available at www.manni.biz).

What happens after we open the bottle?

The processes outlined above go a long way in delivering an oil of great quality with a high level of phenols and a very low level of oxidation until we open the bottle at our home. So what happens after we open the bottle? Today, thanks to international scientific research, we know that the minor compounds of the extra virgin olive oil are important for human health and for the taste and stability of the extra virgin olive oil; the amount of phenolic compounds in extra virgin olive oil correlates strongly with its stability and lower lipid peroxidation. Even so, it is more economical for producers to use large bottles (between 500 cc and 1500 cc), often made of transparent glass. In the hands of the consumer, these economy-size bottles are opened and then kept under lights (UV rays), at room temperature, in direct contact with oxygen, often for months. This kills the oil, destroying its best features, the natural antioxidants, lowering both its shelf life and its beneficial effects on health.

Therefore, we propose a change in habits. The use of a small bottle keeps the oil at its best. The bottle should be opened and the oil used while it is still fresh - before oxygen, temperature and light alter the minor compounds and lipids.

Following this approach, a great result

Taking care of extra virgin olive oil (grove management, fruit pressing, oil storing and bottling) means taking care of ourselves.

The results of this approach can be seen in the chemical values of the oil. We analyze our extra virgin olive oils every four months, publishing most of the data on our Web site. Unfortunately, we know of no other such available data. Normally, extra virgin olive oil is analyzed only after pressing, as required by law for the commercial classification (extra virgin or lower grades). Once the certification has been granted, the oil is not subjected to any other analysis. Therefore, as consumers, we can't be sure of the quality of an oil that may reach our tables ten months after pressing. Moreover, the law does not ask for a phenol profile analysis but only for the total phenol content (making it impossible to check the aging factor - hydrolysis - of the phenols).

At the Oxford Symposium vertical tasting of our 2001 and 2002 oils we presented the data of the phenols through May 2003. The analyses of the phenol components were made by the Department of Pharmaceutical Science of the University of Florence. We were able to show how little the phenol content of the oil changed in the course of eighteen months, after pressing and bottling. Compare also the phenol values of the 2002 bottling of PER ME analyzed at 698 mg. per liter with the minimum legal phenol requirements for classification as "an extra virgin olive oil TOSCANO IGP" (Protected Geographical Indication) set at 60mg. per liter.

Per Mio Figlio Extra Virgin Oil 2001 and 2002 harvests at November 2003

Parameter	2001 Harvest	2002 Harvest	Maximum IGP Toscano limit
Acidity	0.37	0.32	1
No. Peroxides	7.0	7.4	20
K 232	2.09	0.2	2.4
K 270	0.22	0.19	0.2
Delta K	0	0.01	0.01

This oil was created in the context of a scientific research project in collaboration with the Department of Pharmaceutical Science, University of Florence, Italy.

Literature

APARICIO R., RODA L., ALBI, M.A., GUTIERREZ, F., *Effect of various compounds on virgin olive oil stability measured by Rancimat,* J Agric. Food Chem. 1999, 47:4150–5.

BALDIOLI M., SERVILI M., PERRETTI G, MONTEDORO G.F., Antioxidant activity of tocopherols and phenolic compounds of virgin olive oil, JAOCS. 1996 73:1589–93.

BARTOLI L., FERNANDEZ-BANARES F., NAVARRO E. et al., Effect of olive oil on early and late events of colon carcinogenesis in rats: modulation of arachidonic acid metabolism and local prostaglandin E(2) synthesis, Gut. 2000 46:191-9.

BONANOME A, PAGNAN A., CARUSO D. et al., *Evidence of postprandial absorption of olive oil phenols in humans,* Nutr. Metab Cardiovasc. Dis. 2000, 10:111–20.

BOSKOU, D., Olive oil composition. In *Olive Oil: Chemistry and Technology,* Boskou, d., Ed., (Champaign, Illinois: AOCS Press, 1996): pp52-83.

CARUSO D., BERRA B., GIAVARINI F., CORTESI N., FEDELI E., GALLI G., *Effect of virgin olive oil phenolic compounds on in vitro oxidation of human low density lipoproteins.* Nutr.Metab. Cardiovasc.Dis.1999, 9:102–7.

FABIANI, R., DE BARTOLOMEO A., ROSIGNOLI P., SERVILI M., MONTEDORO G.F. AND MOROZZI G., *Cancer chemoprevention by hydroxytyrosol isolated from virgin olive oil through G1 cell cycle arrest and apoptosis.* Eur.J.Cancer Prev. 2002, 11:352-358,

GASPAROLI A., AND FEDELI E., *Preliminary investigation on shelf-life of bottled extra virgin olive oils,* La rivista italiana delle sostanze grasse, 1990, 2.

GIOVANNINI C., STRAFACE E., MODESTI D., CONI E., CANTAFORA A., DE VINCENZI M., MALORNI W., MASELLA R., *Tyrosol, the major olive oil biophenol, protects against oxidized-LDL-induced injury in Caco-2 cells.* The Journal of nutrition. 1999, 129(7):1269–1277.

GORDON M.H., MURSI E., ROSSELL J.B., Assessment of thin-film oxidation with ultraviolet irradiation for predicting the oxidative stability of edible oils. Journal of the American Oil Chemists' Society 1994, 71(12) 1309–1313.

GRUPPO ITALIANO PER LO STUDIO DELLA SOPRAVVIVENZA NELL'INFARTO MIOCARDICO, Dietary supplementation with n-3 polyunsaturated fatty acids and vitamin E after myocardial infarction: results of the GISSI-Prevenzione trial, Lancet.1999, 354:447–55.

GUTIERREZ F, FERNANDEZ JL., Determinant parameters and components in the storage of virgin olive oil. Prediction of storage time beyond which the oil is no longer of "extra" quality. J Agric Food Chem. 2002 Jan 30;50(3):571-7.

GUTIERREZ F., JIMENEZ B., RUIZ A., ALBI M.A., Effect of olive ripeness on the oxidative stability of virgin olive oil extracted from the varieties picual and hojiblanca and on the different components involved. J Agric.Food Chem. 1999, 47:121–7.

JHA P., FLATHER M., LONN E., FARKOUH M., YUSUF S., The antioxidant vitamins and cardiovascular disease: a critical review of epidemiologic and clinical trial data. Ann.Intern.Med. 1996, 124:934.

KANAVOURAS A. AND R. J. HERNANDEZ., *Quality issues and shelf life evaluation of packaged olive oil in glass and plastic containers.* 2002 Annual Meeting and Food Expo - Anaheim, California.

KATAN M.B., ZOCK P.L., MENSINK R.P., *Dietary oil, serum lipoproteins, and coronary heart disease.* AmJClinNutr. 1995, 61:1368S-73S.

KAYA A., TEKIN A.R., ONER M.D., Oxidative stability of sunflower and olive oils: comparison between a modified active oxygen method and long term storage. Food science technology. 1993, 26:464–468.

KIRITSAKIS A., DUGAN L.R., *Studies in photooxidation of olive oil.* Journal of the American Oil Chemists' Society. 1985, 62(5):892–896.

KUBO A., LUNDE C.S., KUBO I., *Antimicrobial activity of the olive oil flavor compounds.* J Agric.Food Chem. 1995, 43:1629–33.

LA VECCHIA C., NEGRI E., FRANCESCHI S. et al., *Olive oil, other dietary fats, and the risk of breast cancer (Italy).* Canc Cause Control. 1995, 6:545-50.

MAESTRO R., GARCIA J.M., CASTELLANO J.M., *Changes in polyphenol content of olives stored in modified atmospheres.* HortScience 1993, 28 (7) 749.

MANNA C., GALLETTI P., CUCCIOLLA V., MOLTEDO O., LEONE A., ZAPPIA V., The protective effect of the olive oil polyphenol (3,4–dihydroxyphenyl)-ethanol counteracts reactive oxygen metabolite-induced cytotoxicity in Caco-2 cells. J Nutr. 1997, 127:286–92.

MARTIN MORENO J.M., WILLET W.C. GORGOJO L. et al., *Dietary fat, olive oil intake and breast cancer risk.* Int J Cancer 1994, 58:774-80.

MASELLA R., CANTAFORA A., MODESTI D. et al., Antioxidant activity of 3,4–DHPEA-EA and protocatechuic acid: a comparative assessment with other olive oil biophenols. 1999 Redox.Rep.:4:113–21.

MONTELEONE E., CAPORALE G., CARLUCCI A., PAGLIARINI E., *Optimisation of extra virgin olive oil quality.* Journal of the science of food and agriculture. 1998, 77(1):31–37.

OKOGERI O, TASIOULA-MARGARI M., Changes occurring in phenolic compounds and alpha-tocopherol of virgin olive oil during storage. Agric Food Chem. 2002 Feb 27;50(5):1077-80.

OWEN R.W., GIACOSA A., HULL W.E., HAUBNER R., SPIEGELHALDER B., BARTSCH H., *The antioxidant/anticancer potential of phenolic compounds isolated from olive oil*. Eur.J Cancer; 2000, 36:1235–47.

OWEN R.W., MIER W., GIACOSA A., HULL W.E., SPIEGELHALDER B., BARTSCH H., Phenolic compounds and squalene in olive oils: the concentration and antioxidant potential of total phenols, simple phenols, secoiridoids, lignans and squalene. Food Chem. Toxicol. 2000, 38:647–59.

PETRONI A., BLASEVICH M., SALAMI M., PAPINI N., MONTEDORO G.F., GALLI C., *Inhibition of platelet aggregation and eicosanoid production by phenolic components of olive oil*. Thromb.Res. 1995, 78:151–60.

PIRISI F.M., ANGIONI A., BANDINO G., CABRAS P., GUILLOU C., MACCIONI E., RENIERO F., *Photolysis of alpha-tocopherol in olive oils and model systems*. Journal of agricultural and food chemistry. 1998 46(11):4529–4533.

PSOMIADOU E, TSIMIDOU M., *Stability of virgin olive oil. 2. Photo-oxidation studies*. J Agric Food Chem. 2002 Feb 13;50(4):722-7.

RASTRELLI L., PASSI S., IPPOLITO F., VACCA G., DE SIMONE F., Rate of degradation of alpha-tocopherol, squalene, phenolics, and polyunsaturated fatty acids in olive oil during different storage conditions. J Agric Food Chem. 2002 Sep 25;50(20):5566-70.

STONEHAM M., GOLDACRE M., SEAGROATT V., GILL L., *Olive oil, diet and colorectal cancer: an ecological study and a hypothesis*. J Epidemiol Community Health. 2000 Oct;54(10):756-60.

TATEO F., CUCURACHI A., CUCURACHI S., *Quality and shelf-life problems of the olive oil*. Developments in food science. 1993, 33:451–467.

VISIOLI F., GALLI C., Oleuropein protects low density lipoprotein from oxidation. Life Sci. 1994, 55:1965–71.

Notes

1. Boskou, 1996.
2. Baldioli *et al.*, 1996
3. Visioli and Galli, 1994; Caruso *et al.*, 1999
4. Manna *et al.*, 1997; Giovannini *et al.*, 1999; Masella *et al.*, 1999
5. Jha *et al.* 1996; Gruppo Italiano Studio Sopravvivenza Infarto Miocardico, 1999
6. Owen *et al.*, 2000
7. Katan *et al.* 1995; Petroni *et al.*, 1995; Bonanome *et al.*, 2000; Fabiani *et al.*, 2002
8. Martin Moreno, 1994; La Vecchia *et al.*, 1995; Trichopoulou *et al.* 1995; Bartoli *et al.*, 2000; Stoneham *et al.*, 2000
9. Further information can be found on the European Union website: http://europa.eu.int/comm/agriculture/prom/olive/medinfo/uk_ie/factsheets/index.htm
10. Monteleone *et al.*, 1998
11. Tateo *et al.*, 1993
12. Kubo *et al.*, 1995
13. Kubo *et al.*, 1995
14. Gasparoli and Fedeli,1990
15. Department of Food Engineering and Biotechnology, Institute of Technology, Haifa
16. Gordon et al, (1994); Aparicio et al., (1999). Rastrelli et al. (2002)
17. Okogeri and Tasioula-Margari (2002)
18. Kiritsakis and Dugan, 1985; Pirisi *et al.*, 1998
19. Maestro et al, 1993

Byron, Bread and Butter

Antony Peattie

The poet Lord Byron (1788-1824) objected to shy, awkward British girls:

The Nursery still lisps out in all they utter;
Besides, they always smell of Bread and Butter.'
Beppo, stanza 39

Now condemned as triply wicked (wheat, carbohydrates and dairy fat), bread and butter was once the archetypal nursery food and a classic item at breakfast, the meal taken in the day's infancy.

Bread is, or was the staff of life. Butter mediates, it lubricates transitions, between primordial nature and culture, between suckling infancy and chomping adulthood, as liquid milk is separated and churned to make a solid. Making bread and butter involves using a knife in two paradoxical ways, for the potentially fatal act of cutting, and the conciliatory art of spreading to conjoin the rough and the smooth. As the traditional prerogative of the Mother, and the poor man's meal, 'bread and butter' garnered the metaphorical meaning of livelihood.

Werther had a love for Charlotte,
Such as words could never utter,
Would you know how first he met her?
She was cutting bread and butter.

It was a memorable encounter, but Thackeray was embroidering on the novel *The Sorrows of Young Werther*. According to Goethe, Werther first sees Charlotte cutting slices of bread and distributing them among six children. There is no mention of butter on the 'Schwarzbrot'.

Lewis Carroll refers to bread and butter to evoke the world of childhood in *Alice's Adventures Through the Looking-Glass* and Charles Dickens uses it to highlight the theme of parenting in the second and penultimate chapters of *Great Expectations*. Its significance for Byron reflects his attitude to food in general and highlights a pattern in his relations with women in England.

From late adolescence Byron suffered from recurrent bouts of anorexia nervosa. The illness itself was not recognized or named until 49 years after Byron's death. A retrospective diagnosis of his condition was first made by Wilma Paterson in 1982, and has been generally accepted.[1]

It began when he was 19 and quarrelling violently with his obese, embittered mother. She swung between bullying and spoiling her only child. Byron's closest friend John Cam Hobhouse described it as 'now kicking and now kissing' him.[2] Byron was born into an unhappy marriage. His father Captain Byron only married the heiress Catherine Gordon in 1785 for her money and abandoned his wife and son when the boy was two. Byron was born with a misshapen right foot and he never forgot 'the feeling of horror and humiliation that came over him, when his mother, in one of her fits of passion, called him "a lame brat."'[3] Accurate or not, what matters is what Byron remembered, the 'coldness with which his mother had received his caresses in infancy, and the frequent taunts on his personal deformity with which she had wounded him'.[4]

Precociously, Byron repeatedly found consolation in idealised passions for girls, who were older, related to him and called Mary. Before he was eight, he fell in love with his distant cousin Mary Duff, a 'lovely Peri' or fairy.[5]

When he was nine he was sexually abused by his nurse May Gray, who was also 'perpetually beating him,' so that 'his bones sometimes ached from it'.[6]

The 5th Lord Byron died in 1798 and Byron inherited the title. He was ten. Mrs Byron and her son moved from Aberdeen and rented a house in Southwell, near Newstead Abbey, the Nottinghamshire estate that came with the title. Byron entered English society embarrassed by his mother, his limp and his Scottish accent. When Mrs Byron gave a party, her son '"was so shy that she had to send for him three times before she could persuade him to come into the drawing-room, to play with the young people at a round game."'[7] He bit his nails, which prompted her 'sudden and violent Ejaculations of Disgust accompanied by a Box on the ear or Hands.'[8]

At the age of 12 he fell in love with his cousin Mary Parker. One 'of the most beautiful of evanescent beings', she 'died about a year or two afterwards' from consumption and 'looked as if she had been made out of a rainbow... – all beauty and peace'.[9]

He was described as 'a fat, bashful boy, with his hair combed straight over his forehead'.[10] It looked as though Byron had inherited his mother's plumpness. His bashfulness never left him. When he was 34 he impressed an American woman as 'a sensitive, gracefully bashful boy – a young Jove, hiding his thunderbolts.'[11]

Another of the ways Byron coped with women was to pursue the unavailable. At 15 he fell in love with his distant kinswoman and neighbour Mary Chaworth, who was about two years older than he was. The relationship was blighted: her ancestor had been killed in a duel by the fifth Lord Byron and she was already engaged to marry someone else. It ended when Byron was either told of, or overheard, her saying to her maid, 'Do you think I could care anything for that lame boy?' The remark struck him, he said, 'like a shot through his heart.'[12] Mary Chaworth's marriage later broke down. When she wrote to Byron, he fled from her advances.

Byron began to express dissatisfaction with his figure in adolescence, almost as soon as he started to complain that he was oppressed by his 'despotic' mother.[13]

A month after he went up to Trinity College, Cambridge in October 1805 he was weighing himself regularly and was annoyed, when the family lawyer John Hanson called him 'Jolly'. In the first letter that Byron wrote from Cambridge to his half-sister the Hon. Augusta Byron he explained: 'that fool Hanson in his *vulgar Idiom*, by the word Jolly did not mean Fat, but High Spirits'. Far from 'increasing', putting on weight, Byron boasted that he had lost one pound (0.45 kilo) in a fortnight.[14]

In January 1807 he weighed 14 stone and 6 lb (202 pounds; 91.63 kilos) though he was only 5 feet eight and a half inches tall (1.74 metres). He was obese, according to the Body Mass Index, which recommends, 'Should lose weight'.

He only began to diet, when he felt trapped in Southwell with his mother. During the previous summer he had escaped by running away to London. But his accumulated debts would not even allow him to return to Cambridge. Reduced to the dependent status of an infant, Byron established and manifested his independence by altering his shape.

Within a year he lost four stone (56 pounds; 25.4 kilos). The chubby child turned into an emaciated adult, whose pallor made him resemble an 'Alabaster Vase lighted up within.'[15] Freeing himself from his inherited body, the 'bonds of clay' (as he put it), should have signified his escape from the '*Fetters* of [his] domestic Tyrant Mrs Byron'.[16] But the change remained skin deep: the process would have to be repeated.

While he was abroad, 1809 -1811, Byron engaged in a platonic affair with an older, married woman in Malta, but otherwise conformed to local habits and slept with boys. He continued to diet obsessively, occasionally binging, then purging and starving himself and his 'use or abuse of Acids' damaged his health.[17] 'I told him of the baneful effects of vinegar &c,' a sympathetic witness reported, four years after his first diet, 'but he tells me he would rather not exist than be large; and so he is a pale, languid-looking young man who seems as if he could not walk upright from sheer weakness.'[18]

Samuel Rogers invited Byron to his house on 4 November 1811. 'When we sat down to dinner, I asked Byron if he would take soup? "No; he never took soup;" - Would he take some fish? "No; he never took fish." - Presently I asked if he would eat some mutton? "No; he never ate mutton." - I then asked if he would take a glass of wine? "No; he never tasted wine." - It was now necessary to inquire what he *did* eat and drink; and the answer was, "Nothing but hard biscuits and soda-water." Unfortunately, neither hard biscuits nor soda-water were at hand; and he dined upon potatoes bruised down on his plate and drenched with vinegar.'[19]

Biscuits and soda-water represent an epicure's version of that standard starvation diet, bread and water – 'which by the way', Byron remarked in 1823, '– are very nourishing – and sufficient – if good of their kind.'[20] He tried to limit his intake to six biscuits and four bottles a day in 1813.[21]

His shyness with women was exacerbated when he grew 'foolishly fond' of one of the servants at Newstead Abbey. She was unfaithful to him. On 16 February 1812 he forbade a friend to mention a woman again in any letter, or even allude to the existence of the sex. He also refused to read a word of the feminine gender.

In his fiction he continued his first strategy for dealing with women, to idealise them. As early as 1830 John Galt remarked on 'the icy metaphysical glitter of Byron's amorous allusions' and his 'bodiless admiration of beauty, and objectless enthusiasm of love'.[22] The pattern endured for much, but certainly not all, of Byron's life and work. He wrote *Beppo* and most of *Don Juan* during a prolonged period of normal eating. But all his life Byron 'disliked seeing women eat, or to have their company at dinner'. An observer explained that this was 'from a wish to believe, if possible, in their more etherial nature'.[23]

The Maniac and the Mathematician

His poem *Childe Harold* was published at the beginning of March 1812 and attracted the particular attention of two formidable women, the 27 year old mother of two young children,

Lady Caroline Lamb, and the virginal, 20 year old Annabella Milbanke. Byron had a passionate affair with one of them and married the other. They were cousins and apparently opposites, in terms of character and experience. But they both stood out from the crowd by not pursuing him, at a time when, as Lady Morgan observed, 'The women suffocated him.'[24]

Lady Caroline Lamb, the wilful, beautiful daughter of the Third Earl of Bessborough and niece of the famous Georgiana, Duchess of Devonshire, had married William Lamb M.P. seven years before. She insisted on meeting the author of *Childe Harold*. 'I was one night at Lady Westmoreland's', she remembered later; 'the women were all throwing their heads at him. Lady Westmoreland led me up to him. I looked earnestly at him, and turned on my heel.'

Lady Holland presented her to Lord Byron on 24 March and he visited her the next day at Melbourne House. There, another young lady, who was more simply dressed than the rest of the assembly, kept her distance from him. Anne Isabella Milbanke, known as Annabella, a spoilt, only child, was born 15 years into her parents' marriage, when her mother was already 40, after a long and difficult labour. Her father was Lady Melbourne's brother; William Lamb was her cousin.

Byron fell in love with Lady Caroline Lamb – 'the cleverest most agreeable, absurd, amiable, perplexing, dangerous fascinating little being that lives now or ought to have lived 2000 years ago'.[25] For the first time he was attracted to a woman of his own rank and intellectual reach. But Lady Caroline was also the first of the wild women in his love life, as 'dangerous fascinating' as the savage animals he favoured as pets, such as ferocious dogs, a bear, a civet-cat, a badger and a fox.

Byron once complained that he had been more ravished than any body since the Trojan war. The scenario recurred so often that it suggests he sought it out, that he was excited *and* threatened by a potential fiendishness in the women he loved. 'Mrs Byron *furiosa*' was the first in Byron's gallery of dominant females.[26] 'And femininely meaneth furiously,' his Assyrian self-portrait Sardanapalus remarks, 'Because all passions in excess are female'. (*Sardanapalus*, III, i, 380f)

The liaison between Byron and Lady Caroline Lamb burned fiercely. But her increasingly outrageous behaviour threatened to involve both of them in scandal. She had to be persuaded to loosen her grip.

That autumn Byron had a brief affaire with an Italian artiste of the Opera. 'I only wish she did not swallow so much supper,' he complained, 'chicken wings – sweetbreads, – custards – peaches & *Port* wine – a woman should never be seen eating or drinking, unless it be *lobster sallad* & *Champagne*, the only truly feminine and becoming viands.'[27]

Lady Caroline was not to be diverted. Only Byron's marriage would help him escape. His thoughts turned to Annabella Milbanke. He never saw a woman whom he '*esteemed* so much'.[28] She declined his proposal and rejection helped Byron to see matters objectively. She was an intellectual, a cold virgin, an 'amiable Mathematician' and 'Princess of Parallelograms'.[29] A month later, he had no regrets: 'That would have been but a *cold collation*, & I prefer hot suppers.'[30]

Lady Oxford

That autumn of 1812, Byron found solace and sustenance in the arms of Lady Oxford, another, younger version of Lady Melbourne, a wise, experienced, married woman of 40 with numerous children by different lovers. Lady Oxford used to say '*seriously*' that 'a *broken heart* means nothing but *bad digestion*.'[31] He stayed with her and her tolerant husband at Eywood, their estate in Herefordshire, for four weeks from 24 October and over Christmas.

Byron felt comfortable with Lady Oxford and called Eywood the palace of Circe.[32] He relished his first experience of happy family life, read, laughed and played at blindman's buff with the children, while 'a month slipped away in this & such like recreations'.[33] He spent his time 'scrambling and splashing about with the children'.[34] And he grew 'much *fatter*'; he could not even think of starving himself down.[35] Given 'the necessity of conforming to a less Eremitical regimen' than he observed on his own in London, he 'lived on tea & bread & butter.'[36] In June 1813, having stayed with Lady Oxford once again, he reported that he was 'in the most robust health – have been eating & drinking – & fatten upon ill fortune.'[37]

Lady Caroline continued to hound him. 'The Devil, & Medea, & her Dragons to boot, are possessed of that little maniac',[38] Byron complained. But he later admitted that he would 'have preferred Medea to any woman that ever breathed'.[39] Medea killed her children and their father, when he left her for another woman. Byron's fascinated ambivalence may reflect the 'tender and peremptory' treatment he received from his mother and his nurse.[40]

Lady Caroline's 'persecution' made Byron consider quitting England. If he didn't travel, he would take orders. Lord and Lady Oxford left London at the end of June. Byron stayed in town to see his half-sister Augusta.

Augusta and Baby B

Byron and Augusta became lovers. She offered him the same kind of unquestioning, maternal support as Lady Oxford, while he was still 'haunted with hysterics'.[41]

Augusta and Byron were born four days and four years apart, and shared the early loss of their father. Six years later, he would look back and assure her, 'I have never ceased nor can cease to feel for a moment that perfect & boundless attachment which bound & binds me to you – which renders me utterly incapable of *real* love for any other human being – what could they be to me after *you*?'[42]

They were linked by a sense of humour, as well as by lineage. When she hoped that Byron would reform, he replied: 'we laugh too much for hopes'.[43] In the summer of 1813, before she knew what was going on, Annabella approved of his 'playful and affectionate manner towards' Augusta.[44]

Augusta looked 'very much older' than Byron, probably because, as Lady Shelley noted in December, she did 'not make the most of herself. She is dowdy in her dress, and seems to be quite indifferent to personal appearances.'[45] In this she resembled Byron's mother. Augusta also treated Byron as her child: 'Mrs Leigh has evidently great moral influence over her brother, who listens to her occasional admonitions with a sort of playful acquiescence.... Her manner towards him is decidedly maternal; it is as though she were reproving a thoughtless child.'[46] His nickname, used by both Augusta and Byron, was 'baby' Byron.[47] The relationship held a mutually parental flavour: he addressed her as 'Child'.[48] Augusta boasted to Annabella that she was 'thoroughly *his* enfant gâté [spoilt child]'.[49] Augusta occasionally persuaded him to relax his rule of abstinence (vegetarianism): staying with her during Lent he ate a 'collar of brawn one evening for supper (after an enormous dinner too)'.[50]

'Everything in this life depends upon the weather & the state of one's digestion', Byron remarked on 20 August,'... – I have been eating & drinking – which I always do when watched for then I grow fat & don't show it – & now that I am in very good plight & Spirits – I can't leave off the custom though I have no further occasion for it'.[51] His *'fattening'* was noticed by Lady Holland.[52]

217

Byron, Bread and Butter

In November 1813 Augusta told Byron that she was pregnant. He may have been the father. He spent Christmas with her and her family at Six Mile Bottom in cramped conditions. There, with Augusta five and a half months pregnant, the claustrophobia which prompted his first diet in 1807 seemed to have returned. He slept all day and wrote poetry all night, 'Living chiefly on biscuits and soda water'.[53]

Augusta gave birth to her fourth child, Elizabeth Medora, on 15 April 1814. It seems likely that Byron believed he was the father. He was briefly tempted to leave England and elope with Augusta. At almost the same moment, on 13 April, Annabella transmitted her father's invitation to Byron to visit them at Seaham. Byron agreed, knowing that the visit would imply a matrimonial motive.

Byron remained committed to Augusta; his heart was not available to Annabella: he was 'perplexed about *2* – and would rather have both', he admitted, as he did not 'see any use in one without a chance at least of the other.'[54] He wanted to marry, principally to ward off Lady Caroline and to shield his affair with Augusta under the cover of Annabella's famous virtue – she was 'the most prudish & correct person' Byron knew.[55] Sin sanctified by marriage constituted the Regency recipe for decorum. Lady Melbourne owed her son William Lamb (and Lady Oxford several of her children) to extra-marital affairs.

Annabella rejected Byron's second proposal on 10 August. In September he enquired whether there was 'any line or change of conduct which could possibly remove' her objections to marrying him. He merely wished 'to learn a possibility', he wrote carefully.[56] She did not answer his question. Instead, characteristically, Annabella interpreted Byron's willingness to be guided as his third proposal of marriage, which she promptly accepted.

But when Byron visited her family, after a pointed delay of six weeks, he was disappointed in just the feature he most needed. 'I fear she won't govern me –', he wrote to Lady Melbourne on 4 November, '& if she don't it will not do at all'.[57] His valet Fletcher commented, 'I never yet knew a lady that could not manage my Lord, *except* my Lady.'[58] Annabella tried to learn, when he told her that his sister always treated him like a child and that she herself reminded him of Augusta, when she was 'playful.'[59] But for most of the time she presented herself as a 'grave, didactic, deplorable person' (in her words).[60]

Despite his misgivings, Byron married Annabella on 2 January 1815. He had regrets, even before their 'treaclemoon' began and set about punishing his wife for her delay in accepting his proposal *and* for accepting it. On the other hand, there were moments when husband and wife succeeded in recreating the bower of bliss that he had found in the arms of Lady Oxford and Augusta.

Lord and Lady Byron stayed with her parents between 21 January and 9 March. Annabella was inclined to be greedy. She once ordered so many mutton-chops that she 'frightened the waiters'.[61] The Milbankes were fond of 'hot luncheons'.[62] Byron occasionally insisted on eating on his own – his mother-in-law tactfully 'never taking it amiss', when he did so.[63] But he began to eat more regularly. Annabella said that her mother 'would go to the bottom of the sea herself to find fish for B.'s dinner.'[64] Augusta was impressed: 'I am so glad he allows himself to dine', she wrote to Annabella on 8 February, '– *improvement* the first!' She was 'quite convinced that if he would condescend to eat & drink & sleep *like other people* he would feel ye good effects – but you know his way is to fast till he is famished & then *devour* more than his stomach in that *weak* state can bear – & *so on* – but I really do hope your wise & judicious endeavors will bring about a reformation on those points.'[65]

Byron and Annabella played games on the beach. She remembered Byron 'jumping & squeaking on the sands';[66] he became 'a wild mirthful boy when climbing the rocks & defying me to follow him in scrambling'.[67] At some point in the marriage Byron told his wife, 'I believe you feel towards me as a mother to her child, happy when it is out of mischief.'[68]

They played a parlour game of 'bout-rimés', composing alternate lines of verse. In her contributions, printed in italics, Annabella made a great effort to be playful but, while she gleefully notes Byron's consumption of nursery food, he regrets that they ever married:

Perplexed in the extreme to find a line
A different destiny is yours and mine.

If rhymes be omens what a fate is ours –
And bread and butter eagerly devours.

My husband is the greatest goose alive
I feel that I have been a fool to wive.

219

The moment was a watershed. From then on, indulgence in bread and butter was increasingly replaced by biscuits and soda water. In March Byron was 'grieved and tortured' to discover that Augusta refused to sleep with him after his marriage.[69] Even Annabella never doubted this.

The marriage had lost its main purpose. But husband and wife could still be happy together, when they lived on their own in London. Annabella discovered that she was pregnant and remembered that Byron 'was kind again – kinder for about ten days...than I had almost ever seen him.'[70] When Augusta came to stay, however, a frustrating, claustrophobic ménage à trois was recreated. Byron's 'black agitation' returned, exacerbated by increasing financial worries.

Once Augusta left, at the end of June, Lord and Lady Byron again lived happily together, in a domesticity marked by gluttony. Annabella was '"afflicted with a raging appetite and rapid power of digestion"'. But she was not alone. She told her mother that a goose-pie was '"highly approved and gratefully acknowledged by B.'s voracious stomach."' Byron was said to eat 'very heartily of *meat*, bread, and biscuit, allows himself half-a-pint of claret at dinner, when at home (and he seldom dines out), has abjured brandy and other spirituous liquors.'[71] On 7 July Byron admitted to Thomas Moore that he had, since his marriage, 'lost much of my paleness, and, – "horresco referens" (for I hate even *moderate* fat) – that happy slenderness, to which when I first knew you, I had attained'.

And then the later stages of his wife's pregnancy exacerbated Byron's antipathy to seeing women eat. 'For four or five months before my Confinement, he objected unkindly to dine with me, though I was willing to conform to his hours, and once when his dinner was accidentally served at the same table with mine, he desired his dish to be taken into another room (in my presence, & the servants attending) with an expression of rage.'[72] The crisis came at the end of August, when Annabella's pregnancy had reached almost exactly the same stage as Augusta's had in December 1813. According to Annabella, Byron was 'perfectly ferocious towards' her for 4 days, Annabella remembered, and as for 'the nights he ordered a bed apart.'[73] Byron denied that he had ever treated her badly, but he admitted he had a 'Vile temper & that he is told his head is not right which he believes may be the case says his Stomach is in a Bad way.'[74] She blamed his 'vitiated stomach' for Byron's depression and his love of tormenting. It suggests that he resumed his extreme form of diet, supplemented by brandy.[75]

In her labour Lady Byron thought that Byron was throwing soda water bottles at the ceiling of the room below, 'in order to deprive her of sleep'. Hobhouse inspected the ceiling and reported that it 'retained no mark of blows; and Lord Byron's habit of drinking soda-water in consequence of taking magnesia in quantities, and of knocking off the heads of the bottles with a poker, sufficiently accounted for the noise.'[76]

Augusta Ada was born on 10 December 1815. Five weeks later, after husband and wife had stopped talking, Lady Byron left London with her daughter and returned to her parents. He never saw either of them again. Four days after Annabella left, Augusta tried to reassure her sister-in-law that Byron was getting better: 'now he is gone to eat mutton broth for dinner', she reported on 19 January 1816.[77] 'I have seen him but a moment today', she added on 21 January, 'when he was eating a stewed knuckle of Veal with broth & rice'.[78] The details of the food speak for its rarity.

Rumours of all sorts circulated, and were sanctioned by Lady Byron's silence on the causes of the Separation. Eventually, Byron felt driven to leave England. One of the last people to see him was the composer Isaac Nathan, in April 1816. 'After visiting his Lordship it occurred to me that as he was particularly fond of biscuits, some Passover Cakes would be acceptable on his voyage; I accordingly sent some to him'. The unleavened bread is 'denominated by the Nazarenes *Motzas*'.[79] Byron was delighted with Nathan's 'very seasonable bequest', and promised he would rely on their efficacy as 'a charm against the destroying Angel wherever I may sojourn'.[80]

Notes

1. Wilma Paterson, 'Was Byron anorexic?', World Medicine, Vol. 17, No. 16, 15 May, 1982, 35 - 38; Walter Vandereycken and Ron van Deth, From Fasting Saints to Anorexic Girls: The History of Self-Starvation,1994, p227f; Jeremy Hugh Baron, 'Illness and Creativity: Byron's Appetites, James Joyce's gut, and Melba's meals and mesalliances', British Medical Journal, vol.315, no. 7123, 20-27 December 1997, pp. 1697-1703; Arthur Crisp, 'Commentary: Ambivalence toward fatness and its origins', BMJ, no. 7123, 20-27 December, 1997, p.1703.
2. Leslie Marchand, *Byron: A Biography*, 3 Vol., 1957, I, 62n.3
3. Thomas Moore, Letters and Journals of Lord Byron: with Notices of His Life, 2 Vol., (1830), 1837, I, 25
4. Moore, I, 136
5. Journal, 26 November 1813
6. JH to Mrs Byron, 1 September 1799, Rowland Prothero, 'The Childhood and Schooldays of Lord Byron', *The Nineteenth Century*, vol.XLIII, no.251,Jan. 1898, 76
7. Elisabeth Pigot, Moore, I, 55
8. Megan Boyes, *My Amiable Mama*, 70
9. Detached Thoughts, 79
10. Moore, I, 55

11 Catherine P. Stith, His Very Self and Voice, Collected Conversations of Lord Byron, ed. Ernest J. Lovell Jr., 1954, 294
12 Moore, I, 48.
13 To AB, 18 August 1804.
14 To AB, 6 November 1805.
15 Detached Thoughts, 15 October 1821.
16 To AB, 6 November 1805.
17 To JH, 1 October 1814.
18 Mary Hopwood to Penelope Hind, before 8 October 1811, Sarah Markham, A Testimony of Her Times, Based on Penelope Hind's Diaries and Correspondence, 1787– 1838, 1990, 98f.
19 Samuel Rogers, Recollections of the Table Talk of Samuel Rogers, ed. Alexander Dyce, 1887.
20 To DK, 18 January 1823.
21 Journal, 17 November 1813.
22 John Galt, *The Life of Lord Byron*, 1830, 15, 16.
23 The Reminiscences and Recollections of Captain Gronow..., 2 Vol., 1889, I, 150.
24 *Lady Morgan's Memoirs*, 2 Vol., 1862, II, 200.
25 To Lady Caroline Lamb, [April,1812?]
26 To John Pigot, 9 August 1806.
27 To Lady Melbourne, 25 September 1812.
28 To LM, 13 September 1812.
29 To LM, 18 October 1812.
30 To LM, 14 November 1812.
31 To LM, 12 January 1813.
32 To Francis Hodgson, 3 February [January] 1813.
33 To LM, 18 November 1812.
34 To LM, 5 April 1813; cf to AM, 12 December 1814.
35 To LM, 10 [11] November 1812.
36 To LM, April-2 May 1813.
37 To LM, 8 June 1813.
38 To JCH, 17 January 1813.
39 To TM, 19 September 1818.
40 To Henrietta D'Ussières, 8 June 1814.
41 To LM (a), 6 July 1813.
42 To the Hon. Augusta Leigh, 17 May 1819.
43 To AL, 19 December 1816.
44 Malcolm Elwin, *Lord Byron's Wife*, 1962,161f.
45 Richard Edgcumbe, *The Diary of Frances Lady Shelley*, 2 Vol., 1912, I, 53.
46 The Diary of Frances, Lady Shelley, I, 53.
47 To AL, 6 November 1816; *HVSV* (*see* footnote 11: C. P. Stith: 334); Hunt, 81.
48 To AL, 2 September 1811.
49 AL to Lady Byron, 11 January 1815.
50 To LM, 8 April 1814.
51 To LM, 20 August 1813.
52 To LM, 1 October 1813.

53 Journal, 9 January 1822, Maria Gisborne & Edward E. Williams, Shelley's Friends: Their Journals and Letters, ed. Frederick L. Jones, 1951, 124.
54 To LM, 16 May 1814.
55 To LM, 10 June 1814.
56 To Annabella Milbanke, 9 September 1814.
57 To LM, 4 November 1814.
58 Moore, II, 223n.
59 Mayne, 124.
60 AM to Lord Byron, 19 November 1814, Elwin (see footnote 44), 234.
61 Mayne, 23.
62 To AM, 28 November 1814.
63 Lady Byron's annotation of January 1851 to Medwin's Conversations of Lord Byron, ed. Ernest J. Lovell, Jr., 1966, 42n.105.
64 LyB to FH, 15 February 1815, Rev. James T. Hodgson, Memoir of the Rev. Francis Hodgson, B.D., Scholar, Poet, And Divine, 2 vol., 1878.
65 15 February 1815, Elwin (see footnote 44), 282.
66 AL to LyB, 19 February 1815.
67 1818, Elwin, 286.
68 Mayne, II, 544.
69 To LyB, 17 May 1819.
70 Elwin, 299.
71 AL to John Cam Hobhouse, 5 July 1815, Elwin (see footnote 44), 309.
72 Elwin, 326.
73 1816, Elwin, 317.
74 Mrs Clermont to Lady Noel, 5 February 1816.
75 LyB to AL, c.8 November 1815, Elwin, 323.
76 Broughton, II, 279.
77 AL to LyB, 19 January 1816, Elwin, 357.
78 AL to LyB, 21 January 1816, Elwin, 368.
79 Isaac Nathan, Hebrew Melodies, Fugitive Pieces and Reminiscences of Lord Byron..., 1829, 89.
80 To Isaac Nathan, April 1816.

What Ibn Jazla Says You Should Eat

Charles Perry

To traditional medicine, all foods are medicinal. At one time, it was usual to view this as sad, outdated superstition, but these days the badge of modernity seems to be the contrary, to look for the wisdom of accumulated experience in traditional diet. In fact, both sober empiricism and desperate magical thinking are always in play.

The irrational elements probably had a practical function, though no longer of use to us. At a time when people believed implicitly in the doctrine of the humours, its arid schematicism – which at times can seem a Rubik's cube of contraindications with no solution – served the same function as the absurd theoretical complexity of astrology: It established the authority of a diagnosis while allowing the better practitioner leeway for acknowledging things he has noticed that don't fit the theory. A successful medieval physician had (in addition to luck) a certain knack, based on a lot of experience, which he used in a given situation. The scheme of humoral oppositions provided a method of justifying and understanding it, which was probably as important to himself, in terms of giving him the confidence of his diagnosis and therefore a good bedside manner, as it was to his patient. Modern medicine, of course, wants cures to be independent, as far as possible, of an inexplicable knack.

Medieval Arab medicine, heir to both Persian and Greek traditions, recognized a vast pharmacopoeia, including not only simples and compounds but sweets, stews and other everyday dishes. Some of their purported powers are recognized today; we still suck on sweets for a sore throat, and nutritionists would certainly agree that dishes containing sugar and fat are 'heating'. It would be harder to sell them on the corollary, ordained by the doctrine of the humours, that sour things have positive 'cooling' powers.

But some medieval Arab treatments were clearly symbolic in nature. In Minhāj al-Bayān, the medical encyclopedia compiled by the prominent 11th-century Baghdad physician Yahyā ibn Jazla, reddish ingredients replenish the blood. Ibn Jazla prescribes rummāniyya (a stew flavored with pomegranate juice) for hemorrhage and summāqiyya (flavored with sumac berries) for cases of spitting blood. By the same token, he prescribes whitish semi-liquid foods: rice pudding (aruzz bi-laban), almond pudding (khabīs al-lauz), wheat porridge (harīsat al-hinta) and chickpea broth (mā al-hummus) to produce semen, chickpea broth conveniently producing milk as well.

Ibn Jazla usually gives a recipe for a dish he prescribes. Soon after his encyclopedia was published, scribes excerpted these recipes and circulated them on their own as a cookbook, and in later centuries cookbook writers freely plundered these recipes. Although the later books usually (but not always) omit the medical information, it was probably the original reason for the recipes' popularity – apart from the fact that they were more exactly written than most medieval recipes, being, in effect, prescriptions. No more need to note how heating, cooling, moistening or drying all the ingredients in a dish are and analyze their possible conflicts and contraindications, a sometimes maddeningly complex consequence of the doctrine of the humours. Ibn Jazla made it simple; for spitting blood, serve rummāniyya.

The leading medical conditions for which Ibn Jazla prescribed food treatments were, understandably, states of the digestion: stomach ache, constipation and diarrhea. He also prescribed that versatile chickpea broth for two other abdominal conditions: to stimulate the menses or expel the fetus in labor.

His recipes to treat stomach ache were isfīdhabāj (a soothing plain stew of meat cooked with onions, chickpeas and no spice but coriander), tuffāhiyya (meat stewed with sour apple juice), tannūriyya (lamb or veal, stewed in the tandoor with chickpeas, spices and dill) and jawādhib al-tamr wal-rutab (dates stewed with honey, sugar, breadcrumbs and walnuts to a thick consistency, sandwiched between layers of flatbread and baked under roasting meat).

For constipation, jawādhib al-tamr wal-rutab again, jawādhibal-khubz (bread pudding baked under roasting meat), khabīs (crumbled semolina bread stewed with sugar and either milk or almond oil), sughdiyya (an elaborate dish of red meat and chickens stewed together with chickpeas, topped with strips of smoked meat and a layer of ground almonds and egg whites, then dotted with the yolks) and kurunbiyya (meat stewed with cabbage).

For diarrhea, the treatment might be boiled rice (but not rice pudding, which is laxative), aqit (a cheese made from sour milk), semolina bread, tabāhajāt hāmida (fried strips of meat flavored with spices and a sour fruit juice), rummāniyya (which we have met before), summāqiyya (likewise; Ibn Jazla notes that it has a constipating effect if purslane and citron leaf are in the stew but not if Swiss chard and spinach are used), hisrimiyya (meat stewed with sour grape juice), and in fact most stews containing a sour fruit. Amīrbārisiyya, made with barberry, Ibn Jazla declares 'the best-flavored costive'.

What Ibn Jazla Says You Should Eat

If you suffered from cough, Ibn Jazla would prescribe hintiyya maslūqa (boiled wheat), itriya (small soup-type noodles, at least when mixed with sugar and almond oil or butter or broth of isfīdhabāj), tuffāhiyya or isfānākhiyya (meat stewed with spinach; he warns that it causes gas) and several sweet dishes: the bread pudding jawādhib al-khubz, jawādhib al-khashkāsh (a pudding flavored with poppy seeds, baked the same way, Ibn Jazla recommending that it be made with sugar, almond oil and chicken fat; he also says this dish is good for insomnia, possibly by association with the fact that the poppy plant produces opium); khabīs (for dry cough), zulābiyā (fried batter, soaked in honey or date syrup; for moist cough) or nātif (unlike the modern Arab nātif, a sort of sugar frosting colored brilliant white with soapwort, Ibn Jazla's nātif was sugar syrup cooked to the hard crack stage and then kneaded with nuts; he singles out the versions using sesame seed and walnuts as effective).

Among other ailments that can be treated with food are catarrh and burning urine (poppy seed nātif); swelling after surgery (fresh cheese); emaciation (jawādhib al-khubz); hangover (laimāniyya and hummādiyya, stews flavored with lemon and citron juice, respectively; Ibn Jazla remarks with some asperity concerning fuqqā, a sort of spiced near beer, 'People might use it on the idea that it settles hangover, but it is not so'); and putrid sores, hip pain and women's pain (murrī, the Arab soy sauce; fūdhaj, the rotted barley from which murrī is made, benefits the itch, if kneaded with wine vinegar and rose oil and painted on the body).

What is particularly interesting about Ibn Jazla is that he often suggests dishes or foods that complement the dish he is discussing – presumably so that its medicinal effect would be countered if you were not actually suffering from a particular disease. These complements would balance the humours of those who were not ill, in other words. His suggestions probably affected medieval menus, at least among those who were keen to follow the most authoritative diet advice.

They often make aesthetic sense, since the doctrine of the humors is based on contrasts of flavors and textures. Sour pomegranate juice or sikanjubīn (a mixture of vinegar and honey) should be served with crepes or zulābiyā. Ibn Jazla recommends that various sweet or fatty dishes be accompanied by particular stews flavored with sour fruits, and sour stews are likewise complemented by fatty stews or sweetmeats.

Some associations are less self-evident. Lemon juice and sesame oil go with bunn, the paste from which soy sauce is expressed (mutajjan was a dish of meat cooked with sesame, soy and lemon, and possibly there is a connection with this prescription, one way or another). Sugar counters the harm of starchy things, such as rice pudding, fried bananas and harisat al-hinta (wheat porridge with meat). Muthallath (grape juice boiled down by two thirds, like the Roman defrutum or the modern Arab dibs 'inab) has all the virtues of wine without being intoxicating, so this sovereign fluid suits fresh fish, ashcake, sanbūsaj (samosa), bazmāward (a sort of giant canapé of meat in bread with a sour flavoring), liftiyya (turnip stew), kurunbiyya (cabbage stew), noodles and hummādiyya (which harms the elderly, who might therefore prefer to treat hangovers with laimūniyya).

In some cases, the humoral element is a fairly hard to see, and the treatment may be based on pragmatic experience, or perhaps even aesthetic taste. Dates (bad for the throat, voice and blood, cause headache) should be accompanied by almonds and poppy seeds and followed by lettuce and cucumber with vinegar. That doesn't sound medicinal, but it does sound quite good.

References

All page references are to the copy of Minhāj al-Bayān at the British Library, no. Add 5934.

rummāniyya: 109a
summāqiyya: 125a
aruzz bi-laban: 21a
khabīs al-lauz: 83b
harīsat al-hinta: 217a
mā al-hummus: 192b
isfīdhabāj: 24b
tuffāhiyya: 53a
tannūriyya: 53b
jūdhābat al-tamr wal-rutab: 66b
jūdhab al-khubz: 66a
khabīs: 83a
sughdiyya: 119b
kurunbiyya: 175b
tabāhajāt hāmida: 144a
hisrimiyya: 75a
amīrbārīsiyya: 33b

hintiyya maslūqa: 79a
itriya: 29b
isfānākhiyya: 22b
jūdhab al-khashkāsh: 66b
zulābiya: 114a
nātif: 207a
laimūniyya: 187b
hummādiyya: 77b
fuqqā jayyid: 159a
murrī: 195b
fūdhaj: 160a
sikanjubīn: 122b
mutajjan: 200a
sanbūsaj: 127b
bazmāward: 43b
liftiyya: 186a

Images of Infant Nutrition
Sightings of food in group & child portraits

Gillian Riley

This paper attempts to evaluate things to eat in family groups, individual portraits of children and images of childbirth. We shall look mainly at material from the Low Countries in the 16th and 17th centuries, with flashbacks to glimpses of mothers and babies in early religious art. Not all the paintings mentioned are available as slides, but their contents are described to give some idea of the visual evidence they present. Feeding the young, in times of high infant mortality, was a major preoccupation. Documentary evidence is available for some periods, and medical and medicinal handbooks and memoirs can help to flesh out the statistics. Paintings also help.

Food in still life and genre paintings is often dismissed by art historians as a mere accessory, valued more for its symbolic meanings than evidence of gastronomic practices, but food historians are grateful for all this visual information, where procedures not always spelt out in cookery texts can be seen clearly. The custom of larding a bird with simple bits of pork fat on one side, and spiced and highly flavoured lardoons on the other is seen clearly in many still lifes, and the ornate architecture of a pie which is implicit in Robert May's recipes but not done justice to in the crude wood cuts which illustrate them, is frequently depicted in careful detail in paintings of the return of the prodigal son, or the rich man and Lazarus. In this talk we shall try and find some kind of balance between an excessive credulity around the symbolism and an over-literal acceptance of the appearances of items of food and drink.

Paintings of the Virgin and Child, or the birth of the Virgin, or of Saint John, can show evidence of contemporary practices. In many devotional paintings we see a chubby Christ child in cool and hygienic wrappings, or none at all, reaching for the breast, or contentedly clutching some fruit, usually apples or grapes, but we need to be wary of the built-in symbolism which dictated their appearance, while the preternatural liveliness of the newborn child, suitable for a divinity but odd in an infant only a few hours old, is also misleading.

We see an exhausted but contented mother, propped up in bed in her best clothes and clean linen, relaxing whilst devoted attendants vie with each other to bathe and swaddle the infant before passing it to the buxom wet-nurse. Visiting friends and neighbours gather in a procession bearing gifts and more importantly nourishing food for the mother. It is to be hoped for the infant's sake that the wet-nurse is equally well fed.

Masaccio's towering image of the Virgin in the National Gallery in London almost overshadows a tiny but robust infant stuffing his face with black grapes from a bunch in his mother's hand. These might have been a nourishing and harmless snack, but they are also symbols of the wine of the Eucharist, and of Christ as the fruitful vine, and the juice on the babe's fingers reminds us of the blood shed by Christ on the cross. These are not a reliable clue to infant feeding, but we might consider that Masaccio's renown was based on his realism, his depiction of events from the bible in the here and now, with people wearing contemporary or vaguely classical clothes, rather than the ornate fancy dress of medieval painters. This realism is seen also in his frescos in the Brancacci chapel, where a serious young mother, living dangerously, carefully holds a bare-bottomed child dressed only in a diaphanous little smock, a perilous way of avoiding nappy rash.

Masaccio's realism is certainly credible in his painted decoration of a birth tray, the wooden platter on which ceremonial gifts, including food and drink, were brought to the new mother. This is contemporary life around 1427, a celebration of a real birth in a comfortable middle class Florentine home, with a wealth of realistic detail, prized for its accuracy in commemorating an actual rather than a mythical or biblical event. Trumpets announce the arrival of richly dressed visitors, followed by servants bearing gifts, a tray or platter containing, perhaps, a tart or pie, and a bowl of, perhaps, comWts or nourishing broth.

Sugared comfits, valued for their healthy sweetness, and a condensed chicken broth, (brodo ristretto, prescribed in cookery texts and medical handbooks, as nourishing invalid food), were offered to ensure the mother's recovery from her ordeal and renew her strength for yet more confinements. If she nursed the child herself it too would have benefited from the nourishment.

Another birth tray is depicted by Paolo Uccello in a fresco in Prato cathedral (The Birth of the Virgin, c. 1436) The mother is enjoying a ritual hand wash, while attendants bring a tray of cordials, a dish of food covered with a napkin, and a pie or covered tart and a bowl of something white, possibly bianco mangiare, an expensive dish made from chicken breasts, ground almonds, sugar and rosewater.

Images of Infant Nutrition

Jacqueline Musacchio has found images from frescos, paintings and ceramics, illustrating the rituals of childbirth in Renaissance Italy which give us some idea of the food offered to mothers and babies[1]. Her study is not primarily concerned with food, but nourishment figures in many scenes of childbirth designed to encourage and comfort the mother, with reassuring images of birth as an intimate, enjoyable experience, celebrated among supportive, congratulatory women friends.

In many images comforting food is brought to the mother in maiolica bowls and dishes which were produced in nesting sets of five pieces or more to commemorate the birth and reward her success. In the previous century the Black Death had wiped out a large proportion of the population, a demographic disaster, and a busy manufacturing town like Florence was desperate to renew its workforce. So the pregnant woman was cherished and made much of, the newborn babe was worshipped, coddled and protected, and this affectionate and wholly self-interested process was depicted by the artists who decorated the maiolica wares. They painted midwives helping the child into the world, the care of the newborn babe by a host of attendants, bathing, drying with a cloth warmed before the fire, swathing in linen bands, then displayed to friends, relatives and brothers and sisters, showing at the same time the care, praise and respect due to the mother. The inside of a maiolica scodella from Casteldurante shows a mother tucked up in bed with an attendant bringing a covered bowl of food, while in the foreground a wet-nurse feeds the infant while rocking it in a crib, images of nurture based on contemporary practice. A tagliere, the flat cover to a deep bowl, a sort of tray upon which other dishes could be stacked, shows a mother eagerly receiving a bowl of food, while two delighted siblings tend to the baby in its cradle.

Musacchio quotes accounts kept by Tribaldo de' Rossi in 1490 showing what he spent in preparations for the birth of his child: 16 soldi on a set of maiolica birth bowls, quantities of grain to fatten chickens (presumably for the broth) and quite a sum on sweetmeats from the apothecary for his wife Nanina and her guests[2].

Paintings of the Virgin and Child by Carlo Crivelli, who was working in the Italian Marches during the mid fifteenth century, combine the rich decorative tradition of the International Gothic style with the new realism of the Italian Renaissance. His mothers are beautiful, modest young women, holding plump babies, scantily clad in contrast to the embroidered and jewel-encrusted clothing of the attendant saints and martyrs. Often the child grasps a fruit, and apples, pears and cucumbers hang meaningfully from the surrounding architecture. Fresh from the lush orchards of the Marche these fruit have more symbolic than nutritional value, the apples are there to remind us of the fecundity of the Virgin Mother and the cucumbers of the purity of her son; they can hardly be seen as nourishment for the still suckling infant.

Fecundity was cherished in the Low Countries during the 16th and 17th centuries for similar reasons. A prosperous trading nation, threatened by foreign aggression and natural hazards, depended on a healthy and vigorous population. Family portraits show this conscious pride in fertility; the father as head of the household, surrounded by several generations – parents, his own children, and a few grandchildren, particularly blooming and lively, amidst symbols of fecundity and evidence of material prosperity[3]. Both painter and sitters would have known the verses from Psalm 1:

> Blessèd is the man that walketh not in the counsel of the ungodly, nor standeth in the way of sinners, nor sitteth in the seat of the scornful. But his delight is in the law of the Lord; and in his law doth he meditate day and night. And he shall be like a tree planted by the rivers of the water, that bringeth forth his fruit in his season; his leaf also shall not wither; and whatsoever he doeth shall prosper.

They would also have been familiar with Psalm 128:

> Blessèd is every one that feareth the Lord; that walketh in his ways. For thou shalt eat the labour of thine hands; happy shalt thou be, and it shall be well with thee. Thy wife shall be as a fruitful vine by the sides of thine house, thy children like olive plants round about thy table. Behold, that thus shall the man be blessed that feareth the Lord. The Lord shall bless thee out of Zion; and thou shalt see the good of Jerusalem all the days of thy life. Yea, thou shalt see thy children's children, and peace upon Israel.

So a family at table, numerous, pious, prosperous, will naturally show, in close proximity to the father, the tree planted by the rivers of water, with the fruitful vine twining around the areas associated with the wife, and the fruits of that vine, bunches of grapes, displayed prominently by her or her children, some of them also brandishing olive branches.

This is where the waters start to get muddied, for bunches of grapes had a multiutude of meanings, and the diligent pursuit of these meanings by eminent art historians has resulted in blood all over the floor and tidal waves of acrimony. As food historians we relish the erudition, pity the walking wounded, and help ourselves to the spoils of war. Grapes could signify fruitfulness in marriage, a desirable aspiration; they could also mean the virginity of a young unmarried woman, and when portrayed in a family context these bunches of grapes could imply a virtuous and chaste wife enjoying what some historians quaintly refer to as a 'second virginity', a relationship in which sex is strictly for procreation rather than enjoyment. So these family groups might simultaneously be celebrating the teeming fruits of an active sexual partnership, and also the virtues of abstinence, leaving some historians understandably sceptical[3].

Where did all these grapes come from? Climate change might account for their profusion upon dinner tables and market stalls, and often in outdoor situations, but the numerous contemporary paintings of skating scenes, with canals and rivers rock hard throughout a long hard winter, indicate that grapes were likely to be either imported luxuries or hot-house fruit enjoyed only by the wealthy, not children's everyday food.

What about the rest of the fruit and nuts scattered over laden tables, or prominent in group portraits? Were they everyday fare, an early sighting of the 'five-a-day' maxim or allowed in as symbols of fertility and lush profusion?

Apples seem innocuous and healthy enough; they are often held by a small child, or seen amongst the scatter of nuts and comfits on a table. Many calm domestic interiors are focused on a woman peeling an apple for a child, usually a little girl, and though we might wish to approve of this healthy snack the reasons for its appearance are not nutritional but symbolic. The apple was seen as a symbol of both good and evil; it caused the fall of man, and so indicates temptation and downfall. But as the fruit of the tree of Knowledge it can be benign, enabling the acquisition of wisdom and learning, not to mention wealth, and it can also remind us that we have in our spiritual lives the capacity to choose between good and evil. The business of peeling it, paring away outer show, the ruddy skin, to reveal the pure white interior, could be seen as attempts to follow the path of virtue. So the neat and dutiful mother peeling an apple is attending to her daughter's moral welfare, not just topping the child up between meals.

A cynic might well wonder at this point about the significance of a mother, watched by a small daughter, scraping carrots and parsnips. This is not an image of woman as drudge, as downtrodden subordinate, she is bringing her child up to perform worthy domestic duties, competently and with decorum, in a role prized and praised by poets painters and preachers. Woman is seen here engaged in household tasks as guardian and trustee of the moral welfare of the family, of her realm within doors, while the father, merchant, mariner or warrior, imposes order and discipline on the outside world.

Providing food for their children is both a duty and an indicator of success at getting great wealth. So the hams, roast meat and fowls and the great pies and hothouse fruit on the table round which the grateful family is seen saying grace are to be taken literally, as evidence of wealth, the reward of virtue. The virtuous woman participates in this, the slattern transgresses, providing much picturesque detail for artists, particularly Jan Steen, who relished the way flaunted wealth can breed chaos, physical as well as moral. Some of his more riotous domestic scenes show parents behaving badly, and children creating mayhem, mother slumped in a comatose state of alcohol-fuelled exhaustion, father dallying with a pie and a loose woman in the background, children feeding a cat with another pie, an equally expensive chunk of cheese lying unheeded on the floor, while a bowl of costly blue and white porcelain full of hot-house fruit is in peril from a rootling pig. Misuse of food is shown here as a symptom of moral turpitude, but the food itself is likely to be the normal fare of a comfortably-off household, and gives some idea of what these mischievous children had to eat.

Jan Steen used his wife and children as models in his outrageous paintings of dysfunctional family life, cunningly working into them enough moral messages to justify these popular renderings of mayhem, a refreshing change from the calm ordered behaviour of people in the interiors of Vermeer and De Hooch.

Steen's 'Feast of Saint Nicholas' depicts in wonderful detail all the breads and confectionery offered as rewards for good behaviour in the past year to smug well-behaved children, but sternly withheld from the delinquent child on the left (a self-portrait). Gaitri Pagrach-Chandra has a vivid account of traditional Sinterklaas bakery, immediately recognisable in the painting[4]. It is depressingly likely that these were a more constant article of diet than the symbolic bowls of fruit.

But to get back to the carrots; the interest here is not in the symbolism, even if crudely phallic, but in their significance as a recently improved root crop. The fertile reclaimed land of much of the Netherlands was cultivated with sophisticated skill. Even in times of war and occupation the market and kitchen scenes of the Low Countries show an abundance of root vegetables (different kinds of carrots, parsnips, skirrets, salsify, various turnips), also cabbages, lettuces, onions and the newly perfected young broad beans and peas, artichokes and asparagus). So a neat, modest woman peeling carrots or parsnips is not making do with humble root crops but feeding her children a fine local product. The painting shows a pride in both advanced horticulture and self-suffciency.

A wider worry is how to interpret the other things on the table in group portraits. The bread and wine can be sacramental as well as the usual accompaniments to a meal. The cheese and butter would be normal fare while symbolising the peace and plenty of a land all too often threatened with invasion and natural disasters. Joints of meat, hams, pies, biscuits, comfits, fruit pastes, were all part of an average meal for the comfortably off, but even so could trigger off a spate of tedious moralising. Comfits and biscuits could, as well as indicating wealthy indulgences, speak of the vanity of such vain pleasures. Walnuts carry quite a heavy moral burden, for the hard wood of the shell can symbolise the wood of the cross, and the soft meat within the love of Christ for mankind, or walnuts held by a child can imply the harsh rigours of stern schooling, which produce salvation for the soul.

Family portraits round a table are intended to show food as a sacrament, with all members except the babies at prayer, an apt illustration of psalm 128, showing the family of a virtuous man enjoying the fruits of his labours, with the wife as the fertile vine and the children literally carrying olive fronds. The things to eat can be read as the worldly goods that the man's wise conduct and subsequent wealth entitle them to enjoy, so as well as being symbolic the food is realistic and to us quite informative.

An anonymous Flemish 16th century family group from a private collection in Great Britain, known to me only in a murky monochrome reproduction in the Witt library of the Courtauld Institute, is a useful corrective to the obsession with fruit. Here a man and his wife sit at the centre of a long table, with an elderly couple to his right, the man holding a small child on his knee; to the wife's left are a girl and four lively boys, the youngest holding a leafy frond which might just be an olive branch, similar to a frond directly in front of the father. The hands of all are joined in prayer, except the father, who may have both arms encircling mother and wife. The family pets are there – a very individual cat curled up under the grandfather's chair, and a dog hopefully entangled with a walking stick behind the eldest son. The detail of the portraits is sufficiently clear to make one confident in the details of the food on the table, which in the absence of colour are however hard to decipher: a somewhat floppy joint, probably boiled, perhaps veal or lamb, a smaller joint, this time a fowl, partly obscured by the boys' heads, and a large ham, the outer rind removed, and the fatty layer beneath studded with cloves, showing the characteristic circular opening from which slices or rather chunks would then be carved. (We see this way of dealing with a ham in many still life paintings, sometimes with the bite-sized lumps of meat on a plate, a sensible way of offering food to be taken up with fingers or the point of a knife). Various kinds of bread, salt in an ornate cellar, pewter plates and one wine glass and several folded napkins complete the table setting, with a large ornate ewer of wine sitting in a cooler on the ground. As well as the undoubted symbolic significance of the food, we can see at a glance that it is that of a family of substance, and that the numerous children will get to enjoy plenty of bread, wine and a lot of meat.

Another murky reproduction of an inaccessible painting in a collection in Poland is worth describing since the theme of nurture is obviously very carefully represented. A couple and their children are shown out of doors in a rural setting, a little girl with a basket of fruit, two boys, one with his golf club and ball and a lively dog, and the parents who sit at a stone table with a casually draped cloth, a jug of wine, a glass, a bread roll and a pretzel, the primly dressed wife looking demurely towards her husband whilst breast-feeding a tiny baby, and the hatless, towsel-headed father triumphantly meeting our gaze. The sinister woodland vegetation in the foreground, the frog on the table, wild birds in flight, and the rustic building in the near distance all seem to provide motifs, along with pretzels, golf and tame dogs, (all burdened with double meanings) for a sermon on the family's role in taming or correcting the dark forces of nature. Good and evil slogging it out in the fresh air with a little help from male power and authority and submissive female wholesomeness. This is the only image I have found showing a baby at the breast in a formal group.

A family portrait in the Rijksmuseum shows a neatly laid table with the usual bread and wine, a large roast, and a bowl of cherries, as well as the token nuts and apples. The youngest of the four children sits on its mother's lap holding a symbolic branch, this time of cherries rather than grapes. Wholesomeness is again the word that springs to mind, bonny children and serious parents surrounded by all the appropriate signs of virtue rewarded.

Another group portrait, a generation earlier, painted in 1563 by Cornelis de Zeeuw, of Pierre de Moucheron aged 55 years, and his wife aged 45, offers a head count of twenty not including themselves. Allowing for various members of an extended family, brothers and sisters of husband and wife, grandparents, grandchildren, we still see an impressive gathering, grouped on one side of a long table. There is an abundance of fruit, some fowl on a dish, and the remains of a shallow pie in the centre. The body language is complicated; no hands are arranged in prayer, but many are holding fruit, cherries, apples, or blossoms, while a young woman plays the virginals, and a sister protectively embraces a sibling. The father holds cherries, and his wife a lemon, in a way that reminds us of the Jewish etrog and its complicated symbolism. An older man, who might be Pierre de Moucheron's father, gestures towards a young boy reaching for a pretzel, the two youngest children brandish toys. Fruitfulness and harmony, and concern for the moral welfare of the young. As for their diet, this painting like so many others tells us less than we wish to know, though the profusion of fruit is interesting.

A family at table, by an anonymous 17th-century artist, has a great deal more to say for itself, the table being something of a pronk still life in its own right. No trailing vines and only a few grapes, but still a wealth of symbolism, the sacramental bread and wine, a son playing the lute, another meaningfully holding a lemon, a faithful dog carrying a tulip, daughters with blossoming roses, and the submissive wife reaching out for her husband's proffered glass of wine. The food is a mixture of honest down to earth fatherland fare – bread of various kinds, cheese, butter and salt, a contrast with a carefully larded chicken with its liver tucked under its wing, and a profusion of luxurious fruit – cherries, strawberries, raspberries, pomegranates, apples, pears, plums, apricots, melon, lemons, and a pair of attractive pink crayfish.

A painting by Gortzius Geldorp executed in Catholic Cologne in 1602, Grace before the meal, shows a pious family seated round a table, with five children at one end, a baby in a cradle, and two diminutive figures standing in the foreground next to fronds of palm or olive (they may represent deceased infants), with an open door to the right through which the tree and the river are clearly seen, together with the fruitful vine twined round the threshold. A devotional painting hangs behind the father, and a display of silver gilt objects on the dresser on the background represents various heroic Christian virtues. The seated mother, with standing companion, an elderly woman, looks pale and tired. The food on the table is the lavish spread one would expect as the rewards of righteousness – a large ham, some roast meat, and a dish of fowls, along with the usual bread and wine and some bowls of fruit. The family dog takes a drink of the water from the wine cooler.

Lush hothouse fruit is central to a family group in an open air setting during the 1650s. For once the female element is almost overwhelming, unlike some portraits which show handsome, virile men and women pale and prematurely aged, wearied by the attrition of multiple births. Here we see four generations of women, blooming and serene, the men either worn out or vacuous. The unmistakable shared likeness of the women, an elderly lady seated in front of a haggard man (son in law?) standing next to his wife, who looks towards her daughter, a young woman in the full prime of life, with a rosy-cheeked child grasping a bunch of grapes on her knee, pointing with conscious pride to another daughter standing by the grandmother whose elderly fingers join with the child's to display a branch of apples. This plenitude of female fecundity is reinforced by the direction of their gaze, a circular journey from one woman to another around the symbolic bowl of fruit, while the men look away in various degrees of resignation and acceptance.

A more homely scene painted by Hendrick Sorgh in 1663 is of Jacob Bierens and his family in their kitchen, a large modern room lit from the left with high windows through which we can just glimpse the tendrils of a wandering vine; there is a wide open fireplace with tiled surround, a marble tiled floor, a sink connected to a water supply in one corner, landscape paintings on the wall, and a profusion of food fresh from the market – cabbages and lettuce, artichokes, asparagus, a bowl of freshwater fish, and the proud begetter of this bounty arriving with his youngest son and a tray of fresh haddock from the fish-market. Mother sits peeling apples, daughter is preparing a chicken, eldest son plays his viol, indicating concord and harmony, and a contented cat sits by the glowing fire, the unbiddable tamed. A prosperous if not patrician household, demonstrating a benign practical application of the virtuous behaviour extolled in the Psalms, the foundation of a just and affluent society, and at the same time almost sending up the pretentiousness of some of the pompous family groups we have been looking at. For once it seems as if the food painted here is indeed the normal diet of a comfortable bourgeois family. The artist had a huge output, including many picturesque scenes of low life in barns and taverns, taking a delight in the pile-up of pots and pans and vegetables, and rendering their form and texture with bravura. He also painted several kitchen scenes, and it is a pleasant paradox that a client of some standing should choose to be portrayed with his family in a kitchen setting.

Another client of high rank, Eeuwout Prins, a prosperous burgher and civic dignitary of Rotterdam, was painted with his wife and two small daughters by Sorgh in 1661. The father is seen in the background, silent and still in a book-lined study, glancing towards the bustle and noise in the foreground, where his wife, not particularly pretty or buxom, but with a touching grace, restrains a hyperactive little child teetering on the edge of a red-covered table, at the same time gently instructing an older girl how to reward an obedient begging dog with a biscuit. Food here as a reward for good behaviour for the biddable, while affectionate control tames natural high spirits. Nature, nurture and a bit of nutrition for good measure.

Portraits of individual children are numerous, but few of them have anything to eat in them. Distinguishing between the sexes is sometimes tricky; boys were not warped for life by being kitted out in skirts, aprons, ruffs, ribbons and trinkets; this was unisex apparel for all young infants, distinguishable sometimes only by what they hold. One portrait shows an intrepid two-year-old setting off for a round of golf with a silver ball and an ornate club, dressed in a dark brown velvet overmantle, with slashed red satin sleeves, a lace-trimmed ruff, an apron with lace edgings and inserts, a matching bonnet under a wide-brimmed brown velvet (moleskin?) hat, and as always, coral bracelets to ward off evil influences. The golf is not a mere pastime, something to keep them out of the way at weekends, for the disciplines involved in hitting the ball in the right direction are those a child needs to direct itself towards the right moral path. This is righteous instruction not fun and games.

Both boys and girls are shown with a pet dog, basket of fruit, and sometimes a biscuit or cracker for the animal. One child has a dog on a lead, symbol of both fidelity, obedience and the ability to learn from instruction. In the other hand she holds a large pretzel. The story of the pretzel is too complex to be investigated here; the pagan origins of strips of bread dough formed into a decorative and symbolic knot can be looked at in our context in the light of later Christian usage. Simon Schama reminds us that the German for bracelets is bretzelen, that these were worn on a child's wrists, along with coral bracelets, to ward off the powers of evil on All Souls' Eve[5]. The Dutch word for what we call pretzel however is krakeling, derived from krakeel meaning to quarrel or fight; the implied conflict and destruction is what happens when two children hook a little finger into the loops of a krakeling and tug, as we would a wishbone, tearing the friable biscuit apart. The inherent violence of play can be tamed by education into moral strength rather than negative mayhem, so the krakeling can imply the educational value of rough games. But the krakeling also appears in books of emblems and wise sayings, where the image of two hands pulling at the biscuit can mean the forces of good and evil competing for the soul of the child, and we know all too well that children's behaviour can be diabolical or angelic.

Schama, proud parent of very young infants at the time of writing this, was not taken in by Cuyp's idealized children, he reminds us of the little terrors painted by Jan Steen and Judith Leyster:

'These 'Haarlem' children are what adults fear: mischievous imps equipped with worldly knowledge, merciless instincts, and inexhaustible energy. Their portraits talk back. To the truly fearful they seem to be little demons. Their opposites, then, must be what adults dream of: little angels. Cuyp's versions are so exquisite that they seem made of powder and rose water: the blond-tressed, snub-nosed, types that, via the valley of pseudo-Renoir, made their relentless route-march through the lower reaches of pastel-tinted bourgeois taste.'

Judith Leyster probably used her own brood as models, but there is affection rather than horror in her painting of two children with emblems of unbiddableness and disobedience. These merry delinquents are playing with a long-suffering kitten and an eel, the little girl taps her forehead, meaning her brother's crazy, while he grins knowingly up at an admonishing adult. 'Hilarity unsettling gravity' as Schama puts it. Moralists might see cats, impossible to tame or discipline, as symbolic of primitive, ungovernable natures and the slippery eel as the unpredictability and intransigence of life, but Leyster makes us laugh with her children as well as at them, thus shaking the moral message to its foundations.

The final images show two very different children; one is a good little boy, bearing up very well, at the age of two, in his best clothes, with starched ruff and clean muslin apron, carrying a basket of fruit in his left hand, and with his right offering a rusk to a pet dog. The dog represents faithfulness and obedience, the biscuit could be its just reward, and the fruit perhaps the child's future as a wise and prolific parent. It might be as well not to make too much of the dietary implications for boy and animal, but the overall impression is of a nice healthy child starting off the way he is meant to go on.

This can hardly be said of the second portrait. A younger infant, perhaps less than eighteen months, is firmly restrained in a stout, heavy baby-chair. We are not fooled by the pink cheeks and merry grin. Those little piggy eyes are blazing with hate – rage at whoever confined him to the ignominious seat, kitted out with slashed sleeves, blue ribbons, the inevitable coral bracelets, and a dangling crucifix, and loathing of the artist taking so long over his tedious task. Unlike the static child portraits we have seen, this radiates movement and noise. The little feet drumming against the base of the wooden chair, the podgy hands crushing the elaborate cookies offered as a bribe for good behaviour, (the little horror is not eating them, he is destroying them). A paediatrician might be able to interpret this hyperactivity as symptom of an eating disorder or food intolerance, the starch and sugar in the rich biscuits stimulating the behaviour they were intended to quell.

This is a sombre note on which to end; but a reminder that there is evidence in art for child, and adult, nutrition which can be collected and evaluated, and perhaps widen our understanding of both disciplines.

References

1. Jacqueline Marie Musacchio, The Art and Ritual of Childbirth in Renaissance Italy, Yale University Press, New Haven & London, 1999.
2. Musacchio p. 120.
3. Jan Baptist Bedaux, 'Fruit and fertility: fruit symbolism in Netherlandish portraiture of the sixteenth and seventeenth centuries, *Simiolus* XVII; 2-3, 1987, p. 150–168.
4. Gaitri Pagrach-Chandra, Windmills in my Oven, a book of Dutch baking, Prospect Books, Totnes, 2002, p. 155.
5. Simon Schama, The Embarassment of Riches, Collins, London, 1987, p. 550.

My brother always made Blue Peter's potato curry. He still does.
Cooks, Home-cooking and Becoming a Cook

Frances Short

Introduction

> When I was little I would go into the kitchen and my Mum might be baking and there would be a bit of leftover pastry and I would make jam tarts. I remember ... grey little pastry tarts because your hands were dirty as you rolled the pastry and Dad having to eat them and say they were lovely.
>
> Sue

Laying the table for Sunday dinner in the dining room, bringing home fish and chips with Dad, licking cake-mix from the bowl, and making chapattis with grandmother: home is where food skills are learned, children are nurtured into cultural foodways and family customs and culinary skills are passed from one generation to the next ... or is it?

Noddy yoghurts, microwaveable chips, dinosaur spaghetti, 'lean cuisine', and chicken tikka pizza: today's food writers and experts continually lament the proliferation of pre-prepared foods, the increasing insignificance of regional and national cuisines, a growing trend for eating alone and 'on the run', and the decline of domestic cooking and culinary knowledge. Worries abound about children who cannot explain where garlic or tomatoes come from, cannot bake a potato or boil an egg and parents who are no longer able to show them or tell them how (see Bell, 1998; Lawson, 1998; Leith, 1998; Lyon, Colquhoun and Alexander, 2003; Seeley, 2003). A recent article in the Guardian, in a series focusing on contemporary food issues, announced 'the death of cooking' (Fort, 2003).

The state of domestic cooking has in recent years become a focus of both academic debate and popular, social commentary. Both in the UK and all over the world concerns (and sometimes rejoicings) prevail about the increased availability and use of pre-prepared, convenience foods and modern kitchen technologies such as the microwave and what is seen as an accompanying debasement of home-cooking and the home-cooked meal and the subjugation (or is that emancipation?) of the domestic cook. Social and family interactions and relationships, people's ability to follow dietary guidelines and eat a healthy diet, and children's acquisition of culinary skill and knowledge are all said to suffer (Baderoon, 2002; Lang and Caraher, 2001; Leather, 1996; Stitt et al., 1996, Perinau, 2002)

But what is 'being able to cook'? Does it involve reaching certain standards and if it does, whose? What is 'cooking'? Does it refer simply to the transformation of food by heating? Should 'cooking' only refer to the preparation of fresh, raw foods and ingredients? What makes a 'good' cook – technical skill, creativity and flair, or an ability to help with home-work, wash-up and feed the cat and a family of five simultaneously? What is a 'culinary skill'? Does it require more skill to search through recipes and prepare a perfect fennel and vodka risotto and vin santo ice-cream for lunch with friends than to make a vaguely edible chocolate cake on a wet Saturday afternoon with some grumpy kids? And how do children acquire culinary ability? How are cooking skills transferred inter-generationally?

Knowledge about contemporary domestic cooking and cooks is, as many experts have pointed out, severely limited and often reliant on speculation (Dickinson and Leader, 1998; James and McColl, 1997 and Murcott, 1995 and 2000). The study upon which this study is based aimed to establish an empirically researched and theoretically based 'way of thinking' about domestic cooking and cooking skills that would contribute to understanding and the development of current discourse. Thirty domestic cooks (defined as people who prepared food – any food and with any frequency – on a domestic basis) living in England spoke in detail about their values and beliefs about cooking and the skills and knowledge they use to prepare and provide food for themselves, their families and friends.

This paper uses some of the findings of the study to explore four concepts, or themes, integral to any debate about cooking, nurture and future generations of home-cooks. The first three themes – 'the meaning of cooking', 'culinary skills and cooking ability', and 'good cooks and good cooking' – enhance the discussion of a final theme – 'acquiring cooking skills and becoming a cook'.

The meaning of cooking

> If I'm cooking for myself I'll just cook pasta and have it with pesto" said Kirsty, "I very rarely cook for myself" she went on to say, stressing the word cook, "I never really experiment cooking wise

All the cooks who took part in the study, including Kirsty, used and understood 'cook' in a number of different ways. It could refer to 'food preparation in general' (as in "cooking for myself") or the application of heat (as in "cook pasta"). It could also be used to refer to a type of more highly valued 'proper cooking' (as in "I very rarely *cook* for myself"). 'Proper cooking' was associated with greater effort and with such things as using recipes, special shopping trips, preparing different and interesting food and food preparation for special occasions. It was often associated with a higher use (than was 'usual' for the individual concerned) of fresh, raw foods. However, 'proper cooking' did not necessarily involve the sole use of fresh, raw foods. For Dean for example, pasta carbonara is the only thing that he has "ever really *cooked*", though he makes it clear that he uses a 'packet sauce mix' to do so.

Some cooks, usually those involved in the preparation of food on a daily and all-day basis, often interpreted the term 'cook' as meaning '*all* food preparation and provision' in the course of their interviews. Pouring cereals, making coffee and packed lunches, re-heating baby food and cartons of soup, grilling fish fingers and searching through the fridge for leftovers with which to make a sauce for pasta were all deemed 'cooking'.

This complexity of the use and understanding of the term cook hints at the corresponding complexity of contemporary domestic 'cooking culture' as a whole.

Today's domestic cooks (the research revealed) find the use of 'pre-prepared' foods entirely acceptable and do not expect to cook such food as bread, sausages, fruit yoghurts, pasta and breakfast cereals 'from scratch'. In fact they often prefer the taste and appearance of pre-prepared foods. Mayonnaise, paneer, lemon meringue pie, pizza, gingerbread men and chicken soup were all referred to as pre-prepared foods thought preferable to home-made versions. Underpinning people's use of 'raw' and 'pre-prepared' foods is a set of guidelines based around the perceived importance of different cooking occasions, the effort it is felt should be applied on that occasion, and the reward it is felt will be received in return[131]. In contemporary domestic cooking culture 'variety', 'interesting' and 'different' are highly valued concepts, recipes are seen as 'right and proper', and cooking is something that the cook can 'get right' or 'get wrong' (titled 'dishes' and recipes and foods that can be bought pre-prepared are most likely to be judged in this way; combinations of foods without a title and more tenuously linked with a specific cuisine, such as 'meat and two veg', less so).

Despite these general, cultural approaches, cooking also means many different things to different people. Though influenced by such things as food provision responsibilities, gender, life-stage, ethnic heritage and cooking experience, cooking is individualist. Some cooks see themselves as 'creators', others as 'providers' or 'learners', yet others as 'experimenters' and 'strugglers'. David described himself as "gadget mad" whereas Moh said he viewed cooking as 'trying out recipes', as something to "tackle". "A bored cook" is how Gay described herself. She is weary, she explained, of endlessly thinking of new foods and recipes to cook for her family. Mick, on the other hand, described himself as a "not interested" cook and appeared faintly bemused by the idea of cooking as a hobby. "I would never think 'ooh lets cook lamb madras. Turn off the telly, turn off the phone and lets get going'" he laughed.

These personal approaches can clearly be seen in the following descriptions of preparing a casserole (people were asked if they were confident about making a casserole or something similar, and if so, what they would do). The first is from a 'self-confessed foodie' who seemed to want to reveal his knowledge of techniques and methods.

> I get a piece of lamb, cube it and brown it off. Then I take that out of the pan and in goes onion, in goes garlic. Then I might use some kind of pulse, some haricot beans or something. I put the lamb back, and I'd have pre-cooked the beans, so I add those with the cooking liquid. I add red wine and I put a little bouquet of parsley, thyme and bay leaf in there. I tie that up and drop that in. Then I let it all cook through. (Patrick)

The second is from a woman who appeared keen to identity herself as a 'provider' of family food and to emphasise how she cooks economically, efficiently and without instruction.

> I buy a dish of diced lamb or pork from the supermarket and I fry that with a bit of garlic and then put it into a casserole dish. Then I chop up a couple of potatoes, some carrots and some onion and throw that in with a few, dried herbs. Next, I crumble up a couple of stock cubes, put that in and pour some boiling water over. If I've got a bit of leftover red wine, some vegetable stock or some soup I'd made that was left over, then I'd put that. (Liz)

Culinary ability and cooking skills

Do we still know how to cook? We asked people how long it takes to soft boil an egg. 74% gave the wrong answer. The average time given was just over 3 minutes. 9% of 18 – 24 year olds thought it would take 6 – 10 minutes. (The Guardian, 2003)

'Making a white sauce', 'preparing vegetables', 'boiling an egg', 'grating cheese', 'microwaving', 'poaching', 'cooking rice', 'stir-frying', and 'making a cake' – many studies that have focused, at least in part, on domestic cooking have described practical tasks and techniques such as these as, or used them as examples of, 'cooking skills' (see Adamson, 1996; Dunmeyer-Stookey and Barker, 1994; Fort, 2003; Lang et al., 1999; Nestle Family Monitor, 2001; Nicolaas, 1995; Rodrigues and de Almeida, 1996; Wrieden et al., 2002). Taking this approach, making a pizza might then be understood to involve such 'cooking skills' as 'kneading' and 'rolling dough', 'chopping tomatoes', and 'grating cheese'. However, Martin's description of making a pizza 'from scratch' had little mention of technical, 'cooking skills' and abilities such as these. Rather, his words revealed his ability to judge when a pizza is cooked, "forage around" for suitable topping ingredients, organise its preparation to fit in around other household tasks and so on. Similarly, when Kate described how her three year-old son is 'learning to cook' she made no reference to his practical abilities. *"He knows that the cooker is hot [and] wants to look in and see things happening"*, she explained, *"he's trying to grasp a concept of times and how long things take."* Likewise, Jen's one-year-old daughter is *"well aware of what food you need to cook and what food you don't"*.

Skills experts point out that practical skills can be described and understood at different levels of detail; there being general agreement that the skills involved in practical tasks are complex and consist not only of mechanical, technical abilities but also academic knowledge and 'tacit' perceptual, conceptual and planning skills (acquired through the application of mechanical skills) (Gabriel, 1990; Pinch, Collins and Corbone, 1996; Singleton, 1974 and Wood, 1982). Useful and insightful skills research, says Lee (1982), is the result of finding and utilising the most informative level of detail for the study in question and understanding that skills can be conceptualised according to the 'requirements of the task' (task centred) or the 'capabilities of the cook' (person centred). In other words, cooking skills and knowledge can be seen as contextual. Making a chocolate sponge to a 'high standard' with the help of a recipe and without interruption would involve different skills to making it with children and no instruction or making it 'fit to sell' in a hectic professional kitchen and with little time to spare. However, all three tasks would involve similar technical 'cooking skills' such as 'mixing', 'beating' and 'baking'.

The cooks who took part in the study that informs this paper were found to use perceptual cooking skills of timing and judgement and abilities to understand the properties of food in terms of taste, colour and texture and how they will react when combined or heated. *"You've got to get the consistency just right for a scone to be nice and light"* Helen remarked, showing an understanding of the link between the texture of the scone dough during the preparation process and the final, cooked result. They also had design and organisational cooking skills, often based on an ability to conceptualise food preparation processes and outcomes – the taste or texture of a combination of ingredients, for example, or the effort involved in a particular cooking task. Design skills took many forms – making a sandwich, for example, recreating a ready-meal seen in a supermarket, or preparing *"a tomatoey based sauce [with] whatever I've got"* to serve with pasta. Organisational cooking skills included the simultaneous preparation of a number of foods, the cooking of foods to be ready for a pre-specified time, and the fitting of cooking into busy days. The cooks also demonstrated knowledge of food hygiene, chemistry, history, geography and nutrition as well as of tastes, flavours and combinations of ingredients considered complementary (within a particular cuisine, that is) – of "what goes with what" as one cook put it.

'More difficult to classify' cooking skills were also evident. An ability to cook to suit the preferences and requirements of others was one such skill used by the cooks: they talked of how families and partners preferred that fish fingers were not to be too black, curry was neither too mild nor too spicy, and tomato 'chunks' were never visible. Cooking under difficult circumstances – whether for an important social occasion, for example, or with small children underfoot – was another. *"When you're at a hot cooker and the kids are trying to pull your legs ... you have to constantly move them away"* said Kate. *"I find cooking can be very stressful"*.

Can the skills involved in cooking fish fingers, frozen chips and peas whilst simultaneously washing up and helping with homework be compared with the devotion of an entire afternoon to preparing sushi 'from scratch' with the aid of a recipe? Is it possible to argue that the person who regularly prepares a nutritious meal for their family with 'what's left in the fridge' is more, or less, skilled than the person who occasionally makes a lemon mousse of a consistency deemed 'correct' by food writers and experts? At what point can the individual be seen as 'having' a cooking skill? What is the criterion for measurement? Can a person be judged as able to poach when they can make food vaguely edible by this technique? Do they have to be able to poach a range of foods, perhaps attaining a certain technical standard, and under pressure of time? Should they know how poaching fits into British or French cuisine?

"How good are you in the kitchen?" a newspaper report asked of London shoppers (Bell, 1998). "Can you poach an egg? Make a white sauce? Make gravy?" (Note the culinary specificity of terms such as these that have been used in this and many much larger surveys to appraise culinary skill and knowledge in multi-cultural societies such as the UK.) What is 'being good in the kitchen'?

What is 'being able to cook'? Does it entail an individual being able to cook effortlessly with all the foodstuffs and ingredients available to them in the locale in which they live or shop for food? Does 'being able to cook' refer to an ability to prepare healthy food, that fits dietary requirements, for a family or household? The words of the chef and restaurateur Gary Rhodes (2002) suggest that for him culinary ability involves preparing 'dishes' and the attaining of certain accepted technical standards within the style and preferred tastes of a particular cuisine. *"I believe that young people should be taught to make and cook well-crafted, good quality dishes"*, he says. *"It is important to know about and use foundation recipes. These are the basic recipes that are traditionally used in cooking where the proportions of the ingredients remain the same unless variation is added"* (Rhodes, 2002, 56). But is this approach to culinary skill relevant or related to the home-cook, for food for their family and/or their friends whilst coping with work and other household tasks, restricted by daily schedules and often with limited resources?

Good cooks and good cooking

> I suppose [a good cook can make] a variety of food with novel ideas and nice presentation, looking completely stress free as they were doing it. (Mel)

For contemporary cooks, 'good cooking' (this study found), is about "interesting food", "original food", "a variety of food"; good cooks prepare "food that looks good", "don't need recipes", "cook like professionals", "do great desserts" and are able to cook like "just about everyone on the telly because they make it look so easy when they do really difficult dishes." The concepts of 'good cooking' and 'good cook' are rarely associated with such things as preparing nutritious food and feeding a family. For the cooks who took part in the research that informed this study, even the frequently mentioned quality of being able to make 'something from nothing' is not connected with being economical but with being spontaneously creative and able to "make something interesting from relatively few ingredients."

The most valued food occasions in contemporary cooking culture, it appears, involve special occasions, friends and guests. (Food for the family is thought of as food 'just for us' and is far less likely to be perceived as involving 'proper cooking'.) These are opportunities to exhibit culinary expertise and knowledge and to apply 'effort' knowing that commensurate 'reward' will be gained.

This is a value system which resembles that which Ann Oakley (1985, 58) called the "creative cooking ideal". (She studied cooking practices as part of a study of women and housework). The aim of 'cooking', under this ideal, becomes "how to get beyond the usual range of meals with time consuming inventiveness" rather than "how to get the most nutritious meals prepared in the shortest possible time". In reality however, says Oakley, "husbands demand meals at specific times, small children cry when their stomachs are empty, the hour that might be cooking competes with the hour that ought to be spent washing the floor or changing the beds." In this way, the 'creative cooking ideal', argues Oakley, puts pressure on the cook (the person responsible for domestic food provision) rather than make cooking an enjoyable and pleasant experience. An interesting point considering that contemporary domestic cooks are continually told that cooking (with fresh, raw foods that is) is both interesting and fun and that an 'interest' in cooking will provide an impetus to do so (see Adamson, 1996; Leith, 1998; Lyon, Colquhoun and Alexander, 2003; Street, 1994).

Acquiring cooking skills, becoming a cook

"Few parents teach their kids to cook" proclaims food writer and campaigner Prue Leith in an introduction to a survey of home-cooking by Sainsbury's The Magazine. "Who taught you to cook?" the same survey asks of its respondents (Innes, 1998). "How much, if at all, are your children taught at home about cooking?" questions a recent MORI study (Nestle Family Monitor, 2001). Likewise, an oft-quoted survey by the Health Education Authority (1998 [and see Lang et al., 1999]) enquires of its respondents "when you first started learning to cook, which of any of these did you learn from?": 'mother', 'father', 'articles in magazines', 'booklets from food producers' and 'health centre/doctor' being some of the sources of information for respondents to choose from.

In current commentary about the state of cooking the acquisition of culinary knowledge and cooking skills is conceptualised as 'task centred'; a straightforward teaching and learning process where the focus of research is on understanding more about 'sources of learning' such as 'school cookery lessons', 'grandmother', and 'cook books'. Yet the research upon which this paper is based found that domestic cooks, who rarely set out purposefully to learn to cook, extend their experience of foods and cookery techniques (and hence their tacit skills of timing, judgement, design and organisation) in a haphazard and fortuitous manner. They 'pick up' new ideas and hints about food and cooking by 'flicking through' food articles in magazines and journals, from the casual observance of television cookery programmes, and through informal chats about food with friends or relations. Cookery books and recipes are used but only by some cooks and usually only for special 'cooking occasions' (when they are often a source of inspiration rather than precise instruction). Patrick, for example, explained how he once picked up *Hello Magazine* in his Doctor's waiting room and glanced at a recipe which he has since made, 'in some form or other', on a number of occasions. Another cook, Daisy, described how she once noticed her daughter stud a joint of pork with whole garlic cloves; a "tip", she added, that she now regularly uses herself.

Gaining cooking experience and skills of judgement, timing, creativity and planning is often a process of 'trial and error'. When James, for example, first started to cook he explained, he would *"chop all my vegetables up, the onion and the garlic, and put it all into a pan. And then it would be 'that's cooked but that's not, the onion's raw and the garlic's burnt'"* . *"Eventually"* he said, *"[I] learned to cook things in some sort of order [and] put different vegetables in at different times".*

Are children and teenagers 'taught' to cook by their parents or guardians? Do they 'learn to cook' in a purposeful manner using distinctive sources of learning? Or do they follow the hit-or-miss adult example (described above)?

In the home, children (the research revealed) can acquire cooking skills and knowledge in a number of different ways. 'Learning to cook' at home, it appears, is not about structured cookery lessons and formal 'teaching' but about being informally apprenticed in the ways of the kitchen. Cooking can be a 'play activity'; younger children 'cook for fun' and make such things as cake and jelly with their mother (and it is usually mother). Sometimes children (of all ages) help out in the kitchen – fetching food, opening packets, scrubbing, peeling and chopping, washing up and unpacking carrier bags of food. Younger children often watch food preparation activities; Hal's little girl likes to see food changing colour under the grill and listen for the 'ping' of the microwave. Sometimes older children cook for themselves and their friends; Jez likes to 'cook' himself and his mates 'chicken kievs' and 'oven chips' to eat whilst they watch a video.

What kind of cook – the creator, the provider, the experimenter – 'involves' children the most? Who is best at nurturing the young cook and passing on skills and knowledge to the next generation?

Liz sees herself as a 'provider' of food, and feeding her family well is, she says, the reason why she cooks. Cooking for her, Liz explains, is neither an interest nor chore but just, as she says, *"part of my life"*. Her young children are usually involved in cooking on a daily basis whether she is using pre-prepared foods or cooking 'from scratch'. They stir saucepans of pre-prepared pasta sauces, add extra, favourite toppings to pizza, whip-up packet desserts and fetch fish fingers from the freezer as well as help make pancakes, scrambled egg and packed lunches.

Margaret makes the point that when cooking with children *"you have to mind about not doing things properly ... you have to just enjoy it and hope things come out edible"*. "I'm not terribly good at that" she admits. Martin finds that cooking with his four-year-old daughter "can be difficult". *"It's a kind of balancing act between letting her think she's helping and actually not letting her help at all"*, he says. For Patrick cooking is about accomplishment and success; using pre-prepared foods is not 'cooking'. He loves to cook, he says, and prefers to cook alone especially on important 'cooking occasions' because he likes the food he prepares to be 'his'. Patrick feels that food gets "ruined" if his children help or participate.

Making cakes is an enjoyable way of spending a rainy afternoon with her son says Maureen, and, though perfectly able to bake a cake 'from scratch', they usually use a packet mix. They are better suited to his attention span, she explains, and he loves all the little envelopes, cake cases, different mixtures and cartoon characters almost as much as she does.

Current knowledge provides little detail of *how* children acquire culinary ability and knowledge in the home. The nurture of young cooks into cultural foodways is a subject that deserves far greater attention. Certainly, passing on culinary ability and knowledge to following generations involves numerous skills and abilities in itself.

Perhaps the transference of useful cooking skills and knowledge, beneficial for health and well-being, from one generation to the next is less about practical and technical skill levels and the use of 'raw foods' and 'pre-prepared foods' than about personality and approaches to cooking. The key to the nurturing and apprenticeship of future cooks who can enjoy good food and provide themselves with a healthy diet may not lie with formal 'lessons' in the domestic kitchen, technical standards and achievement, and an avoidance of pre-prepared foods. Rather, the key may lie in 'getting involved', tasting, watching, smelling, fetching, being patient, feeling, understanding, playing, not worrying about culinary 'success', helping, enjoying and an appreciation of the numerous and varied skills involved in preparing and providing food, on a daily basis, to family, friends and self.

References

ADAMSON, A., (1996), Food, Health and Cooking: why it matters, in *Get Cooking! In Newcastle*, a report of a conference held in London, February 1996, (London: National Food Alliance).

BADEROON, G. (2002), Everybody's mother was a good cook: meanings of food in Muslim cooking, in *Agenda* 51, <www.agenda.org.za.Gabeba>

BELL, A (1998), Storm in an egg cup as Gary says Delia's cookery advice is 'insulting', in *The Independent*, October 27.

DICKINSON, R. AND LEADER, S. (1998), Ask the Family, in *Consuming Passions: Food in the Age of Anxiety*, Griffiths, S. and Wallace, J. (eds.), (Manchester: Manchester University Press), pp. 122 – 129.

DUNMEYER-STOOKEY, J. AND BARKER, M. E., (1994), *Socio-cultural factors affecting food choice: the role of culinary knowledge*. Working paper for the School of Health and related research, University of Sheffield.

FORT, M. (2003), The Death of Cooking, in Food, the Way We Eat Now, *The Guardian* (supplement), May 10, p. 11.

GABRIEL, Y., (1990), *Working Live in Catering*, (London: Routledge).

GUARDIAN, THE, (2003), A Diet Based on Worry, in *Food, the Way We Eat Now*, (supplement), 10 May, p. 3.

HEALTH EDUCATION AUTHORITY, (1998), *Health and Lifestyles: a Survey of the UK Population 1993*, (London: Health Education Authority).

JAMES, W. P. T. AND MCCOLL, K. A. (1997), *Healthy English Schoolchildren: A new approach to physical activity and food*, (Aberdeen: Rowlett Research Institute).

LANG, T., CARAHER, M., DIXON, P. AND CARR-HILL, R., (1999), *Cooking Skills and Health*, (London: Health Education Authority).

LANG, T. AND CARAHER, M., (2001), Is there a culinary skills transition? Data and debate from the UK about changes in cooking culture, *Journal of the Home Economics Institute of Australia*, Vol. 5, No.2, pp. 2–14.

LAWSON, N., (1998), Can't cook, don't want to, in *The Guardian*, October 13, pp. 6-7.

LEATHER, S., (1996), The making of modern malnutrition. An overview of food poverty in the UK, (London: the Caroline Walker Trust).

LEE, D., (1982), Beyond deskilling: skill, craft and class, in Wood, S., (ed.), *The Degradation of Work? Skill, deskilling and the labour process*, (London: Anchor Press), pp. 146 – 162.

LEITH, P., (1998), *Cooking with Kids, in Consuming Passions: Food in the Age of Anxiety*, Griffiths, S. and Wallace, J. (eds.), (Manchester: Manchester University Press), pp. 58 – 65.

LYON, P., COLQUHOUN, A. AND ALEXANDER, E (2003), Deskilling the domestic kitchen: national tragedy or the making of a modern myth, in *Culinary Arts and Sciences* IV, Global and National Perspectives,

Edwards, J. S. A, and Gustafsson, I-B (eds.), pp. 402 – 412, (Bournemouth: Worshipful Company of Cooks Research Centre).

MURCOTT, A., (1995), Raw, cooked and proper meals at home, in *Food Choice and the Consumer*, Marshall, D. W, (ed.), (Glasgow: Blackie Academic and Professional), pp. 219 – 234.

MURCOTT, A., (2000), Is it still a pleasure to cook for him? Social Changes in the household and the family, in the *Journal of Consumer Studies and Home Economics*, 24, pp. 78 – 84.

NESTLE FAMILY MONITOR, (2001), Carried out by MORI on behalf of Nestle UK, No. 13.

NICOLAAS, G., (1995), Cooking, Attitudes and Behaviour, a working report on the OPCS omnibus survey data produced on behalf of the Nutrition Task Force for the Department of Health, London, Crown Copyright.

OAKLEY, A., (1985), *The Sociology of Housework*, (Oxford: Basil Blackwell).

PERINAU, L. (2002), Dining with the Doom Generation, in *Gastronomica. The Journal of Food and Culture*, Vol. 2, No. 4, <www.ucpress.edu/gastro>

PINCH, T., COLLINS, H. M. AND CORBONE, L., (1996), Inside knowledge: second order measures of skill, in *The Sociological Review*, Vol. 44, No. 2, pp. 163 – 186.

RHODES, G., (2002), Famous Last Words, Rhodes from School, in *Cook School: The Food Education Magazine*, the Design Dimension Educational Trust, launch issue, p. 56.

RODRIGUES, S. S. P. AND DE ALMEIDA, M. D. V., (1996), Food habits: concepts and practices of two different age groups, in Edwards, J. S. A. (ed.), *Culinary Arts and Sciences*. Global and National Perspectives (ICCAS96), (London: Computational Mechanics Publications), pp. 387 – 397.

SEELEY, A. (2003), Stress Free Cooking, Ashford, in *Let Us Eat Cake!* News letter of the Food Poverty Network (Sustain, the alliance for better food and farming), issue 28, pp. 14 – 15.

SINGLETON, W. T., (1978), The Study of Real Skills. Volume 1 The Analysis of Practical Skills, (London: MTP Press Ltd).

STITT, S., JEPSON, M., PAULSON-BOX, E., AND PRISK, E., (1996), *Research on Food Education and the Diet and Health of Nations*, (Liverpool: John Moores University Consumer Research).

STREET, P. A., (1994), An investigation into the prevalence and degree of cooking skills in North Reddish. With particular reference to mothers on a low income with young children, dissertation for the Department of Food and Consumer Science, Manchester, Manchester Metropolitan University.

WOOD, S. (ed.), (1982), The Degradation of Work? Skill, deskilling and the labour process, (London: Anchor Press).

WRIEDEN, W. L., ANDERSON, A. S., LONGBOTTOM, P. J., VALENTINE, K., STEAD, M., CARAHER, M., LANG, T., AND DOWLER, E., (2002), Assisting dietary change in low-income communities: assessing the impact of community-based practical food skills intervention (CookWell), working report to the Food Standards Agency.

Commercial Nurturing:
The Culinary Education of America's Youth

Andrew F Smith

Introduction

Three massive shifts simultaneously jolted the United States during the last half of the 19th century. The first two were demographic: an internal population migration of people from farms to the cities; and a massive immigration into American cities from Southern and Eastern Europe. The third was the industrial revolution, which provided employment for those arriving in American cities and created vast quantities of low-cost goods that had to be sold.

These shifts affected every aspect of American life, especially that of food production and consumption. Through the 19th century, most Americans grew a substantial portion of their own food on farms or in garden plots. Small general stores catered to those who were not self-sufficient or who desired luxuries not grown or raised in the local area. Food was mainly sold as generic products measured out from unmarked barrels, sacks and jars. This changed as food production was industrialized. Food processors and manufacturers grew rapidly after the Civil War (1861-1865) as massive agricultural surpluses flooded the market and technology lowered the cost of production. The result was the rise of large food manufacturers, who converted generic foods into branded products.

These shifts set in motion a multitude of changes in American society, and they specifically altered the way young Americans learned about food and its consumption. For millennia, culinary wisdom – what to eat, and how to obtain, store, prepare and consume it– had been passed down orally from one generation to the next, usually from mother to daughter. In American cities at the beginning of the 20th century, this traditional system broke down. Generations were often separated by great distances, and the culinary wisdom based in rural or "old country" lifestyles was not necessarily useful in American cities, where qualities and quantities of ingredients differed as did the ways in which food could be prepared and consumed.

Commercial Nurturing

Jumping into this void were food processors, who were extremely interested in selling their branded products. To make these more expensive new products financially viable, consumers had to be convinced to purchase them. To accomplish this, food companies began advertising their products nationally and regionally through newspapers and magazines, and locally through circulars, billboards, and promotion at points of sale. Food advertising became a major source of American knowledge about what, when, and how to eat.

Almost from the beginning, children became the favorite target of advertisers, especially for selling particular products, such as breakfast cereals, snack foods and soft drinks. Later, fast food was added to this list. Most of those foods had high concentrations of fat, sugar and/or salt, which appealed to children's uneducated tastebuds. Inexpensive items, such as candy and sodas, could be purchased directly by some children. When children lacked funds to purchase products, they influenced their parents through "pester power." Advertisers found it easy to manipulate children, who have not yet developed the intellectual skills to distinguish fantasy from reality in advertisements.[1] Focusing on children also had another potential long-term effect from the advertiser's standpoint: children will often continue to purchase these familiar products throughout their lives.

Food advertisers reached children in a variety of ways. They have, for instance, mounted point-of-sale displays, placed billboards in strategic places where children will see them, and circulated a vast array of printed material, including flyers, posters, coloring books, trade cards, picture books, comic books, and stamp albums. Almost from the beginning food companies advertised in children's magazines.

From the early decades of the 20th century, food advertisers have also tried to reach students in schools. Some food manufacturers have tried to introduce their products into the school through school lunch programs. Recently, candy and soda manufacturers have placed vending machines selling their products on school campuses. The school makes money on the operation, gaining funds needed for educational materials and supplies. Other manufacturers sponsor athletic teams and send representatives to campuses seeking student workers. Food manufacturers also produce vast quantities of "educational" material that promotes their products; these are intended for circulation though the schools.[1] Finally, Channel One Network– a commercial educational television network watched by students during school time–broadcasts numerous commercials for snack food, cereal, fast food and soda manufacturers, such as Mars, Kellogg Company, Pizza Hut, and PepsiCo.

When radio became America's prime source for entertainment, food advertisers sponsored children's programs. When television emerged, food companies advertised on children's programs. Since the 1950s, television has dominated the advertising market targeted at children. One recent study found that 33 percent of American children watched twenty or more hours of television weekly. On a typical Saturday morning, a young American TV viewer may be exposed to over one hundred commercials. Annually, American children are exposed to more than 10,000 food and beverage commercials. The majority of these commercials promote foods high in fat, sugar and calories, such as potato chips, chocolate bars, and sugar-coated breakfast foods, while less than two percent of children's commercials promote healthy foods, such as fruit, milk, and vegetables.[3]

Food advertisers use many techniques to persuade American youth to purchase their products. Here are some successful examples of such campaigns.

Selling Soup

From the earliest days of American food advertising at the beginning of the 20th century, children have been used to sell products. One early food advertiser who did so was the Campbell Soup Company. In 1904, Theodore Wiederseim, an advertising agent, convinced Campbell's executives that the way to sell soup was to target women through "child appeal." Wiederseim's wife, illustrator Grace Drayton, drew plump, rosy-cheeked children and presented the drawings to Campbell's. The concept was accepted and the company launched what would become known as the Campbell Kids. The Kids appeared on advertisements in early 1905 and have been a part of Campbell's advertising ever since. The not so subliminal message was simple: kids who consume Campbell's Soup are healthy and happy. The initial advertisements were aimed at adults, but children themselves became the target in 1910, when Campbell's Kids' likenesses were first sold as dolls. Subsequently, their likenesses appeared on a vast array of promotional items, such as balloons, bells, cards, clocks, cookie jars, dolls, jewelry, lunch boxes, mugs, music boxes, napkins, pails, planes, puzzles, t-shirts, thermoses, toys, and watches, – to name but a few. By any standard, the Campbell's Kids are among the most successful American advertising icons, although recently they have been slimmed down as concern with obesity has increased in America.[4]

Selling Confections

Cracker Jack, a confection of popcorn, peanuts and molasses, was trademarked in 1896. At the time, it was a product sold locally in Chicago. Within two decades, it had become the "World's largest selling confection." The main reason for the snack's rise from obscurity to the pinnacle of success was advertising. At first, the company's adverting was aimed toward adults. It was promoted in magazines as "a healthful, nourishing food-confection." In 1910, the company placed coupons in Cracker Jack packages that could be redeemed for over three hundred "varieties of handsome and useful articles, such as Watches, Jewelry, Silverware, Sporting Goods, Toys, Games, Sewing Machines and many other useful Household articles." Redeeming the coupons, however, was cumbersome for the consumer and costly for the company, so they scrapped that promotion and instead began to enclose a children's toy in every package. Packaging also played a part in targeting children. In 1916, the familiar little boy in a sailor suit, along with his dog, Bingo, first appeared in ads; three years later the characters became part of the design of the Cracker Jack box. Sales soared. By 1926, the Cracker Jack Company was selling more than 138 million boxes annually.[5] Cracker Jack has declined in importance as a snack food, but the combination of food and toys as a magnet for young consumers has greatly increased in significance over the years. The most spectacular example is McDonald's.

Selling Hamburgers

In 1960, the McDonald's franchise in Washington, D.C. sponsored a local children's television program called *Bozo's Circus*. Sales in Washington grew by a whopping 30 percent per year during the next four years. In 1963 the television station dropped *Bozo's Circus*, which had lagged in the ratings. The local McDonald's franchisee decided to keep the clown in the public eye by producing television commercials starring Bozo. These were the first commercials initiated by a McDonald's franchisee. The clown was renamed Archie McDonald, which offered an allusion to the McDonald's Golden Arches symbol, but there was a sportscaster in the Washington area named Arch McDonald, so another name had to be found. Ronald McDonald, with its pleasing memorable rhyme, was selected instead. Ronald McDonald's first television commercials were broadcast in October 1963.

When the national McDonald's Corporation sponsored the television broadcast of the Macy's Thanksgiving Day Parade in 1965, the commercials featured Ronald McDonald. Previously, no fast food chain had advertised on national television, and it was a risk because McDonald's did most of its business in the summertime, not in the fall. Also risky was the direct appeal to children, who were not then considered an important target of fast food promoters. The Thanksgiving Day advertisement produced immediate nationwide results and this convinced McDonald's to focus more of their ads toward children. Ronald McDonald became the company's "official spokesman" in 1966. His image appeared on television commercials and on a vast array of products, including coloring books, comic books, cups, dolls, frisbees, games, mugs, napkins, postcards, puppets, records, toy parachutes, trains, and trucks, and the famous "Flying Hamburger."[6]

In addition, McDonald's in-store Playlands – in-store playgrounds in McDonald's restaurants – featured Ronald McDonald and a cast of other mythical characters. While none of the other characters achieved the prominence of Ronald McDonald, the Playlands strengthened McDonald's dominance in the fast food market. In 1979, McDonald's inaugurated the Happy Meal, a special children's meal packaged with toys. The Happy Meal was a resounding success. It was copied by other fast-food sellers and McDonald's program is still in effect today. Thanks to the Happy Meal, McDonald's is the world's largest toy distributor. Ninety-six percent of American children recognize Ronald McDonald. As for the success of the chain's advertising campaigns, just do the math: every month more than 90 percent of American kids eat at McDonald's, and most children bring their parents along with them.

Selling Candy

McDonald's and other fast food establishments have also tied their marketing activities to major children's motion pictures. In these cases, toys related to the film are mass produced along with many other promotional materials. There's also the huge industry of "product placement" in movies. By far the most successful example was the big-budget feature film *E. T.* In 1981, Universal Studios approached Hershey's Food Company for assistance with making a new film. The main character in the film was a lovable alien, and the filmmakers wanted to have the children in the film lure the creature with a trail of candy. The producers had previously contacted Mars, Inc., requesting the use m&ms, but Mars refused. So Universal turned to Hershey for permission to use Reese's Pieces instead, and Hershey agreed. Reese's Pieces consequently received national visibility in the blockbuster film, which set box office records; it was a cheap marketing triumph.[7]

Selling Peanuts and Peanut Butter

Food companies and their marketing experts have frequently created brand names expressly to appeal to children. Joseph L. Rosefield, for instance, selected the name "Skippy" for his peanut butter. Most likely, the name was derived from a children's comic strip also called "Skippy," launched by Percy L. Crosby in 1923. Rosefield's use of the name "Skippy" generated several lawsuits, which were eventually settled out of court. But the name "Skippy" appealed to kids, and sales have been high ever since. Today, "Skippy" is the second largest peanut butter brand in the world.

The only brand surpassing Skippy's sales is Peter Pan. The E. K Pond Company manufactured peanut butter beginning in 1920, but its sales were limited. The lackluster sales encouraged the company to change the name to something catchier, "Peter Pan" after the popular fantasy character popularized in the 1903 James M. Barrie play and the 1920s silent film. As soon as the new name appeared, sales took off. In 1940, a major marketing campaign was inaugurated. The product was advertised nationally in the mid-1940s. The radio program, "Sky King," was sponsored by Peter Pan. When the program moved to television in September 1951, Peter Pan continued to sponsor it. The company issued coloring books in 1960, comic books by 1963 and games by 1969. It recently spent $400,000 on posters associated with the "Rescuers" television program.

Another example of targeting children is Planters Peanuts, which was launched in 1906 by two Italian immigrants, Amedeo Obici and Mario Peruzzi. In 1916 Planters conducted a contest to develop a trademark, offering a prize worth $5 for the best designed symbol. The winner was a 14-year-old boy named Anthony Gentile, who submitted a drawing of "a little peanut person." With this image as a starting point, Planters hired a Chicago art firm, which commissioned a commercial artist named Andrew Wallach to draw several different characters. Wallach added a top hat, monocle, cane, and the look of a raffish gentleman, who was subsequently named "Mr. Peanut." Planters applied for a trademark on March 12, 1917. During that year, Mr. Peanut made his debut in New England newspapers and on advertising posters in New York City subway trains. A national advertising campaign followed. This was so successful that Planters increased its advertising budget for each succeeding year, spending hundreds of thousands of dollars on ads in the best newspapers and magazines in the country. Within a few years, salted peanuts and confections bearing Mr. Peanut's picture became known "everywhere in this broad land of America." Planters opened a store on the Boardwalk in Atlantic City, New Jersey. A man dressed in a Mr. Peanut outfit greeted visitors outside the store and became one of the most memorable figures along the Boardwalk. By the mid-1930s, Mr. Peanut had become the symbol for the entire peanut industry.[8]

Since his origin, Mr. Peanut has been on virtually every Planters package, container, premium, and advertisement. As a result, the Mr. Peanut character has become one of the most familiar icons in advertising history. His likeness graces mugs, pencils, pens, and tote bags that are available by redeeming product wrappers. Planters offered a variety of premium items with its products: glass jars, charm bracelets, clocks, metal tins, wristwatches, ashtrays, plastic whistles and display figures with monocles which light up. By the mid-twentieth century, Mr. Peanut had become a children's hero and an American culinary icon.

Effects of Children's Advertising and Promotion

Today, according to the Centers for Disease Control and Prevention, nine million American children, aged 6 to 19, are overweight. This is three times the number 20 years ago. While there are many causes for the increase in obesity among American children, one obvious cause is the consumption of fast food, snack foods and soft drinks. As Eric Schlosser states, the fast-food industry spends billions of dollars every year marketing high-fat, unhealthy food to children.[9]

The United States may be a good example of a national "nurturing system" that has gone awry, but a number of potential solutions have been advocated. There is a major effort under way, for instance, to ban the sale of snack foods and sodas on school campuses. Perhaps the United States can follow the lead of other nations that have banned or restricted commercials on children's television programs, such as Norway, Sweden and Austria.

Notes

1. Ratner, E. M., et al., FTC Staff Report on Television Advertising to Children (Washington: Federal Trade Commission] : for sale by the Supt. of Docs., U.S. Govt. Print. Office, 1978).
2. Sheila Hart, Hucksters in the Classroom; A Review of Industry Propaganda in Schools (Washington, DC: Center for Study of Responsive Law, 1979).
3. Vessey, Judith A., Paula K. Yim-Chiplis, and Nancy R. MacKenzie, "Effects of Television Viewing on Children's Development," Pediatric Nursing 23 (September/October 1998): 483.
4. David Young and Micki Young, Campbell's Soup Collectibles: A Price and Identification Guide. (Iola, Wisconsin: Krause Publications, 1998); for more about the Campbell's Kids advertising see Andrew F. Smith, Souper Tomatoes: The Story of America's Favorite Food (New Brunswick: Rutgers University Press, 2000), 95-6.
5. For more information about Cracker Jack advertising, see Andrew F. Smith, Popped Culture: A Social History of Popcorn in America (Columbia: University of South Carolina Press, 1999), 86-88.
6. For more about the Happy Mal toys, see Gary Henriques and Audre DuVall, McDonald's Collectibles; Identification and Value Guide (Paducah, KY: Collector Books, nd); Meredith Williams, Tomart's Price Guide to McDonald's Happy Meal Collectibles. Revised and Updated (Dayton, Ohio: Tomart Publications, 1995); Terry Losonsky, and Joyce Losonsky, McDonald's Happy Meal Toys around the World (Atglen, PA: Schiffer Publishing, Lttd., 1995);
7. Joël Glenn Brenner, The Emperors of Chocolate; Inside the Secret World of Hershey & Mars (New York: Broadway Books, 2000), 273-8.
8. For more about Planter's Peanuts, see Jan Lindenberger with Joyce Spontak, Planters Peanut Collectibles 1906-1961 Second edition (Atglen, Pennsylvania: Schiffer Publishing, Ltd., 1999); Jan Lindenberger with Joyce Spontak. Planters Peanut Collectibles Since 1961 (Atglen, Pennsylvania: Schiffer Publishing, Ltd., 1995). For more information about peanut and peanut butter promotion in general, see Andrew F. Smith, Peanuts: The Illustrious History of the Goober Pea (Urbana: University of Illinois Press, 2002), 42-3.
9. Eric Schlosser, Fast Food Nation; the Dark Side of the All-American Meal (Boston & New York: Houghton Mifflin Company, 2001).

Mumbling

Colin Spencer

"To mumble rabbits and chickens" was to enable them to be consumed by toothless gums whether old or young. Recipes exist and their appearance in the cookery books reflects the history of false teeth, their availability and efficiency, for once dentures were reasonably inexpensive and comfortable, the recipes vanish as does the meaning of the word 'mumble – to chew or bite softly as with toothless gums', though the word is used in literature up to and including the 19th century. However the cookery books of the gentry in the 17th century cannot quite bring themselves to include a Mumble; similar recipes appear but under other names, my inference being that there was something vulgar about both the word and the dish.

We have long ago lost the meaning and definition of 'to mumble' as a gustatory activity. By the 16th and 17th centuries its use had become commonplace. 'Before his bait be mumbled by a fish.' 'Sitting as it were alone mumbling on a crust'. 'My master picked him up before a puppet-show, mumbling a half penny custard.' (The character, Dufoy, later uses the word 'dariole' to describe his custard tart.) 'And gums unarmed to mumble meat in vain.' . Later Sir Walter Scott in his novel *Woodstock*, mentions 'A child mumbling gingerbread' (1826), and Lord Lytton in his novel *Lucretia* 1847 'His glove fell to the ground, and his spaniel mumbled it into shreds'. But for the dog to have shredded the glove he must have had teeth and the word explicitly means to maul with toothless gums. But Lord Lytton was a careless novelist, though a brilliant playwright. The word was used rarely in the second half of the 19th century and this meaning of it lapsed entirely in the 20th. But this reflects accurately the history of the denture (see below) and its use by a growing number of people. But the word 'mumbling' also gave its name to certain dishes and a method of preparing both rabbit and chicken. When did the act of mumbling give its name to the dishes themselves? The OED cites Eliza Smith in her *Compleat Housewife* of 1727: 'to mumble Rabbets and Chickens...'

Her method is to stuff either the rabbit or chicken then to boil it so that it is tender enough for the meat to come off the bones. Then the boned meat and stuffing is added to a little of the stock, some white wine, chopped herbs and reheated, adding egg yolks to thicken. Serve on sippets. These were a medieval adjunct to many dishes, pieces of bread soaked in the sauce. But the word, ' mumble' was much in use the century before, so surely the idea of making flesh meat small enough to be swallowed without being gnawed at by teeth, had become fixed to a method of cooking. For the word 'mumble' to be transferred from the act of chewing to making food chewable seems the most natural process.

Yet a brief search of 17th century cookery books beginning with the Countess of Kent, *A True Gentlewomans Delight* (1653) brought not a mention of the mumbling recipe, yet other recipes To Bake a Hare for example from Kent's *Choice Manuall* (1653) is very similar.

'Take out his bones and beat the flesh in a mortar with the liver, then season it with all sorts of spices, then work it up with 3 or 4 yolks of eggs, then lay some of it all over the bottom of the pie, then lay on some lard and so do until you have laid on all, then bake it well with good store of sweet butter.'

Another similar recipe is 'How to Stew Rabbits.'

Half roast it, then take it off the Spit and cut it in little pieces, and put it into a dish with the gravy, and as much liquor as will cover it, then put in a piece of fresh butter and some powder of ginger, some pepper and salt, 2 or 3 Pippins minced small, let them stew an hour, then dish them upon sippets.

A chicken is done in a similar way, but flavoured with cloves, mace, barberries and grapes. Barberries, I noticed, was much used as a flavouring and a sauce with various rabbit recipes.

Other cookery books of the period, *The Compleat Cook* (anon, 1655), Hannah Woolley *The Ladies Delight* 1672, and a 1683 reprint of Gervase Markham's *The English Huswife* first published in 1615, Elizabth Moxon's *Housewifery* (1749) all had similar methods of cooking rabbit and chicken but never called it mumbled.

The main difference between them and the Eliza Smith recipe was the fact that there was no stuffing used in the sauce, but all the recipes would have been suitable for toothless gums to chew and masticate. They were called either a fricassee or just baked or stewed, but they involve being half cooked, then the meat is taken from the bone, cut up small and placed into a spicy sauce, reheated and thickened with egg yolks, bread crumbs or cream. We forget how the sophisticated cooking of the past had to take into consideration the fact that people lost some of their teeth at a relatively early age and needed food that could be swallowed easily.

Nevertheless, to name a group of dishes as specifically for the toothless might have been a mite crude for polite society. So I speculate that perhaps the word 'mumbled' was somehow too vulgar a word to be used in books which are imbued by social aspiration, perhaps because it was too graphic in calling up a toothless diner. Its usage, so historically brief, ended when dentures became reasonable enough in price and comfortable enough to wear.

False teeth were known in the ancient world, these were real teeth taken from others strung together with gold wire, but they were ugly, ill-fitting and therefore inefficient . However, the demands of an affluent elite, determined to eat well and look beautiful, ensured that physicians throughout history would continue to attempt to refine the technique of gaining the immaculate smile. The Etruscans were adept at making gold bridges, each tooth was surrounded at its base by a gold ring with an extra ring holding the two natural teeth either side, human teeth were used or else teeth carved from the teeth of an ox. Roman and Arabian physicians copied the technique.

Advances in artificial dentistry accompanied the development of the French aristocracy. The French surgeon, Ambroise Pare (1510-1590) made artificial teeth from the ivory of the hippopotamus or walrus. His pupil, Jacques Guillemeau (1550-1613) made teeth from a compound mixture of wax, mastic, white coral and ground pearls. Pierre Fauchard in his book *Le Chirurgien Dentiste* (The Surgeon Dentist) 1728 explains how he created the crown which was fixed to the root by a wooden pivot, the denture being carved from the long bone of an ox or from ivory, while springs were used to keep it in place. But whatever slight improvements were made false teeth were still difficult to wear and it is doubtful that they had any cutting edge at all. George Washington wrote in 1798 to his dentist, John Greenwood, in Philadelphia, to complain of his sore mouth and of the 'pouting and swelling appearance' given to his lips, the upper lips being forced out 'just under the nose.' In 1788 Dubois de Chemant exhibited dentures of baked porcelain and after 1810 great advances were made in England, France and the United States in the manufacture of porcelain teeth, which quickly displaced the old teeth of ivory. After 1850 banded crowns were made of gold which encircled the root of the tooth which formed the two, extremities of the bridge. 'Crown and bridge' work became the dominant feature of dental prosthetics throughout the second half of the 19th century. By that time recipes for mumbled dishes had quite disappeared.

But not quite, I found one last recipe and one which poor Eliza Smith would not have recognised, but still one perfectly suitable for the toothless diner. It appears in The Encyclopaedia of Practical Cookery, edited by Theodore Francis Garret published in 1890.

Mumbled Rabbits

> To the minced meat of 2 boiled rabbits add lemon rind, nutmeg, butter and nine beaten eggs and butter, stir until done (scrambled) garnish with fried bread.

So this recipe is really only scrambled eggs with minced cooked rabbit, a savoury perhaps. But nothing like the highly flavoured dish of diced rabbit and chicken in a wine sauce enriched with cream and egg yolks with its various textures of meat and savoury stuffing that was the original mumble.

Nuts for the children:
the evidence of the Talmudic literature[1]

Susan Weingarten

I want to look here at nuts in the Talmudic sources, and the way in which they appear to have been seen as a food particularly associated with children. To do this I have looked at all the places where nuts appear in the Talmud, and excluded purely agricultural references and metaphorical ones. We are left with a very few sources that refer to nuts as food for people in general, adults as well as children, and rather more sources that refer to nuts as food particularly associated with children – whether particularly suited to them or simply particularly desired by them.

But first, a word about Talmud for the uninitiated. Apart from the religious laws found written in the Bible, Jewish tradition had further laws, originally preserved orally but eventually written down in a collection called the Mishnah, which was finally edited in the 2nd-3rd centuries of our era. To site it in the world of food, the Mishnah received its final form in Palestine at the same time as Athenaeus was writing his *Philosophers at Dinner* in Egypt. The laws found in the Mishnah cover many aspects of everyday life. However, they are written very concisely and in Hebrew, whereas the everyday language of Jews in the Roman and Persian Empires was Aramaic (or Greek). So further explanation was needed, and a further body of legal and moral discussion and commentary on the Mishnah grew up and was eventually written down by rabbis in both Palestine and Babylonia around the 4th and 7th centuries respectively, to become the Jerusalem and Babylonian Talmuds. In Palestine there was also another legal compilation called the Tosefta, and legal and moral commentaries on different books of the bible called Midrashim.

Since not everyone could understand the original Hebrew, the Talmudic literature often included translations of terms, and since rabbis did not always agree with each other the discussions they had were also recorded. Many of these discussions are related to food. Talmudic literature was written in the same world as Graeco-Roman or Persian literature, but it differs from this in one important respect. The other literature was written by aristocrats for other aristocrats – no-one else could read or write. Thus they were not interested in how food was prepared – this was the province of women and slaves – only in the finished products, and in luxury products in particular. Talmudic rabbis, on the other hand, were often very poor men themselves, and they were interested in every aspect of daily life in order to bring it under religious control. So from them we can learn about the everyday food of ordinary people.

There are a large number of references to nuts – *egoz*, pl. *egozim* – in the Talmudic literature, and a survey of these references shows quite clearly that they were regarded as food for children in particular. *Egozim* can mean nuts in general, or the word can refer specifically to walnuts[2]. Other nuts mentioned in Talmudic sources are almonds and a sort of pistachios – but apart from one case which we will discuss later none of these seem to be connected with children in particular. Perhaps children, particularly in poorer homes, were not able to be fussy, and just took whatever nuts they could get, or if the reference is to walnuts, this could mean that these were the commonest nuts available. Nuts are, of course, extremely good concentrated sources of both fats and proteins, and some nut-trees, such as the terebinth, a variety of pistachio, and the almond have grown in Middle East at least since biblical times[3]. The *egoz* –tree is mentioned in the biblical Song of Songs, and the rabbis of the Talmud commented on this book, each rabbi giving a different interpretation[4]. Thus Rabbi Berekhiah, a third century rabbi from Palestine, writes that *egozim* have four quarters and a vacant space in the centre, which certainly sounds like walnuts. However elsewhere in the same passage another, anonymous rabbi talks of *egozim* as being soft, medium and hard. This sounds more as if he is talking about nuts in general, rather than walnuts, which are not exactly soft. (There is another rabbi who notes that nuts cannot escape custom duty, being betrayed by their rattling!) Since it is hard to decide what is being referred to in any one case, we shall just refer to them as nuts.

Of course it was not only children who ate nuts – adults ate them as well, and this is reflected in the Talmudic sources. There are a few references to the use of nuts in prepared dishes of food – one of these talks of adding nuts to honey with sesame seeds. This may be done for a sick person on the Sabbath, provided they do not reduce it to a pulp, according to the Tosefta (Shabbat 12,14). However, the Babylonian Talmud writes that nuts on their own are considered to be bad for a sick person (BT Avodah Zara 29a) – they are supposed to send him straight back to his illness, (together with a long list of other things which are said to do the same including fat meat, roast eggs, shaving, bathing, cheese and liver). So either these Babylonian rabbis disagreed with their Palestinian predecessors, or it was just unalloyed nuts that were considered to be bad, not nuts mixed up with sesame and honey. Excess of nuts, like excess of eggs, was certainly bad – eating forty of either of them would give you a heart attack! (Masekhet Kallah, i, 13) An eleventh century rabbi interprets the Talmudic food *kisnin* or *kisanin* as pockets of dough filled with sugar, nuts and almonds but the presence of sugar here would seem to imply that he is interpreting this food in terms of his own day, not the time of the Talmud[5]. The Jerusalem Talmud discusses whether flavouring unleavened bread eaten on Passover and disguising the original taste is allowed. It lists several possible flavourings, including liquids and sesame seeds – and it also mentions nuts[6]. However, as often in Talmudic discussions, it is unclear whether people actually baked their unleavened bread with nuts or whether this is merely a theoretical possibility. I could find no other evidence of nuts in prepared dishes. There are rather more references to the use of nuts by themselves as a last course – what the Greeks called τρωκτά (*trôktá*)– things nibbled after the main course of the meal. Here nuts appear accompanied by parched corn and dates and even sometimes mushrooms and pigeons in what must have been a rare feast for a rich rabbi.

The Seder meal eaten on the eve of the festival of Passover was a very special meal, 'different from all other nights' we are told. One of the differences was that food normally eaten was specifically **not** eaten on this night – unleavened bread was eaten instead of leavened bread, only bitter herbs were eaten instead of a variety of herbs and the usual dessert was not eaten. This is made clear by the Babylonian Talmud Pesahim 119b-120a which discusses the *afikoman,* the dessert, and makes it clear what is **not** to be eaten after the Passover meal:

> Shemuel said: mushrooms for myself and pigeons for Abba; R Hanina b Shila and R Johanan said: [things like] dates, parched ears of corn and nuts. It was taught following R Johanan: you must not conclude after the Passover meal with things like dates, parched ears and nuts.

The rabbis here start by talking about the foods usual for the last course eaten after the main course. Shemuel liked to eat mushrooms and Abba, who must have been a rich rabbi, liked pigeons. We know from Athenaeus that it was usual in the Greek world to eat this sort of thing after the main course, together with little cakes (*Deip*.xiv). Rabbi Johanan makes it clear that ordinarily the sort of things eaten for the last course things were nuts, dates and parched corn. So, having made it quite clear what was usually used to end a meal, the rabbis tells us that we must **not** eat **any** of these after the main course at the Passover meal, which was 'different from all other nights'. The only 'dessert' allowed was a further special piece of unleavened bread. We shall come back to the Passover meal later, but now I want to continue to look at other uses of nuts, still with adults in mind.

Hospitality was very important in the world of the Talmud, and the Tosefta discusses whether someone is allowed to measure out food on the Sabbath, including nuts, dried corn and dates (Tos Shab 17, 7). The conclusion is that this is allowed, unlike other sorts of measuring:

> A man may take out from [the store] he has in his house and measure out for his guests nuts, dates and parched corn even on the Sabbath, when other sorts of measuring are not allowed.

In Babylonia (BTSukkot 10a) nuts were also used as decorations on the harvest festival of Sukkot in the autumn, together with figured cloths which were hung up with almonds, peaches, pomegranates, bunches of grapes, wreaths of ears of corn and other decorations. Since almonds are referred to here separately from nuts, *egozim*, presumably *egozim* is being used here to mean walnuts.

Nuts are also referred to metaphorically – there are many fables and parables (for example the commentary Songs Rabbah vi, 11 we quoted before) where the Jewish people is compared to a nut, since even if it falls on the ground and is trampled in the dirt, the sweet kernel is preserved unharmed. And of course there are references to nuts in various agricultural contexts, as well as references to nut oil, which was seen as inferior to olive oil for lighting (eg JTShabbat ii, 4b, 2).

But apart from all these there are also a very large number of references to nuts and children and it is clear that for the rabbis of the Talmud nuts were particularly associated with children. This association is clear from all the Talmudic literature, both in ancient Palestine and in Babylonia.

To begin with the Mishnah, completed in the third century CE. Mishnah Bava Metzia chapter four is dealing with laws about fair trading practices, going into details about what is and is not acceptable.
The Mishnah writes:

> R Judah says: a shopkeeper may not distribute parched corn or nuts to children, for he accustoms them to come [only] to him. But the Sages permit it.[7]

It is clear that Rabbi Judah regards the bribe or free gift of nuts addressed particularly to children as unacceptable. But the sages disagree with him.

267

We cannot know from this typically concise Mishnah just why the sages disagreed. However, because so many laws in the Mishnah are expressed in this very brief form, the rabbis would often add further comments to explain why, so we can look at the Talmud to explain our Mishnah. The Babylonian Talmud Bava Metzia 60a explains why the sages disagreed: there is no reason, they say, why, if one shopkeeper hands out nuts to children, his rival cannot hand out plums!

So perhaps the association of nuts with children is just accidental, as it might just as well be plums? Well, the Jerusalem Talmud Pesahim x, 37b 1, discusses the injunction of another Mishnah, 'On a festival, a man is required to make his wife and children happy.' (This in itself is based on the biblical commandment 'You shall rejoice on your festival.') The Mishnah continues, asking 'With what does he make them happy? With wine. [But] Rabbi Judah says: 'Women with what is appropriate for them and children with what is appropriate for them. ' In other words, the Mishnah is telling us that a man should take care that his family has something to rejoice about on the festival. He must give his wife and children what they want. And what **do** they want, or in the words of the Mishnah, what is appropriate for them? The Mishnah itself does not say, but the Jerusalem Talmud commenting on it explains it for us. Wives want shoes and doves, the Talmud explains, and the sort of things that please children are nuts (presumably walnuts here), almonds etc. [8]

Thus nuts were certainly seen as a treat that children particularly enjoyed – you could be sure that they would make them happy on a festival. In another source, nuts are specified as one of the things a particularly spoiled child wants: BT Ta'anit 23a describes a spoiled child who

> acts petulantly before his father, who gives him whatever he wants. Thus he says to him: Father, take me to bathe in warm water; wash me in cold water; give me nuts, almonds, peaches, pomegranates – and his father gives them to him.

Clearly this is a child so spoiled he hardly know what he wants. He asks to bathe in hot water – and we should note that the Romans always saw hot water as a symbol of luxury and decadence – Tacitus tells us that providing hot baths was one of the ways the Romans managed to enslave the British[9]. However the moment this child has his hot water he wants cold water! And then he nags his father for a long list of treats – and the first one he thinks of is nuts. Since our spoiled child also includes almonds in his wants list, we may deduce that he is using *egozim,* nuts, here to mean walnuts.

Nuts for the children

Since nuts were so evidently desirable it was not only the shopkeepers who used them as bribes – ordinary parents would do the same. The festive Passover meal we referred to earlier included long rituals and recitals before getting to the meal. BT Pesahim 109a, for example, specifically says that children should be kept awake through the long rituals by giving them nuts and parched corn so they won't fall asleep[10]. The meal, as we saw before, was to end not with these desirable nuts and parched corn but with a special piece of unleavened bread that was symbolic of the Passover lamb. This was presumably not much of an incentive for the children to stay awake, so the parents are recommended to turn the ritual into a game and pretend to steal and hide this last piece of *matzah,* unleavened bread. Nowadays it is still traditional for everyone to try to steal the *matzah,* and since the meal can't end without eating it the celebrant is forced to bargain with the child who holds the trump card. This is certainly worth staying awake for.

And talking of games, nuts were perhaps so popular because they could also be played with by children, and not just eaten. The midrashim refer on a number of occasions to nuts as 'the plaything of children and the amusement of kings' – and the Midrash called Pesikta Rabbati 11 expounds on this – when the Jews are good, 'kings will be their nursing fathers' – this is a verse from Isaiah – but if the Jews are bad, they will become the plaything of the nations. (And while we are on the subject of nuts and games, my 91 year old father tells me that when he was a child it was traditional to be given nuts to play with on a Jewish festival, particularly on the festivals of Hanukah and Passover.) To return to our Talmudic sources, women too are shown as playing with nuts in BT Eruvin 107a – something not allowed on the Sabbath, in case they start digging in the earth to make a flat surface, which is work which is not allowed. Children also played with the abandoned nutshells – Mishnah Kelim 3,2 discusses children who use nut shells and acorns and dried pomegranate skin as cups for playing in the sand.

Nuts and children are thus clearly closely associated in the Talmudic sources. As well as being toys and treats, nuts are used several times in tests. In one case in BT Gittin 64b we see that nuts are used in developmental testing of children – a child who understands will throw away a pebble in order to take a nut, whereas a very small child will not know the difference between them.

Nuts are also used to distinguish between children, between boys and girls. A story is told in Midrash Proverbs 1 of the Queen of Sheba testing the wisdom of King Solomon.

Nuts for the children

She brought before him boys and girls, all of the same appearance, all of the same height, all clothed the same and told him to distinguish the boys from the girls. He told his eunuchs to bring him nuts, and began to hand them out to the children. The boys unashamedly lifted up their tunics to collect the nuts in it. The girls were embarrassed to do this, and modestly collected them in their scarves. He told the queen 'These are boys and these are girls. She said to him 'My son, you are a great sage.'

There is another use made of children's liking for nuts in a legal ceremony in a passage mentioned a few times in the Talmudic sources[11]. If a man sold his family land, or married a woman beneath his social rank, his relatives would symbolically cut him off by bringing jars of nuts and parched corn and breaking them in the presence of children. The children would pick up the nuts and say 'This man has been cut off from his inheritance or from his family'. If he later bought back the land or divorced his wife they would repeat the ceremony of breaking the jars, and this time the children would pick up the nuts and corn and say 'This man has returned to his possession or to his family.' When the children grew up, their memory of this ceremony, re-inforced by eating all those nuts, would be admissible as evidence in a court of law, even though they had been under-age witnesses at the time.

Nuts, of course, are ideal provisions to take on a journey even for adults, as they do not go bad and do not need cooking. Midrash Genesis Rabbah 60,11 shows us how valuable they were in this context. The Bible gives a list of the valuable things Abraham's servant took with him when he set off to go back to Mesopotamia to find a wife for his master's son Isaac. When he arrived at his destination and found Rebecca, Isaac's future wife, he gave her brother and her mother silver and gold and garments and what the A.V. calls 'precious things.' The rabbis explain these 'precious things' as nuts and parched corn. Were nuts and parched corn really so valuable? someone asks. Yes, comes the answer, if a man goes on a journey without them he will suffer!

Here the traveller who provisions himself with nuts is obviously a grown man, but nuts were clearly so strongly associated with children that there are some sources which show them as special provision for **children** on a journey. Thus the Mekhilta de Rabbi Shimon bar Yohai 12 (39) describes the haste in which the Jews left Egypt at the Exodus: they could not bake proper loaves of bread, just 'hasty bread' which was unleavened because they could not afford the time to wait until it rose. They did not take proper provisions and they had nothing in hand for the way – not even nuts and parched corn for the children.

Nuts for the children

The Talmudic sources have shown us the value placed on nuts for children by both the children themselves and by adults. Jewish sources in general have no problems with the enjoyment of good food, unlike many of their contemporary ascetic Christian writers, who often inveigh against meat and wine in particular. So it is interesting to find that on the subject of nuts and children there is a parallel to the picture we have seen in the Jewish sources in the *Confessions* of Saint Augustine. Augustine, who lived in North Africa, is writing about the trials of growing up, and says:

We may exchange our infant teachers and school teachers, nuts and footballs and singing birds for prefects and kings, for money, land and slaves; but the same desires stay with us through all the stages of our lives, just as severer penalties replace the beating of a schoolmaster... *Confess* 1, 19

In this passage infant teachers and school teachers are paralleled to prefects and kings, those who rule our lives, while 'nuts, footballs and singing birds,' the prized possessions of the child, become the adult's 'money, land and slaves.' Is it reading too much into Augustine to say that nuts here have become the currency of the child?

To sum up: we have seen how, although adults ate nuts often as dessert or when on a long journey, the Talmudic literature saw nuts as particularly associated with children. They were seen as extremely desirable for children, who would want them to celebrate festivals. They could be used as bribes in order to get the children to behave as adults wanted – whether by shop keepers to entice them into their shops, by their parents to keep them awake or to reinforce their memories of important rituals. Nuts could also be used in testing children. They were also convenient foods to take for children on a journey. For their part, children put them at the head of their 'wants' list, perhaps because after eating them they could also use the shells as toys. The contemporary Christian St Augustine appears to present nuts as the currency of the child.

In conclusion: we saw earlier how one Midrash showed that nuts were seen as food particularly appropriate for children going on a journey. This same thought is expressed even more beautifully in another Midrash on the Book of Exodus, Shemot Rabbah iii,4. Here Moses is discussing with God what provision there will be for the Children of Israel if he leads them out of Egypt. I think it is most appropriate for a conference on 'Nurture' to end with this passage:

Moses said to God: You tell me to go and bring out Israel [from Egypt]. Where can I give them shelter in summer from the heat and in winter from the cold? Where shall I get enough food and drink? [Look] how many midwives they have! And how many pregnant women! And how many little ones! What food have you prepared for the midwives? What kind of delicacies have you prepared for the pregnant women? How many nuts and parched corn have you prepared for the little ones? ... God said to him: [When you see] that the hasty bread which they will take with them from Egypt will last for thirty days, you will know how I will lead them!

Notes

1. An expanded version of this paper dealing with children's food in general in the Talmudic literature will be published in *Feast, Fast or Famine: Food and Drink in Byzantium* (eds. W. Mayer, S. Trzcionka and F. Harley, Adelaide, 2004).
2. Andrew Dalby has pointed out to me that in Greek too the word for walnut, *karyon*, can also mean nuts in general.
3. Remains of two varieties of *Pistacia* nuts and wild almonds have been found on a mid-Pleistocene site in Israel together with acorns and what looks like evidence of nut-cracking: N. Goren-Inbar, G. Sharon, Y. Melamed, M. Kislev 'Nuts, nut cracking and pitted stones at Gesher Benot Ya'aqov, Israel' *PNAS* 99/4 (2002) 2455-2460.
4. Songs Rabbah vi, 1, 11.
5. A. Kohut (ed) *Aruch Completum* (NY, 1955). This is a modern edition of an 11th century dictionary written in Rome. The entry for *kisan/kisnin* (BT Berakhot 41b etc.) cites Rabbenu Hannanel (d.1055) of Kairouan in present-day Tunisia, who interprets them as pockets filled with sugar and nuts. Among the alternatives for *kisnin* considered in the dictionary entry are cannabis seeds.
6. JT Pesahim 29b.
7. Mishnah Bava Metzia iv, 12.
8. All the main texts of the Talmud (P Schäfer, H-J Becker *Synopse zum Talmud Yerushalmi* ii, 1-4 (Tübingen, 2001) p.174) here have *mesanin* shoes, which makes good sense in the context. But perhaps it is a comment on what some commentators thought women should be entitled to that there have been attempts to alter this to *kesanin* ears of corn (Jastrow), or *besanin* fine linen (Bokser *tr.*, citing Epstein, HaShiloah 4 (1925) 399-402, which I have not seen). At least 'fine linen' has some support from the parallel passage in the Babylonian Talmud.
9. Tacitus: Agricola 21
10. Midrash Sechel Tov Shemot 12,10
11. JT Ketubot ii, 26d, 10; JT Qiddushim i, 60c, 5; Ruth Rabbah vii, 11; Yalqut Shimoni Ruth 447

'But I saw it on TV!'
How do you get children to eat real food?

Mary Whiting

Education is a form of civil defence against media fallout
Marshall McLuhan

We must all have heard that the health of children in Britain today is a matter of rapidly growing concern. For decades, we have known that they have the worst teeth in the EU due to high sugar consumption, and it has also long been known that, because of poor diet, our children also risk suffering in later life from heart disease, diet-related cancers, obesity and a range of diseases of the digestive system.

But recently, concern is increasing as some of the results of our children's diet become more obvious. Most noticeably, our children are getting fatter. In England, 13.5% of girls and 9% of boys are now overweight. (In the US it's even worse – 25% of children are overweight with 10% officially obese. The US government's Centers for Disease Control have said that obesity comes second only to smoking as a leading cause of preventable death[1]). Over here, Dr Susan Jebb of the Cambridge-based think-tank Human Nutrition Research says 'Obesity is the most enormous threat to public health; it's also costing an estimated £2 billion a year'.

The figures climb dramatically, year on year. According to a study published in the British Medical Journal, children's waists have expanded by an average of over two inches (over 6 cm) in the last ten years, particularly in girls. Also, type-2 diabetes (also known as maturity onset diabetes) which is a close relative of obesity, and which previously chiefly affected older adults, has now assumed epidemic proportions and is for the first time, and almost unbelievably, attacking teenagers. In turn, diabetes is a major cause of blindness, kidney failure, disability, damage to the arteries and heart disease. It is largely preventable.

Diabetogenic foods
Most cases are caused by the excessive consumption of diabetogenic foods: sugar-laden foods such as soft drinks, sweets, chocolate, processed breakfast cereals and the like. An

American study in 2001 showed that 'for each additional can or glass of sugar-sweetened drink that [children] consumed every day', their obesity risk jumped by 60%.[2]

It is extremely worrying that over the last 50 years, children's consumption of biscuits has risen by four times, confectionary by 25 times and soft drinks by 34 times, while their consumption of bread, red meat, green vegetables and milk has declined.[3] The loss of milk in favour of fizzy drinks is disastrous for children's bone development: not only do children lose the plentiful calcium (along with many other nutrients) in milk but the phosphorus in fizzy drinks effectively destroys calcium. A recent American study found that low intake of milk during childhood and adolescence was associated with a twofold greater risk of bone fracture.[4]

A meeting of specialists held last spring at the Royal College of Paediatrics and Child Health heard that a whole generation of British children could be described as 'pre-ill', since, because of faulty diet, they were extremely likely candidates for a range of serious chronic diseases. They were literally 'eating themselves sick'. More than two thirds of pre-school children were fed a diet of white bread, chips and sweets, and rickets had returned in some age groups. Many children were suffering from the potentially lethal combination of being both overweight and malnourished, and some specialists feared that poor nutrition would have long lasting effects on children's mental development and learning ability. And as well as heart disease, obesity, cancer and diabetes, it was predicted that some children could suffer from old-age diseases such as osteoporosis while still in middle life.

However did this situation arise?

Role of the food industry
It has to be chiefly the fault of the food industry – and also successive post-war governments for allowing it get so out of control. The food industry has increasingly loaded our diet with seemingly cheap, but profitable, energy-dense processed foods that are stuffed with sugars, salt and fat, and which are low in fibre and nutrients including micronutrients. Our diet has become calorie-heavy but impoverished.

Foods created especially for children are now a large and money-spinning part of the industry's market. One would expect something called 'children's food' to be especially nutritious and designed to build health. In fact the opposite is true. 'Children's foods' as a group would appear to be the worst foods on sale and they are marketed directly and determinedly at our children. It is known that children are particularly vulnerable to advertising and so manufacturers use this knowledge to boost profits. 'Pester power' is now a specialist area and manufacturers are unashamedly urged to use it. A spokesperson at Saatchi & Saatchi was quoted in the Guardian as saying: 'Children are much easier to reach with advertising. They pick up on it fast and quite often we can exploit that ... and get them pestering their parents.'[5]

Marketing to children is taken very seriously by manufacturers. Thus the packaging, with it's child-enticing artwork featuring story-book and cartoon characters, 'free' gifts, collections to make, puzzles to do, endorsements by sports stars and so on results from highly sophisticated and meticulous planning. The final product becomes extremely hard for a child to resist. The child may first encounter it through its being repeatedly hyped during children's television programmes. If the child's friends have it, perhaps in their school lunch boxes, the urge to have it grows even stronger. It is disturbing to see how desperate a child can become to have a certain brand of yoghurt or breakfast cereal – or rather the packaging and the 'gifts'. Pestered parents may give in for the sake of peace and quiet. Some mothers have told me they just get tired of being the meanie who's always saying 'No'.

But mother is targeted too: she may notice a 'flash' across the product which proclaims 'With added iron!' or 'With extra vitamin C!'. These 'flashes' are effective in persuading her to think the thing has at least some benefit and to give in. So it's a two-pronged attack: the pictures and puzzles target the child, the 'flash' targets the adult. In fact the amounts of these boasted-of nutrients are tiny – usually the smallest the manufacturer can put in and legally make the claim. They are also usually not ones that most British children go short of – but it doesn't say that on the packet.

With older children, other techniques are used: teenagers are targeted by using sports heroes or stars of the entertainment industry, or being offered prizes in competitions. Fast foods appear in adverts as 'cool' or 'must-have'. Companies may sponsor sports and pop music events. The trick overall is to cover all ages and a range of interests. For example, here are some of the techniques McDonald's have used to target children: they sponsor children's TV, advertise during children's TV and cinema, link with popular films (Disney) and offer free cinema tickets, run email promotions, offer collectable toys with children's meals, run birthday parties, sponsor children's football clubs, offer fast food as 'rewards' to children for achievement in school. They make the food as widely available as possible, adapt it to local cultures and sell it cheap. From America to Lithuania, Barbie dolls help promote MacDonald's 'Happy meals' to young girls.[6]

The advertising budgets of the top players can be immense. In the year 2000, Coca Cola, Nestlé, McDonald's and Mars each had an advertising budget of over $1 billion. Pepsi and Coca Cola between them spend $2.2 billion on advertising, globally in a single year.[6] The most heavily advertised foods are confectionary, pre-sweetened breakfast cereals and fast foods. To quote Sustain's report TV Dinners,[7] 'Advertising during children's programming continues to present a grossly imbalanced nutritional message.' Parents may try to keep their children away from adverts by, for instance, allowing them to watch only non-commercial TV channels, but advertisers are now learning how to by-pass parents by such ploys as speaking directly to children via their mobile phones and by email.

Role of school and leisure activities

And then there's school. Here, food companies are filling the funding gap and school dining halls can be shrines to the fast-food industry; soft drinks machines decorate the corridors. Schools may ask children's parents to buy massive quantities of a certain brand of chocolate or crisps in order for the school to be 'given' an item of (sometimes not very expensive) equipment. In design and technology lessons (formerly domestic science or home economics), companies are, appallingly, taking over the curriculum. Frequently children are required to do such tasks as 'designing' meals and snacks suitable for sale in supermarkets. Teachers frequently dislike this new aspect of the curriculum but know their hands are tied.

At sports and entertainment venues, in shops of various kinds including chemists, and at most kinds of public events we find displays of the same high-calorie, low-nutrient, tooth-rotting, waist-expanding, disease-building, seductively-packaged, heavily-advertised glop. Indeed getting anything else to eat or drink may be impossible. And in the face of all this mass production, if genetically engineered food or irradiated food becomes available, how could we ever enable children to avoid it?

In addition, portions are getting bigger. According to the Journal of the American Medical Association, February 2003, in the last 30 years portion sizes have increased by over 50% for soft drinks and by 60% for salty snacks. This gives each drink an extra 90 calories, which means that someone having one soft drink a day could have gained as much as half a stone in just nine months.

The profit motive

Why does all this happen? Money, is the short answer. For caterers and retailers, it's easier to buy in frozen, chilled or well-sealed packets of ready made food and drink than to buy fresh, perishable ingredients and to cook on the premises. Next to no skills are required on site, so staff can be few, unskilled and cheap. For manufacturers, processed foods are much more profitable than fresh ingredients. If you compare the price of potatoes with a bag of potato crisps you get the idea. It's called 'added value'! Actually, of course, much – even most – of the real value of the original food has been lost in processing, and the only usual additions are refined carbohydrate (especially sugar), salt, hydrogenated fat, water and a range of additives – plus the packaging and increased price.

Additives, and addiction

Additives are a problem in themselves. For years the Hyperactive Children's Support Group has said they can 'cure' eight out of ten children just by removing something from their diet, often additives. Now government sponsored research has found that certain additives, E102, E110, E122, E124 and E211, do indeed produce hyperactivity. (There is a fascinating summary of this report in issue 59 of The Food Commission's Food Magazine.) The cost to parents, schools and society in general of young people regularly consuming such additives surely must be enormous.

There's also another, more sinister side. With regard to diabetes, for example, in addition to the manufacturers and retailers who greatly benefit from selling diabetogenic foods, it is also profitable for the pharmaceutical industry which sells drugs to treat the disease and its various complications, and also for the emerging xenotransplantation industry which hopes to supply animal hearts and kidneys for people whose own have been destroyed.

In addition, we are now hearing that the food industry may have known for some time that some ingredients in its big-selling foods are addictive. According to a Sunday Telegraph interview with Dr Neal Barnard of George Washington University Medical School, head of the US-based Physicians Committee for Responsible Medicine and author of a new book on the science of food craving, Breaking the Food Seduction, manufacturers have knowingly exploited the bio-chemical effects of such foods as cheese, sugar and chocolate. This is because these foods contain compounds that trigger responses in much the same way as addictive drugs. Such foods are widely used in snacks and fast foods and, says Dr. Barnard, are used to enhance the appeal of foods they are added to (such as adding a slice of cheese to a burger, and chocolate to cereals). He adds 'Many carbohydrates – including those promoted as a means of reducing fat intake – are known to affect hormone levels in a way that rapidly re-awakens hunger. It's not just a question of a bit of indulgence – it's bankrupting our health services as well as our personal well-being.'

Response of the food industry and the BBC

The food industry's response to all this is always predictable. Their mantra goes like this: (a) it's parents' fault for buying the products (never mind who invents, makes and relentlessly advertises them); (b) these foods are only meant to be 'treats'; (c) obesity is caused by lack of exercise, not diet; and (d) famously: 'There's no such thing as a bad food'! It is fine, apparently, to make and advertise health-endangering food, as long as (e) it's eaten 'as part of a balanced diet' and 'looked at in context.'.

BBC Worldwide, in a recent letter defending why they were endorsing foods which exceeded Government guidelines in sugar, salt and fat, wrote: 'Licensed foods tend to be products that form treats or are occasional extras within the context of a balanced diet…allowing parents and children to choose a couple of treats alongside a wide range of staple foods.'. But they don't tell parents that a particular food isn't actually very good and should only be bought occasionally. If it were on the packaging and on adverts they might have a point.

Most people have no idea how poor a food is because they don't read the nutrition labels. But these labels always look insignificant, have tiny print, and can be difficult to both find and understand. (Manufacturers have always resisted calls to make the information more comprehensible by, for example, presenting it as a bar chart.)

Most parents I've talked to about fruit yoghurts think they make a good dessert for a child. When I point out that one small tub can contain the equivalent of six sugar lumps, they are amazed and sceptical, but of course it is very hard to work out anything meaningful from the label. In discussing such ready-made foods parents may exclaim 'But it's made for children!' and 'It can't be that bad or it wouldn't be on sale!'. I have no idea where such trust comes from, but food manufacturers and retailers are very much protected by it.

I would like to challenge BBC Worldwide (and others who hide behind parents' trust, and the 'it's only a treat' excuse) to write on the label 'Warning!! This food may seriously damage your child's health! Only to be eaten as an occasional treat.' Fat chance!

However, there may be a glimmer of hope as, for the first time, the industry has become worried about being sued by obese people for their ill health much the same as the tobacco industry was sued by smokers. One or two companies have announced changes to their products. Fear of the courts may save us yet, but as they say, don't hold your breath. Meanwhile, people who would like to see children eat better are (still) dismissed variously as food fascists, food Stalinists, food Leninists, the food police, health food freaks, nannies, and always as a small, biased minority. I think they should be called food guardians, but I doubt the food industry will take to that one.

Food guardians of children

Parents who try to keep rubbishy food away from their children have a steeply uphill task, and can feel sabotaged, helpless and furious. Whatever can they do to protect their children?

The first thing I would say to parents is: know the food industry agenda. When you understand the sheer profitability as well as the dangers of so much modern mass-produced food and of 'children's food' in particular, it is easier to shun it. With knowledge comes determination.

Next, make a battle plan. Knowing your family, decide what you'd really like your children to eat and drink and then provide it: you, as parent, are in charge after all, and indeed you must take charge of what is eaten in your own home. One excellent idea is to write each week's menu for every delicious and nutritious meal, every snack, every drink, and from that write the shopping list. For those unused to doing this it can be a salutary experience, exposing as it does one's habits hitherto. It can also save money. It takes a little time at first but soon speeds up as it becomes the weekly routine.

It does of course speed up shopping, and parents who shop with children in tow find that there is less time for their children to get bored or be distracted by seductive packaging. It's a good way of putting you, the parent, in charge. If there's something you'd rather your children didn't have, then simply don't put it on the list and don't buy it. It's much easier to say no to something when it's not in the house. If pestered, simply say 'It's not on the list', perhaps adding 'Maybe next week…'. Don't ever say 'What shall we have?' – if you get an answer you don't want, whatever can you reply? Older children might enjoy planning some meals, perhaps in their school holidays.

Shopping is easier too if you don't shop when any of you are hungry: perhaps take food with you in case hunger strikes while you're out, or buy something such as dried fruit when you enter the store for children to nibble on. You could involve children by asking them to find or choose things within a limited range of choices. You could say 'Choose a fish for dinner' or 'Pick out three different kinds of fruit, or 'We need about a dozen mushrooms'.

If you need to make sizeable changes to the family's eating habits, either make these gradually over a period of weeks or months (sneak it in on them), or, depending on the children concerned, tell them what you're up to. Take them into your confidence and explain that you've learned more about some of the foods you've all been eating and that one or two things must be improved – perhaps having chips less often or not having such sugary cereals any more.

Always blame yourself for having to make changes. Say it's your fault for having let them get used to something and not knowing about it earlier. Make it clear it's not a punishment, it's because you love them and don't want them to be ill. Explain, simply, what's wrong with some foods and what's right with others. Even the youngest children could be told something like 'Fizzy drinks stop your bones growing properly but milk makes them fantastic and strong so they won't break easily.'.

And then talk about some of the nice foods you've planned as replacements. And cook! Any talk about 'Oh I don't have time to cook' or 'I'm not very good at cooking' has to go straight out of the window. I know several extremely busy mothers who are either working full time or studying and working part time – and who still put a home-cooked dinner on the table every night. How do they do it? They're organised! They have a cache of dinner recipes that can be made in 30-40 minutes or that can be cooked super-slowly all day and be ready in time for the evening meal. They (sometimes) involve their older children in cooking or preparation, they (occasionally) have help from their men folk – and they wouldn't be caught dead buying a ready meal. If you can't cook, learn – it's never too late; and doing it daily leads to speed. I think it is vital that our children grow up with the idea that dinner is something that you make yourself, not buy, massed produced, in a box.

Food industry's warning

The food industry has given us a warning: several years ago on TV, one of their representatives said something like this (the final sentence is, as I remember, his exact words): 'Two hundred years ago, everyone made their own clothes. Now, no one makes their own clothes unless it's their hobby. I would say that in about 50 years' time no one will cook – unless it's their hobby. We are working towards that.'

Indeed they are, because ready-made meals are more profitable than raw ingredients. The industry recites a mantra on this subject. They tell us that nowadays we are all far too busy to cook, and that no one wants to 'slave' 'for hours' over a 'hot stove' any more. So, for our convenience (no other motive is mentioned) they have created ready meals.

Of course, if we become de-skilled in cooking, we shall have to buy ready meals, and profits will be assured. And, as Colin Spencer so vividly documents in his recent history, British Food, cooking skills can be lost in a generation. If mother isn't to be found cooking dinner each day, then cooking dinner won't seem like a normal daily activity. Already there are children growing up whose mothers never cook and who therefore have been brought up with a taste for mass-produced food and not a clue as to how to tackle the simplest kitchen task. In turn, they will have nothing to pass on to their own children. One useful thing parents can do is to involve children in cooking as a fun activity from an early age so that they acquire at least some basic skills and familiarity with utensils. It will stand them in good stead when they leave home.

The role of children

Children can be included in other ways including helping to grow food – or at least seeing some kinds of food growing in their parents' garden, and perhaps helping to pull and shell peas, or pick red currants or cut a few chives to decorate a dish.

I think it's useful to keep the subject of food on the agenda. For example, when you see farm animals in a field or visit a farm park, chat about the way animals can be kept. Mention the subject of food labelling and packaging when you go shopping and when you watch TV, explain how advertisements are only about selling. This is excellent consumer education and a life skill.

One extremely important thing is to try to keep family mealtimes happy. To this end, I should like to pass on a few practical tips collected from both parents and professionals which have been found to work well.[8]

An excellent way of avoiding a number of mealtime problems, discovered by professionals, is to avoid putting food directly onto children's plates. Instead put it on (heated) serving plates in the middle of the table and let the children – and adults – help themselves. It has been found that children as young as two are quite able to do this, and by the age of four, most children can judge how much they can eat. This method removes from the child any feelings of challenge or dismay at being presented with someone else's choice of portion size and content. A few rules make it work well for everyone:

Rule one is fair shares. Everyone can have as much or as little as they want of their share of the food on the table at that time. This means, of course, that everything put out is good food. If a child wants the crispy topping but not the underneath – fine, but what he can't have is anyone else's share of the topping.

Rule two: fairness aside, no comments or criticisms of what someone has taken or how much they ate of it. This seems to have a relaxing effect on children who can become more adventurous, and it has sometimes solved the problem of picky eaters.

Rule three: importantly, no substitutions. This is the meal, cooked with the family in mind, and there is nothing else until the next meal except water. (One or two parents have told me they do allow the choice of bread, cheese and an apple if a meal is really disliked, although other parents have said No! This is the meal and that's that.) Of course, this means that the children should be hungry for their next meal. It also means that mother cannot be wheedled into offering anything else. There is absolutely no question of having to prepare different types of food for different people in the family, nor can the children go off and play if they say they're not hungry. Babies over the age of one can (usually) have the same meal as everyone else, mashed or chopped as necessary. Of course, any sugar or salt should not be added until the baby's portion has been taken out.

Overall, this method is seen as helping children to become more independent, more socially aware, allowing and encouraging them to take responsibility for their actions (it's also a brilliant introduction to early mathematics!).

Obviously, it is only fair that the food provided is delicious as well as nutritious. Vegetables need careful presentation: they must not be overcooked and there should be variety. A big lump of real butter on the vegetables is one good way of making sure they're all eaten. Fruit (which can always serve as dessert) must be fully ripe, colourful and varied. Fish must be cooked slowly and never over-cooked or it will smell and taste disgusting. In collecting ideas from parents for the book Dump the Junk! I discovered scores of delicious and ingenious cooking and presentation tips for getting children to enjoy healthy foods and for fending off the rubbish.

Outside the home, however, there are plenty of opportunities to eat badly and few to eat well. Since the Thatcher government removed the nutritional requirement for school dinners, most schools now serve the cheapest mass-produced 'novelty' or 'children's' foods, mostly deep-fried, coated stuff, chips, burgers, sausages, and sugary 'desserts'. Fresh fruit, vegetables and salads usually appear only as an option. Head teachers now have the responsibility for all food and drink consumed on school premises, though this new, non-teaching extra job is not one most relish, and none were trained for it. Nevertheless, dissatisfied parents should always complain first to the head teacher about a school's poor food. Parents can also approach a school's Parent Teacher Association and the school governors to try and get things changed. Beyond that, organisations such as the Health Education Trust can be invaluable.[9]

As for packed lunches and snacks, a school can lay down guidelines about what it will and will not allow to be brought onto school premises. Some schools now say 'fresh fruit only' as snacks and water only as drinks (British tap water is now fine in taste and quality). Some schools forbid confectionary and drinks at any time, and on the whole, it is something parents heartily approve.

Dealing with children's friends and their parents – not to mention one's own family members – can be another problem area. Much diplomacy may be required plus, on occasion, a compromise or two. Sometimes, however, it can be easier than is feared, and can simply be a matter of explaining your position to relatives or to another parent and then sticking to it. There might be unexpected agreement and support.

Parents, take charge!

Overall, parents need to take charge of their children's food in order to protect them from the current very serious threats to their health. After all, if they don't, who will? As well as providing the best possible food at home, they should also seize every opportunity to complain to venues that promote fatty, salted, sugary foods, to their local council about such places, to food companies, to the Government via their MP, to the Advertising Standards Agency…and to anyone and everyone who directly or indirectly peddles sickness-producing food and drink to children. In fact everyone can join in. This is a great battle to join and we can all help to win it!

Notes

1. United States Department of Health and Human Services, Public Health Service, Office of the Surgeon General (2001): The Surgeon General's call to action to prevent and decrease overweight and obesity.
2. Luwig, DS; Petersen, KE; Gortmaker, SL (Feb.2001) 'Relation between consumption of sugar-sweetened drinks and childhood obesity: A prospective observational analysis'. Lancet 357: 505-508
3. Avon Longitudinal Study of Parents and Children (ASPAC) 2002
4. Kalwarf, H et al. 'Milk intake during childhood and adolescence, adult bone density and osteoporotic fractures in US women'. American Journal of Nutrition 2003: 77:257-265
5. Guardian: November 22nd 1999: Should our children be spared Ronald?
6. Broadcasting Bad health: why food marketing to children needs to be controlled; IACFO, 30 pages; July 2003. Available in pdf format on The Food Commission website: <www.foodcomm.org.uk>
7. TV Dinners: What's being served up by the advertisers? 2001. Available from Sustain, the alliance for better food and farming: <www.sustainweb.org>
8. Mary Whiting, Dump the Junk!, (Forest Row, Sussex: Moonscape Books, 2003).

9. The Health Education Trust: 18 High Street, Broom, Alcester, Warwicks, B50 4HJ; fax: 01789 773915; <www.healthedtrust.com>

Count Rumford's Soup

Bee Wilson

Count Rumford by Gainsborough[1]

Benjamin Thompson, aka the Graf von Rumford of the Holy Roman Empire (1753-1814), was a brilliant, vain and insanely ambitious scientist, whose invention of a new soup to combat pauperism briefly became the talk of the Western world during the period after the French Revolution and before Waterloo. Rumford soup, as it came to be known, was really nothing more than barley, potatoes and dried peas, all cooked in a large volume of water, with vinegar, salt and a little dry bread added at the end. If you were to be served now with a bowlful of this gloopy, homely mixture, you might not guess that it was meant to constitute a great scientific invention, a masterpiece of both nutrition and philanthropy. Yet in its day, Rumford soup was compared in its epoch-changing significance to the inventions of the steamship and vaccination.[2] Rumford soup was thought by some as brilliant as the lightning rod, which would have pleased Rumford, who from his youth had modelled himself on Benjamin Franklin, as an inventor, essayist, public reformer and all-round citizen of the globe.

If Count Rumford is remembered now, it is chiefly for his experiments involving heat, which disproved the then prevalent theory that heat was a substance; for his founding of the Royal Institution in England; and for his kitchen inventions, including the closed oven range, the double-boiler and the drip method for coffee.[3] His contemporary fame, however, was largely connected to his eponymous soup, which inspired other philanthropists to set up soup kitchens for the poor all over Europe and America. After he died, the inscription on his tomb called him 'The celebrated physicist and enlightened philanthropist, whose discoveries on light and heat made his name illustrious, and whose work to help the poor will always be dear to the friends of humanity'.[4] His "work to help the poor" was intimately connected with his soup, which was first devised as a way of feeding the poorest classes of Munich.

Like Benjamin Franklin, Rumford[5] was an American of modest origins who felt most at home abroad. An "ingenious young man", he was keen from the earliest age to escape the farming stock he was born into in Woburn, Massachussetts.[6] His youth was spent in unsuccessful mercantile apprenticeships – he worked for a while in a dry goods business in Boston. Things looked up when, with a scientifically-minded friend, Loammi Baldwin, he founded a society 'for propagateing learning and usefull knowledge'[sic].[7] He married an older widow as a way of furthering himself, but his career really only took off during the Wars of Independence when he fought on the loyalist side, and ingratiated himself with the British, such that he soon found work as a spy and go-between in London, and in 1784 was even knighted. He would be adored in France, too, where, late in life, he was admitted to the Academy of Sciences and made a foolish second marriage to Mme Lavoisier, the widow of the great chemist, whose charm proved short-lived and whom Rumford later described as 'the female dragon'. But it was in Bavaria that he really found himself, and here that his great soup was conceived. After his successes in England, Rumford had taken a job in 1785 as an aide-de-camp of Carl Theodor, Elector of Bavaria. To start with Rumford wisely kept a low profile, perfecting his French and German and slowly making himself invaluable to Carl Theodor. He was rewarded with a splendid villa in the *Schwabinger Gasse* and in 1786 was presented with the Royal Order of St Stanislaus. Meanwhile, he had begun to experiment in earnest on heat and light. Around this time, he wrote to his mentor in London, Lord Germain, with astonishing self-satisfaction:

> I hardly know what there is left for me to wish for. Ranks, titles, Decoration, Literary Distinctions, with some degree of literary and some small degree of military fame I have acquired...and the road is open to me for the rest. No man supports a better moral character than I do, and no Man is better satisfied with himself.[8]

The sheer smugness of it takes one's breath away, especially from a man still in his early thirties (and one whose moral character was actually far from spotless, since he had fathered at least one illegitimate child). But it was this bumptiousness that propelled Rumford forwards and made his eventual philanthropy possible. With nothing more 'to wish for' on his own account, he applied himself to the problems of the world, starting with Bavaria. At that time, the place was a mess, afflicted with grotesque poverty and civil disorder, saddled with an overweening Catholic hierarchy, a cluttered and feckless Court and an army which bred hooliganism and beggary in place of law and order. Rumford surveyed this chaos with a canny eye. He realised that it would be career suicide for him to attack the Church or the Court. But this still left the army, and he wrote a detailed memo detailing everything he found wrong with Bavarian military life, before sending it to Carl Theodor. This was a daring act, and Rumford knew there was every chance that such criticism would inflame Carl Theodor's autocratic vanity. As things turned out, however, it pleased Carl Theodor that this fledgeling scientist was prepared to take the work out of governing for him. To his amazement, Rumford woke up one morning 'to discover that he had been appointed Minister of War, Minister of Police, Major-General, Chamberlain of the Court, and State Councillor, with sufficient powers to do what he liked with the Bavarian army'.[9] He now had *carte-blanche* to reform the Bavarian economy, and started work straight away.

The trouble with the organisation of the Bavarian military, Rumford decided, was that it was fundamentally antisocial. Soldiers were paid a pittance and given horrible food and spent most of their time in idleness away from home, which led to outbreaks of petty crime and fragmented families, both caused by boredom. Rumford concluded that the way to make

Bavaria strong was to turn soldiers into citizens and citizens into soldiers. He established permanent garrisons throughout the country, so that soldiers could stay close to their wives and children. Instead of lazing around when they were not needed in war, Rumford employed them in road-making, marsh-draining and repairing river banks. The most decisive change of all was in feeding. Rumford encouraged soldiers to eat together in their messes and to take their food, which was perforce very cheap, in the form of soup. Most commonly, they would have beef, boiled with herbs and their allocated 'ammunition bread'. On this diet, the Bavarian military became, or so Rumford claimed, 'the finest, stoutest and strongest men in the world'.[10] Moreover, each garrisoned private and NCO was given his own potato bed of 365 square feet in the military garden of the garrison. Through this initiative, the potato, which was already gaining in popularity, became the staple food of Bavaria, mainly in the form of dumplings. On this hearty diet of beef soup, bread and dumplings, the military did indeed transform itself into a cadre of model citizens – or at least improved its discipline to a remarkable extent.

The lessons Rumford learned feeding the military proved invaluable in his next project, which was eliminating beggars from the streets of Munich. The poor of Bavaria were 'not just deprived, they were destitute and starving'.[11] Mendacity had become a 'highly organised racket', with beggar-chiefs kidnapping children and maiming them to make them more pitiful and therefore more profitable beggars.[12] The main responsibility for improving matters seemed to lie with the Church whose attitude was that poverty was a necessary concomitant of lack of virtue. Clerical alms-givers preached virtue first, then happiness. How effective this was may be judged by the fact that alms-seekers just kept on multiplying. 'It was often said that in Bavaria there were as many priests, nuns and monks begging for alms to give the poor as there were poor begging for themselves'.[13] Rumford, an intellectual Protestant, was unusual in having 'the courage to break with the feudal philosophy that the poverty of the common people was a God-willed necessity'.[14] His ideas about poverty mixed cold utilitarianism with enlightened despotism. He believed in pleasure and pain as the basic units of human experience but also believed that he had the power to dole them out, or withhold them – in the form of soup. Those who persistently failed to turn up on time to the workhouse would be denied their delicious soup. 'Rewards and punishments are the only means by which mankind can be controlled and directed'.[15]

Rumford entirely reversed the Catholic attitude to begging, using arguments not dissimilar to Jeremy Bentham's:

To make a vicious and abandoned people happy, it has been generally supposed necessary first to make them virtuous. But why not reverse the order? Why not make them first happy, and then virtuous? [16]

The thing was to make the poor honest and industrious. But to do this, Rumford argued, 'the utmost caution will be necessary to prevent their being disgusted'.[17] The main tool against disgust, he felt, was the 'pleasure of eating'.

On New Year's Day, 1790, infantry officers combed the streets of Munich arresting every beggar they could find. Rumford boasted that in less than an hour, no beggars remained on the streets. Each beggar was given a number and told to report to the new workhouse, where they would learn a trade, and would be given in return shelter, warmth (Rumford had strong views on the civilising effects of warm rooms) and, most importantly, a good meal. To the question of what this meal should be, Rumford applied the whole of his scientific mind. As he wrote in his essay *Of Food*, 'There is...no subject of investigation more interesting to mankind' than 'the nourishment and growth of plants and animals', including the human animal.[18]

With his admiration for potatoes, Rumford was rather fond of Irish 'calecannon' as a food for the poor, giving a recipe which included ginger as well as greens, butter, onions and potatoes.[19] But however delicious it might be, this dish was still relatively expensive, on account of the butter, and did not offer the most nourishing food for the least money. He was also fond of polenta and macaroni, and lamented the fact that they were so often seen on the tables of the rich in England and Germany, while the poor, who 'ought to be considered as having almost an exclusive right to them...are kept in perfect ignorance of them' (a complaint which could still be made today).[20] But his experiments in the workhouse at Munich convinced him that 'the cheapest, most savoury, and most nourishing food that could be provided was a soup composed of pearl barley, pease, potatoes, cuttings of fine wheaten bread, vinegar, salt and water, in certain proportions'.[21] It was no surprise that soup should turn out to be the cheapest food. After all, soup had been served in bread and broth kitchens to the poor since medieval times. Rumford's real breakthrough, or so he believed, was that soup was disproportionately more nourishing than other cheap foods. His point of true originality – or, if you prefer, his moment of real madness – was in his claim that what made soup so nourishing was the water in it.

Rumford was under the impression that he had unearthed a real discovery relating to the role of water in nutrition. He observed that water seemed to act as a 'food' for plants.[22] In vegetation, water was not just a vehicle of nourishment, but a nourishment in itself. Why, then, should it not perform the same role for humans? Why shouldn't water be 'food'?

Clearly, Rumford saw, water was not the *only* element in a good soup: 'no great relief would be derived from drinking *crude* water to fill up the void in the stomach.' To extract the goodness from water, it was necessary to cook it wisely with some solid matter. It was also essential to insist on 'a proper choice of the ingredients, and proper management of the fires in the combination of those ingredients' in order to make a soup that was 'rich' and 'palatable'.[23] Rumford's directions for making his soup were impressively exact.

The method of preparing this soup is as follows; The water and the pearl barley are first put together into the boiler and made to boil; the pease are then added, and the boiling is continued over a gentle fire about two hours;--the potatoes are then added, (having been previously peeled with a knife, or having been boiled, in order to their being more easily deprived of their skins,) and the boiling is continued for about one hour more, during which time the contents of the boiler are frequently stirred about with a large wooden spoon, or ladle, in order to destroy the texture of the potatoes, and to reduce the soup to one uniform mass. – When this is done, the vinegar and the salt are added; and last of all, at the moment it is to be served up, the cuttings of bread.

The soup should never be suffered to boil, or even to stand long before it is served up after the cuttings of bread are put into it. It will, indeed, for reasons which will hereafter be explained, be best never to put the cuttings of bread into the boiler at all, but, (as is always done at Munich,) to put them into the tubs in which the soup is carried from the kitchen into the dining-hall; pouring the soup hot from the boiler upon them; and stirring the whole well together with the iron ladles used for measuring out the soup to the Poor in the hall.

It is of more importance than can well be imagined, that this bread which is mixed with the soup should not be boiled. It is likewise of use that it should be cut as fine or thin as possible; and if it be dry and hard, it will be so much the better.[24]

The bread used by Rumford in Munich was very hard 'semel' bread, which bakers donated for free once it had gone stale. The hardness was useful, he believed 'for it renders mastication necessary; and mastication seems very powerfully to assist in promoting digestion: it likewise *prolongs the duration of the enjoyment of eating,* a matter of very great importance indeed, and which has not hitherto been sufficiently attended to.'[25] Just how enjoyable it is to masticate hard stale bread is a moot point; but these things are all relative. Compared to no bread at all, this soup-dampened chewy *semel* must have been nectar for the gods.

What really took Rumford aback, though, was 'the discovery of the very small quantity of solid food which, when properly prepared, will suffice to satisfy hunger and support life and health, and the very trifling expense at which the stoutest and most laborious man may, in any country, be fed'.[26] To start with, Rumford had included a little meat in his beggar's soup, as was the Bavarian custom; but as he developed his cooking technique, he soon decided that this could be dispensed with without making the 'victuals' much less nourishing.[27] 'I never heard that the poor complained of the want of it'. Rumford believed that soup – and particularly his special soup – had the power to alleviate hunger in a way that the same ingredients taken 'dry' could not. Rumford ran tests to see whether an active grown man could survive on 4½ ounces of bread a day taken with plain water. He found that on these rations the workers grew faint and weak. But when the same 4½ ounces of solid food were cooked into a soup, the eaters were somehow able to keep going and lead productive lives.[28]

Rumford backed up this revelation with the German practice of feeding cattle with liquid mixtures, called *drank* or *drink,* pottages made from a lot of water cooked with bran, oatmeal, brewer's grains, mashed potatoes, mashed turnips, rye meal, and barley meal.[29] What worked for cattle must work for paupers too! One can see why a friend once said of Rumford that 'He judged people the way a planter judges his slaves'.[30] He admired what he saw as the 'Chinese' system of government, in which a subject people was ruled by a learned elite.[31] He was such a control freak that after a recipe for 'Indian pudding', he even gave instructions on precisely how to eat it, 'beginning at the circumference of the slice, and approaching regularly towards the centre'.[32] Rumford believed wholeheartedly that he knew best and that his soup could transform the public feeding of the world. He happily boasted of the way that the poor of Munich treated him as their saviour, setting aside an hour every evening after their work to pray for him!

Imagine my feelings, upon hearing of the confused noise of the prayers of a multitude of people, who were passing by in the streets, upon being told that it was the poor of Munich, many hundreds in number, who were going in procession to the church to put up public prayers for me – public prayers for me! For a private person! A stranger! A Protestant! ... I dare venture to affirm that no proof could well be stronger than this that the measures adopted for making these poor people happy were really successful.[33]

Rumford did not give much consideration to the possibility that the gratitude of the Munich-poor might have had as much to do with being given *anything* to eat at all, as with the exact composition of his soups. The formula for these soups, he argued, should be applied to hospitals as well as workhouses. Public kitchens should be set up 'in all towns and large villages throughout the kingdom' where the 'poor might be fed *gratis*' and where 'the industrious inhabitants of the neighbourhood might be furnished with food at so cheap a rate as to be a very great relief to them at all times'.[34] In times of scarcity, the frugal soups emanating from these kitchens might even be enough to prevent famine, guarding the public against the effects of hoarding and speculation.[35]

To a very considerable extent, the idea of Count Rumford's soup did take off. *Soupe-maigre* had been fed to the poor for centuries, but Rumford soup seemed something new - an excitingly scientific solution to the new levels of indigence in an industrialising world, partly because it was so wonderfully cheap, and partly because Rumford's new ovens made the work of cooking so much easier. Soup kitchens proliferated in all the major cities of Europe. The public kitchens of Switzerland issued meal tickets engraved with the name and portrait of Rumford, something which, he wrote to his daughter Sarah in 1801, smugly as ever, made him feel 'deeply affected'.[36] Rumford soup was an established enough thing to inspire the rage of that other social campaigner, William Cobbett, who referred to the famous soup as 'dirt and bones' and called it an outrage that any Englishman, no matter how poor, should ever be insulted by being offered this insipid brew.[37] After his death, a satirist wrote that ' those who can swallow the Count's dinners can swallow anything'.[38]

Yet Rumford soup continued to influence the feeding of the poor throughout the 19th century, even when the precise recipes of the count were not followed. 'Rumfordizing' came to mean philanthropic feeding of all kinds. In 1899, an American follower of the count could write that 'no real advance on the foundation that he laid seems to have been made until near our own time'.[39] In Berlin in 1890, there were 15 public kitchens on the Rumford model, serving 2,724,419 portions of soup per year. Temperance campaigners saw Rumford kitchens as a possible tool against drunkenness. Rumford's ideas were also applied to feeding in schools and colleges.

Now, however, the soup is more or less forgotten, or, if remembered, it is derided. A recent scientific biography of Rumford described his theory on the nutritive properties of water as 'his one error of judgement', and deemed it 'odd' that 'someone with Rumford's scientific background and experience could ever have persuaded himself to accept such an erroneous view'.[40] But is it really so odd? Even though Rumford was wrong to think of water as nourishing, surely he had hit on something special about the power of soup to comfort and to feed. He was right that a well-made soup will nourish better than a carelessly thrown-together hotch-potch. He was right that the poor deserve better than dry bread and 'thin wash'. He was right that food is a more congenial tool for producing work than religion. He was also right that a raging hunger on a cold winter's day is better met with a warming barley-broth than with the same calorie's worth of cold bread and water.

It was a pity that he then generalised these truths into the theory that more water meant more nourishment. The greater pity, however, was that he never recognised that there was something fundamentally grotesque in doling out his specially calculated soups to the poor, as if they were just fodder for his experiments. Rumford may have filled thousands of stomachs, but in doing so, he paid scant attention to the human hunger for dignity. Rumford was adamant that soup kitchens should be run strictly on a voluntary basis, rather than by governments, as a way of preserving freedom. Yet he did not see that stuffing the poor with pease and barley broth three times a day might in itself be a threat to individual liberty – the liberty of taste.

Like many great philanthropists, Rumford had little feeling for other human beings. When he died, he had no more than two or three friends, despite all the hundreds of Bavarian beggars who had supposedly worshipped his watery soup. It was said that 'although Rumford disliked people to his dying day, as much as they disliked him, he loved humanity'.[41] By the same token, while he loved the idea of 'feeding' as a way of improving the lot of man, he did not have a great feel for gustatory enjoyment, (apart from coffee, about which he was fanatical). Indeed, he admitted that

> Although I have written a whole chapter on the pleasure of eating, I must acknowledge what all my acquaintances will certify, that few persons are less attached to the pleasures of the table than myself. If, in treating this subject, I sometimes appear to do it *con amore*, this warmth of expression ought, in justice, to be ascribed solely to the sense I entertain of its infinite importance to the health, happiness and innocent enjoyments of mankind.[42]

You would never find a true gastronome such as Brillat-Savarin disavowing the 'pleasures of the table' in this way. But nor would Brillat-Savarin, with his fat lawyer's stomach, ever have mustered the astonishing social drive of Count Rumford in trying, however imperfectly, to salve the hunger of the world.

Short Bibliography

G.I. BROWN, Scientist, Soldier, Statesman, Spy: Count Rumford, The Extraordinary Life of Scientific Genius, (London, Sutton Publishing, 1999).

SANBORN C. BROWN, Benjamin Thompson, Count Rumford, (Cambridge Massachussetts and London: The MIT Press, 1979).

GEORGE E. ELLIS, Memoir of Benjamin Thompson, Count Rumford, (reprinted Boston: Gregg Press,1972).

CHARLES FOURIER, The Theory of the Four Movements, edited by Gareth Stedman Jones and translated by Ian Patterson, (Cambridge: Cambridge University Press, 1996).

EGON LARSON, An American in Europe: The Life of Benjamin Thompson, Count Rumford, (New York: Rider & Company, 1953).

J.R. POYNTER, Society and Pauperism: English Ideas on Poor Relief, 1795-1834, (London: Routledge, 1969).

BENJAMIN THOMPSON COUNT RUMFORD, The Collected Works of Count Rumford, edited Sanborn C. Brown, (Cambridge, Mass.: Belknap Press of Harvard University Press, 1968-70).

THE RUMFORD KITCHEN LEAFLETS, Boston (Whitcomb & Barrows, Mass, 1904) (1899).

Appendix: Ingredients and Costings for Count Rumford's Soup

(Taken from Rumford (1970) vol V).

Soup No. 1

Ingredients	Weight avoirdupois		Cost		
	lbs.	oz.	£	s.	d.
4 viertels of pearl barley, equal to about 20 1/3 gallons	141	1	0	11	7 ½
4 viertels of peas	131	4	0	7	3 ¼
Cuttings of fine wheaten bread	69	10	0	10	2 ¼
Salt	19	13	0	1	2 ½
24 maasse very weak beer, vinegar, or rather small beer turned sour, about 24 quarts	46	13	0	1	5 ½
Water, about 560 quarts	1077	0			
Fuel, 88 lbs. of dry pine-wood, the Bavarian klafter (weighing 3961 lbs.) at 8s. 2¼ d. sterling			0	0	2 ¼
	1485	10	1	11	11 ¼
Wages of three cook-maids At twenty florins (37s. 7 1/2 d.) A year each, makes daily			0	0	3 2/8
Daily expense for feeding the three Cook-maids, at ten kreutzers each, according to an agreement made with them			0	0	11
Daily wages of two men servants, employed in going to market, collecting donations of bread, etc., helping in the kitchen, and assisting in serving out the soup to the poor			0	1	7 ¼
Repairs of the kitchen and of the kitchen furniture, about 90 florins (8l. 3s. 7d. sterling) a year, makes daily			0	0	5 ½
Total daily expenses, when dinner is provided for 1200 persons			1	15	2 ¼

Soup No. 2

Ingredients	Weight avoirdupois		Cost		
	lbs.	oz.	£	s.	d.
2 viertels of pearl barley	70	9	0	5	9 ½
2 viertels of peas	65	10	0	3	7 5/8
8 viertels of potatoes	230	4	0	1	9 9/11
Cuttings of bread	69	10	0	10	2 4/11
Salt	19	13	0	1	2 ½
Vinegar	46	13	0	1	5 ½
Water	982	15			
	1485	10			
Expenses for fuel, servants, repairs, etc., as before			0	3	5 ½
Total daily expense, when dinner is provided for 1200 persons			1	7	6 2/3

Note: a *Viertel* is a twelfth part of a *schäffel*, and a Bavarian *schäffel* equals 6.31 bushels; thus, 1 viertel = 19.140 litres.

Notes

1. Portrait of Count Rumford, taken from rumford.com: ' Count Rumford by Gainsborough, a copy of which is on display at Count Rumford's birthplace, Woburn, Massachusetts. The painting, formerly in possession of Countess Rumford, is now in the collection of the Reverend Sheafe Walker, Concord, New Hampshire'.
2. Fourier (1996) p. 315.
3. For more on Rumford's legacy, see the website devoted to him, www.rumford.com.
4. Quoted, Larson (1953) p. 169.
5. I will refer to him as Rumford throughout, for the sake of clarity, though in fact he was not ennobled with that title until 1791.
6. Brown (1979) p. 1.
7. Ibid. p. 7.
8. Quoted, Brown (1979) p. 106.
9. Larson (1953) p. 53.
10. Rumford (1968-70) volume V p. 198.
11. Brown (1979) p. 123.

12 Larson (1953) p. 52.
13 Brown (1979) p. 123.
14 Larson (1953) p. 58.
15 Rumford (1968-70) vol V p. 129 (Of the Fundamental Principles on which General Establishments for the Relief of the Poor may be Formed in all Countries).
16 Ibid. p. 59,
17 Poynton 91969) p. 89.
18 Rumford (1970) Vol V p. 171.
19 Rumford (1970) Vol V pp. 371-375.
20 Ibid. p. 217.
21 Ibid. p. 173.
22 Ibid. p. 172.
23 Idem.
24 Idem.
25 Idem.
26 Idem.
27 Ibid. p. 193.
28 Brown (1979) p. 160.
29 Idem.
30 Quoted Brown (1979) p. 59.
31 Larson (1953) p. 169.
32 Quoted Larson (1953) p. 77
33 Brown (1979) p. 161.
34 Rumford (1970) Vol V p. 181.
35 Idem.
36 Brown (1999) p. 112.
37 Cited, Ellis (1972) pp. 506-507.
38 Brown (1999) p. 113.
39 Rumford Kitchen leaflets (1899) p. 156.
40 Brown (1999) p. 113.
41 Ibid. p. 161.
42 Larson (1953).

Feeding the Artist

Carolin Young

Now, as violence, worry and ignorance threaten to snuff out the flame of civilization, it is difficult to not to feel that the gods, or God, by whichever name we call him, have retreated to the heavens, leaving us to a dark and uncertain fate. We live in what Roberto Calasso, in *The Marriage of Cadmus and Harmony*, an exploration of the meanings of story, myth and metaphor threaded through Greek mythology, defines as, "The third regime, the modern one … that of indifference, but with the implication that the gods have already withdrawn, and, hence, if they are indifferent in our regard, we can be indifferent as to their existence or otherwise."[1] If the Muses hide themselves in a forgotten cave on Mount Helicon and Apollo no longer visits us with his lyre how are we to find inspiration today?

At the end of World War II, Caresse Crosby, the poet, gallery director, arts patroness and hostess famous as the co-publisher, with her husband Harry, of the Black Sun Press, founded the literary magazine *Portfolio* to catalyze trans-Atlantic creativity after the long years of destruction. In the introduction to her first issue, she implored, "Never before has so much depended on the courageous vision of the artist. In every age, there have been men to lead peoples into treacherous conflict, but human achievement lives on through the medium of the artist, be he historian, poet, or painter."[2] One could argue that never since that time have her words held such resonance as they do today.

Although not a gastronomic journal, from its outset *Portfolio* emphasized the table as a forum for artistic invention. In "The Staff of Life" (an excerpt from *The Air-Conditioned Nightmare*), Henry Miller, justifying the appeal of expatriate Parisian life, declares, "What do I find wrong with America? Everything. I begin at the beginning with the staff of life, bread. If bread is bad, the whole of life is bad. On the whole, Americans eat without pleasure. They eat because the bell rings three times a day."[3]

Artistic endeavor, in its myriad forms, is cultivated from the primal, animal act of feeding. The German *fressen*, is elevated through taste, care and ritual to the human *essen*. Good food is a solid start but as the timeworn expression states, "Man does not live on bread alone." Feeding the artist requires more than a meltingly succulent menu. For this reason

Caresse Crosby, renowned hostess and muse, placed food last, after (1) guests, (2) drink and (3) entertainment, on her list of requisites for party giving.[4]

In the revised edition of *How to Cook a Wolf*, originally written to promote hospitality during World War II rationing, M. F. K. Fisher declared: "I believe that one of the most dignified ways we are capable of, to assert and then reassert our dignity in the face of poverty and war's fears and pains, is to nourish ourselves with all possible skill, delicacy, and ever-increasing enjoyment. And, with our gastronomical growth will come, inevitable, knowledge and perception of a hundred other things, but mainly of ourselves. Then Fate, even tangled as it is with cold wars as well as hot, cannot harm us."[5] Unlike Miller, Fisher *is* typically categorized as a food writer, yet it was her concern with nurturing creativity, the exchange of ideas and goodwill that both inspired her and gives her work continued resonance. "Now, of all times in history," she counseled," we should be using our minds as well as our hearts in order to survive… to live gracefully if to live at all."[6]

Almost 500 years earlier, the 15th century Florentine philosopher Marsilio Ficino, who translated Plato, authored *Three Books on Life* (with dietary recommendations for the health-seeking scholar), and earned the moniker "Friend to Mankind", admonished, "If we did not allow Man himself, that is the soul, to perish from hunger while we feed the body, the dogs, and the birds, then each man would live content and plenished; just as now no one is content."[7] Ficino's words remain as poignant and intractably relevant as the elusive dream his patron Cosimo 'il Vecchio' de' Medici maintained of healing the rift between the Eastern and Western Churches. Toward that harmonic end, the untitled, second-generation banker invited the Eastern Patriarch, the Pope, the Emperor of Byzantium and every reigning European statesman he could muster to banquet in the shadow of Brunelleschi's recently erected dome in Florence in 1439. Though these entertainments failed in their official purpose (and how different history, had they succeeded) the infusion of Eastern influences, particularly discussions with the philosopher Georgius Gemistus Plethon, inspired Cosimo to sponsor young Ficino's study of Greek and subsequently Plato.

The banquet, ancient forum for religious celebration, remains a place from which we, like Crosby, Miller, Fisher, Ficino and Cosimo de' Medici before us, may attempt to conjure the Muses to our side. In a letter to the Aristotelian philosopher Francesco Tebaldi, Ficino noted that the Peripatetic philosophers "discussed the soul after a banquet as if they thought that the body should be refreshed before the soul could be brought into being."[8] "For my part," he continued, "although I created the little soul of this letter before dining, I nevertheless agree with them about the order of creation." Indeed, he acknowledged that it was a banquet on 7 November 1468, the anniversary of Plato's birth and death, held in the Medici villa at Careggi, which inspired him to write *De amore*, his commentary on *The Symposium*, which reconciled the Greek philosopher's precepts with Christian theology so that they re-entered the lexicon of Western learning.[9]

"Only the meal embraces all parts of man," Ficino declared, "for … it restores the limbs, renews the humors, revives the mind, refreshes the senses and sustains and sharpens reason."[10] He did not, however, mean just any meal. In his original Latin text, Ficino used the word *convivium*, the etymological ancestor of "conviviality," and carefully specified that this comprised not just the ingestion of food and drink but "a sweet communion of life." "The *convivium*," he explained, "is rest from labors, release from cares, and nourishment of genius: it is the demonstration of love and splendor, the food of good will, the seasoning of friendship, the leavening of grace and the solace of life." Ficino knew that to feed the artist we must consciously invite the Muses to banquet with us.

Erato "the lovely," muse of lyric and love poetry, Thalia, "the flourishing," deity of comedy and pastoral poetry, and Calliope, "the fair-voiced," guardian of epic poetry, Clio, "the proclaimer," keeper of history; Euterpe, "the giver of pleasure," goddess of music and lyric poetry; Melpomene, "the songstress," lady of tragedy; Polyhymnia, "she of many hymns," divine inspirer of heroic hymns and sacred poetry, Terpischore, "the whirler," steward of dancing and song; and Urania, "the heavenly," priestess of astronomy—the Muses must be venerated at the table because their shimmering gift, the spark of inspiration, occurs in that magical space between the words, at that time when the body has been fed. The 17th century author of *L'Art de bien traiter*, known only as L. S. R., eloquently described the phenomenon. At dessert, he states, "the spirit revives, the wittiest words are spoken, the most agreeable topics debated … [I]t is then that the funniest stories are told … [A]s they say, between the pear and the cheese, a thousand pleasantries are invented to pass the time and entertain good company, which provide the greatest charm in life."[11] In the 19th century, Brillat-Savarin elaborated:

At the beginning of the meal, and throughout the first course, each guest eats steadily, without speaking or paying attention to anything which may be said; whatever his position in society, he forgets everything to become nothing but a worker in the great factory of Nature. But when the need for food begins to be satisfied, then the intellect awakes, talk becomes general, a new order of things is initiated, and he who until then was a mere consumer of food, becomes a table companion of more or less charm, according to the qualities bestowed on him by the Master of all things.[12]

So too, the venerated gastronome upheld the immutable connection between the table and the Muses. He therefore bequeathed them a new sister, Gasterea, the Tenth Muse, who reigns over "the delights of taste."[13] Although Gasterea's worshippers enjoy the greatest triumphs of cuisine, the staggering beauties of the temple and lilting music, Brillat-Savarin tells us that at her feast day they derive their principle happiness from the conversation: "No man is seated beside the woman to whom he has already said all he has to say."[14] (Unlike his Florentine antecedent, he mixes the sexes at table when promoting mealtime banter.) Her banquet is populated by stimulating companions, "the savants of both sexes who have enriched the art with new discoveries, hosts who graciously fulfill the duties of French hospitality, cosmopolitan sages to whom society owes useful or agreeable imports, and those charitable men who nourish the poor with the rich spoils of their superabundance."

The Muses are the daughters of the Titaness Msemosyne (Memory) who for nine consecutive nights lay together with Zeus, the powerful god who swallowed the whole universe and spat it back out. They are ladies in waiting of the banquet, where the act of breaking bread forges occasion, which in turn creates memory, indelibly demarcating a moment in life from all others. The sense of taste reaches powerfully beyond the articulated word into the nether-reaches of the subconscious and the wellspring of memory. Perhaps Gasterea is not a sister of the Muses, after all, but their mother, Msemosyne, called by a different name. Marcel Proust, in his famous passage about the madeleine, in which a bite of the cake soaked in tea suffices to flood the narrator's mind with vivid images of his childhood argues, "when from a long-distant past nothing subsists, after the people are dead, after the things are broken and scattered, taste and smell alone, more fragile but more enduring, more unsubstantial, more persistent, more faithful, remain poised a long time like souls, remembering, waiting, hoping, amid ruins of all the rest; and bear unflinchingly, in the tiny and almost impalpable drop of their essence, the vast structure of recollection."[15]

Ficino believed, "enjoyment is the seasoning of things, it is the food of love, the kindling of genius, the nourishment of will, and the strength of memory."[16] For this same reason, early Arab poets such as Hafs al-Umawi and 'Ubayd Allah Ibn Qays al-Ruqayyat incorporated the image of the remembered banquet into the form of the *nasib*.[17] These proto-Romantic poets luxuriated in melancholic nostalgia, intertwining food and memory, ritual and art:

> I stopped at the abode, but what I found
> Was only recollection,
> the figment of a dream.

> All was decay, all desolation, where once
> > reigned cheer and fellowship,
> And empty stood the lofty halls
> > Of nations past.[18]

A novel, a poem, a painting, a song—all these and more can be nurtured at table. But if we forget to imbue meals with the ineffable spirit of inspiration and focus only upon fleeting sensory gratification we endanger the essence of our humanity.

Brillat-Savarin posits that the biological act of eating evolved into the ritualized act of dining because of humankind's need to tell stories. "It was the meal," he surmised, "which was responsible for the birth, or at least the elaboration of languages, not only because it was a continually recurring occasion for meetings, but also because the leisure which accompanies and succeeds the meal is naturally conducive to confidence and loquacity."[19]

Roberto Calasso even more daringly attributes the introduction of the alphabet in Greece to the mythological feast that gives his book its title, the wedding banquet of Cadmus, the Phoenician, to Harmony, a daughter of Aphrodite, at which gods and goddesses dine together with mere mortals. The monumental legacy of this unforgettable occasion, by legend the first mortal wedding attended by gods, was written language itself. In Calasso's words, "Cadmus had brought Greece 'gifts of the mind': vowels and consonants yoked together in tiny signs, 'etched model of a silence that speaks'—the alphabet. With the alphabet, the Greeks would teach themselves to experience the gods in the silence of the mind, and no longer in the full and normal presence, as Cadmus himself had the day of his marriage."[20] The birth of the alphabet, springboard of poetry and literature, required no mere banquet but a feast in the presence of the divine.

Calasso tells us that after the marriage of Cadmus and Harmony the separation between mortals and the gods became more distinct. "Man's relationship with the gods passed through two regimes: first conviviality, then rape," he explains.[21] In this second phase Zeus might appear disguised as the bull or as the unknown guest welcomed at one of the primitive meals to which Brillat-Savarin attributes the emergence of hospitality. The god could not be seen in his own form but he could still be sensed and experienced; he was present at the table. The possibility that one might be hosting Zeus or Elijah must certainly have elevated the art of dining and lent a keen frisson to any feast. The myth of the divine or holy stranger who arrives unexpectedly for supper without revealing his identity stretches across borders and religions, repeating its call to graciousness in every variation. The resulting stories survive as myth, legend, and holy texts.

We, who live in Calasso's third regime, the modern era of indifference, must strive to conjure the Muses metaphorically, as Ficino did, and in so doing perhaps, if we are very lucky, we, too, may inspire a Renaissance in our own time. Ficino explained that according to his beloved Plato, "the Muses should be understood as divine songs; thus they say 'melody' and 'muse' take their name from song."[22] Song, he elaborated, was vital to the *convivium* because it is "most like the food of the gods"; wine helped ply the soul into flight; and conversation provided nourishment for the mind. Toward that end, he took his cue from Varro and proclaimed that the ideal number of banqueters "should be neither fewer than the three Graces not more than the nine Muses." "Moreover," he continued, "from this fellowship of the Graces and the Muses, it is quite clear what kind of people these participants should be: they should be graced by the Graces, gifted by the Muses, and men of letters."[23] Above all, Ficino advised, "everything should be seasoned with the salt of genius and illumined by the rays of mind and manners, so that, as was said about the dinner of Plato and Xenocrates, the fragrance of our meal [*convivium*] may spread further and be sweeter the next day."[24]

We must by no means believe that inciting the Muses to join us at table is easy or without risk. Calasso warns us:

After that remote time when gods and men had been on familiar terms, to invite the gods to one's house became the most dangerous thing one could do, a source of wrongs and curses, a sign of the now irretrievable malaise in relations between heaven and earth. At the marriage of Cadmus and Harmony, Aphrodite gives the bride a necklace which, passing from hand to hand, will generate one disaster after another right up [to] the massacre of the Epigoni beneath the walls of Thebes, and beyond. At the marriage of Peleus and Thetis, failure to invite Eris leads to the Judgment of Paris in favor of Aphrodite and against Hera and Athena, and thus creates the premise for the Trojan War. Lycaon's banquet, where human and animal flesh are served up together, brings about the Flood. Tantalus's banquet, were little Pelops is boiled in the pot, marks the beginning of a chain of crimes that will go on tangling together ever more perversely right up to the day when Athena casts the vote that acquits the fugitive Orestes.

What conclusions can we draw? To invite the gods ruins our relationship with them but sets history in motion. A life in which the gods aren't invited isn't worth living. It will be quieter, but there won't be any stories. And you could suppose that these dangerous invitations were in fact contrived by the gods themselves, because the gods get bored with men who have no stories.[25]

It is a dangerous sport and an unreachable goal nevertheless we must feed the artist along with the beast. As Ficino ended his banqueting treatise: "To what end is all this written about the *convivium*? Simply, that we who live separated lives, though not without vexation, may live together in happiness as one."[26] Can we succeed in lofty idealism where Cosimo il Vecchio and Ficino failed? No. But their examples demonstrate success within failure. As the darkness encroaches let us use every means possible to reach for the space between the words when we gather together at table. To do so is, "giving birth in beauty, whether in body or in soul," which the wise old woman Diotima in Plato's *Symposium*, concludes is the "real purpose of love".[27] She promises, "The love of the gods belongs to anyone who has given birth to true virtue and nourished it, and if any human being could become immortal, it would be he."[28] *The Symposium* was a work inspired by a banquet, which subsequently catalyzed Ficino and his fellow humanists to organize their own feast. Let us, as they did, remember the words of Plato's host, Agathon: "Love fills us with togetherness and drains all of our divisiveness away. Love calls gatherings like these together. In feasts, in dances, and in ceremonies, he gives us the lead."[29] So that we, like the 14th century Persian poet Háfiz, may cry out:

Excuse all the seventy-two nations at war.
They did not see the truth, and took the road of fable.

Thank God that peace has fallen between us.
The celestials danced and drank the cup of gratitude.[30]

Selected Bibliography

BRILLAT-SAVARIN, JEAN-ANTHELME, *The Physiology of Taste*, translated by Anne Drayton, (London: Penguin Books, 1970, reprinted 1994).

CALASSO, ROBERTO, *The Marriage of Cadmus and Harmony*, translated from the Italian by Tim Parks, (New York: Vintage International, 1994).

CONOVER, ANNE, *Caresse Crosby, From Black Sun to Roccasinibalda*, (Santa Barbara: Capra Press, 1989).

CROSBY, CARESSE, *The Passionate Years,* (New York: The Ecco Press, 1953).

FICINO, MARSILIO, *The Letters of Marsilio Ficino*, translated from the Latin by members of the Language Department of the School of Economic Science, London, Volumes 1—5, (London: Shepheard-Walwyn, 1975—1994).

------. *Commentaire sur le banquet de Platon*, French translation by Raymond Marcel from the original Latin manuscript *De amore*, (Paris: Les Belles Lettres, 1978).

FISHER, M. F. K. *The Art of Eating: The Collected Gastronomical Works of M. F. K. Fisher,* with an Introduction by Clifton Fadiman, (Cleveland: The World Publishing Co., 1954).

HÁFIZ- I SHÍRÁZÍ, KHWÁJA SHAMS UD-DÍN MUHAMMAD, *The Green Sea of Heaven: Fifty ghazals from the Díwán of Háfiz,* translated by Elizabeth T. Gray, Jr. with an introduction by Daryush Shayegan, (Ashland, Oregon: White Cloud Press, 1995).

PLATO, *The Symposium,* translated with introduction and notes by Alexander Nehamas and Paul Woodruff, (Indianapolis: Hackett Publishing Co., 1989).

PROUST, MARCEL, *Remembrance of Things Past,* the definitive Pléiade edition translated by C.K. Scott Moncrieff and Terence Kilmartin. Three Volumes, (New York: Vintage Book, 1982).

R., L. S. *L'Art de bien traiter,* reprinted in *L'Art de la cuisine française au XVIIe siècle,* edited by Gilles and Laurence Laurendon, (Paris: Payot & Rivages, 1995).

STRETKEVYCH, JAROSLAV, *The Zephyrs of Najd: The Poetics of Nostalgia in the Classical Arab Nasib,* (Chicago: The University of Chicago Press, 1993).

Notes

1. Calasso: pp. 52—53.
2. Caresse Crosby quoted by Conover: pp. 113—114.
3. Henry Miller quoted by Conover: p. 114.
4. Crosby: pp. 305—306.
5. M F. K. Fisher: p. 350.
6. Ibid: p. 192.
7. Ficino, *Letters*: I: 26.
8. Ibid: 96.
9. Ficino, Prologue to *De amore*: p. 136.
10. Ficino, *Letters*: 2:42.
11. Author's translation of L. S. R. in Laurendon: p. 168.
12. Brillat-Savarin: p. 162.
13. Ibid: p. 290.
14. Ibid.
15. Proust: I, pp. 50—51.
16. Ficino, *Letters*: I: 105.
17. Stretkevych, p. 65.
18. 'Ubayd Allah Ibn Qays al-Ruquayyat in Stretkevych, p. 101.
19. Brillat-Savarin: p. 161.
20. Calasso: pp. 390—391.
21. Ibid: p. 52.
22. Ficino, *Letters*: I: 7.
23. Ibid: 2:42.
24. Ibid: 2: 42.
25. Calasso: p. 387.
26. Ficino, *Letters*: 2: 42.
27. Plato: Lines 206B—C, pp. 52 & 53.
28. Ibid: Lines 212A—B, p. 60.
29. Ibid: Line 197D, p. 37.
30. Háfiz: Ghazal 29.

Symposium Events

Apart from the keynote speech, panel discussions and workshops, at which papers were presented and discussed, there were various events and entertainments for symposiasts to enjoy.

On the Friday night prior to the Symposium, Jeffrey Steingarten, author of 'The man who ate everything' and 'It must have been something I ate', delivered a public lecture, **You are *not* what you eat**, at the Said Business School. The lecture was preceded by a Wine Reception.

The highlight of the Symposium was
Sunday Lunch in honour of Alan Davidson
A lunch was held in honour of Alan Davidson's being awarded the Premium Erasmianum. This anticipated the actual award on November 5th in Amsterdam. The menu was based on his favourite foods, beginning with Rempeyek, a crunchy Indonesian snack made by Sri Owen, Alan's first Prospect Books author. The menu included many seafoods such a smoked eel and kippers; and excellent cheeses with oatcakes, The lunch concluded with Alan's all-time favourite, Scots trifle, magnificently constructed by St Antony's kitchen staff, who excelled themselves.

Thanks to the inspiration and hard work of Geraldene Holt, Chairman of Trustees, tributes to Alan and Jane Davidson from over 60 friends and symposiasts had been collected into a volume entitled "Funschrift", and this was presented to them to their great delight.

The Symposium Organiser, Silvija Davidson, and all those who helped her and contributed wine and food, are to be thanked and congratulated.

The Symposium dinner on Saturday night was 'hatched' by Caroline Conran and Elisabeth Luard, and included that ultimate symbol of nurture, tetilla, a Spanish cheese in the shape of a woman's breast.

Symposium Events

Eating like a Child – an interactive performance was staged by Marlena Spieler. The idea was to help participants get in touch with their inner child by engaging in various forms of childhood eating behaviour.

The Seven Tables Paula Claire, Oxford's "concrete" poet, led the Symposium in a participational poem based on objects depicted in the Dutch and Flemish still-life paintings in the Ashmolean Museum, Oxford. Participants were reminded of the ephemeral condition of fruit, flowers, meat, fish and drink, often emphasised by flitting butterflies, caterpillars and flies (tempus fugit), whose beauty and abundance make them emblems of the Heavenly Feast. The Seventh Table, envisioned by the mind's eye, represented Seventh Heaven.

The boy who wouldn't eat and his hovering mother was a performance in four acts, created by Alicia Rios and performed with the assistance of Raymond Sokolov. Nothing would persuade the boy to eat the delicious food prepared by his mother, until she threatened to give it to the children of the third world. The child's reluctance to eat was thus overcome and he could not be restrained.

Four films relating to the theme of Nurture were shown:

Bon A Petite by **Henrik Feldmann,** a fascinating study in film of a child eating, presented by Alicia Rios.

Nilesh Patel's *A Love Supreme*, a tribute to his mother's culinary skills. Her hands are the film's only character, and we watch as they prepare traditional Indian samosas with great dexterity. Presented by Nilesh Patel.

Film report on **Chez Chartier**, a family run *bouillon* (cookhouse) in Paris. A day in the life of this busy, highly successful *bouillon*, it's staff, customers and atmosphere. Presented by Andrew Dalby, with an accompanying summary in English.

Make yourself at home, film of a hilarious performance by **Bobby Baker**, presented by Paul Levy.

Menus from the Saturday night dinner and Sunday lunch are shown on pages 308-313.

Oxford Symposium on Food & Cookery 2003

Saturday Evening Dinner
13 September

on the theme of
Nurture

Sweet-cured herring fillet with radishes and soured cream
dark rye bread

Meantime White beer

Truffled boudin blanc with sautéed new potatoes
and hot beetroot

Meantime Red beer

Salad of red and white chicory

Fougasse

Wines selected by St Antony's Steward available to purchase

Tetilla D.O. Pérez Oliveira with Membrillo

Buffalo milk ice cream
With crushed cinnamon sugar

Piebald chocolate with rose petals

Finca Ana La Huerta Estate Guatemalan coffee

Notes on suppliers:
Herring fillets from Aberdeen Sea Products;
Truffled boudin from Rosslyn Deli, NW3;
Tetilla and Codonyat membrillo from Brindisa;
Ice cream by Labelle Rouge;
Chocolate by The Chocolate Society;
Coffee from Union Coffee Roasters;
Breads by Dan Schickentanz of De Gustibus;
Vegetables, salads, sauces and dressings by St Antony's chef and staff.

Menu hatched by Caroline Conran and Elisabeth Luard

Oxford Symposium on Food & Cookery
2003

Sunday Lunch

in honour of

Alan **D**avidson

14 September 2003

Rempeyek Kacang & Rempeyek Kacang Hijau
produced by Sri Owen

1999 Nierstein Riesling
contributed by Dr Alexander Michalsky Weingut St Antony, Nierstein

Avruga
contributed by Land & Sea

Ortiz anchovies: cured Cantabrian anchovy fillets
contributed by Brindisa

Smoked eel
by Brown & Forrest Brown
donated by Sri Owen

Smoked mussels
contributed by Frank Hederman of Belvelly Smokehouse

Smoked organic salmon
contributed by Frank Hederman of Belvelly Smokehouse

Scottish Salmon Rillettes
contributed by Forman & Field

Loch Fyne Kippers
contributed by Loch Fyne restaurant, Oxford

Breads
contributed by Dan Schickentanz of De Gustibus

"Per Me" extra virgin olive oil 2002
contributed by Armando Manni

Bisol Molera di Valdobbiadene 2002
contributed by Gianluca Bisol

Cashel Blue farm produced cheese
contributed by Jane and Louis Grubb

Montgomery's Cheddar
contributed by Jamie Montgomery

Vignette
contributed by Jonnie Archer of the Huge Cheese Company

Cabra del Tietar
contributed by Brindisa of Exmouth Street & Borough

Oatcakes
produced by Laura Mason

Betty's Yorkshire Oatcakes
contributed by Betty's and Taylors of Harrogate

Worcester apples and Victoria plums
contributed by Marks & Spencer

Scots Trifle
with a Bearsden's twist
produced by St Antony's kitchen
crystallized rose petals contributed by The Chocolate Society

Fazenda Rainha estate Brazilian coffee
contributed by Union coffee Roasters

ଓ ✱ ଞ

With special thanks to Symposiasts
Myrtle Allen, Ann Barr, Sarah Freeman, Ursula Heinzelmann, Mark Lake
Laura Mason, Sri Owen, Gae Pincus - and to Helen Saberi
for divulging Alan's favourite foods

About the Authors

Melitta Weiss Adamson is Associate Professor of German, Comparative Literature, and History of Medicine at the University of Western Ontario, London, Canada. She has published widely on food and preventive medicine in the Middle Ages. Her books include *Medieval Dietetics* (Lang 1995), *Food in the Middle Ages* (Garland 1995), *Daz buoch von guoter spise (The Book of Good Food): A Study, Edition, and English Translation of the Oldest German Cookbook* (Medium Aevum Quotidianum 2000), and *Regional Cuisines of Medieval Europe* (Routledge 2002).

Joan P Alcock took a first degree in History and subsequently degrees in Archaeology and Education. As a university lecturer she lectured on History, Archaeology and Environmental subjects before researching and writing books and articles on food history. In connection with her research she has travelled widely in Europe and the Far East. She is a Fellow of the Society of Antiquaries, a member of the Guild of Food Writers and, as an Honorary Visiting Fellow of London South Bank University, she works with the university in an advisory capacity.

Tony Blake has degrees in Chemistry and Biochemistry from the University of Oxford. He worked for 20 years with Unilever in research and marketing positions with their flavour operations and for the last 18 years, for Firmenich in Geneva where he is Vice President for Food Science and Technology. He is concerned with studying the interactions between flavour molecules and food matrices and recently on the psychology of flavour perception and the learning of flavour and food preferences. In 2001 he was appointed a special professor at the University of Nottingham's School of Biosciences. Professor Blake is a fellow of the British Society of Flavourists, and an enthusiastic self-taught chef.

Barrett P Brenton is an Associate Professor of Anthropology at St John's University in New York City and a Vincentian Research Fellow on Poverty and Social Justice. As a specialist in nutritional and medical anthropology his cross-cultural research is focused on international food security and the health consequences of dietary change. He has conducted applied fieldwork in North and South America, Europe, and Africa. Dr Brenton has published widely, is co-editor of the international journal *Ecology of Food and Nutrition*, and is currently President of the Society for the Anthropology of Food and Nutrition.

Liza Debevec is a social anthropologist, currently finishing her PhD on experiences of everyday life in southwest Burkina Faso at the University of St Andrews in Scotland. She has carried out extensive fieldwork in Burkina Faso, Croatia and Slovenia. In addition to food related issues, her research focuses on kinship, gender, identity, modernity and hope. She has published articles on family meals in Burkina Faso and on the place of food in West African novels.

Daphne L Derven is Director of Program and Development at Stone Barns Center for Food & Agriculture in Pocantico Hills, NY. She was a field archaeologist for over 20 years. Her research specialties are food and food related technology with a focus on the Americas. She has worked extensively in museums and educational institutions: The AIWF, the California Academy of Sciences, COPIA. In 2003 she was appointed Project Scholar for California for the Smithsonian travelling exhibition *Key Ingredients: America by Food*. The forthcoming Thames and Hudson publication, *Seventy Inventions of the Ancient World*, will contain her contribution on the origins of cooking.

Margaret Drabble novelist and critic, has published many articles and written 14 novels. She won a scholarship to Newnham College, Cambridge, where she read English. Her novel *The Millstone*, first published in 1965, won the John Llewelyn Rhys Prize. She also received the James Tait Black and the EM Forster awards and was awarded the CBE in 1980. She was editor of *The Genius of Thomas Hardy* (1976) and of the fifth edition of *The Oxford Companion to English Literature* (1985). Her biography of the novelist Sir Angus Wilson was published by Secker and Warburg in 1995.

Alexandra Grigorieva was born in Moscow in 1974. Experimented with cooking and languages from early childhood. In 1991 entered the department of Classics (Moscow State University). Besides Latin and ancient Greek studied English, German, French, Italian and modern Greek. In the meanwhile became hooked on food history, wrote gastronomic articles and supplied some Moscow restaurants with historic menus. Completed her Ph.D. thesis (culinary terminology of Apicius) in 2000. Since 2001 has been teaching Latin and Medieval

Latin at the department of Byzantine studies (Moscow State University) and writing articles and books on wines and food.

Natalie Halbach, a native of Minnesota, received her B.A. in both International Studies and French from the University of North Carolina at Chapel Hill. While studying, she helped establish the UNC Dance Marathon as the university's largest student-run fundraiser. As captain of the varsity gymnastics team, Natalie earned the National Collegiate Athletic Association's highest academic honour, the Walter Byers Postgraduate Scholarship. Her 16-year gymnastics career sparked her passion in nutrition, hunger and healthy behaviours. After a year of teaching in France, she plans to pursue both this passion and her commitment to service through further study of public health.

Ursula Heinzelmann was born in West Berlin in 1963. She started to cook even before she could read. In her earlier lives she trained and worked both as a chef and sommelier and has run her own restaurant in the south of Germany. In her present life – after building up a French wine and cheese shop in Berlin – she is a freelance journalist and author, writing about food and wine for various newspapers and magazines. She lives in East Berlin and is currently working on her first book, a culinary autobiography about one German's search for her own taste.

Maurice Holt is professor emeritus of education at the University of Colorado at Denver. His particular interest is the improvement of public education, with regard both to its process in schools and its organization as a public service. He was the first principal of a Hertfordshire comprehensive school, then a consultant on curriculum and organization. After three years as director of the American Academy, Cyprus, he moved to Denver in 1991. He now lives in Oxford and continues to write on educational topics.

Philip Iddison is a civil engineer who has worked in several overseas countries over the last 26 years, particularly in the Middle East. Spare time has been devoted to the study of the culinary culture of these countries across a broad spectrum including ethnography and ethnobotany. Papers and publications have detailed subjects such as desert truffles, dairy food in the UAE, records of Bedouin food, the interface between food and folklore and the minor food products of Thailand and Turkey. Phil received the Sheikh Mubarak bin Mohamed Al Nahyan Award for 2002 for his publications on the food culture of the UEA.

Cathy Kaufman is a professional chef and culinary arts instructor at the Institute for Culinary Education in New York City. Currently the chairperson of the Culinary Historians of New York, she is an associate editor of the *Oxford Encyclopedia of Food and Drink in America* and is presently working on a cookbook of ancient recipes for the Greenwood Press. Before earning an honest living in the kitchen, she practiced law for 11 years in New York.

Sam Kilgour works as a freelance food writer and lives in North London. Sam is a keen supporter of Farmers' Markets, enjoys buying direct from suppliers and is involved with efforts to improve school meals. When not cooking, her interests include walking and climbing, music and books. Sam is married to Adam and they have three children.

Walter Levy is Professor Emeritus of English, at Pace University, in New York City. Levy has written on the environment, literature, and drama. His current interest is the picnic, where he can find one in literature, art, music, and cookery.

Pia Lim-Castillo is a Filipino freelance writer on food and travel who resides in the Philippines. While her background is in agricultural economics specializing in the marketing of agricultural produce, she finds more fulfillment in experimenting with local food ingredients and in researching on Philippine culinary history. She has attended the Oxford Symposium on Food and Cookery for the last four years encouraged by her mentor, the late eminent Filipino food anthropologist, Doreen G Fernandez. She has presented papers that document, both in print and in digital video, Filipino culinary history and traditions.

Máirtín Mac Con Iomaire is a lecturer and tutor on the Culinary Arts programme in the Dublin Institute of Technology. Máirtín has over 15 years experience working as a chef at the highest levels both in Ireland and internationally. Having travelled extensively he is a keen contributor on food in the media, and is engaged in food training consultancy. Areas of interest include mentoring, Irish food history and customs, oenology, education, ethnic cookery and ballad / traditional 'sean-nós' singing. Máirtín is currently researching 'an Oral History of Dublin Restaurants 1922 – 2002' for his PhD in the Dublin Institute of Technology.

Armando Manni is a filmmaker and passionate gourmet, who became one of the noted photographers of the '80s. Elvis & Merilijn, his first feature film, has an international cult following and has earned high critical praise, becoming one of the most prize-winning Italian films of recent years. Next Manni devoted himself to olive oil making through a partnership with the University of Florence. His limited-production extra virgin olive oil is very highly regarded by famous chefs such as Thomas Keller, Jean-Georges Vongerichten, Charlie Trotter, and Heston Blumenthal.

Antony Peattie is a freelance writer and lecturer. He helped found *Opera Now* magazine, devised surtitles for *The Ring* at Covent Garden and for many works in Scottish Opera's repertory. He co-edited *The New Kobbe's Complete Opera Book* with Lord Harewood and is Series Editor for Opera Bites, introductions to opera on CD, that are published by Glyndebourne's education department. His translation of Verdi's *Ernani* was used by ENO and recorded by Chandos. He is currently writing a book about Lord Byron.

Charles Perry studied Middle Eastern languages at Princeton University, the University of California, Berkeley, and the Middle East Center for Arab Studies, Shimlan, Lebanon. From 1968 to 1976 he was an editor at Rolling Stone Magazine. Since then he has been a food writer, specializing (as far as the market will allow) in Middle Eastern food history; currently he is on staff at the Los Angeles Times. He has presented papers at 14 Oxford Symposia.

Gillian Riley was born in Yorkshire in 1933 and lives in London N16. Her published works include a translation of Giacomo Castelvetro's *The Fruit, Herbs and Vegetables of Italy*, Penguin, 1989 and the National Gallery Cookbook *A Feast for the Eyes*, National Gallery Publications, London, 1997. Bumping slowly along in the pipeline are the British Library Cookbook *Eat your Words*, a translation of Maestro Martino for Octavo, and *The Oxford Companion to Italian Food*.

Alicia Rios, from Madrid, Spain, is an academician, cook, restaurateur and writer. She has published many books on olive oil, and on gastronomy. She is an olive oil taster and consultant. As a food performance artist and historian, she is renowned for her surreal and provocative edible food art events throughout the world. Her creations belong to the genre of "devorations", her exclusivity. Among her edible trompe l'oeils feature: "The Temperate

Menu: an edible garden"; "An edible olive grove"; "The Edible Library"; "A ceremony of Pictophagy", "Cooking and eating Madrid" and "Cooking and eating Melbourne".

Frances Short. After more than 15 years working with food – as chef, recipe developer and teacher – Frances Short obtained a PhD in Food Policy with a study of domestic cooking. She researches, writes and lectures about the different and vary varied 'cooking lives', experiences, abilities and food choices of cooks today. She is a Visiting Researcher at London Metropolitan University, an Honorary Research Fellow of City University, London and a member of the Guild of Food Writers.

Andrew F Smith is a freelance writer and lecturer on food and culinary history. He teaches culinary history at the New School University in Manhattan. He is the author of nine books on food history. His most recent is Peanuts: The Illustrious History of the Goober Pea, published by the University of Illinois Press. He serves as the general editor for the University of Illinois Press's Food Series and is currently the editor-in-chief of the Oxford University Press's Encyclopedia on Food and Drink in America.

Colin Spencer is a novelist, painter and playwright. He was first published in The London Magazine at the age of 21, then went on to do a series of drawings of Writers of our Time for the Times Literary Supplement. He has had nine novels published, five plays produced and 23 books of non-fiction including 15 cookery books. He wrote a food column for The Guardian from 1980 to 1993. He has traced the history of vegetarianism in *The Heretics Feast* (Grub Street). His latest book is *British Food – an extraordinary thousand years of history* (Grub Street).

Marlena Spieler is a food writer and broadcaster. Dividing her time between Britain and the USA, she contributes to a variety of publications (Bon Appetit, Saveur, among others). Her column, The Roving Feast, runs in The San Francisco Chronicle and in syndication, and is the basis for her classes at The San Francisco Chronicle Cooking School. She often travels doing television, radio, and personal appearances. She is a prolific author, whose books have frequently been short-listed for awards and who is a twice-winner in The Association of Food Journalists.

Susan Weingarten belongs to the research team of the Sir Isaac Wolfson Chair of Jewish Studies, Tel Aviv University, Israel, working on an interdisciplinary historical study of daily life in the Talmudic sources. She is looking at Food Preparation in the Talmud, using collateral evidence from ancient Greek, Roman and Arab sources and archaeological finds from late antique Palestine and Babylonia. In 2003 she was awarded the Sophie Coe Prize for a paper on ancient tracta, to be published in Food and History 2 (2004). Her research this year is supported by a bursary from the Jane Grigson Trust.

Mary Whiting is an experienced teacher of young children and also runs cookery courses for adults. She is the author of several books on food including *The Nursery Food Book* and 'Teach Yourself: Healthy Eating for Babies and Children', both with Dr Tim Lobstein, and *Entertaining Single-handed*. Her latest book is *Dump The Junk!* which was runner up for the 2004 Derek Cooper Award. She also writes regularly for child-care magazines on the subject of food and children's health.

Bee Wilson is a Research Fellow in the History of Ideas at St John's College Cambridge, specialising in the history of early socialism in France, on which she did her PhD. Her interest in Count Rumford came from studying the socialist Charles Fourier, who greatly admired the notion of Count Rumford's soup. Bee Wilson writes a weekly food column in the Sunday Telegraph magazine. She has also written a book on ideas about honey and bees, *The Hive: The Story of the Honeybee and Us*, published by John Murray (September 2004).

Carolin C Young is the author of *Apples of Gold in Settings of Silver: Stories of Dinner as a Work of Art* (Simon & Schuster, 2002). She lectures at Sotheby's Institute of Art and other cultural venues, for which she often recreates the historic banquets she discusses with special attention to the settings, entertainment, and etiquette in addition to the menus. *The New York Times* describes her as "one of a new breed of food studies scholars who view meals not as ephemeral events of passing biological significance but rather as windows onto a culture's most pressing concerns."